D1319127

TOKYO RISING

TOKYO RISING

THE CITY SINCE THE GREAT EARTHQUAKE

EDWARD SEIDENSTICKER

HARVARD UNIVERSITY PRESS
CAMBRIDGE, MASSACHUSETTS
1991

First Harvard University Press paperback edition, 1991

This edition published by arrangement with Alfred A. Knopf, Inc.

Grateful acknowledgment is made to the following institutions for permission to
publish illustrations supplied by them appearing on the following pages:
Tokyo Prefectural Archives: pp. 9, 12, 22, 24, 28, 47, 52, 54, 56, 69, 80, 91, 92, 101,
105, 113, 118, 130, 222, 269, and 289; *Asahi Shimbum:* pp. 34, 64, 74, 110, 126, 140,
157 (top), 183, 196, 200, 204, 211, 237, 249, 285, 286, and 326; *Asahi Hyakka Nihon
no Rekishi:* pp. 151, 154, 173, and 207; *Asahi Graph:* p. 157 (bottom); *Tokyo Prefectural
Government:* p. 347.
English translation by Edward Seidensticker of excerpts from *Collected Works* of
Nagai Kafū. Originally published by Iwanami Shoten, Tokyo, Japan.

English translation by Edward Seidensticker of excerpts from *Collected Works* of Takeda
Rintarō, and excerpts from *Collected Works* of Kawabata Yasunari.
Originally published by Shinchosha, Tokyo, Japan.

Grateful acknowledgment is made to the following for permission
to reprint previously published material:
Chuokoron-Sha, Inc.: English translation by Edward Seidensticker of excerpts from
Collected Works of Tanizaki Junichirō. Copyright 1934 by Tanizaki Junichirō. Reprinted by
permission of Chuokoron-Sha, Inc., No. 2-8-7, Kyobashi Chuo-ku, Tokyo 104, Japan.
Keiso Shobo, Ltd.: English translation by Edward Seidensticker of excerpts from
Collected Works of Takami Jun, Vol. XIX, 1974. Reprinted by permission
of Keiso Shobo, Ltd., Tokyo, Japan.

Library of Congress Cataloging-in-Publication Data

Seidensticker, Edward, 1921–
Tokyo rising: the city since the great earthquake/Edward
Seidensticker.—1st Harvard University Press pbk. ed.
p.   cm.
Includes bibliographical references (p.   ) and index.
ISBN 0-674-89461-8 (pb)
1. Tokyo (Japan)—History.   I. Title.
DS896.64.S43   1991
952'.135—dc20
91-8497   CIP

CONTENTS

PREFACE

This book is a sequel to *Low City, High City*, which told of Tokyo between the Meiji Restoration of 1867 and 1868 and the great earthquake of 1923. Most people who vaguely remember the title of the earlier book seem to think that it is *High City, Low City*, probably because "high" comes before "low" in so many conventional locutions. The reversing of the two was intentional. The book is elegiac, its emphasis on the part of the city which was the cultural center of Edo, predecessor of Tokyo, and was ceasing to be any sort of center at all.

Low City, High City makes no claim to be political or intellectual history, and little more to be literary or economic history. It might possibly be called social or cultural history. So might this one, although, with the growing ascendancy of the High City—the wealthy hilly districts—politics and intellectual matters are bound to figure more prominently. The ascendancy is now virtually complete. The Low City, the less affluent flatlands, offered something to talk about as late as the years between the two world wars. The center of popular culture was there, in Asakusa. Since the Second World War it has offered very little indeed. The words before the comma in the earlier title have been almost completely eclipsed by the words after.

There was another reason for the emphasis on the Low City: a fondness for the place. It follows with a certain inevitability that when there is little to say about the place one is fondest of, things must be said of places of which one is less fond. Many interesting things have happened in the High City, certainly, and Tokyo, which for cultural purposes is now the High City, goes on being the city among them all in which one has the least excuse to be bored. Yet the effort has been continuous to keep grouchiness from creeping in at the ways in which the city has chosen to spend its money. If I have not been entirely successful, and if a certain grouchiness does creep in at, for instance, the internationally famous architects, I can only hope that it is balanced by affection for people like Enoken.

Low City, High City could have ended with the end of the Taishō reign, three years and a few months after the earthquake. The earthquake was the end of so much more than was the end of the reign, however, that it prevailed. If it had not, then this book might have been, more neatly, about Tokyo in the recently ended Shōwa reign. That is what it is mostly about in any event. Nothing is said about the end of the Shōwa reign because it had not occurred when the manuscript was finished. All that seemed practical was to go back and put the reign in the past tense.

The problem of what to call Tokyo has been a nagging one, since the city of Tokyo ceased to exist as a political and administrative entity in 1943. In that year the municipal government and the prefectural government were amalgamated. The prefecture may be divided broadly into the "ward part" and the "county part," the twenty-three wards as they have been since 1947, and the rest of the prefecture, off to the west of the wards. In the chapters having to do with the postwar period, I have tried to use "prefecture" whenever a government agency is referred to and whenever precise distinctions seem called for. Sometimes "city" has been a convenience. When the word is used it may be taken as referring to the ward part of the prefecture.

The annotation is like that for *Low City, High City*: minimal. The sources of direct quotations are given, and the notes contain little else. A disproportionate number refer to the writings of well-known authors, disproportionate in the sense that the passages cited are less conspicuous in the text than in the notes. It will be observed that notes become less frequent toward the end of the book. Fewer memorable things seem to be said about the city as time goes by. The well-known authors have died, chief among them Nagai Kafū, to whose memory *Low City, High*

City was circumspectly dedicated, and as writers about Tokyo they have not had successors. The point is made in the book that Tokyo is not the subject for distinguished writing that it once was.

The Japanese name order, with the family name first, is used throughout. Modern life, for all its complexities, does produce a simplification from time to time. One has been the tendency of writers not to have "elegant sobriquets." This means that when a single element of a name is used it can be, as in the West, the family name. "Nagai Kafū" is the major exception. "Kafū" is a sobriquet. In accord with Japanese practice, it is used when the whole name is not.

The Tokyo Archives have been very helpful in the assembling of illustrations. So has the *Asahi Shimbun,* in particular Mrs. Notoya Ryōko, of the staff of the weekly magazine *Asahi Hyakka Nihon no Rekishi (The Asahi Encyclopedia: Japanese History)*. Where no credit is given, illustrations are from postcards in my collection or photographs by Mr. Fukuda Hiroshi.

TOKYO IN 1927

THE TOKYO WARDS,
1932—1947

Tokyo Prefecture as it has been since 1947. Certain offshore islands, not shown here, are also part of the prefecture. The four surrounding prefectures, reading clockwise from the west, are Yamanashi, Saitama, Chiba, and Kanagawa.

Nos. 3 through 25 are the twenty-three wards, as follows.

3. Chiyoda	15. Shibuya
4. Chūō	16. Suginami
5. Minato	17. Nakano
6. Shinjuku	18. Toshima
7. Bunkyō	19. Nerima
8. Taitō	20. Itabashi
9. Sumida	21. Kita
10. Kōtō	22. Arakawa
11. Shinagawa	23. Adachi
12. Ōta	24. Katsushika
13. Meguro	25. Edogawa
14. Setagaya	

The remaining portions are what was after 1932 the "county part" of the prefecture. The unnumbered portion at the extreme west is all that remains of West Tama County. Everything else is now incorporated cities, except for No. 41, which is two incorporated towns. No. 44 is Hachiōji, the oldest incorporated city in the county part. The Taishō and Shōwa emperors are buried in the western part of Hachiōji. Mitaka, of the celebrated train wreck, is No. 26. Higashimurayama, wherein reposes the reservoir that has replaced the one at the Shinjuku Westmouth, is the southern of the two Nos. 35. Tachikawa of the big (the newspapers said notorious) American air base is the eastern of the two Nos. 39.

TOKYO RISING

1

THE DAYS
AFTER

In a few years the governor of Tokyo, the council, and the bureaucracy will move their offices out beyond the western limits of the old city.

Despite opposition from the eastern wards, the decision was made in 1985. Unless there are delays in building the somewhat grandiose new offices, the move will take place in 1991. The governor will then be nearer the population center of his constituency than he is now. However one may regret the departure from the old city, the reasons for the move are good ones.

The city has moved westward in the century and twenty years since it became Tokyo. So the governor recognizes the facts, and will go where the people who elect him have gone. American city halls tend to stay put. The New York city hall has not moved north or east with the spread of population, and the Philadelphia city hall has remained where William Penn put it. Perhaps the Japanese are more realistic and flexible in these matters.

Yet one does have regrets, for the move and for the shift that has made it seem realistic. Edo, the seat of the Tokugawa shoguns, became Tokyo in 1868, after the overthrow of the shogunate. The Low City, mostly reclaimed flatlands, was where the lesser orders lived, the merchants and artisans or workmen. It was the crowded part of the city, and the lively part. The hilly High City, to the west of the castle, was sparsely populated. A line north and south from the old magistracies (there were two of them) would have had the larger part of the population east of it, and the centers of commerce and culture as well. The aristocracy in the great castle complex and the High City had money and taste, but it was not imaginative or inventive. It was in the Low City that the things which interest us a century and a half and two centuries later were made and done.

By "aristocracy" is here meant the military class, the court and its courtiers having stayed in Kyoto. The military class was on the whole conservative. Its tastes and the tastes deemed appropriate to it were antiquarian and academic. What was new and interesting in Edo, the cultural center of the land under the last six or seven Tokugawa shoguns, was mercantile. The daimyo patronized Nō drama and the tea ceremony. The wealthy merchant patronized Kabuki and the entertainments, often of very high quality, provided by the geisha, whether in the licensed pleasure quarters or the less strictly regulated "private" quarters. Nō and the tea ceremony were elegant and elevated pursuits, but during the Tokugawa Period they became highly ritualized and formalized. If they changed, it was almost imperceptibly. Kabuki changed and grew, and so did the music and dance of the pleasure quarters. It has become common in our day to think of Kabuki, like Nō, as a crystallization of unearthly beauty, but it can be earthy, erotic, and ribald. More important, new and good things were constantly being added to it, and to the art of the geisha, as they were not to Nō and the tea ceremony. The former were living and growing, the particular treasures of the Low City.

In Meiji the governance of Tokyo Prefecture moved slightly westward, to Marunouchi. Meiji is the era designation for the first reign after the upheaval of 1867–68. The Meiji emperor died in 1912, and the era name changed to Taishō. The prefectural government, along with the city government when there has been one, as there has not been since 1943, has been in Marunouchi ever since. And now it will move much further west, to a part of Shinjuku that was not brought within the city limits until 1932.

Even if the governor and government were not moving, we would have to admit the fact, melancholy for some of us, that the Low City has fallen far behind. It was the cultural center of Edo, and the new prefectural offices will lie beyond the old High City, beyond even the first of the old post stations on the highway to the mountain province of Kai.

Although already declining, the Low City was still important enough in Meiji that a cultural history of Meiji Tokyo could not leave it out.

The simplest and the best explanation for the decline of the Low City is economic. Money departed. Kabuki stayed behind and so did the best geisha, but rich merchants, such as the Mitsui, moved to the High City when the class structure of Tokugawa disappeared. The chief sources of patronage came to be the entrepreneurial and bureaucratic classes of the High City. In 1923 mansions of the wealthy and aristocratic stood along the Sumida, central to the arts and pleasures of the old Low City. Most of them then disappeared. The new Sumida Park and a brewery came to occupy the tract on the east bank of the Sumida where the greatest of them, the river villa of the Mito Tokugawa family, had stood.

Except for the regions immediately east of the outer moat, now filled in, not many would notice if the Low City were to disappear completely from a postwar history. Only the omission of Ginza, just east of the old castle complex, would be certain to bring complaints. Ginza is geographically in the Low City, since it lies east of the hills that begin in the palace (once the castle) grounds, but it belongs to the whole city. If the city, sprawling and decentralized, has a center today, it is probably Ginza and districts nearby.

Amusing things were still going on in the Low City during the interwar period, but they fall in the realm of popular culture, amusing enough for an evening, but ephemeral, not likely to be of much interest to anyone except very specialized antiquarians two centuries from now. So, even without insisting upon them, the story of Tokyo since 1923 must implicitly be about the decline of the Low City and the rise of the High City.

The Low City did almost completely disappear for a time late in the Taishō reign, which ended on Christmas Day 1926. Fires raged through it for two days following high noon of September 1, 1923, and left almost nothing behind save modern buildings along the western fringes. The fires followed upon the great Kantō earthquake, which struck at a minute and a few seconds before noon on September 1. The great shift to the High City was already in process and would have occurred even without the disaster, but the disaster sped it along. The novelist Tanizaki Junichirō was born in Nihombashi, the heart of mercantile Edo, between the old castle complex and the Sumida. He remarked in 1934 that he could no longer think of Nihombashi, or indeed Tokyo, as home. The place where he had spent the most impressionable years of his boyhood now lay under asphalt, in the middle of a thoroughfare cut through after the earthquake. It is an extreme instance, but symbolic of what happened to the whole Low City. The sites were there, but denuded, stripped of history and culture.

Old things would probably, most of them, have vanished in any event. Except for grand public structures like temples, buildings were not meant to last long and did not last long. But they would not have gone so quickly. Crowded and flimsily built, the Low City could not be protected against the fires that broke out immediately after the earthquake. The High City fared better. It too was largely built of wood, but broken topography and irregular building patterns reduced the damage.

The financial, entrepreneurial, and merchandising center of the city —Nihombashi, Ginza, and Marunouchi—also fared better. The offices of governor and mayor, in Marunouchi, came through so solidly that no one within was immediately aware of what had happened. Lights swayed, but it was the news that automobiles were unable to get through to the east that brought the first sense of disaster. Presently, people on their way to the safety of the palace plaza were dying of burns and having babies under the mayor's windows.

Marunouchi was less severely damaged than Nihombashi, and so the managers and entrepreneurs started moving westward, even as the city did. Marunouchi derives its name from the fact that the district lay within the outer revetments and moat of the castle. Developed in Meiji by the Mitsubishi enterprises, which bought it from the government, Marunouchi now emerged clearly dominant over Nihombashi, where the merchant class of Edo had been most affluent and powerful. The stock exchange and the Bank of Japan stayed in Nihombashi, but Marunouchi more and more became the right address for the big managers.

The Yamanote loop line of the National Railways, joining the center of the city with transfer points to the western suburbs, was finally finished in 1925. The last link joined Tokyo Central Station with Ueno, the point of departure for the north. Marunouchi thus became the *genkan,* the "front door," for the whole nation. The front door of the station faced Marunouchi and, from 1926, a broad avenue leading to the palace plaza. Nihombashi, on the east side of the station, did not even have a back door. The number of big companies with offices in Marunouchi doubled between 1922 and 1924. Almost three decades, since the completion of the first Mitsubishi brick building in 1894, had been required to reach the 1922 figure.

Nihombashi was also losing out to Ginza as a retail district. It had Mitsukoshi and Shirokiya, the energetic Meiji pioneers in the new, Western kind of retailing, but department stores in quick succession established main or branch stores in Ginza. Mitsukoshi was among them. As the lesser parts of the Low City, save only Ginza, were left further and further behind by the High City, so was proud—some might have said, arrogant—Nihombashi.

There was talk of more shattering change, spiritual and man-made this time—the physical disaster could scarcely have been more complete. Kyoto was still officially the capital of the land in 1867, when the shogunate collapsed. There was talk of having the capital somewhere other than Edo, seat of the shoguns and the actual seat of power. It was stilled when the emperor took up residence in Edo, and not revived until 1923.

With the city so grievously damaged, might it not be better off without the national bureaucracy, and the bureaucracy without the snarls and tangles of the great city? It should be easy to find a new capital less prone to disasters. Tokyo lies in earthquake country. Another flattening earthquake was bound to come. It has not come in the more than sixty years since the last one, but the assumption that it will come someday is universal.

Among nonseismic arguments for moving the capital was that Kyoto, or elsewhere in the Kansai, would be nearer the center of the Japanese empire, by which was meant Taiwan and Korea as well as the home islands. There even seems to have been talk in the armed forces—already feeling the spur of ambition—of moving the capital to the continent. Dispersal was suggested (and again today, when concentration in Tokyo has come to seem extreme and unhealthy, it is a popular subject). Kyoto had been all this while going on thinking of itself as the Western Capital. A measure of reality might be given to the claim. The government could be in both Kantō and Kansai.

On September 12, 1923, a royal proclamation said that Tokyo would remain the capital. This is the official translation: "Tokyo, the capital of the empire, has been looked upon by the people as the centre of political and economic activities and the fountainhead of the cultural advancement of the nation. With the unforeseen visit of the catastrophe, the city

7

has entirely lost its former prosperous contours but retains, nevertheless, its position as the national capital. The remedial work, therefore, ought not to consist merely in the reparation of the quondam metropolis, but, in ample provisions for the future development of the city, completely to transform the avenues and streets." The regent, the next emperor, took a drive through the burnt-over wastes of the Low City. (He was to do it again, as emperor, in 1945.)

The city burned for some forty hours, and before the last embers were out reconstruction had already begun. It was used to and indeed rather proud of fires, known as "flowers of Edo," and proud as well of the speed with which it recovered. The proper merchant insisted upon speed in these matters. If a shop had not resumed business within three days, common mercantile wisdom held, it had no future. Prepared for what must come sooner or later, merchants kept reserves of lumber east of the Sumida River. The lumberyards were very watery, and reserves of lumber had a chance of surviving the worst conflagration, as also did inventories in somewhat fireproof warehouses. Department stores quickly put up emergency markets. Ginza and Asakusa almost immediately had street stalls again, as they had them before. Already on September 3 there was a sign in the wastes of the central fish market, in Nihombashi, summoning such fish dealers as survived to discuss plans for reopening.

> Completely burned out. But see:
> The son of Edo has not lost his spirit.
> So soon, these rows and rows of barracks,
> And we can view the moon from our beds.

So went "The Reconstruction Song," popular in the months after the earthquake.

Late in September a newspaper account based on a police report said that thirty thousand "barracks" had already gone up. Here and in "The Reconstruction Song" the English word is used, in the singular, to signify a building erected hastily on the site of a disaster. The new barracks were most numerous in Asakusa, Shitaya, and Honjo wards, the northern tier of the old Low City. The smell of new wood was everywhere,

Barracks begin to go up in Hongō Ward after the earthquake

faces were black from clearing the ashes, though the wares offered for sale were skimpy.

More than ashes had to be cleared away. The tallest building in the city, the Asakusa "Twelve Storeys," broke in two, at the eighth storey, during the earthquake. The novelist Kawabata Yasunari was off for a look at Asakusa a scant two hours afterward. He was less impressed with the destruction than with the refugees, especially the courtesans and geisha who poured in from the north, "like a disordered field of flowers." The great Yoshiwara quarter, to the north of Asakusa, was completely destroyed and several hundred of its women were incinerated, but the fires stopped just short of Asakusa proper, where Kawabata wandered in his field of flowers.

He did describe the final disappearance, the following year, of the Twelve Storeys. It seems to have been a rather festive occasion. More properly the Cloud Scraper, the Twelve Storeys was a pleasure and retailing center, a somewhat ungainly brick tower completed in 1890. Army demolition squads completed the destruction.

A character in Kawabata's *Scarlet Gang of Asakusa (Asakusa Kure-*

naidan), published at irregular intervals between 1929 and 1935, is speaking:

> "All around us and as far as we could see were burned wastes. A few shacks had gone up here and there, but nothing blocked the view of the park from the school roof. The elevated portion of the roof was crowded with spectators. We must have waited an hour or so. There was an explosion and a cascade of bricks. The wall at one side had not fallen. It was like a thin sword. Another explosion and the sword fell. The crowds on the school roof cheered, and then how we all did laugh! As the sword collapsed a black mass of people raced up the mountain of rubble."

Individual enterprise was so swift and forceful that some of it got in the way of larger plans. Charles Beard, the American historian, was also swift and forceful, generous with his advice. A telegram from him crossed with one from Gotō Shimpei, the home minister, now in charge of reconstruction. Mayor of Tokyo until shortly before the earthquake, Gotō had once before asked Beard's advice. He was known as "the mayor with the big kerchief," which might be rendered as "the mayor with all the plans." At his invitation, Beard studied the city administration for six months in 1922 and 1923 and submitted a report early in 1923. Now Gotō summoned him back. He came, and the telegram, a stern one, preceded him. Sentimentality about the old must not be allowed to interfere in any way with plans for the new: no new buildings were to be allowed until a new street plan had been drawn up. But of course barracks were already appearing at a rate of close to ten thousand per week, if that police report was accurate.

The earthquake came at a time of political disarray. The admiral who had become prime minister in the summer of 1922 died late in August 1923. It was the age of what historians call "Taishō democracy," a somewhat liberal age between the authoritarianism of Meiji and that of the thirties and early forties. Political parties were for the first time experiencing the delights of power, and they were much given to squabbling. A successor cabinet was not easily arranged. On September 2, while the city still burned, a cabinet headed by another admiral took office. It lasted only until early 1924, but under it, and especially Gotō, the national government assumed the lead in the rebuilding. It would probably have done so even without the services of Gotō, since the city did not have the money.

Gotō's original plan covered the whole city, including the relatively undamaged High City, and almost every lesser category imaginable—streets, parks, rivers, canals, transportation. A grand arterial highway some two hundred yards wide was to run north and south through the city proper from beyond the city limits at either end, passing just to the east of Ginza and the main part of Nihombashi. For a politician, Gotō was curiously unrealistic. The budget was scaled down from several billion yen to about a half billion for Tokyo, and an additional amount for the still more grievously injured Yokohama. The main emphasis in the more modest plans was upon getting roofs over people's heads and widening streets. The width of Gotō's grand avenue was reduced to a little over half, and its length greatly reduced as well. Known as Shōwa Avenue from the era designation for the reign just recently ended, it runs past Ginza and Nihombashi and on to Ueno in Shitaya Ward.

Less than the half billion yen was finally approved. The new Reconstruction Agency was not of a single mind. Some thought that matters of little immediate concern were included and that the requisitioning of land for the widened streets would be a great bother. One of the two major political parties agreed. Why, it asked loudly, should so small a part of the country make demands upon the whole country? Widened streets and some new parks remained of Gotō's dreams. The street pattern was similar to that of Edo.

The rebuilding of the city may seem like a case study in lost opportunities. It would not do, however, to suggest that nothing at all was accomplished. The city *was* rebuilt, after a nondescript fashion, and it was to an extent redesigned. Nor would it do to leave the impression that the city did nothing at all for itself. The national government took responsibility for main thoroughfares, new and widened, and the city for lesser streets. In the end almost a quarter of a million residences were moved. The proportion of streets to total area was much higher after the earthquake than before. Three big new parks were financed by the national government, all in the Low City, near or along the Sumida. The city built more than fifty small parks, many of them by waterways now gone, most of them near schools. Motomachi Park, in what was then Hongō

Ward, near Ochanomizu Station, is perhaps the only one of the small parks to survive in its original form. Opened in 1930, it is a charming Art Deco composition, with something in it of Frank Lloyd Wright's Imperial Hotel as well. The erection of a memorial hall on the site east of the river where the largest loss of life occurred was the mayor's idea. It took seven years to complete, but already by the first anniversary of the quake it was receiving pilgrims to its mass graves.

One of Kawabata's short-short stories, which he called "palm-of-the-hand stories," is set on the first anniversary of the earthquake. A woman whose whole family died in the earthquake has become the companion of a clever and skillful Asakusa beggar. They go off to the memorial site. The man removes one of his shoes, and tells the woman that her questions about this eccentric behavior will soon answer themselves. He uses the bare foot to pick up coins that have been tossed at but missed the offertory box, and puts them in the shoe. A royal emissary arrives. So do the home minister and the mayor. All of them read messages at the altar. There are wreaths from ambassadors. "At two minutes before noon all vehicles in the city stopped for one minute. The whole city prayed in silence."

An anniversary service at the Earthquake Memorial Hall east of the Sumida, site of the largest loss of life in the fires following the earthquake

The novelist Nagai Kafū tells in his diary how it was on that first anniversary, a day of apprehension for the superstitious. "The citizenry was in terror. Banks locked their doors, greengrocers and fishmongers took a holiday. The weather was good, with a fresh autumn wind."

The climax to Kafū's *The Woman in the Rented Room,* written in 1927, also occurs on September 1, 1924. "It was already dark, but the back alleys were ridiculously silent. The Yotsuya geisha quarter was, on the surface at least, taking a holiday. That was not all: even on the main trolley street there was none of the usual bustle of night stalls and shops. The trumpet from the grounds of the Military Academy, beyond Tsuno-kami Hill, seemed very near." The woman of the title, through whom we observe the silence of this dread anniversary, is a kept woman, and the fact that she does not expect her patron to come calling this night of all nights causes him, after a sequence of almost ludicrous mishaps, to discard her.

The origins of the panic of 1927 may be traced directly to the earthquake. The causal relationship between the two was not inevitable, but the behavior of the government gave it the look of inevitability. The Yamamoto cabinet, which took office on September 2, declared a limited debt moratorium. Under certain conditions and in certain areas payment could be deferred. In effect, the Bank of Japan was required to guarantee losses by commercial banks, and its own losses were guaranteed by the government up to a specified limit. The time limit for these arrangements was extended repeatedly. Because the value of uncollected and uncollectable instruments far exceeded the official guarantee, the Bank of Japan was affected, and through it the commercial banks.

In March 1927 the finance minister did a peculiar thing. He said in the Diet that the Watanabe Bank, an important commercial bank, would be forced to close its doors in a few hours. This was untrue. The Watanabe Bank was in trouble, but not such critical and immediate trouble. He seems to have said it to divert attention from a bank still more heavily burdened with bad instruments. There was a run, and the Watanabe Bank was forced to suspend payments. So, after a time, was the second bank, the Bank of Taiwan, in the interests of which the minister had spoken his untruth, and half the capital of which came from public funds. Efforts to bail it out were declared unconstitutional by the Privy Council. Other banks failed, including one of the five largest in the land. It was the worst financial panic in the history of modern Japan, and its

remote origins were in the earthquake. The cabinet resigned, to be succeeded by that of Tanaka Giichi, an army man and an early advocate of
assertive policies on the continent. So the political and economic effects
of the earthquake reached far. The politicians who said that the damage
to the capital was of little concern to them and the nation were wrong.

Through a moratorium, actions by the Bank of Japan, and a bit of
trickery, the crisis presently came under control. The banks that reopened did so with ostentatious piles of cash by their teller windows.
Much of the money was printed only on one side, for there had not been
time to print both sides.

It is possible—though to state it as fact we must put complete cre-
dence in the professed motives of the culprit—that the most sensational
crime of the post-earthquake years was also caused by the earthquake.
On December 27, 1923, the regent, after 1926 the emperor, was on his
way to the opening of a Diet session. As he passed Toranomon, "Tiger
Gate," a young man pushed his way out of the crowd and fired point-
blank at the regent, who escaped injury. This attempted assassination is
known as the Tiger Gate Incident, from the site of a castle gate on the
outer moat. (Both gate and moat are long gone.)

The young man was from a good provincial family, the son of a Diet
member. He later said that he had to do what he did, and that he did it
out of anger at the treatment of laborers and Koreans after the earthquake. However matters were with laborers, Koreans were very badly
treated indeed: they were massacred, as many as two thousand of
them.

The would-be assassin was pummeled by the crowds and arrested.
Not quite a year later, in November 1924, he was hanged at Ichigaya
Prison, and that evening given a pauper's burial east of the Sumida, in
the northeastern suburbs. The river embankment was very pretty, it is
said, with police lanterns.

Only after the sentence was handed down did the defendant break
his silence. This he did with two shouted words encouraging revolution.
So the theory that he might have avoided execution had he been less
vehemently revolutionary is not supportable. The court was not prepared
to be merciful to someone who had done such a thing.

Nagai Kafū, a quirkish man, had his own thoughts in the matter,
and set them down in his diary.

November 16. Sunday. Sunny. Big play given in all the newspapers to the execution of Namba Daisuke. Daisuke is the student who was arrested after trying to shoot the regent at
Toranomon last year. Some denounce the act as the vilest treason,
but I do not think it anything so very astonishing or reprehensi-
ble. The assassination of monarchs is no rarity in the West.
Everything about modern Japanese life is superficial imitation of
the West. Daisuke's behavior is but another instance of imitation.
What is there to choose between him and a Westernized woman
out dancing?

It is interesting to note, by way of comparison, what happened to
earlier and later would-be assassins. In 1891 a policeman in the town of
Otsu, just east of Kyoto, slashed the czarevitch of Russia with a sword.
The Otsu trial was swifter than the Tiger Gate one, but the assailant
was sentenced to life imprisonment rather than death. Though the prosecution asked the death penalty, the judge allowed only a charge of simple
assault, holding that this attack on royalty was no different from an
attack on anyone else. The fact that extraterritoriality was still in effect
may have influenced the decision. The judge wished to demonstrate the
independence of the courts from political pressures, and therefore
the superfluity of extraterritorial consular courts. The fact remains that
the Tiger Gate court did not follow the Otsu precedent.

On January 8, 1932, the emperor (the 1923 regent) was the victim of
another attack. A Korean threw a hand grenade at his cavalcade as he
was returning from a military parade. No one was injured, though one
of the automobiles, not the emperor's, was damaged. The incident bears
the name of another of the old palace gates, the Sakurada or Cherry
Orchard Gate. The Tiger Gate precedent, and not the Otsu one, was
followed: the assailant was put to death. The conclusion seems hard to
escape that not all royalty is equally royal. The cabinet resigned after the
1923 incident, and attempted to resign after the 1932 one. It was persuaded to stay on in the latter instance because of the outbreak of hostil-
ities in Manchuria.

The Tiger Gate Incident had an effect on the culture of the nation
that could not have been foreseen. The chief of the Tokyo police was
dismissed, as was the assistant chief in charge of the patrolling forces.

The latter was Shōriki Matsutarō, who set forth on a new career that brought him fame and power, in the media and in entertainment. He became president of the *Yomiuri Shimbun* in February 1924. It was a time when aggressive Osaka journalism seemed to be having everything its way. Two Osaka newspapers, the *Asahi* and the *Mainichi*, each passed a million in nationwide circulation the year after the earthquake. The largest Tokyo newspaper had a third of a million. The two Osaka papers ganged up on it, undermining it so successfully that the *Yomiuri* took it over. The Osakans next turned their energies on another distinguished Tokyo newspaper, and the *Nichinichi*, the Tokyo edition of the *Mainichi* (both names mean "daily"), took that one over.

Shōriki went quickly to work. He sought to give the *Yomiuri* a common touch, without the intellectual tendencies of the Osaka newspapers. His *Yomiuri* had the first women's page and the first advice-to-the-troubled column. He also did wonders with sports, giving the *Yomiuri* a professional baseball team which the whole nation loves. He made it into the largest paper in the city. Since the war it has become the largest in the land.

So all manner of remarkable sequences of events (Shōriki was also to become a pioneer in commercial television) are traceable to the earthquake, if we may assume that the Tiger Gate Incident is traceable to it. But to return to the immediate aftermath. The governor of Yamaguchi Prefecture, whence the assailant came, docked his own pay for two months. The governor of Kyoto Prefecture, where the man had lingered on his way to Tokyo, was reprimanded. The man's father resigned from the Diet and withdrew into the stoic seclusion of the dishonored samurai. The village in which he had been born forwent all New Year festivities by way of atonement. The principal of his elementary school—he had graduated a decade earlier—resigned.

The trail of punishment and contrition following the Otsu Incident is altogether less exaggerated. The home minister resigned, and the governor and police chief of Shiga Prefecture, of which Otsu is the capital, were dismissed: and that was that. All of these people may in some measure be held responsible, whereas it is hard to think the governor of Kyoto and the rural school principal responsible for what happened at Tiger Gate.

·   ·   ·

The Taishō period, the reign of the Taishō emperor, stands almost exactly midway through the first Tokyo century, 1868 to 1968. The whole of the Meiji reign and the portion of the Shōwa reign that falls within the century are of almost equal length. Taishō stands at midpoint in another sense. The city has not ceased changing since the end of Taishō, and the early years of Shōwa were to bring a disaster that almost destroyed it once again. Taishō may have been the era when change was fastest. There is no device for precise measurement of such phenomena as cultural change. Yet one has a "sense" that it must be so. The last year of Taishō must have seemed more different from the first than 1912 did from 1897, or 1925 from 1940. The things of late Taishō and early Shōwa, the institutions and the modes of behavior, have a familiar look about them that those of the Russo-Japanese War do not. Even "Taishō democracy," which surrendered so meekly to the reaction of the thirties, seems familiar. It has come again. We have similar extravagances today. Only a prophet can say whether or not indignant, righteous men with guns will try one of these days to work a similar reaction.

The Taishō emperor was mentally incapacitated—from how far back in his not very long life (he was born in 1879) we do not know. His birth

The Taishō emperor

was difficult and he was given up for dead. So it may be that he was retarded from infancy. He had already withdrawn from public life before the future Shōwa emperor became regent, late in 1920 and some months after his twentieth birthday. There was little stir over the Taishō emperor's death, certainly very little compared with that which accompanied his father's last illness. The announcement that he had pneumonia came early in December 1926. He was taken to the royal villa at Hayama, on Sagami Bay, south of Tokyo. (The villa disappeared, a victim of arson, in 1971.)

In his diary, Nagai Kafū indicated disapproval of the announcement.

> December 14. Cloudy and cold. Toward evening it began to clear.
> I went in the evening to Ginza, which was noisy with hawkers of newspaper extras. I suppose they informed us that His Majesty's death approaches. The detail with which newspapers, morning and evening, have reported the royal illness is extreme. They do not hesitate to tell us the state of his appetite and of his defecatory processes. This sort of reporting began with the death of the Meiji emperor. With the encouragement of the authorities, the newspapers told us that the emperor suffered from uremic poisoning, and that his august countenance had turned a muddy purple. . . .
> If my opinion were asked I would give it. I would say . . . that a national legend is thus destroyed. While he lives our sovereign is revered as a god, and to tell us that he has died a victim of uremic poisoning shatters the poetry. . . . Why must these facts about appetite and defecation be made public as the royal death approaches?

The emperor died very early on Christmas morning, and so the first year of Shōwa was only a week long. Among the curiosities one comes upon in flea markets are diaries and memorandum books for the year that failed to be, the sixteenth year of Taishō. It was too late to print books for the second year of Shōwa, and so people made do with ones printed before the royal death and the change of era names.

It has been the practice since 1868 to have era names coincide with reigns. In earlier centuries they were changed more frequently. The designation "Shōwa," meaning literally "Clarity and Harmony," and conveying a hope for peace at home and amity with all nations, comes, like most of them, from the Chinese classics. It is the longest-lived era name in Japanese history, and it is an inadvertency. The royal household got scooped and was embarrassed. Among the common Japanese ways of coping with an inadvertency is to pretend that it did not occur. A newspaper published the name originally chosen, Kōbun, before it was officially released. The alternative name Shōwa was therefore substituted on a moment's notice and was with us for more than six decades. Kōbun, suggesting an age of brilliant letters, might have been more descriptive of the reign than Shōwa.

The Taishō emperor was buried in February 1927 with suitable reverence and pageantry, and great crowds in which people were trampled to death, but without the public outpourings that accompanied his father's obsequies. There had been disagreement about where the Meiji emperor should be buried. There seems to have been none in the case of the Taishō emperor. His grave is in the western suburbs of Tokyo. Lavish undertakings for a memorial to the Meiji emperor produced the Meiji Shrine and Gardens. No one took the trouble in the case of the Taishō emperor. General Nogi Maresuke, the greatest of modern military heroes, committed suicide on the first day of the Meiji emperor's funeral. The poet and scholar who composed the official threnody died the day before the Taishō emperor's funeral began, but not by his own hand.

All in all, a hush surrounds the Taishō emperor. It is not easy to assess the political importance of the Meiji emperor, but his name rallied the nation for the great efforts of the late nineteenth century. The Taishō emperor is by comparison a slight, sad figure.

Interment of the Taishō emperor at Hachiōji, February 1927

He was, however, the first Tokyo emperor. His father was reared in Kyoto and buried in the outskirts of that city. The Taishō emperor lived his whole life in Tokyo, to the extent that anyone in this mobile age lives his whole life anywhere. His grave lies in Tokyo Prefecture. No one remembers much about him except that he was kept out of sight, but in this one regard he was unique, an original.

2

HAPPY

RECONSTRUCTION DAYS

The official view was that the reconstruction of Tokyo from the great earthquake was complete by 1930. A "reconstruction festival" took place in March of that year. The emperor, who had been regent at the time of the earthquake, was among those who addressed a reconstruction rally in the palace plaza. The mayor addressed a gathering in Hibiya Hall, a few hundred yards to the south. The citizenry was not much a part of these rallies, but the celebrations went on for several days and included events to please everyone—parades and "flower trolleys" and the like. These last were elaborately decorated trolley cars that went all over the city.

The emperor took an inspection tour, and expressed taciturn satisfaction with all that he saw by way of reconstruction and hopes for a future of unity and progress. He used the word "capital" to particular effect, as if to emphasize that there was to be no more talk of a capital elsewhere. The organizers of the tour shielded him from the masses with a thoroughness at which the Japanese are very good. Some fifteen thousand people with whom it was conceivable he might come into contact were vaccinated for smallpox. An estimated quarter of a million people were in some way involved in the planning and execution. The tour took him through the flat Low City, the regions most cruelly devastated by earth-

The Shōwa emperor, then regent, on an inspection tour after the earthquake; he is standing next to the chair

quake and fire. He stopped, among other places, at Sumida Park and the earthquake memorial (see page 12).

The park is a product of the earthquake, one of the two big new parks beside the Sumida River. It runs for not quite a mile along the right, or Asakusa, bank, less than half that distance along the left bank. The shorter, or left-bank, portion has been the more successful as a park, because it contains venerable religious institutions and the famous line of cherry trees. A new start had to be made on this last. The fires of 1923 destroyed the old one almost completely. Much of the right-bank portion is on reclaimed land. The Arakawa Drainage Channel of mid-Taishō had removed the threat of floods and made reclamation possible. When, in recent years, an ugly concrete wall was put up to contain the river, the incentive was less a fear of waters rushing down the river than of waters rushing up from the bay during stormy high tides. Title to the land for Hamachō Park, the other of the two, on the right bank downstream, presented few difficulties, since there were only three landowners. Getting rid of all the little places that had rights of tenancy was more complicated. Much of the Hamachō geisha district happened to sit upon the tract, and geisha and their patrons can be strong-willed and influential people. The quarter was rebuilt a short distance to the west.

If the official view is accepted, the city did not have long to enjoy its new self. The reconstruction had taken seven years. Only a decade and a little more elapsed before the Second World War started pulling things apart once more. Happy days were few. It may be, indeed, that the years of the reconstruction were happier than the years that followed, for the latter were also the years of the depression, the assassinations, and the beginnings of war.

The Japanese word that is here rendered as "reconstruction" is also rendered by the dictionaries as "restoration." Perfect restoration of a city is probably impossible. There may be attempts to redo a city exactly as it was before whatever made restoration necessary. There have been such attempts in Europe since 1945. The results may be faithful to all the evidence of what was lost, but they are somehow sterile. The life that produced the original is not there.

Nothing of the sort was attempted in Tokyo. Probably it would have been impossible except in limited neighborhoods. We may be grateful that the city was allowed to live and grow, and not forced back into molds it had outgrown. Yet, though few people now alive are old enough to remember what was there before September 1, 1923, one has trouble believing that the old city was not more pleasing to the eye than what came after. If perfect restoration is probably impossible, a reconstruction is generally less pleasing than what went before it. In Tokyo the reasons are not mysterious. They have to do with the fact that Tokyo and Japan had opened themselves in the decade of the 1860s to a deluge of devices and methods from a very alien culture. These had much to recommend them. They were ways of fending off political encroachment. They also tended to be cheaper and more convenient than old devices and methods. So with each reconstruction jerry-built hybrids became more common.

The citizenry seems on the whole to have been rather pleased with the rebuilding, as it was again to be in 1945 and after. Everything had become so cheerful, all that white concrete replacing all that dark plaster and those even darker tiles. Sukiya Bridge, west of Ginza, with the new *Asahi Shimbun* building reflected in its dark waters like a big ship, and the Nichigeki, the Japan Theater, like a bullring, was the place where all the *mobo* and *moga*, the modern boys and girls (for these expressions see page 40), wanted to have their pictures taken.

Fully aware that there are no rulers for measuring, and at the disadvantage of not having been there, we may ask just how much it did all change. The opinions of the best-informed and most sensitive are not unanimous. Most of what survived from Edo had been in the Low City, because that is where most of Edo was. Therefore most of it disappeared. So much is beyond denying. It is in the matter of the rebuilding and the changes it brought to the physical, material city and to its folkways— changes in spirit, we might say—that opinion varies.

In the early years of Shōwa, Nagai Kafū was spending many of his evenings in Ginza, at "cafés," which today would more likely be called bars or cabarets. In 1931 he put some of his experiences and observations into a novel, *During the Rains (Tsuyo no Atosaki)*. An aging character who is in many ways a surrogate for Kafū himself—although Kafū was younger, and never served a prison term for bribery, as the character has —muses upon the Ginza of recent years. Every day something changes;

Kyōbashi, as rebuilt after the earthquake

the sum of changes since the earthquake is like a dream. The Ginza of today is not the Ginza of yesterday. The old gentleman's interests are rather narrow. He is chiefly concerned with the cafés which sprang up in large numbers after the earthquake, most of them on burnt-over tracts, and which, being outposts of the demimonde, were highly sensitive to new fashions and tastes. He speaks for Kafū, however, and Kafū found the changes devastating. The old pleasure centers were gone, and good taste threatened to go with them.

Tanizaki Junichirō, a native of the city who had been away most of the time since the earthquake, felt differently. Change had not lived up to his predictions. On September 1, 1923, he was in the Hakone Mountains, some fifty miles southwest of Tokyo. He had a famous vision of utter destruction and a splendid flapper-age rebuilding. What he saw and wrote of in 1934 was disappointing, or would have been had he still been in his 1923 frame of mind. He had changed, and was glad that changes in the city had not been as extreme as he had hoped and predicted. The Tanizaki of 1934 would have been disappointed, this is to say, if the Tanizaki of 1923 had not himself changed.

So ten years and one have now gone by. The decade which seemed so slow as it passed came to an end on September 1 of last year. I am forty-nine. And how are things today with me, and how are things with Tokyo? People say that the immediate future is dark, and that nothing is as it should be; yet looking back over the meditations in which I was sunk on that mountain road in Hakone, I feel somewhat strange. I do not know whether to be sad or happy at the irony of what has happened. My thoughts then about the extent of the disaster, the damage to the city, and the speed and form of the recovery were half right and half wrong. . . . Because the damage was less than I imagined, the recovery in ten years, though remarkable, has not been the transformation I looked for. I was one of those who uttered cries of delight at the grand visions of the home minister, Gotō Shimpei. Three billion yen would go into buying up the whole of the burned wastes and making them over into something regular and orderly. They were not realized. The old tangle of Tokyo streets is still very much with us. It is true that large numbers of new bridges, large and small, now describe their graceful arcs over the Sumida and other rivers and canals. The region from Marunouchi through Ginza and Kyōbashi to Nihombashi has taken on a new face. Looking from the train window as the train moves through the southern parts of the city and on past Shimbashi to the central station, I cannot but be astonished that these were lonely wastes where I would play half a day as a child. People back from abroad say that Tokyo is now a match for the cities of Europe and America. . . . The daydream in which I lost myself on September 1, 1923—I neglected to think even of my unhappy wife and daughter, back in the city—did not approach the imposing beauty I now see before me. But what effect has all this surface change had on the customs, the manners, the words, the acts of the city and its people? The truth is that my imagination got ahead of me. Westernization has not been as I foresaw. To be sure, there have recently appeared such persons as the stick girls of Ginza, and the prosperity of bars and cafés quite overshadows that of the geisha quarters, and movies and reviews are drawing customers away from Kabuki; but none of these places, and even less the casinos and cabarets, bears comparison with even the Carleton Café in Shanghai. . . . How many women and girls wear Western dress that really passes as Western dress? In summer the number increases somewhat, but in winter you see not one in ten among shoppers and pedestrians. Even among office girls, one in two would be a generous estimate.

(Since Tanizaki was born in 1886, his age is obviously by the Oriental count. "Stick girls" were female gigolos. Like walking sticks, they attached themselves to men, in this case young men strolling in Ginza.)

So Tanizaki's feelings are mixed. He is sad that he must admit his inadequacies as a prophet and sad too that with regard to Nihombashi, at least (see page 5), his predictions were not exaggerated. Yet he does not see changes in customs and manners as Kafū does.

Writing also in the early thirties, Kawabata Yasunari is more interested in physical change, and is a subtler chronicler of it, than Kafū or Tanizaki. (Kafū was twenty years older than Kawabata, Tanizaki thirteen.) In Hama Park he comes upon a kind of revivalism directed not at Edo and the Japanese tradition but at early Westernization. He finds Western tendencies, in other words, that have become thoroughly Japanized.

Everything is new, of course, Hama Park being one of the two new ones along the banks of the Sumida. Nothing is unchanged except the sea gulls and the smell of the water. Yet nostalgia hangs over the place. The new Venetian pavilion is meant to recall a famous Meiji building lost in the earthquake, the offices put up by Josiah Conder for the Hokkaido Development Bureau. Conder, an Englishman, was the most famous of foreign architects active in Meiji Japan. The music and revelry from the riverboats of Edo are too remote for nostalgia.

Kawabata does not tell us what he thinks of Sumida Park, the other new riverside one, but quotes a friend who is an unreserved booster. With its clean flowing waters and its open view off to Mount Tsukuba, Sumida Park, says the acquaintance, is the equal of the great parks beside the Potomac, the Thames, the Danube, the Isar (which flows through Munich). Give the cherry trees time to grow and it will be among the finest parks in the world. In his silent response Kawabata is perhaps the better prophet. Tsukuba is now invisible and concrete walls block off the view of a very dirty river. Only in cherry-blossom time do people pay much attention to the park, and even then it is not noticed as is the much older Ueno Park.

Kawabata has a walk down the whole length of the new Shōwa Avenue, from Ueno to Shimbashi. Some liken it to the Champs-Elysées and Unter den Linden. Kawabata does not. "I saw the pains of Tokyo. I could, if I must, see a brave new departure, but mostly I saw the rawness of the wounds, the weariness, the grim, empty appearance of health."

Famous old sweets, offered for centuries along the east bank of the Sumida, are now purveyed from concrete shops that look like banks. (Though Kawabata does not mention it, the mall in front of the Asakusa Kannon Temple was also done over in concrete, in another kind of revivalist style, the concrete molded to look like Edo. The main building of the National Museum of Ueno, finished in 1937, is among the most conspicuous examples of the style.) The earthquake memorial on the east bank of the Sumida, where those tens of thousands perished in the fires of 1923, is a most unsuccessful jumble of styles, also in concrete. Is it no longer possible, Kawabata asks of a companion, to put up a building in a pure Japanese style? "But all these American things are Tokyo itself," replies the companion, a positive thinker. And a bit later: "They may

*Shōwa Avenue (Shōwadōri), looking northwards from the
freight yards at Akihabara*

look peculiar now, but we'll be used to them in ten years or so. They may
even turn out to be beautiful."

Kawabata does think the city justly proud of its new bridges, some
four hundred of them. Indeed they seem to be what it is proudest of. In
a photographic exhibition about the new Tokyo, he notes, more than half
the photographs are of bridges.

In 1923 Tokyo was still what Edo had been, a city of waters. The
earthquake demonstrated that it did not have enough bridges. There
were only five across the Sumida. They all had wooden floors, and all
caught fire. That is why more people died from drowning, probably, than
directly from the earthquake. On the eve of Pearl Harbor, with the

completion of Kachitoki Bridge, there were eleven. Kachitoki means "shout of triumph," but the name is not, perhaps, quite as jingoistic as it may seem. Those who chose it in 1940 may well have had in mind the shout of triumph that was to announce a pleasant end to the unpleasantness on the continent, but the direct reference is to a triumph that actually came off, that over the Russians in 1905. The name was given to a ferry established that year between Tsukiji and filled lands beyond one of the mouths of the Sumida. The name of the ferry became the name of the bridge, a drawbridge that was last drawn almost twenty years ago. By the late fifties automobile traffic to and from Ginza was so heavy that there was congestion for two hours after a drawing of the bridge.

Nor were there enough bridges across the Kanda River and the downtown canals. These waterways did not claim the victims that the Sumida did, but they were obstacles to crowds pressing toward the palace plaza. Of the streets leading westward from Ginza toward the plaza and Hibiya Park, only three had bridges crossing the outer moat. The moat was now bridged on all the east-west streets, as also was the canal that bounded Ginza on the east.

Moat and canal now are gone. There was some filling in of canals from late Meiji, as the city turned from boats to wheels for pleasure and for commerce. Between the earthquake and the war several canals in Nihombashi and Kyōbashi were lost, but one important canal was actually dug, joining two older canals for commercial purposes. Other canals were widened and deepened. Both in 1923 and in 1945 canals were used to dispose of rubble, that reconstruction might proceed. It has been mostly since 1945 that Tokyo of the waters has been obliterated. In the old Low City the Sumida remains, and such rivers or canals as the Kanda and the Nihombashi, but the flatlands are now dotted with bus stops carrying the names of bridges of which no trace remains. Venice would not be Venice if its canals were filled in. Tokyo, with so many of its canals turned into freeways, is not Edo.

It was after the earthquake that retail merchandising, a handy if rough measure of change, went the whole distance toward becoming what the Japanese had observed in New York and London. Indeed it went further, providing not only merchandise but entertainment and culture. Mitsukoshi, one of the bold pioneers in making the dry-goods stores over into department stores selling almost everything, has had a theater since its post-earthquake rebuilding. Most department stores have had amusement parks on their roofs and some still have them, and all the big ones have gardens and terraces, galleries and exhibition halls.

The great revolution occurred at about the turn of the century, when Mitsukoshi and the other Nihombashi pioneer, Shirokiya, started diversifying themselves. What happened after the earthquake is modest by comparison, but a step that now seems obvious had the effect of inviting everyone in. Everyone came.

The change had to do with footwear, always a matter of concern in a land whose houses merge indoors and outdoors except at the entranceway, beyond which outdoor footwear may not pass. Down to the earthquake the department stores respected the taboo. Footwear was checked and slippers were provided for use within the stores. There were famous snarls. They worked to the advantage of smaller shops, where the number of feet was small enough for individual attention. After the earthquake came the simple solution: Let the customer keep his shoes on.

Simple and obvious it may seem today, but it must have taken getting used to. Never before through all the centuries had shod feet ventured beyond the entranceway, or perhaps an earth-floored kitchen.

Smaller shops had to follow along, in modified fashion, if they were to survive. In earlier ages customers had removed their footwear and climbed to the straw-matted platform that was the main part of the store. There they sat and made their decisions. Customer and shopkeeper were both supposed to know what the customer wanted. It was fetched from warehouses. Now the practice came to prevail of having a large part of the stock spread out for review. Floor plans changed accordingly. There was a larger proportion of earthen floor and a smaller proportion of matted platform, and customers tended to do what they do in the West, remain standing and in their shoes or whatever they happened to bring in from the street with them.

Private railways were beginning to put some of their profits from the lucrative commuter business, which in Meiji had been largely a freight and sewage business, into department stores. In this they were anticipated by Osaka. The Hankyū Railway opened the first terminal department store at its Umeda terminus in 1929. Seeing what a good idea this was—having also the main Osaka station of the National Railways, Umeda was the most important transportation center in the Kansai region—the private railways of Tokyo soon began putting up terminal department stores of their own. Thus they promoted the growth of the western transfer points—Shibuya, Shinjuku, and Ikebukuro—and their control over these most profitable of places.

The department stores discontinued old services. The bourgeois matron from the High City now had to come to the store. Fewer and fewer stores would come to her, as all of them had in the old days. New services were added as the railways began to open their stores and competition became more intense: free delivery, even free bus service to and from stores. If it asked that the matron set forth and mingle with the lesser orders, the department store made the process as painless for her as possible.

External architecture changed along with floor plans. Tiled roofs began to disappear behind false fronts. The old shop signs, often abstract and symbolic and always aesthetically pleasing, gave way to signs that announced their business loudly and unequivocally. Advertising was now in full flood. Huge businessman and little businessman alike had taken to it, and the old subdued harmonies of brown and gray surrendered to a cacophony of messages and colors. This seems to have been truer west than east of the Sumida. In the conservative eastern wards rows of black-tiled roofs were still visible from the street. The west bank was said after the earthquake and rebuilding to resemble a river town put up by the Japanese in Manchuria.

The first vending machines were installed at Tokyo and Ueno stations early in 1926. Like advertising, whose origins in Tokugawa and Meiji were so simple that they were almost invisible, vending machines have become an insistent presence in the years since. They now offer an astonishing variety of wares, from contraceptives to a breath of fresh air.

Like the practices and habits of shoppers, those of diners-out changed. The restaurant in which one eats shoeless and on the floor is not uncommon even today. Yet new ways did become common at the center, Ginza, and spread outward. Good manners had required removing wraps upon entering a restaurant, or indeed any interior. Now people were to be seen eating with their coats and shoes on, and some even kept their hats on. Before the earthquake women had disliked eating away from home—it was not good form. The department-store dining room led the way in breaking down this reticence, and the new prominence of the working woman meant that women no longer thought it beneath them to be seen by the whole world eating with other women. Before the earthquake a restaurant operator with two floors at his disposal tended to use the upper one for business and the lower one for living. Now the tendency was to use the street floor for business. An increasing number of shopkeepers (a similar trend in Osaka is documented in Tanizaki's *The Makioka Sisters*) used all the floors for business and lived elsewhere, most often in the High City. So it was that money departed the Low City.

The habits and practices of the Buddhist clergy were also changing. The priests of some sects had long married. Now there was an insurgency in a stronghold of Tendai, one of the sects that had remained celibate.

The Kaneiji Temple once occupied most of the land in Shitaya Ward that is now Ueno Park. There it ministered to the souls of six Tokugawa shoguns, whose graves lay within the premises. It was almost completely destroyed in the "Ueno War" of 1868, when the Meiji government sub-dued the last Tokugawa holdouts in the city. Sorely reduced in scale, the temple was rebuilt and came through the earthquake without serious damage. In the Edo centuries there were fifteen abbots, even as there were fifteen shoguns. All of the abbots were royal princes, and all were celibate, at least to appearances, though dubious teahouses in the dis-tricts nearby seem to have catered to the needs of the Kaneiji clergy. In Meiji the abbots started taking common-law wives. In 1932 one of them made bold to enter into a formal, legal marriage. The appointment of his successor was the occasion for a struggle between the Kaneiji and Tendai headquarters on Mount Hiei, near Kyoto. Hiei demanded that the Kaneiji candidate choose between marriage and career, and did not prevail. He had both. The Hiei abbots have gone on being celibate.

The female work force was expanding rapidly. In that day when Taishō democracy was dying but not quite dead, a few people were beginning to have ideas about the equality of the sexes. Already in Meiji, women had taken over nursing and the telephone exchanges. In the years before and after the change of reigns "red-collar girls" appeared. These were bus conductors, and their trade was almost entirely feminine until its extinction after the Second World War. Up and down Shōwa Avenue, the wide new street cut through from Shimbashi to Ueno after the earthquake, were gas-pump maidens. The day of the pleasure motorist had come, and pretty maidens urged him to consume. The day of the shop girl had also come. Sales in the old dry-goods stores had been entirely in the hands of shop boys.

The question of the shop girl and whether or not she was ideally liberated added much to the interest of the most famous Tokyo fire between the gigantic ones of 1923 and 1945. The "flowers of Edo," the conflagrations for which the city had been famous, were not in danger of extinction, but they were becoming less expensive and less dramatic. Firefighting methods improved, the widening of streets provided fire-breaks, and, most important, fire-resistant materials were replacing the old boards and shingles. Except for the disasters of 1923 and 1945, there have since the end of Meiji been no fires of the good old type, taking away buildings by the thousands and tens of thousands within a few hours. The number of fires did not fall remarkably, but losses, with the two great exceptions, were kept to a few thousand buildings per year.

The famous fire of early Shōwa occurred in a department store. It affected only the one building and the loss of life did not bear comparison with that from the two disasters. It was, however, the first multiple-storey fire the city had known, and the worst department-store fire anywhere since one in Budapest late in the nineteenth century.

The Shirokiya, an eight-storey building constructed after the earth-quake, was the chief rival of the Mitsukoshi through the years of diver-sifying and expanding. On the morning of December 16, 1932, a fire broke out in the toy department on the fourth floor. The end of the year had traditionally been a time of giving gifts, and Christmas gifts had of recent years been added to those based on older customs. The Taishō emperor brought Christmas Day into prominence by dying on it. Christ-mas Eve was now becoming what New Year's Eve is in the West. The Shirokiya was bright with decorations. A technician was repairing Christmas lights and a tree caught fire. The fire spread to the celluloid toys, and the whole fourth floor was soon engulfed. Fortunately this happened at a few minutes after nine, before the store had filled with customers. A watcher from a fire tower nearby saw the fire before it was reported. Firemen were changing shifts, and both shifts rushed to the scene. Presently every pump in the city was on hand. Not much could be done to contain the fire. The floors of the Shirokiya were highly inflammable and all the top ones were quickly in flames. The fire was extinguished a few minutes before noon.

Utility poles and wires along the main streets, and the narrowness of

The Shirokiya fire

side streets, made it difficult to use ladders, though some rescues were effected. Ropes and improvised lines from kimono fabrics in the store inventories brought people down and slings up to bring more people down. Army planes came by with ropes, although, according to the fire department, they were too late to do much good. It may be that no one except a single victim of asphyxiation need have died. The other thirteen deaths were by jumping and falling. The bears and monkeys on the roof came through uninjured, to demonstrate that the roof was safe enough throughout. The jumping was of course from panic. The falling had more subtle causes, having to do with customs and manners—in this instance, the slowness of women in converting to imported dress.

All shop girls in those days wore Japanese dress and underdress, wraparound skirts in various numbers depending on the season. Traditional dress for women included nothing by way of shaped, tight-fitting undergarments to contain the private parts snugly. The older ones among the Shirokiya women, also being bolder, made it safely down the ropes. Some of the younger ones used a hand for the rope and a hand to keep their skirts from flying into disarray. So they fell. In 1933 the Shirokiya started paying its girls subsidies for wearing foreign dress, and required that they wear underpants.

From about the time of the earthquake, advertising men had been pushing Western underdress for women, which they made a symbol of sexual equality. But a disaster like the Shirokiya fire was needed to effect decisive change. It demonstrated that women were still lamentably backward, and the newspapers loved it. Underpants became one of their favorite causes and enjoyed quick success, though the reform would actually seem to have begun earlier. Kawabata noted that all the little girls sliding down the slides in Hama Park were wearing underpants.

Some years earlier another department store, the new Matsuya in Ginza, which was to be the Central PX for the American Occupation, had provided the setting for another new event. The Shirokiya had the first modern high-rise fire, and the Matsuya the first high-rise suicide. It occurred on May 9, 1926. In a land in which, ever since statistics have been kept, there has been a high incidence of suicide among the young, suicides have shown a tendency toward the faddish and voguish. Meiji had suicides by jumping over waterfalls, and the closing months of Taishō a flurry of jumping from high buildings.

In May 1932 a Keiō University student and his girlfriend, not allowed to marry, killed themselves on a mountain in Oiso, southwest of Tokyo. The incident became a movie, *Love Consummated in Heaven,* and the inspiration for a popular song.

> With you the bride of another,
> How will I live? How can I live?
> I too will go. There where Mother is,
> There beside her,
> I will take your hand.
>
> God alone knows
> That our love has been pure.
> We die, and in paradise,
> I will be your bride.

At least twenty other couples killed themselves on the same spot during the same year.

Early in 1933 a girl student from Tokyo jumped into a volcanic crater on Oshima, largest of the Izu Islands. Situated in and beyond Sagami Bay, south of Tokyo, the islands are a part of Tokyo Prefecture. The girl took along a friend to attest to the act and inform the world of it. A vogue for jumping into the same crater began. By the end of the year almost a thousand people, four-fifths of them young men, had jumped into it. Six people jumped in on a single day in May, and on a day in July four boys jumped in one after another.

On April 30 two Tokyo reporters wearing gas masks and fire suits descended into the crater by rope ladders strengthened with metal. One reached a depth of more than a hundred feet before falling rocks compelled him to climb back up again. They found no bodies. After more elaborate preparations the *Yomiuri* sent a reporter and a photographer into the crater a month later. Using a gondola lowered by a crane, they descended more than a thousand feet to the crater floor. There they found the body of a teenage boy.

The year of all these suicides seems to have been a nervous and jumpy one in general. It was the year in which Japan, having rejected the Lytton Report, left the League of Nations. The report demanded that Japan withdraw from Manchuria. Feelings of isolation and apprehension seem to have swept the land. Yo-yos were bobbing everywhere. Peak sales ran to five million a month. During the summer, the withdrawal from the League having come in the spring, everyone was out in the streets and in the parks, hopping about to the accompaniment of the great hit song of the day, "Tokyo Ondo" ("Tokyo Dance"). The music of this is by Nakayama Shimpei, generally held to be the founder of modern Japanese popular music, and the lyrics are by Saijō Yaso, a poet of such distinction that he is given three pages in a one-volume encyclopedia of modern Japanese literature.

The lyrics do not say very much. Half of them and a bit more are meaningless chants to keep rhythm by: *sate ya-a to na sore yoi yoi yoi*, and that sort of thing. Interspersed among them are fleeting references to places and things and combinations of the two, such as the moon upon the Sumida, the willows of the Ginza, and Tsukuba and Fuji, the mountains that are supposed to adorn the Tokyo skyline but seldom do.

Advised that the dancing in Hibiya Park was disturbing His Majesty's rest, the Marunouchi police ordered it to desist at nine o'clock. At Asakusa the police did the opposite, protected the dancers. They had had reports that the movie theaters, most of whose potential customers were out in the streets dancing, had hired men from underworld gangs to break the dances up. In parts of town the dancing crowds stopped traffic, and the police were powerless either to disperse or to protect.

The number of Tokyo suicides doubled during the first decade of Shōwa. The number of attempted suicides doubled in three years toward the end of the decade. Despondency, illness, and family difficulties were the predominant motives. The effects of economic depression are to be detected in the last category. The number of suicides began to fall with the approach of war and continued to fall during the war.

The most famous suicide of early Shōwa occurred in the northern suburbs of Tokyo. On July 24, 1927, the writer Akutagawa Ryūnosuke killed himself with an overdose of "Veronal, etc.," as accounts of the event uniformly have it. He did not, as General Nogi did, choose the day of the emperor's funeral, but his passing has widely been taken as symbolic of the passing of the Taishō reign.

A remarkable Kawabata essay, "Akutagawa Ryūnosuke and the Yoshiwara" ("Akutagawa Ryūnosuke to Yoshiwara"), published in 1929, associates the Akutagawa suicide with the horrors of the earthquake, and so makes it yet more symbolic.

Hirotsu Kazuo describes in a recent story how he and Akutagawa Ryūnosuke, having seen Uno Kōji to a hospital, went off for a look at the Tamanoi district and its unlicensed prostitutes. . . . I had an account directly from Mr. Hirotsu, and the impression it left was more powerful than that of the story. The conclusion had a certain ghoulishness about it, with the women of Tamanoi turning pale as Akutagawa passed, and whispering to one another: "A ghost, a ghost!"

Akutagawa had by then completed preparations for his suicide, and so I wanted to attach all sorts of meanings to the anecdote, and of course I remembered how, some five or six years ago, I went with him to look at the Yoshiwara. . . .

I had been taking long walks through the city every day from September 1. There cannot be many who saw as well as I did what the earthquake had done. I believe I was sitting on the veranda of the Akutagawa house describing a little of it. Akutagawa himself suggested, I think, that he and Mr. Kon and I go look at the bodies in the Yoshiwara pond. Akutagawa was wearing a striped kimono and a helmet. The helmet was incongruous, like a gigantic toadstool perched on the thin face and figure. Walking along in those great strides of his, swinging his body as if about to take flight, he looked like a villain setting forth on some evil mission. He was a war-horse striding past the devastated wastes, up streets that were a tangle of charred electric lines, among survivors tired and dirty as war refugees. I was a little annoyed with him and the briskness that put him in such contrast with everyone and everything else. As I ran after him, I thought what fun it would be if a policeman or a person from the vigilance committees were to stop him and question him.

The pond beside the Yoshiwara quarter was one of those horrible pictures of hell which speak only to someone who has seen the real thing. The reader should imagine tens and hundreds of men and women as if boiled in a cauldron of mud. Muddy red cloth was strewn all up and down the banks, for most of the corpses were those of courtesans. Smoke was rising from incense along the banks. Akutagawa stood with a handkerchief over his face. He said something, but I have forgotten what. Probably it was something light and sarcastic, well worth forgetting.

He came upon a policeman in the Yoshiwara. For a kilometer or so on our way back they walked side by side, and he drew forth all manner of information about the earthquake. The policeman was an accommodating sort who answered all his questions. . . .

For me who had so little to do with Akutagawa while he lived, the picture that comes first to mind, now that he is dead, is of that helmeted figure striding vigorously along with no regard for his surroundings. There was in it a lightness and briskness that contained no hint of death.

But when, two or three years later, he had made his resolve to die, the picture must have come back into his mind, I am sure, of those horrible corpses piled on one another in the Yoshiwara pond. He seems to have deliberated all sorts of ways to die in search of one that would leave a handsome corpse. In contrast to the handsome death, its antithesis, were those corpses in the pond.

That was the day in his life when he saw the largest number of them.

And I who was with him in observing the most repellent of deaths can perhaps visualize his handsome death better than those who have been spared the repellent kind.

All of the other persons mentioned were well-known writers. Tamanoi is a district east of the Sumida River, then in the suburbs. Until 1945 it contained an unlicensed pleasure quarter. It is the setting of Nagai Kafū's A *Strange Tale from East of the River* (see pages 52–53).

The Taishō era needed a literary symbol, and Akutagawa was a good one, embodying (or so it is widely held) the sometimes neurotic refinement and intellectualism that were products of the great Meiji endeavor to encompass and catch up with the West. The common view has therefore been that his suicide, more than the death of the emperor, brought an end to an era. It is not easy to establish that Akutagawa's mental illness was peculiar to the era. Yet he will do as a symbol, as the poor emperor will not. The emperor's illness ran in the direction of retardation, which will hardly do for either Meiji or Taishō. The Akutagawa suicide provides reasonable grounds for considering the unlikely Taishō reign an independent and in some measure self-contained cultural period.

The new and popular words of the post-earthquake years were mostly foreign. This seems proper for that relatively cosmopolitan day of Taishō democracy; people did not have to be apologetic about importing their neologisms. Things were rather different in the late thirties. The Japanese language has always been hospitable to new words. Tokyo, where the lords of the media and of advertising have their seats, has coined most of them and helped others to spread. Numbers of Osaka words have made their way into the standard language, but they have had to be adopted by Tokyo before prevailing in the provinces.

Here are some popular words and expressions from late Taishō and early Shōwa: "It," "shan," "mobo" and "moga," "Charleston," "manne-quin girl," "modern life," "stick girl," "casino." The significance of some should be clear enough, some require explanation. (Among the pleasures of modern Japanese is that its use of one's own language so often requires explanation.) "It" refers to the Clara Bow quality. "Shan" is from the German *schön*. It is a masculine term referring to feminine beauty. The mannequin girl is a particular kind of beauty, the fashion model. Though models had been used in advertising even before the earthquake, the modeling business really got started in 1929. From the spring of that year all the big department stores began using them. Curiously, an early photograph of the Mannequin Club—like most other people, models quickly formed a club which had as its chief aim the exclusion of every-one else—shows almost all of the ladies in Japanese dress. "Stick girl" will be found above, in Tanizaki's remarks about his native city. "Mobo" and "moga" are acronyms, and among the words that might be thought symbolic of the age itself. They are from "modern boy" and "modern girl" (*garu*): the advanced young people of the day, the ones most sensitive to fad and fashion, they who went strolling in Ginza and had their pictures taken at Sukiya Bridge.

Many a neologism has had its brief day and gone, but all of the above remain in the language and are to be found in any dictionary. "Casino," from French rather than Italian or English, might be rendered "music hall." A neologism that did not gain immediate currency but has since become very much a part of the language was first used in a women's magazine in the spring of 1929. Before the earthquake "mama" was already supplanting native words for "mother." "Mama-san," adding the common appellative, now came to indicate the lady in charge of a café or bar, also often called a "madame."

Taishō was a time of great change. Such places of entertainment as the cafés make Ginza, for instance, come to seem near and familiar. And, given that wars, especially lost ones, and economic miracles are always potent engines of change, there has been no paucity in this re-spect in the years since. A 1929 survey of Tokyo *sakariba* shows us a city that is in important and interesting respects different from the city of today. The biggest of Japanese-English dictionaries gives "a bustling place" as one of its definitions of *sakariba*. These are places where crowds gather, and where revelry and shopping occur with the greatest intensity.

The *sakariba* covered are Ginza, Shinjuku, Ueno, Asakusa, Shibuya,

Ningyōchō, and Kagurazaka. No one today would include the last two, and Asakusa would be a borderline case; and no one would leave out Ikebukuro or Roppongi. Omissions and inclusions tell of the westward march of the city. Now among the gigantic transfer points in the old western suburbs, Ikebukuro was slower to get started than Shibuya and Shinjuku, those other western giants. To the huge profit of the Seibu Railway, one of the private commuter systems, it has grown hugely this last half century. The southern wards contained no bustling places in 1929. Shibuya lay beyond the city limits. Roppongi is in the old Azabu Ward, but it is a latecomer which got its start as a camp follower. This was in the late nineteenth century, when war (a victorious one in this instance) brought military barracks to the district. It has really emerged since the Second World War, as the most highly amplified of the *sakariba* and among the ones dearest to the very young.

Ningyōchō was lively in Meiji and has been in decline since the earthquake. So has most of the old Nihombashi Ward, the recognized center of mercantile Edo. Ningyōchō is as good a place as any to go in search of the mood and flavor of the old Low City, but it is not the smallest competition with a place like Shinjuku in the matter of drawing crowds. Kagurazaka, in Ushigome Ward, to the northwest of the palace and not far from the western limits of the old city, was for a time after the earthquake among the leading *sakariba*. It was one of the uptown geisha districts for which the knowledgeable Nagai Kafū had great contempt. Their geisha were, he thought, without accomplishments other than those of the bedroom. Kagurazaka had its period of prosperity with the destruction in the earthquake of the Low City pleasure quarters. It lay near a station on the western suburban line of the National Railways, but was not a transfer point, and so was outstripped by Shinjuku, which was.

The 1929 survey was made in the afternoon at all the places except Ningyōchō, where it was done in the early evening. In none of them do women outnumber men. Shinjuku in midafternoon has the highest proportion of women, 43 percent, and of these only a third are recognizable as housewives. In Ginza at four o'clock, young men account for almost half, young women only a little over a tenth; and so those who went strolling seem to have done it mostly by themselves or with male companions. *Mobo* were most commonly without *moga*. Asakusa, as noted above, would today be a borderline instance. It drew big crowds a half century ago but does no more. In 1929 the golden age of the music halls was just getting underway; yet the survey contains ominous signs. The proportion of young men is much smaller than in Ginza, and that of middle-aged men higher. Already so early, it may be, the blight was setting in. The middle-aged crowd may spend more generously, but it is the young crowd that sets the tone and ensures that there will still be crowds for a while. When the young start to abandon a place, it is in for bad times.

The sex ratio would be different today. Ours is a much more womanized age. At four in the afternoon women would probably outnumber men in any of the places that still draw great crowds, except just possibly Ueno. Asakusa, Ningyōchō, and Kagurazaka do not.

The survey also spelled out categories, which would seem to show that a great uniformity has settled over Japanese crowds this past half century. Here is a full list of them: provincials, soldiers (Ueno had the most), shop boys, laborers, young boys, male students, youths (other than students, presumably), middle-aged men, old men, old women, housewives, young women, female children, female students, serving maids, geisha, and working women. They obviously are not carefully enough defined to be mutually exclusive, but we may assume that the surveyors could confidently, albeit vaguely, distinguish the categories one from another. Many of them would be indistinguishable today—students from other young men and women, for instance, and housewives from serving maids, or shop boys and laborers from other young men the same age. Many a provincial these days could easily cross the line and pass as a Tokyo person. There has been a leveling process which some might call democratic and others might call conformist.

Another survey of 1929, of department stores, also reveals a few interesting things. There were as many men as women. Today there might just possibly be on a Sunday afternoon, if an uncommonly large number of wives were able to drag their husbands forth on shopping expeditions. There certainly would be at no other time. The categories, again, call for notice: gentlemen, merchants, provincials, housewives, working women, serving maids. Again they are obviously rough, and they cannot be all-inclusive. Why are there no children and no students, who were in those days, as they are not now, easily detectable by their uniforms? Yet the categories are more distinctive than they would be today. Almost two-thirds of the men are in Western dress, but only a sixth of the women—and only 2 or 3 percent of "adult women," which category is not defined. The tendency of women to stay longer in traditional dress than men seems to be universal, and was clear in Japan from the beginning of Meiji. Cosmetics seem to have been a way of distinguishing the urban lady from the provincial. Heavy applications were the mark of the provincial.

Since 1898 Tokyo had had a mayor who presided over the "ward part" of the prefecture, the fifteen wards of the Meiji city, whose limits remained almost unchanged until 1932. Appointed governors had jurisdiction over the whole prefecture, including the "county part," the towns and rural regions that lay outside the city limits. Population was already spilling beyond the city limits in 1923, and did so ever more rapidly in the years that followed. The city wished to go west, and indulged the wish more and more.

Already in 1923 the prefecture was growing faster than the city. The process speeded up after the earthquake. Because the suburbs suffered relatively light damage, many of the 1923 refugees did not return, and population increase tended toward places where land was cheaper. With 1918 considered as 100, the population of the wards stood at only 90 in 1932. It fell by about a sixth immediately after the earthquake (though this was by no means as drastic a fall as that during and after the upheavals of 1867 and 1868 and the disaster of 1945). It quickly began to recover, but at no time before 1932 had it returned to the 1918 level. The population of the prefecture, again with 1918 as the base, stood at 156 in 1932, and the population of the city as its limits were redrawn in 1932—the population, that is, of the fifteen old wards and twenty new ones—stood at 322. Even what remained of the counties, to the west of the newly enlarged city, had risen to 129 as against 100 for 1918.

In 1920 the city still contained more than half the population of the prefecture. In 1930 the proportion had fallen to between a third and two-fifths. Four towns on the edges of the fifteen wards had more than a hundred thousand people in 1930. Fifteen had fifty thousand to a hundred thousand. The expansion of 1932 lagged far behind the facts. The city was much larger than the area the mayor had jurisdiction over.

As the old city filled up and spilled over, so did its cemeteries. The big new ones of Meiji, along the western limits of the city, were filling by the end of Taishō. Plans were completed on the eve of the earthquake for a new one, out in the "county part" of the prefecture, not far from the Tama River. It too was filling before the new reign was a decade old. This time the city looked eastward. A tract was purchased at a place named Yasumi in Chiba Prefecture. Yasumi seems a most pleasant and appropriate name for a cemetery. The commonest word for "rest" is homophonous.

The western and southern suburbs were growing more rapidly than the northern and eastern ones. So once more we have evidence of the decline of the Low City. The northern and eastern suburbs were an extension of the Low City, the southern and western ones of the High City. The southern suburbs, on the way to Yokohama and in the industrial belt that lay between the two cities, were growing fastest of all. The town of Ebara, immediately beyond the southern city limits, had more than fifteen times the population in 1932 that it had had in 1918. Only one town to the north and east had an increase of more than sevenfold during the same period.

The suburbs, particularly the western and southern ones, were the realm of the *bunka jūtaku,* the "cultural dwelling," a euphemism for the kind of dwelling the "salaryman" or office worker was expected to be happy in. ("Salaryman" is a coinage from English which seems to have come into use during the First World War.) A cultural dwelling typically had three or four little rooms, one of them in a somewhat Western style, two floors, a floored kitchen, and a bath. In more traditional houses for the middle and lower orders the kitchen had a floor of packed earth. The private bath marks a major departure from tradition. In recent years it has become more economical for a family to bathe at home than to go to a public bath, and so of course the public bath has declined grievously. The public baths of Edo and Meiji were social and even cultural centers. Many cultural dwellings had pink and blue roofs, and so we have the beginnings of the plastic look, to replace the earthen look of the older styles.

At irregular but convenient intervals among all the new cultural abodes were shopping districts, many of them called the Something Ginza. Thatch-roofed farmhouses still dotted the suburbs, and some of them still had lands to farm. In late Taishō there was farming in eleven of the fifteen wards. Today there are truck gardens and a few paddies in the twenty new wards, but none in the fifteen old ones.

Universities began deserting the old city after the earthquake. Burned out in Kanda, the University of Commerce (Shōka Daigaku) moved by stages to the place where, with the name Hitotsubashi from the old site, it now is, far out in the western suburbs. Burned out in Asakusa, the University of Technology (Kōgyō Daigaku) moved out to the paddies in what is now Meguro Ward. Keiō, one of the better-regarded private universities, built itself a second campus in Kanagawa Prefecture, beyond the Tama River. In this it was abetted by one of the private railways, many of which were also energetic real-estate developers. Title to the new land passed, without reimbursement, from the Tōyoko (Tokyo-Yokohama) Railway to the university. Today the Tōyoko is a part of the Tōkyū, or Tokyo Express, system. Keiō retained the original campus in the old High City where it had since early Meiji been an evangelical center for Westernization.

The growth of the suburbs was not only residential and educational. Industry was also moving outward. In 1932, when rebuilding from the earthquake was held to be complete, more of the large factories in the prefecture—factories with more than a hundred workers—were outside than inside the city. By the thirties the district from southern Tokyo into Kanagawa Prefecture was emerging as one of the great industrial belts of the country, and the largest in the Kantō region. Really heavy industry situated itself across the Tama River in Kanagawa, but there were many subcontractors in what from 1932 were the southern wards of Tokyo. By that year the prefecture had passed Osaka in industrial output.

Tokyo bound far the largest number of books, printed far the largest number of pieces of paper, and made far the most pencils in the country. It excelled in what might be called the literate industries. Early in the thirties, chemicals were the largest Tokyo industry. By the end of the decade, with the war approaching, machine tools had emerged as the largest. Of the five wards with the largest industrial output, only one, Honjo east of the river, was in the old city. The largest of all was Kamata, a part of the Tokyo-Kanagawa industrial belt. The district east of the river continued to be one of light industry, while the south was heavy. Most of the printing was done in the old city, because that is where the newspapers were.

The burgeoning of the suburbs has not, as in many American cities, meant the withering away of the center. Ginza, at least, and to an extent

Ueno have held their own against the growth of the suburbs and the places—Shibuya, Shinjuku, Ikebukuro—where office workers on their way to and from suburban cultural dwellings change trains. Because centers yet farther east, prosperous in Edo and Meiji, have declined with the general decline of the Low City, Ginza may no longer be at the center of a cobweb; but the westward movement of the city has not emptied it. Westernmost among the lively centers of Meiji, it is now, with Ueno, the easternmost. It is still a place upon which rapid-transit lines converge, bringing crowds. We hear of a "doughnut effect" in Tokyo. It unquestionably is there, but the doughnut is an eccentrically shaped one, not exactly penannular, but far puffier to the left, as we face the top of the map, than the right. The center is not merely a hole.

If we think of the center as a larger complex than Ginza proper, including Nihombashi to the north and Marunouchi to the west, there has been a shift. This has been remarked upon above. Nihombashi is relatively less important than it was as a retail center, having lost ground to Ginza, and as an entrepreneurial center, having been the victim of a shift to Marunouchi. Yet few people would have been inclined during the interwar years to think of Shibuya or Shinjuku or Ikebukuro as the center of the city. Some might incline toward Shinjuku today, but Ginza would probably come at worst second.

These were the great years of *Gimbura,* another of the acronyms of which the Japanese are so fond and for which they have such a gift. The first syllable is from Ginza, and the other two are from *burabura,* a mimetic word which indicates an aimless wandering or an idling away of time. "Fooling around in Ginza" might do for a translation. The *Gimbura* crowds were young. They may not have had much to spend in the newly risen Ginza department stores, but they were an animating presence. More than any other part of the city, Ginza was the place to be. Yet it was first among peers. Tokyo has always been a city with several centers. That is why it is often called not a city but a collection of villages. "A collection of cities" might better catch the truth.

The Shōwa reign was a year and five days old when, late in 1927, the first Tokyo subway line began service. It was the first in the land, and in Asia. The route was a short one, less than a mile and a half long, between Ueno and Asakusa. Four companies had franchises to dig; only one started digging. The same company extended the line to Shimbashi in 1934. The entrepreneur who owned all the land around Shibuya and brought the private commuter line into it saw his opportunity. Shimbashi must not remain the terminus. So he started digging from Shibuya, and his line was opened to Shimbashi in 1939. There were two Shimbashi stations, without free transfer between them. The two companies were brought together, and the stations united, in 1941, under a public corporation whose capital came from the National Railways and the prefecture. Remnants of the other Shimbashi subway station can be detected a short distance toward Shibuya from the one now in use.

The two halves of the Ginza line, as it is now called, show a certain difference in spirit. The northern half, from Shimbashi to Asakusa, was dug by a company specializing in transportation and interested in pleasing its customers. Some of the stations are rather charming, in Art Deco and traditional styles. The station next south and west from the Asakusa terminus was decorated with the family crests of famous actors. That was deemed in keeping, and one must heartily agree that it was, with the nature of the district served. The stations south and west of Shimbashi are uniformly drab and boxlike, the product of an entrepreneur whose chief interest was in getting hordes of people as rapidly as possible

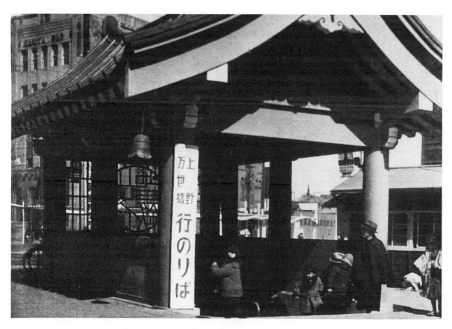

Entrance to the new subway in Asakusa

into the Tōyoko department store, on the third floor of which the line ends. So we might say that the Ginza line symbolizes transition. The northern half belongs to the past, the southern hall to the emerging future.

The earliest section, Ueno to Asakusa, was a huge popular success. It had turnstiles adapted from New York ones. People would go in and out, in and out. They could not do it on Sundays and holidays, however, when a wait of as much as an hour was required to get aboard for a five-minute ride. Stories of subway picnics seem a little unlikely, given the shortness of the route.

The subway company put up high buildings at each of its two original terminuses, Asakusa and Ueno. (For the Asakusa terminus, see page 72.) The Ueno terminus had a department store, on its front a clock, illuminated at night, said to be the largest in the world. It was some twenty meters in diameter. Both buildings have been torn down in the years since the war. Subway people do not seem to have had the heads for retailing possessed by the people of the surface railways.

The Ginza line, not quite nine miles long, was the only line in existence during the war years. Construction did not begin on a second line until 1951, when another reconstruction of the city was underway. Thus well over 90 percent of the splendid system we have today is postwar. Though not badly planned, insofar as it was planned at all and not given over to mercantile ambitions, the Ginza line was not ideally planned to alleviate congestion on the National Railways. Shinjuku was growing more rapidly than Shibuya and would have been a better terminus. The National Railways continued to provide faster transportation from all commuter transfer points except Shibuya than did the subway. Yet it probably helped to keep Ginza at the center of things, and for this we must be grateful. Rapid transit had terminated just south of Ginza when the railway line to Yokohama opened in early Meiji and skirted it when, early in Taishō, the National Railways began service through to Marunouchi. Now it ran north and south under the main Ginza street.

Another change in the transportation system favored the suburbs. Buses grew numerous and important, and, most naturally, the trolley system entered upon the decline that has in recent years brought it near extinction. With the trolley system and the railways heavily damaged by the earthquake, large numbers of little companies sprang up to take people to and from the suburbs—almost two hundred of them, mostly short-lived, in two months. Motorized public transportation was in much confusion. In the mid-thirties there were still several dozen private bus lines, in competition with one another and with the municipal buses.

The private railways, enterprise at its boldest and most aggressive, were getting into the bus business. They still are in it, most profitably. They were also in the department-store business and the real-estate business. In both of these they were anticipated by the Hankyū Railway in Osaka, which was the first company to open a terminal department store. In one Tokyo instance, the real-estate business came first, the railway afterward. A land company that owned huge tracts in the south-western suburbs and on into Kanagawa Prefecture built a railway, the Tōyoko, to push development and, incidentally, to make Shibuya the thriving center it is today. The Tōyoko also developed a garden city, a "city in the fields," which is today one of the most affluent parts of Tokyo. It gave Keiō that new campus, out in Kanagawa Prefecture beyond the Tama River.

With the completion of the Yamanote line in 1925, Tokyo Central Station may have become the front door to the nation, but it did not itself have a back door. The throngs poured forth on Marunouchi, where Mitsubishi had built its brick "Londontown," a showplace of Meiji. As early as the thirties it was beginning to tear Londontown down, and today almost nothing remains; and Mitsubishi was beginning also to lose its monopoly. The proportion of non-Mitsubishi offices in the district rose from a tenth to two-fifths between the wars. We need not pity Mitsubishi, however. Marunouchi had by then become the undisputed managerial and entrepreneurial center of the land.

In 1929 Tokyo Central got its rear or east entrance, facing Kyōbashi and Nihombashi. The new entrance was a limited one. For long-distance tickets people still had to go around to the front, or south to Shimbashi. It was only after the Second World War that the rear entrance began to offer full services. Nihombashi has never recovered from its earthquake losses, but the new entrance has brought a turnabout. The east side of the station, known as Yaesuguchi or "the Yaesu Mouth," has become a much livelier place for shopping and revelling than the older Marunouchi Mouth.

The name Yaesuguchi is an interesting one, and a somewhat mobile one. A Dutchman named Jan Joosten Loodensteijn had his residence and business on an inlet of the bay near what is now Hibiya Park. By the familiar acronymic process and by assimilation with an old word for "fish weir," Jan Joosten's strand became Yaesu. The inlet disappeared in the seventeenth century and so of course did the strand, but the name survived and moved northward and eastward to where it now reposes. Together with the more famous Englishman Will Adams, Loodensteijn served the first Edo shogun.

Unlike most of the High City and the suburbs, Shinjuku suffered heavy damage in the fires of 1923. A part of the district had been incorporated into the city in 1920, but the vicinity of the railway station still lay beyond the city limits. The station, the car barn, and the Musashino, the largest and most popular movie palace in the High City and beyond, were all destroyed. This was probably good for Shinjuku, famous earlier for its horse manure, clouds of which would blow up on windy days like the yellow dust storms of Peking. With wartime prosperity and the beginnings of suburban growth, it was ready to take off. Buses began to run from Shinjuku into the suburbs, and the trolley line westward from the palace was extended to Shinjuku Station. A new station was completed in 1925. It too produced a turnabout. The main entrance had faced south, on the highway westward to the mountains and the province of Kai. The new one faced northward, in the direction of the postwar and post-earthquake boom.

Mitsukoshi opened several emergency markets throughout the city just after the earthquake. In 1924 its Shinjuku market became its Shinjuku branch, the first Shinjuku department store. After a move or two it settled where it is now, a few steps east of the east entrance to the station. The forerunner of the Isetan store was in Shinjuku, on the present Isetan site, in 1926. Two big private railways had come into Shinjuku by 1930. One of them set up a retail business, called the Keiō Paradise, the second word in English, in the upstairs of its Shinjuku terminus.

Old shops were rebuilding and transforming themselves, with an eye to the sophisticated and literate sorts who had to set foot in Shinjuku every working day. The Kinokuniya, an old lumber and charcoal dealer, moved westward from Yotsuya and made itself over into a bookstore, the biggest now in Shinjuku and one of the biggest in the city. A greengrocer near the station became the Takano Fruits Parlor, one of the places everyone knows. The last two words of the name are in English. An insistence upon putting "fruit" when used as an adjective into the plural is a little idiosyncrasy of Japanese English. "Fruits punch" has long been a standard item on the menus of such places everywhere.

A jumble of the old and the new, Shinjuku was already a traffic nightmare in the twenties. Automobiles and construction projects blocked the main streets, stalls and crowds blocked the back streets, lines of sewage wagons backed up each evening. Growth continued even with the panic and depression. Shinjuku took business from such places as Kagurazaka in the old High City. By about 1930 Shinjuku was second only to Ginza as a retail center.

It was one of the "mouths," the last of the old post stations on the way into and the first on the way out of Edo. Pleasure quarters grew up at all of the "Five Mouths." The old Shinjuku quarter straggled along the Kai highway. Shortly before the earthquake it was brought together into a more compact and easily definable and controllable neighborhood, just at the city limits after the 1920 annexation of a part of Shinjuku. Like Kagurazaka, it benefited from the destruction in 1923 of the Low City pleasure quarters. It was the noisy, bustling center of Shinjuku until things began to get lively near the main entrance to the new station.

The Shinjuku of the interwar years, like Asakusa, is often referred to as second-rate, and again the standard of comparison is Ginza. According to such members of the Ginza congregation as the novelist Ooka Shōhei, Shinjuku ran altogether too easily and giddily in pursuit of the modern and "high collar," two expressions meaning very much the same thing. The modern boy and modern girl went to extremes thought unseemly and in bad taste by high Ginza. Certainly it was the place where the Marx boys gathered, as to a lesser degree were the stations along the Chūō line of the National Railways. From precisely these regions was to emerge the new intelligentsia that dominated the media in the years just after the San Francisco Treaty of 1952. The phonograph was far more conspicuous in Shinjuku roistering places than the samisen, and these places were known for their large, ribald women, with limbs such as foreign women were thought to have. Street stalls made the narrow streets yet narrower. By the early years of Shōwa, Shinjuku was probably the most crowded place in the city, at least during the prime evening hours. It had more street musicians than Ginza. It had flower women and children, their wares both real and artificial, and fortune-tellers and beggars, a constant stream through the evening hours.

Shinjuku had all of these in the twenties, and, except that the street stalls are gone, must have been rather as it is today. In the thirties it became a sort of western capital some distance behind the eastern one at Ginza-Nihombashi-Marunouchi. It had a famous slum too, even as Asakusa had one, just north of the temple. The Shinjuku slum was just south of the department stores, a place of cheap inns, bedbugs, and a transient population of day laborers, peddlers, street musicians, hawkers.

The Shinjuku quarter was one of six licensed ones. Two, including the venerable and once-glorious Yoshiwara, now fallen sadly, were within the limits of the old city. Three lay beyond, at three of the old "mouths," or stations. The Shinjuku quarter straddled the city limits. After 1932 they all lay within. Then there were the unlicensed quarters, the "dens of unlicensed whores" (shishōkutsu), the most famous of them beyond the city limits. At about the time Japan went to war with China (the Japanese have preferred to call the war an incident), Nagai Kafū

The liveliest part of post-earthquake Shinjukū, near the old licensed quarter

wrote one of his best works about the Tamanoi quarter, by then within the city limits but before 1932 in the northeastern suburbs. A lady there reminded him of Meiji and his youth, and gave the lie to his contention that Meiji quite disappeared in 1910 or so. Because of Kafū, Tamanoi was the most famous of the unlicensed quarters, but it was second in size to Kameido, a bit to the south. The Kameido district, on the north or back side of the Kameido Tenjin Shrine and its splendid wistaria, gave sustenance to some seven hundred ladies. Tamanoi had fewer than six hundred. Prostitution was quite open in both places. There was little to distinguish them from the licensed quarters, except perhaps that in the latter procedures for obtaining employment were more complicated, hygienic facilities were better, and the ladies did not have to work as hard. The Kameido quarter had been there from late Meiji. Like Tamanoi, it had its best years after the earthquake.

Shinjuku may at certain hours of the evening have had a greater press of bodies than Ginza, and certainly that is one of the things the city loves best, but it was still second-rate Ginza. The high life of the years after the earthquake centered upon the cafés. In these Ginza was preeminent, the place that other places looked up to. The early interwar period was the full summer of the cafés, and this word almost demands the qualification "Ginza."

Shibuya had about it much more the look of the one-company town than Shinjuku. It was quite dominated by the Tōkyū Railway system. As a place for reveling it has always been some distance behind Shinjuku, though polls have shown that the teenage crowd prefers it. In one respect it was at the very forefront of progress. Along with Asakusa, it offered a multilevel transportation, entertainment, and retail complex. Representations of the future as seen from the thirties, with rocketlike objects shooting off in all directions and shooting back again, look as if Shibuya might have been the inspiration.

The Shibuya complex has been described as very Tokyo-like. If by this is meant that it is very crowded and cluttered and difficult to find one's way about in, then the characterization is apt. Shibuya has the only subway station all along the Ginza line that is not underground. Indeed the tracks are high above the ground, the highest of all the tracks in the complex. The Tōyoko department store is mazelike and inescapable. Perhaps that is what the founding magnate had in mind. The arrangement of the station is in another respect not wholly irrational.

What is now the busiest part of Shibuya, still countrified after reconstruction

The use of the hill beyond as a turnabout station and car barn makes it possible to run subway trains in very quick succession. The assumption that everyone will benefit once he or she gets the hang of it all (a little time and study may be required) also seems very Tokyo-like.

At the beginning of Meiji "the flower and the willow" quite dominated the high demimonde. The former was the courtesan and the latter the geisha. It is not easy to say just what a geisha is. The expression is a vague and complex one covering a broad range of prostitutes and performing artists. Geisha of the more accomplished sort, and the literal significance of the word is something like "accomplished sort," were the ones the affluent merchants of Edo and Meiji looked to for elegant and expensive entertainment. Their accomplishments were in traditional music and dance, at their best in the pleasure quarters, whether licensed or "private," and in the theater.

There came Western incursions. Opinions will differ as to whether the nightclub entertainer and the bar girl of our day are as accomplished as was the geisha of old, but the geisha has gradually yielded to them. The story of the high life of this past century might be told as the retreat of the one and the advance of the others. If Nagai Kafū had been a century younger and, as Tanizaki was, a true son of the merchant class, he would probably have spent his bachelor nights among the flowers and willows, to the extent that he could afford them. Being a man of conservative tastes, he did not forsake these people, but far more of his nights during the post-earthquake years were spent among the tinselly flowers of the Ginza cafés.

Ginza, not Shinjuku, would have been recognized by almost everyone —and certainly by Kafū, who did not often go to Shinjuku—as the place for them. The number of drinking spots in Kyōbashi Ward, which included Ginza, was twice in 1930 what it had been in 1920. This is to say that in one decade the accumulation of such places equaled what it had become through all the decades before. The big buildings of Ginza came through the earthquake and fire fairly well, but not the little ones along the back streets; so building and rebuilding were feverish in the half dozen years after. Each day the Ginza of the cafés must have indeed been as the old gentleman of *During the Rains* saw it, not the Ginza of yesterday.

These years also had bars, dance halls, and cabarets, all of these words from either French or English. Distinctions among them, though cultural historians tend to treat them as obvious, are not always clear. In a general way a café was a place, sometimes small and intimate, sometimes big and noisy, but always, when it was doing well, crowded, whose clientele drank, took light refreshments, and enjoyed the company of pretty girls. We have the testimony of Kafū, among others, that many of the girls were scarcely distinguishable from the courtesans, those other flowers of Edo. Their company could be made, if the conditions were right, to last through the night. Café ladies in Kafū's fiction have a way of complicating things for themselves by accepting too many after-hours engagements.

An Osaka influence is discerned in the gaudier of the Ginza cafés. (It was just before the earthquake that Ginza became what it is today, the district on either side of the old Edo–Kyoto highway that lay between two bridges, the Kyōbashi on the north and the Shimbashi on the south. Before then only the northern part had, strictly speaking, been Ginza.)

In a Ginza café

Crowds on the main Ginza street

The Osaka-style bars of northern Ginza were very gaudy and very big, illuminated in many colors with neon lights and flashing bulbs and dancing spotlights. The smaller and more modest Tokyo sort prevailed to the south. Predictably, Tanizaki Junichirō, having departed Tokyo in 1923 and turned vociferously against it, preferred the Osaka version.

> All up and down the back alleys of Ginza are tiny, intimate cafés. . . . To be sure, Osaka cafés with their noisy bands are somewhat vulgar; but no one could possibly call these cramped little places in the smallest degree elegant. It is not as if there were only a scattering of them. They are numberless, each with its own steady little clientele. The Osaka kind may be vulgar, but they do at least require a certain investment. These Tokyo ones do not. Five or six tables crowded together in a tiny room, nondescript furnishings thrown together from nothing, dim indirect lighting to conceal the tatters, a French name to attract ambitious young literary types: such places have sprung up like bamboo shoots after a rain.

It is peculiar for an aesthete like Tanizaki to distinguish between good and bad in terms of money spent, and the passage perhaps does damage to the impression he assiduously cultivated of the quiet classical repose to be found in the Kansai. One may suspect, moreover, that had the Osaka version and the Tokyo version been reversed, he would have preferred the former then too. There was little that he liked, or professed to like, about Tokyo in those years. Yet it does seem to be the case that Osaka capital was quicker than Tokyo to plunge into the entertainment industry—and that little cafés sprang up like (as we would say) weeds.

The principal character of Kafū's *During the Rains*, written in 1931, is a promiscuous café lady. She works in a place called the Don Juan, so crowded in among other cafés that one must be attentive to avoid going in the wrong door. It is in the northern, "Osaka" part of Ginza, and fairly large, the main downstairs room covering an area of some seven or eight hundred square feet. Stepping through the front door—over which, in Roman letters, is the name of the place supported by two naked feminine statues, or paintings, it is not clear which—one has chiefly an impression of clutter. Screens and booths and tables are everywhere, lights and artificial flowers hang from the ceiling, genuine greenery is like thickets on the Kabuki stage. One does well not to enter by the alley and through the kitchen. Bluebottle flies buzz among garbage cans, and an odor of stale cooking oil pours from a hut of corrugated metal that might have been put up just after the earthquake.

Kafū loved dressing rooms. Here is the Don Juan one:

> You kept your shoes on to climb the steep stairway from the earthen floor of the kitchen. At the head of it was a room maybe a dozen feet square all along the walls of which were mirror stands, fourteen or fifteen of them. It was a few minutes before three, the hour of the change of shifts, the morning one to the evening one. The place was so crowded that you could not find a place to sit down. The girls jostled one another as they pushed their faces forward into the mirrors.

The Don Juan seems to have kept long hours. At midday it must have been more like a European than a Tokyo café, and the ladies on the early shift must have had more of the night for sleep than did Kimie, our heroine.

A striking thing about descriptions of Ginza cafés is how familiar they look. Gentlemen with a taste for the high life gather now in Ginza and Shinjuku bars, and gathered then in Ginza cafés. The two seem very much alike. One may find it a little hard to imagine what a "milk bar" of Meiji may have been like, but not a Ginza café of early Shōwa. (Milk bars were places where intellectual and literary people went to read difficult publications and discuss constitutionalism and such things.)

The novelist Takeda Rintarō describes a café in his novel *The Eight Ginza Blocks (Ginza Hatchō),* written in 1934. The title is an up-to-date one, referring to the newly expanded Ginza, eight blocks of it from Kyōbashi to Shimbashi. The café is making its way through a dull Sunday evening.

> From time to time the door would open. Everyone would look up in anticipation of a customer; but always there would be, and in considerable numbers, children selling flowers, and imitators of famous actors and singers, and mendicant priests with boxes inviting contributions to the Church of Light and Darkness, and violinists, and sketchers of likenesses, and lutists, and solemn-

faced young men in student uniform selling pills and potions, and, with babies tied to their backs, women selling horoscopes. They would all of them glance inside and, seeing that there were no customers, be on their way.

The priests, wandering adherents of Zen, would be uncommon today in Ginza and Shinjuku bars, and guitars and accordions would be more likely than violins and lutes. The Ginza café of 1930 or so, however, does not seem so very different from the Ginza bar of today.

Eroguro, sometimes *eroguro nansensu,* is the expression held to capture more than any other the mood of early Shōwa. It is the Japanese equivalent of "Flapper Age." *Nansensu* is the English "nonsense." *Eroguro* is another product of the Japanese talent for acronyms and abbreviations. It is compounded of the first two syllables of "erotic" and the first of "grotesque," the latter made into two syllables by the Japanese dislike of consonant clusters. The radical reactionaries of the thirties were against *eroguro nansensu,* even as they were against money-grubbing. Already before the earthquake there were cries for a return to the solid and austere old ways. After the earthquake, voices were raised telling the city that it was Sodom, punished by the heavens for being so. Tsubouchi Shōyō, a distinguished man of letters and a leader of the avant-garde theater, heard a Diet member remark in London that divine punishment had come for all the looseness and frivolity, all the moral laxness. Shōyō asked why divinity had chosen to punish those tens of thousands of people east of the river who did not have enough money to be frivolous and loose. The reply is not recorded.

As it concerns the cafés, the erotic half of the word is easier to apprehend than the grotesque. Suggestions as to what the latter half signified in their regard are mixed and contradictory. Also in *The Eight Ginza Blocks,* Takeda Rintarō describes a Ginza bar as dark and spooky in an outmodedly grotesque style. This suggests something crepuscularly Gothic; yet the *eroguro* that came from Osaka would seem to have had noise and light as its most conspicuous qualities. We may conclude that "grotesquerie" refers very generally to what made a new cabaret distinctive.

When we turn to the sideshows at Asakusa and their tendency toward what anyone would recognize as grotesque, it does not seem so very new. In the Asakusa park of Meiji there were, among others, a spider man and a woman who smoked through her navel. These we may describe as reasonably grotesque. In *Scarlet Gang of Asakusa,* Kawabata Yasunari describes a worthy successor in the post-earthquake years to the woman who smoked without troubling her respiratory tract. The scene is one of the little huts in the park.

"That it may be of use to medical science," cries the man on the stage, "we will show you right before your eyes how he eats through the mouth in his stomach.

"The man with the hole in his stomach was born in Asahigawa on the island of Hokkaido. The liquor with which he fended off the snow and the cold was pure alcohol. It produced strictures of the esophagus. So the doctors at Hokkaido Medical College opened this hole in his stomach.

"Unfortunately there were no teeth in the mouth the doctors made. So he has this bill, like a bird's."

It was true. The man in white untied the cord of the cloth around the bill, an object like a tobacco pipe inserted into his stomach.

Putting a glass funnel into the pipe, he poured milk and bread crumbs inside.

"Even in his pitiful condition he seems unable to forget the taste of sake. Occasionally he has a cup. He tastes it with the mouth in his face and drinks it through the one in his stomach. . . . Are not the advances of medical science marvelous?"

In another story from Kawabata's Asakusa period a young man back in Asakusa after an absence for his own safety gives a quick impression of how it has changed: "It's gotten to be just like Osaka." Which, if we turn again to Ginza, brings us back to lights and noise.

The grotesquerie is more elusive than the eroticism. It may be that they were put together because they sounded good together, and the first is the dominant half of the *eroguro* pair. This does not seem so very new either, although the borders of the erotic were pushed constantly back as the years passed. It took more to arouse a person. Primly dressed young women who played and sang traditional music were erotic in Meiji, as we may judge from the crowds of young men who poured in to look at them and perhaps listen to them as well. Now a certain expanse of flesh was asked for.

In a society dominated by men, it is most natural that women should dominate the world of sensuous pleasure. The girls in the big, flashy Osaka cafés are said to have had "It," the Clara Bow thing. They were becoming more aggressive and less inhibited. In the early days, when Kafū was frequenting Ginza cafés with English names like Lion and Tiger, the ladies stayed in the background, pleasant to look at and not expected to make much noise. Men went for masculine companionship, much as they must have gone to the coffeehouses of Dr. Johnson's London.

Now the ladies emerged to take charge of the conversation. The age of the waitress gave way to that of the hostess. We are still in the latter age.

There was a "Hostess's Song," the lyrics once more by Saijō Yaso. Here are the first two of four stanzas. The other two are similarly damp and aggrieved.

> I am a bar flower
> That blooms by night.
> Rouged lips,
> Gauze sleeves,
> Mad dancing
> By neon light,
> A flower watered by tears.
>
> I am a bar flower,
> A sad flower,
> By evening a girl,
> By day a mother,
> Tear-dampened sleeves
> Concealing the past.
> They are heavy as the night wears on,
> And not with dew.

Japanese popular music is so flooded with tears that we need not take them very seriously. Though such a world is bound to have its sorrows and uncertainties, Takeda Rintarō tells us, again in *The Eight Ginza Blocks,* that the world of the Ginza cafés was tight and snug.

> The same people worked all the numberless places of the Ginza back streets. They moved from place to place, rarely staying long in any one of them; they all knew all the others. They knew everything about one another: foibles and general disposition, of course, and very private matters as well. It was the same with the customers. If each stronghold had its own little troop, it was a rare customer who limited himself to one place. They moved about, and so customer and hostess and manager were all of them acquaintances. The drinking places of the back streets were one world. For the clientele it was like a club, for management it was like a chain store.

Many if not all hostesses were, like Kimie of *During the Rains,* accommodating. Prices rose as the ladies came forward to dominate the scene, and so did tips. The ordinary "salaryman" could afford to go to one of the fashionable places perhaps once a month, on payday. Takeda Rintarō tells us that students were not welcome at the café of *The Eight Ginza Blocks.* They did not have enough money. Though they were not refused admission, it was hoped that they would sense the chill in the air and depart.

So another institution, the *kissaten,* literally the tea shop, emerged to fill the gap. An impecunious student could spend a whole afternoon for the price of a cup of coffee, and look at pretty girls who did not say much of anything after they had brought the cup. This meant essentially, on the simpler levels of the entertainment and pleasure business, a reversion from the age of the hostess to that of the waitress. It is a remarkable business, leaving no need unfulfilled, providing every commodity and service, and it is what the puritan radicals of the thirties objected to; and the product of their activism has been a society in which they would find much more to object to.

Tanizaki may have been right that the tiny Tokyo-style places all had French names, to attract customers with literary ambitions and pretensions. The bar that is the main setting for *The Eight Blocks of Ginza* is called L'Automne. Some of the famous tea shops also had French names: Colombin, Mon Ami. More had English or American: Columbia, Olympic, Eskimo, and Europe, the last pronounced in a way that established it as English and not French or German. Kafū was fond of a place called Fuji Ice, half of the name a Japanese proper noun and half an English common one.

For a time after 1923 Osaka may have been the first city of Japan. Artists and intellectuals fled to the Kansai district, of which Osaka was the center, in great numbers. They started coming back once Tokyo was comfortable again. Tanizaki was the great exception. He stayed not far from Osaka for most of his remaining years, although he never lived in the city. We have already seen an Osaka influence on the Ginza cafés and on the media. Osaka was largely responsible for the growth of monster newspapers. Only the *Yomiuri* among Tokyo natives stood out successfully against Osaka incursions.

And Osaka may be blamed in part for the decline of the Rakugo comic monologue. Both Osaka and Tokyo had monologues, marvels of versatile mimicry. Even before the earthquake a form called Manzai was replacing Rakugo in Osaka. Dominant in the closing years of the Taishō reign, it advanced upon Tokyo. Not all Osaka influences can be described as baneful, but this one surely was. Manzai performers come in pairs and crack jokes, sometimes funny. The difference between Manzai comedians and good Rakugo performers is that between the stand-up comic and the actor. The latter has skills and devices and puts himself into multiple roles. The former chatters, and if he is successful people sometimes laugh at the chatter. It is perhaps the difference between art and life, the one creating a world of its own, recognizable and persuasive but apart, the other being merely itself. Manzai has not raised the quality of popular culture.

Probably through Manzai, Osaka speech began lending words to Tokyo speech, the national standard. Tourists may not be aware that when they call the traditional livery jacket a "happy" they are using an Osaka word, *happi*. Many Tokyo people are similarly unaware that *shōyū*, almost universal now to indicate the soybean condiment, is an Osaka loan word.

Already in decline before the earthquake, Edo cooking surrendered the realm of high and expensive cuisine to Osaka. The most famous riverside restaurant of Edo was a victim of the earthquake, or, more precisely, the reconstruction. It stood on land marked for the new Sumida Park. Rebuilding elsewhere would have been possible, but the owner took a good price for the land and withdrew. His clientele came in from the river, and, with wheels replacing boats, the river was not what it once had been. Today Edo cooking survives in a few proud old restaurants surrounded by Osaka ones. Here the Osaka influence is not to be called baneful. Osaka cooking is more subtle and imaginative than that of Edo. So is Nagasaki cooking, which also has spread.

But the share of the blame which Osaka must take for the decline of such popular arts as Rakugo is small compared with that which may be assigned to the rise of mass entertainment, whose day had come. Audiences had been small in Edo. Even the biggest Kabuki theaters and the Sumō wrestling tournaments had drawn only a few hundred. Now they swelled to millions.

Among the celebrities who came visiting, to great acclaim, were some whom the new age had created. They were products of the twentieth century and its mass culture, and Japan was part of the twentieth century even as it had been trying hard to be a part of the nineteenth. Entertainers had come from abroad in Meiji, but they had had limited audiences in their native places and had similar audiences in Japan. Without question the foreign visitors who raised the greatest stir in Meiji

Charlie Chaplin tries a Japanese snack during his visit

were General and Mrs. Ulysses S. Grant. Next, perhaps, was an Englishman named Spencer, who did aerial stunts. Possibly the nearest equivalents in early Shōwa to the general and his lady were representatives of high technology and high culture. The *Graf Zeppelin* flew over the city in 1929 and was moored over water some miles to the east. George Bernard Shaw came in 1933. It would be hard to say that either quite captured the eager attention of the nation as the Grants did. They did not pay it as great an honor, and the nation would probably not have been as alive to the honor if, say, Calvin Coolidge had come. All people had to do was look up as the *Graf Zeppelin* flew over; they did not jam the streets for a look at its crew. They did for Mary Pickford and Douglas Fairbanks, who came the same year. Charlie Chaplin was in town on the day in 1932 when the prime minister was assassinated, the third prime minister to be so dealt with in this century, and the second in less than two years. The prime minister's son was supposed to take Chaplin across the river to the Sumō tournament on that beautiful late-spring Sunday. Chaplin went anyway.

The mass audience is not a uniquely Japanese phenomenon, of course. It was not something the Japanese did for themselves. Though one could not reasonably say that it was forced upon them, the way had not been prepared in Tokyo as it had in London and New York. Baseball did not give way to Sumō in New York as Sumō gave way to baseball in Tokyo.

The decline of Sumō is a relative matter. Baseball did not replace it immediately and has never replaced it completely. The only spectator sport in Edo, it has had its ups and downs in the century and more since Edo became Tokyo. The years before and after the earthquake were fairly good ones. There were popular wrestlers. The Kokugikan, "Hall of the National Accomplishment," the Sumō stadium near the earthquake memorial east of the Sumida, was badly damaged in the earthquake. Money for repairs flowed swiftly in. The national accomplishment, which is to say Sumō, has gone through periodic spasms of reform and modernization. The major one in the years after the earthquake led to the formation of a legally incorporated Sumō association. The Tokyo and Osaka bands of wrestlers came together, on the understanding that tournaments would be held alternately in the two cities. This was thought admirably in the spirit of Taishō democracy, but was not sufficient to prevent new crises. Another split came in 1932, a few Kantō defectors going off to Osaka with the Osaka stalwarts to form a new band. The tournaments that resulted were not popular. Neither band had enough celebrated wrestlers to fill the top ranks. A reunion was arranged in 1933, though holdouts sulked in Osaka until 1937.

The crowds that gathered for Sumō, even in the Kokugikan, were small compared with those that were to gather for baseball, which may not call itself the national accomplishment, but is. Among the very young, Sumō was probably still more popular than baseball in the years just after the earthquake. It had a radio following and presently would have a television audience as well. Newspapers did a good business in Sumō extras. It may be that radio audiences for Sumō were as large as for baseball when popular wrestlers were doing well, but here conjecture must prevail. There were no commercials and no ratings, and NHK, the public radio corporation, had a monopoly. But if Sumō was sporadically popular, baseball has been consistently and increasingly so. Sumō is no competition at all when it comes to television huckstering.

Japanese baseball began in Tokyo, and Tokyo has been the baseball capital ever since. The early period was ambiguously amateur. The big teams belonged to the universities. A tourist guide published by the National Railways in 1933 could still say that "the biggest attractions are the matches organized by the leading universities in the spring and autumn." The big baseball universities, Waseda and Keiō, did not stint in their support of promising players. A game in 1905 raised animosity between them to such a pitch that it was thought better for them not to see each other again. They resumed play in 1925, the last full year of Taishō. The best baseball stadium was in the outer gardens of the Meiji Shrine, often called Meiji Park. The shrine and gardens are a memorial to the Meiji emperor. The gardens, complete with stadium, were finished in October 1926, when the reign of Meiji's successor had only two months to go. A three-university league, all of its members in Tokyo, was formed early in Taishō, and by the end of the period, with the accession of the perpetual cellar team, Tokyo University, it became what it is today, a six-university league.

The semiprofessional status of the celebrated university players aside, there were already in late Taishō the beginnings of professional baseball. An organization called the Shibaura Society, named for filled land by the bay where it had its grounds, assembled nonstudent players for whom the game was more than sport. Its first games were with Waseda, which won. Waseda received the larger part of the credit for the sizable crowds. Ahead of its time, the Shibaura Society moved to Osaka. Professional baseball did not really get underway until the mid-thirties. It was not the Shibaura team but a Tokyo one, Shōriki's Yomiuri Giants, named by Lefty O'Doul, that was to become the national team. Wherever they go nowadays the Giants draw crowds, as no Osaka team does except in Osaka, and Osaka teams do better even in Osaka when playing the Giants.

Shibaura is at the southern edge of the Low City, but the Meiji Gardens are on the far southwestern fringes of the old High City. An attempt after the Second World War to give the Low City a baseball park of its own was not well received. Only teams from the non-Giant league played in it, and the crowds did not come. The Giants have their home park on the edge of the High City. So baseball and television, which fill the spare hours of the Low City, do not come from there.

March 22 is "founding day" for radio. On that day in 1925 experimental broadcasts went forth from Atago Hill in Tokyo, the high place just north of the Tokugawa tombs in Shiba Park that had been popular for its view of Edo and of Meiji Tokyo. There were also broadcasts in Osaka and Nagoya. The first program was elevated and eclectic: Beethoven, classical Japanese music, a play by Tsubouchi Shōyō which sought to bring Kabuki and Shakespeare together.

The three regional radio companies were amalgamated the following year into Nihon Hōsō Kyōkai, the Japan Broadcasting Corporation, a public corporation that has always identified itself to its audiences by the English pronunciation of its initials, NHK. Through the war years NHK had a monopoly on broadcasting. Commercial broadcasting came only in 1951, a few months before the first television. Tokyo Rose's popular wartime broadcasts were over NHK.

Movies were first among the forms of popular mass entertainment. So they continued to be until television began having its day. When old people, the lucky few who are able to, reminisce upon good times in Asakusa, they are likely to be talking of the music halls, and the "opera" they offered before the earthquake and the "reviews" after. They do not speak of Asakusa as the great center for movies. That is probably because

live, legitimate forms were very much *of* Asakusa, and movies were everywhere.

Yet Asakusa was the center. In 1930 it had fourteen movie theaters.
The next-largest concentrations were on or beyond the city limits, at
Shinjuku and Shibuya, with four each. A quarter of a century later,
when television was beginning to bring bad days for the movie business
and turn Asakusa theaters into game parlors, Asakusa had fallen a little
behind the Ginza-Marunouchi complex in number of theaters (it was
still ahead in the number that showed Japanese films) and was ahead of
Shinjuku by a bit.

Kawabata did a survey of Asakusa in 1930 which showed theaters
with live performances to outnumber movie theaters. There was a variety
of styles of the former, but no single kind had as many places in which
to show itself as did the movies. Asakusa still had a half-dozen Yose, or
Rakugo variety halls, not as grievous a decline as one might have expected
from the dozen or so of late Meiji. It had a single Kabuki theater, a small
one, whereas it had had almost a monopoly on Kabuki when the shogunate fell. Then there were review places, to be discussed, places offering
traditional music of more than one kind, and places whose chief attraction was swordplay, masculine and feminine, the latter the more popular
because somewhat erotic.

But mostly there were the movies. Asakusa drew its crowds from all
over the city. The High City and suburban places, Shibuya and Shinjuku and the like, got few people from the Low City. Asakusa had a
"theater department store." Three houses under the same management
stood side by side along the main Asakusa theater street. Passageways
joined the three, and for the price of a single ticket the devotee could
make a day of it, wander back and forth among them, and enjoy the
offerings of all. Not much remains of the street from its best days, but,
thanks to their continuing to be under the same management, all three
houses survive, all with yellowish brick fronts, one surmounted by bat-
tlements, one with a plain-bellied front broken only by windows, the
third with decorative windows in an Art Deco style. The connecting
passageways also survive, but they have been left to spiders and rats for
almost half a century. The survival of the middle theater, the plain-
fronted Tokiwaza, is a modest triumph for the conservation movement.
Until 1965 it was devoted to stage productions. Then it became a movie
theater, and in 1984 it closed entirely and demolition was in prospect.

The Asakusa Sixth District in the great age of the movies and music halls; the three theaters shown were joined together, and they still survive—see page 68

Local pressures and donations from wealthy persons with attachments to Asakusa persuaded the Shōchiku entertainment company, owner of the three, to keep it open for recitals and short-run performances.

One Asakusa motion-picture theater was famous for a noisy ceiling fan. It was very popular. The attention the fan called to itself made people feel cool. The *benshi* must have been rather sorely tried, however. These remarkable and very Japanese performers were like Rakugo monologuists. Without the use of amplifiers, they declaimed all the parts on the screen above them, male and female, and told the story as well, so that the audience might be informed. They even spoke in measured phrases, alternating syllable counts of seven and five, like balladeers of old. There were *benshi* contests, one performer per reel. The advent of the talkie brought bad times. The man known as the last of the *benshi* died in the summer of 1987. He was only in his mid-sixties, and so he was a child when talkies came. It may be that others like him still preserve the art somewhere.

69

The first talking pictures from abroad required *benshi*. Between 1929, when the first one came, and 1931, when subtitles were first affixed (to *Morocco*) and when also the first Japanese talkie appeared, the *benshi* went on doing what he had been doing all along, a little more loudly perhaps. A Japanese audience viewing a foreign film had a *benshi* talking away in front of it while Greta Garbo and Gary Cooper were talking away on the screen. Garbo, noisy fan, no amplifier: it must have called for a durable voice, and kept people awake.

A strike by *benshi* against technical progress was in vain. Such strikes always seem to be, and one may wonder why. If it is true, and we are assured by those who remember the good *benshi* days that it was, that people often went to movies as much to hear the *benshi* as to watch the movie, why did there not continue to be a demand for silent movies? The very notion of technical progress seems to disarm resistance except on the part of those whose livelihood is immediately affected. It seems inevitable and it seems good, and those who prefer silent movies, like those who prefer silent radios and television sets, are ashamed to admit the preference.

Silent movies had background music too, and theme songs. The most popular song of very early Shōwa was from a movie, *Tokyo March* (*Tokyo Kōshinkyoku*), which is also the name of the song. It is by the Nakayama-Saijō combination of "Tokyo Dance" (see page 36). There are four stanzas, about Ginza, Marunouchi, Asakusa, and Shinjuku. Here is the Ginza one:

> The Ginza willows bring thoughts of the past.
> Who will know the aging, fickle woman?
> Dancing to jazz, liqueur into the small hours.
> And in the dawn a flood of tears for the dancer.

There is at least one foreign word per stanza. In this one "jazz," "liqueur," and "dancer" are all in English (the transcription into the Japanese syllabary suggests strongly that the second is not French). The fourth stanza, the Shinjuku one, advocates running away from it all via the Odakyū, the Odawara Express, a private railway line opened between Shinjuku and Odawara, at the foot of the Hakone Mountains in Kanagawa Prefecture, in 1927. The railway objected to the recording company that if the name was to be used at all it must be used in full, Odawara

Kyūkō Denki Kidō Kabushiki Kaisha. This did not fit the music very well, and the abbreviation Odakyū prevailed. The song was a huge piece of free advertising for the railway. Today no one calls it anything but the Odakyū. The invitation to flee via it has a stylish, up-to-date ring, for it runs through wealthy suburbs to what in another culture might have been called a hill station.

Some of the Asakusa theaters offered more than *benshi* and music to go with their movies. One burned incense in its pits during funeral scenes, which were frequent, bereavements being frequent. Movies were rated according to the number of handkerchiefs they made sodden with tears. One little theater jiggled and chugged as the view from an observation car passed on the screen.

During his Asakusa period, Kawabata was living just behind Ueno Park, within easy walking distance of Asakusa. He said in 1934 that he went there almost every day for three years. Sometimes he wandered about all through the night. Asakusa was a nightless place, the only part of the city with all-night restaurants. The best chronicler of Asakusa during those years, Kawabata found the crowds interesting even at the most unpromising of hours, the morning ones. Men who had passed the night in the Yoshiwara quarter north of Asakusa were on their way home, and geisha on their way to matins at the great Kannon Temple.

Yet, he said, Asakusa produced nothing of the really highest order. There had been a decline, certainly, since the last years of Edo, when Asakusa had had the best of the theater and, in the Yoshiwara, some of the best chamber performances as well. It may be that Kawabata's most famous Asakusa piece, *Scarlet Gang of Asakusa,* is a little like Asakusa itself. Mannered, diffuse, obscure, inconclusive even as Kawabata novels go, it is second-rate Kawabata; but it is interesting. Asakusa may have been second-rate by Ginza standards, but it too was interesting.

In *Scarlet Gang,* Kawabata quotes a famous songwriter approvingly:

> "Asakusa is the pulse of Tokyo.
> Asakusa markets humanity."

These are the words of Soeta Azembō.
"Asakusa of the myriads flings everything forth in the raw.

All manner of desire dances there naked. All classes and all races mix into one great flow, limitless, bottomless, not distinguishing day from night. Asakusa is alive. The masses edge forward. Asakusa of the masses, melting down old forms to be cast into new ones."

In early Shōwa, Asakusa was still what it had been in Meiji, the most bustling among the *sakariba,* the "bustling places," of the city. It was the great purveyor of inexpensive entertainment. For centuries the grounds of the temple had been a place where people went to amuse themselves, often in coarse and vulgar ways. The doctrine of the temple was easygoing. From Meiji into Taishō there were new entertainments, notably the movies and the Twelve Storeys, the brick tower that fell apart in the earthquake.

The Twelve Storeys acquired a successor in early Shōwa. Here too, as in so many things and ways having to do with Asakusa, there was a falling off. The Twelve Storeys, when it was put up, was the highest building in the city. The tower that arose over the new subway station was by no means the highest. It was only six storeys, or some hundred thirty or forty feet high. Yet from the observation platform on the top floor one could see, on a clear winter day, Mount Tsukuba in the east and Mount Fuji in the west, and in the near distances a great deal of smoke, from factories, from trains, and from the brewery built on the site of the old Tokugawa estate. One riverside villa yet remained on the far bank. The new tower, Kawabata said, was in the Osaka style. All the floors except the top observation one were occupied by eating places.

The movies attracted the biggest audiences, but it was the legitimate theater that interested Kawabata, and is likely to interest us a half century and more later, when the crowds have gone the way of Kabuki and the geisha. Before the earthquake there was the Asakusa opera, and after the earthquake the Asakusa review. We learn in local histories of an opera period and a review period, as if these forms were clearly distinguished from each other. A catastrophe came between, to give the impression of a cultural break, with a conclusion on the one side and a beginning on the other. (So it was to be with the catastrophe of the forties. Before it were the reviews and after it the strip shows.) The reviews had a longer period to die in than did the opera. The reactionaries of the thirties did not approve of such things and the war years brought an end to almost all theatrical performances. Yet the several genres are not discrete. They blend into one another.

The beginnings of the reviews are in the opera, the ancestry of which was Italian. An Italian impresario named G. V. Rossi is the recognized progenitor. Though the word "review" itself seems to have come from English, the reviews were ostensibly of French ancestry. ("Opera" is probably from Italian.)

Rossi never worked in Asakusa. First at the Imperial Theater in Marunouchi and then at a place which he bought near the southwestern city limits, he endeavored to produce Italian opera, including Mozart, using Japanese performers. Some of his disciples transferred the enterprise to Asakusa. The Asakusa performances based on Italian scores must have sounded more like operetta or musical comedy, people with pleasant voices singing in a manner all natural and unrestrained. The best of them had little musical education. The performance whose opening night is considered the birthday of Asakusa opera was definitely light and scattered. The language and the writer were Japanese. It could have been called a review.

Hamamoto Hiroshi, a novelist who died in 1959 and who drew most of his material from Asakusa, said toward the end of his life that the Asakusa opera was ruined by its own most fanatical supporters. Predominantly male—women preferred the movies, where they could all weep into their handkerchiefs—they demanded eroticism. They demanded a "decadent" (Hamamoto's word) something of the singers. Then there were dancers. Singing and dancing continued after the earthquake, but were beginning to look tired. They could not carry it all off by themselves.

A new element was added: bright, fast comedy, thought to be Gallic. So the review came into being. "Eroticism and nonsense and speed," said Kawabata, "and humor in the vein of the topical cartoon, and the jazz song and legs." All the items in the medley except the last are in English. So maybe it is the most important—it and the foreignness, the fact of depending so on a foreign language.

Whether or not the review was greatly inferior to the opera, and whether or not the break between the two is a clear one, the day of the review was the last time Asakusa could be ranked high among the *sakariba*. It may also have been the last time the Low City, center of Edo

An Asakusa review

mercantile culture, could be called the center and the producer of anything cultural at all. (Ginza, as we have seen, is a special instance, in
but not of the Low City.) Asakusa has not done much in recent decades
to return the affection of people like Hamamoto.

July 10, 1929, is the birthday of the Asakusa review, and it was born in
a little place called the Casino Folies. The founders, two brothers, had
been to Paris, and they loved the follies, and combined the Casino de
Paris and the Folies-Bergère to give their theater its name. The Casino
Folies occupied the second floor of an aquarium on a back street, next
door to an entomological museum. "It came to be," says Kawabata in
Scarlet Gang of Asakusa, "that the girls of the Casino Folies passed the
fishes in their tanks and turned in by a model of the sea king's palace to
go to their dressing rooms." They also had to pass "dusty cases of flies,
beetles, butterflies, and bees." The aquarium and the Bug House were
"relics of the old Asakusa Park, left behind in the Fourth District."

What was known as Asakusa Park, not much of it very parklike, was divided into seven districts. The Casino Folies was some distance from the main theater district, which was in the Sixth District, much the most famous and crowded of the seven. The founding brothers, besides their love for Paris and its follies, had a modest amount of money. They rented a place somewhat apart from the main Sixth District street because they could afford it. Kawabata's *Scarlet Gang,* the first part of it serialized in the *Asahi Shimbun* from December 1929, attracted attention to the Casino Folies and made it popular. Those whom Kawabata called Ginza people started coming.

The reviews were to be more popular than the opera had ever been, but the original Casino Folies did not last long. At a disadvantage when theaters nearer the heart of the Sixth District started presenting reviews, and deserted by its most famous performers, it changed management in 1932. Ownership of the property remained with the aquarium, which survived because groups of schoolchildren were taken there to look at goldfish and turtles. Often they had to be rounded up by their teachers after sneaking upstairs and getting themselves in at reduced prices to look at the reviews. Curiously, children watching the reviews did not seem to upset the police as did children going to movies, some of which were forbidden to them.

The Casino Folies produced actors and actresses who were to become very famous. The actress Mochizuki Yūko was in her later years so successful in movie portrayals of troubled mothers that she became known as Japan's mother; she got her start in the chorus line at the Casino. She was the daughter of the caterer who delivered lunch to the troupe; an actor looked at her legs and said she might join. The actor was Enomoto Kenichi, probably the most popular of all Japanese comedians. Enoken, an acronym from the two elements of his name, is how everyone knows Enomoto. He has been called the Joe E. Brown of Japan, but he was more versatile than Brown. Besides having an impish and feckless kind of charm that made people smile before he had uttered a word, Enoken was a rather good singer and a very lithe dancer. Had Danny Kaye been around at the time, he might have been a more appropriate American analogue than Brown. The son of a shopkeeper in Azabu, one of the affluent wards along the southern tier of the old High City, Enoken defied the Azabu notion of what a schoolboy should do and went off to watch Asakusa opera. Though he made his debut at the age of fifteen in one of the Sixth District opera houses, he had to wait for the reviews before he attracted attention, and the reviews had to wait for him. The July birthday assigned to the reviews might better be the November date when Enoken came onstage at the Casino.

He left the Casino Folies in 1930 for the bigger theaters in the Sixth District, where he headed troupes with such Gallic names as Poupées Dansantes and Pierre Brilliant. From them he moved on to the big movie and management companies and the central theaters, the ones near Ginza. The reviews thus became big time, with huge troupes and budgets. The Casino had ten girls or so in its chorus line. In the big theaters there were sometimes as many as a hundred people onstage at one time. Asakusa may not have produced the very best of anything, but performers who went on to be the best at what they did got their start in Asakusa. Though the "crisis" of 1937 and after was not deemed a time when people should be funny in public, and though Enoken was in very bad health in his last years, he did not give up until his death early in 1970, at the age of sixty-five. Not even the amputation of a gangrenous foot stopped him, and indeed he showed great ingenuity in converting his disability into comedy. It was sadder in his case than it would have been for others, because in his prime his versatility included dancing and acrobatics.

An impression that Enoken alone made a success of the Casino Folies and the Asakusa reviews would be wrong. Kawabata certainly helped. Enoken himself was to say in his late years that what really brought in the crowds was a rumor that the girls in the chorus line dropped their drawers on Friday evenings. It was, he said, a false rumor. Reminiscing back over a half century, Mochizuki Yūko said that a girl did in fact one day let the cotton wraparound drop from her breasts. It was an accident, and it may have been the source of the rumor. Falling drawers would not have signified very much in any event, said Miss Mochizuki, because the girls wore their own (and this before the Shirokiya fire) under the uniform stage costume. To give more strongly a sense of Paris, they sometimes wore golden wigs.

Miss Mochizuki described the test, a simple one, which candidates for the line had to pass. They raised their skirts, so that Enoken might have a look at their legs. Legs were what was wanted. They were very young girls, and by all accounts very innocent compared with the ladies of Kafū's café pieces. The average age was sixteen or seventeen. Kawabata tells of a girl who, at eighteen, had never worn cosmetics. Many commuted to the review houses from home. In one of Kawabata's shorter Asakusa pieces several girls pass the night in the narrator's apartment, and it is all very virginal, not in the least suggestive of Kafū's orgies. The erotic element had to do almost entirely with the lower limbs. The shoulders and a patch of the back might have been exposed, but the breasts were obscured by wraparounds of cotton. It was hardly extreme nudity. Yet the police were touchy.

They forbade ad-libbing, for one thing, because they disliked surprises. As a device to forestall it they required that scripts be presented ten days in advance. Ad-libbing had been among the principal techniques of the comedians and it went on despite the ban. They did not have time to learn their lines very well. Besides, it was often the impromptu gag that brought the best laughs.

The police also worried about the garb and demeanor of the girls and handed down regulations. Drawers must cover at least the top ten centimeters of the thigh. Flesh-colored drawers were not permitted. A portion of the back might be exposed, but the whole front of the torso must be covered from a safe distance above the breasts. There might be no suggestive lighting about the hips and pelvis, no kicking in the direction of the audience, and no wriggling of the hips. If the girls wore tights for photographs, they must also wear skirts. And so on, through nine articles. The Casino girls were one day herded off to the Asakusa police station to have their drawers measured. Enoken went with them, and had to stay behind when the measuring was over, to write out an apology for indiscretions.

Two routines in particular put the police on their mettle. One, if it had gone a bit further, would have been consummated in a kiss, right there on the stage before everyone. (It was not until after the war that the movies made bold to show an unexpurgated kiss.) The other was about Tōjin (a translator has rendered this as "Chink"—it indicates a foreigner, or a Japanese whose foreign inclinations pass bounds) O-kichi, the reputed mistress of Townsend Harris, first American minister to Japan. O-kichi has been elevated to martyrdom, on the grounds that in surrendering to Harris she disgraced herself, and did it for her country. She was a good subject for Asakusa, combining nationalism and eroticism, but from the police point of view the writers seem to have provided too little of the former and too much of the latter.

Comedians and chorus girls and staff worked hard. To compete with the movie theaters, the review halls changed their programs every ten days. There were three performances a day. In a short story called "Rainbow" ("Niji," 1934), Kawabata reported that the dancers were required to stay for photographs after the last performance on opening day and that rehearsals for the next program began after the last curtain on the fourth day. So there were only two nights during every run, or six nights a month, when they could go home and fall into bed. Perhaps a half dozen dance routines and an equal number of skits had to be put together. The dressing rooms were full of sleeping dancers, and fainting from exhaustion was not uncommon. A character in "Rainbow" finds conditions so bad that he does not bother to learn his lines. Nothing polished or substantial is likely to come of the effort, and ad-libbing works best.

Here, in a passage from "Rainbow," a choreographer is meditating upon the reviews and the life of the dancers:

> But there was no time for training in any real sense of the term. An amateur would suddenly be thrust on the stage and not so much trained as told to follow the others. Those who had a certain grace would presently acquire a certain facility. The choreographer would have to put five and six dances together in three and four evenings of rehearsal. The process would be repeated three times a month; and in the weariness of it all any sort of trickery was permitted if it worked. To point out faults was taboo. Nakane, only twenty-seven years old, more often felt sorry for himself than angry at the dancers. So in the beginning he warmly argued the merits and shortcomings of the chorus line with the male actors who were in positions of authority; but he found that no one was really listening.

There is a mild inconsistency here with what has been said earlier in the same story. The count of days for rehearsal is not quite the same. That there are not many is clear, as is the slapdash nature of the productions. So is the class structure, the distinction as to status and function between comedians and dancers. Clearest of all is that the dancers have a hard life. What have they to look forward to, Kawabata asks, but to go on kicking?

In *Scarlet Gang of Asakusa*, Kawabata records a fragment of a program at the Casino Folies, six numbers out of eleven. They include a "jazz dance," a dance to "La Paloma," an "acrobatic tango," a "nonsense" sketch called "That Girl," and a comic song.

The changes of costume are so rapid that breasts are openly displayed in the process.

And now we have Number 6, "Jazz Dance. Ginza."

> On a street the width of a sash:
> Sailor trousers, false eyebrows,
> An Eton crop. What fun,
> Swinging the snakewood!

Silk hat at an angle, black velvet vest, red string necktie, collar opened whitely, a thin stick under an arm—it is of course an actress impersonating a man. Her legs are bare. Arm in arm with a pair whose skirts come to their hips and who are stockingless, she sings "Ginza Today." They dance their stroll down Ginza.

Nudity seems to have been more pronounced backstage than onstage. Most of the important nouns in the song—"trousers," "Eton crop," "snakewood"—are in English. Snakewood seems to be a South American wood with snakeskin markings, much used for walking sticks.

Also in *Scarlet Gang* is a complete program from early summer of 1930. The theater is not the Casino.

1. Grand Chorus: A Selection of Famous Songs
2. Fairy Story: The Spirit of the Artist's Brush
3. Musical Comic
4. Magnificent Magic, Made Public for the Very First Time
5. Ocean Dance
6. Dramatic Vignettes
   A. One Wants a Companion on a Journey
   B. Sleeping Car
7. Cowboy Dance
8. Dramatic Vignettes
   C. Falsehood
   D. Lady Angler
9. Cannon: A Sad Tale from the Wars of the Roses

10. Modern Dance: Five Festivals
    A. The New Year
    B. The Doll Festival
    C. The Iris Festival
    D. The Festival of the Stars
    E. Chrysanthemum Festival
11. Daring Aerial Acrobatics
12. Humorous Magic: Egyptian Paradise

This program too is larded with English words. "Cowboy Dance" and "Ocean Dance" are in English. So is the curious expression "Musical Comic." Even "Modern Dance," which, given the subject matter, was probably done in traditional dress, may well have had touches of the foreign. Elsewhere Kawabata speaks of a famous Asakusa dancer who did not imitate the Japanese dance as one got it at Hibiya Hall, the best concert and recital hall in town, but rather that of the port cities, aimed at foreigners.

Kawabata continues:

The New Tsukiji Troupe had been here late in May, with the general theme "What Made Us Come to Asakusa?" It did "What

Another Asakusa review, at the Shōchiku

Made the Girls Do It?" and "A Secret Tale of Tsukuba" and the like.

On banners billowing in the winds before the Kannon Theater in July, "It," written in three ways.

The Nihonkan thought of the effective name Eroero Dance Team, and even the Shōchikuza had to reply, in big black letters, with Dance Ero. "Ero" on all the billboards. The faltering Japanese of foreign performers is better than many things. Those who wish these days to collect the mottoes on the billboards of the specious reviews will find the alleys behind the lake and its theaters the place to do it: "Diary of a Sex Lunatic"—but come along and see for yourselves, all of you, in the evening. One hears that the extortionists are out along these alleys even in broad daylight; and here are the stage doors for the "ero queens." They come out to take the evening cool. My readers will understand that when I call the Danilevskis beautiful, the distortions and illusions of the night lights are at fault. Their legs are darker than those of Japanese.

The program of this Tenshō troupe is, after all, not as specious as some of them. The magicians are marvelously skillful. The expressions the young dancers turn on the audience are studiously beautiful. Alas, Tenshō herself, old enough to be a grandmother, ventures to play a girl student. She appears in every act and throws herself about perhaps a bit too strenuously. Henry Matsuoka's aerial acrobatics are splendid. . . . But what surprised Lefty Hiko most were the wares flung out to the audience from the stage. Sawa Morino, playing the artist in "The Spirit of the Artist's Brush," wound up like a baseball pitcher and flung thirty or forty bags of sweets.

Kawabata had only this one try at a chatty style and an intimate narrative stance permitting frequent intrusions, and he was not comfortable with it. Yet *Scarlet Gang* is full of good reporting. It gives most vividly a sense of what the Asakusa reviews were like, and Asakusa itself. The passage requires comment. The three ways in which "It" is written are the two Japanese phonetic syllabaries and Roman letters. Mount Tsukuba would seem to fit in with the general theme, "What Made Us Come to Asakusa?," because Asakusa was proud of having it on the eastern horizon. Lefty Hiko is a member of the Scarlet Gang, an assemblage of young delinquents.

There were foreign performers in Asakusa, most of them, as the passage suggests, Russian refugees. In that summer of 1930 (it seems to have been June) a pair of Finns, mother and daughter, the latter only ten years old, were a big hit. They, or one of them, did an imitation of Chaplin, and they sang in Japanese and did a Japanese dance. Four Russian sisters did Gypsy, Cossack, Spanish, and "jazz" dances, and sang Japanese songs with a sweet Russian accent. (Kawabata reminisces upon his student days, just after the Russian revolution, when little Russian girls no more than twelve or thirteen were walking the streets and selling themselves at no high price.) The Casino had a popular hula dancer, but she was Japanese. An American diver performed in a sideshow somewhere, and there was a French chanteuse, a dramatic soprano, we are told in English. "Her naked, pearl-white beauty quite radiates eroticism." Asakusa is kind to foreigners, says Kawabata, and especially to foreign children.

The "ero" that is up on all the marquees is of course that of *eroguro*, from "erotic" or "eroticism." The Shōchikuza is one of the grand theaters, the property of the Osaka company that dominated the Tokyo theater and had a large chunk of the movie business as well. Kawabata is saying that this institution, which should be above cheap tricks, must go erotic if that is what everyone else is doing. The sweets flung out so vigorously were aimed mostly at children. That there were children in the audience is interesting indeed, and may seem to go against generalizations about eroticism and grotesquerie. Probably such eroticism as there was, mostly bare legs, passed lightly over the heads of children. Though the Japanese police do sometimes treat foreign manifestations as if they were invisible (the original of *Lady Chatterley's Lover* was sold openly even as criminal litigation was in progress against the publisher and translator of the Japanese version), neither Kawabata nor anyone else tells us that the chanteuse was uncommonly naked.

Asakusa connoisseurs (again our authority is Kawabata) have said that things were actually dirtier back in the days of the Russo-Japanese War. The diving girls in the sideshows of those days were far bolder than the dancing girls of early Shōwa were permitted to be. The garb of the latter was not much different from the bathing dress of the time. And there had been wantonness in the park, right there beside the great temple, at least since the eighteenth century, when Edo came into its own as a cultural center. Wayside teahouses and archery and shooting stalls and the "famed sake places" all had had their pretty girls whose business was not only the announced one.

Yet the police of early Shōwa were being challenged. They had taken a position with regard to nudity, and the impresarios were pushing ahead in that direction as rapidly as they could. The police were also becoming more self-conscious. A spasm of puritanism was coming over the city and the nation, which had been victims of such spasms from time to time through the Tokugawa centuries.

Kawabata remarks upon the conservatism of Asakusa. In the following passage, the speaker, who is addressing a young lady of Asakusa, is Kawabata's alter ego.

"I don't care what you say, Asakusa people are old-fashioned. They look after others and others look after them, they care for people and have a sense of duty, all of them, the dealers and hawkers at the top to the tramps and beggars at the bottom. They're like the gamblers of Edo. I'm told that the toughs in Shibuya and Shinjuku are a newer sort than the ones we have here. They don't have a tradition, and Asakusa does. It may all seem like flash and glitter, but there's nowhere else things are so on the move. It's like the Bug House too. Or an island way off somewhere, or an African village with a chief and a set of rules and bonds the modern world doesn't have."

Two important matters are involved: acceptance of a moral and ethical code, and sensual abandon. It is quite possible to have both. Not even the puritan radicals of the thirties forwent the teahouses and extralegal polygamy. For all its willingness to provide and sell almost anything for and to almost everyone, Asakusa does seem to have had moral groundings. The Bug House to which the man refers is the place with the dusty display cases next door to the aquarium and its Casino Folies.

The sentence about the hawkers and the others contains several words that are almost untranslatable. The people who look after and are looked after are *oyabun* and *kobun,* the surrogate parents and children in the social arrangements of such persons as gamblers, firefighters, construction workers, and extortionists. The qualities of sympathy and duty are the *giri* and *ninjō* so prominent on the Kabuki stage. They come down to something not far from the Golden Rule.

As there were for the reviews, there were rules for the shooting stalls, which had long been covers for prostitution. The temple grounds still contained some forty of them in the early thirties. They could stay open for twelve hours from sunrise. Drinking was not permitted, nor was "wanton" touting and hawking. Only employees were allowed behind the counter. The rules may or may not have been enforced, but the fact that they were there, and that many customers were addicted to the stalls, suggests that they were used for something besides shooting.

Kawabata adverts to Asakusa speciousness and reports upon it. He is also good at scamps and beggars, the bottom of the heap. One sideshow promises nude beach photographs to those who will put down money for tickets; inside are photographs of athletic teams training on beaches. The curious passerby must buy the suggestive magazines at the stalls if he is to see what is in the secret supplements; they contain cooking and knitting lessons. A sideshow (another chronicler, not Kawabata, tells us of this one) offers an underwater strip show; inside, beyond a tank of water, is a painting of a nude woman. The code of Asakusa did not preclude misrepresentation, but it does seem to have forbidden complaining. Those who got cheated did not go to the police or otherwise protest.

When, at least partly because of *Scarlet Gang*, the "Ginza people" started coming to the Casino Folies, beggars and vagrants started going away. Earlier they had drifted in from the park to watch the girls. One caught the smell of them as the audience thinned out.

As for the scamps, there was a young delinquent known as the Mantis. He knew his law. Arrested numerous times, he could not be prosecuted until he was fifteen. Finally he got sent off to Iwo, the remotest place under the jurisdiction of the prefecture. One member of the Scarlet Gang, also a minor, works as a "cherry" for an Indian who peddles jewelry beside the temple. A cherry is a shill, someone who buys wares by prearrangement in hopes of starting a trend. An elderly man befriends him and teaches him a new trade, cat-catching. Skill and patience are required—a little, perhaps, as in fly-fishing. A sparrow on a string lures cats to within grabbing distance. Having seized one, the boy beats it to death and takes it off to the riverbank or a secluded part of the temple grounds, there to skin it. Makers of samisens pay a good price for cat skins, which function as sounding membranes on samisens.

At the end of "The Asakusa Mynah Bird" (*Asakusa Kyūkancho*), the bird of the title, which lives in a department store, is stolen. This exchange takes place:

"Someone stole it? The first time since the place opened that a bird's been stolen."
"You don't say."
"Only in Asakusa."

The last remark catches Asakusa nicely. It seems to have been proud of its scamps. A history of the ward published in 1933 finds evidence of old-style verve and gallantry in the fact that Asakusa produced so many "knights of the town," as one dictionary defines the members of the underworld gangs.

In *Scarlet Gang* there is a labor demonstration. Asakusa did have its little touches of fashionable left-wing radicalism. From the sheet-metal roof of a theater marquee, a performer agitates the passing crowds. Unless the system is reformed, he shouts, they will all starve to death. The harangue over, several of his fellows join him, there on the roof, for a display of swordsmanship. He is not of the reviews, whose lower orders would have had every right to demonstrate against the class system of which they are victims. He is rather from one of the swordplay troupes that were another Asakusa attraction.

Kengeki means literally "swordplay," if "play" is understood in the sense of "dramatic performance." There were several such troupes in Asakusa. Like O-kichi, swordsmen appealed to old virtues, and thus satisfied the police, the radicals of the right, and the Asakusa masses. Female swordplayers were more like O-kichi than the men. They brought in eroticism, as the men could not easily do. Like plucky little Orientals overwhelming huge ugly Occidentals in Bruce Lee movies, they were always overcoming adversaries more muscular than they, and they appealed to the sympathy for the underdog which was a part of the image the son of Edo and Tokyo had of himself. Best of all, they managed, wielding their swords, to show their legs every bit as generously as the review girls were permitted to do.

Singers of Naniwabushi, Osaka narrative balladry, also answered to right-wing tastes. They were very popular in Asakusa, if not everywhere. In the late thirties a Naniwabushi man was unsuccessful in Hibiya Hall, the place for advanced performances and awarenesses, but filled the Kokusai, the largest theater in Asakusa. The heroes of their ballads were strong on old virtues—loyalty, sacrifice, duty.

All of these attractions, and more, were available in Asakusa. The movies drew the biggest crowds, as they did everywhere, but it is well to note that Asakusa, in these its last good days, offered a variety of things.

After Enoken's departure the Casino Folies went arty. The choreographer had studied under Pavlova. There were dramatizations of socially conscious novels. There were ideological pieces aimed at the May Day crowd, the early years of Shōwa still being a time when the proletariat took to the streets of a May Day.

Sometimes the suggestion is strong that the reviews were not entirely serious even about artiness. On a stage other than the Casino, Kawabata saw two Heian courtiers, one of them Genji of the long romance that bears his name, the other the great lover Narihira. To all appearances they are in Heian dress, but under their arms they each have a walking stick hidden. They sway (not wriggle) their hips and sing. No, they are not courtiers at all. Observe these, their blue collars. And these weapons are not for elegant swinging, they are for smashing. The chorus line makes sedate Heian motions, and suddenly one of its number breaks into a Charleston, so earnestly that she falls exhausted. There ensue discussions of society and politics, a fox-trot, and a final "jazz chorus" and dance.

Artiness, however, may have had something to do with the untimely demise of the Casino Folies. Asakusa was not the place for that sort of thing. Shinjuku was. Shinjuku also had a review house, the Moulin Rouge, which opened on New Year's Eve 1931. The choice of opening day was an indication that it meant to be very advanced. New Year's Eve in Japan has traditionally been somewhat akin to Christmas Eve in the West, a vaguely religious night for family gatherings. Having done what they could by way of cleaning house and clearing debts, people stayed at home and perhaps went out to a shrine. Now they were invited to go to Shinjuku and watch the girls.

The Moulin Rouge was initially an offshoot of the Casino Folies. The first manager was a Casino man, and the first shows were scarcely distinguishable from the Asakusa sort. Shinjuku, however, was a place with middle-class crowds. It was also a student and intellectual center. Waseda University lay not far away. There were railway stations nearer the Waseda campus, but crowds draw crowds, and Shinjuku had the big ones. So the Shinjuku reviews gradually became sharper and more bracing than those of Asakusa. Eroticism waned as the challenge to the mind waxed. It was the sort of thing that brought radicalism of the left and of the right together. Both disliked venal politicians and money-mad businessmen. The police do not seem to have worried about it as they worried about the girls and their drawers at the Casino Folies.

3

DARKER
DAYS

Until 1926 the mayor was appointed upon royal command from a list of candidates preferred by the city council. The practice was to appoint the candidate at the top of the list—the one who had the strongest backing from the council. After 1926 the mayor was actually elected by the council. During the four and a half decades until, in 1943, there ceased to be mayors, the city had seventeen of them, or eighteen, if the one who had two separate tenures is, like President Cleveland, counted twice. So the average term was a little over two years, and for the early years of the Shōwa reign, down to the reorganization of 1943, it was even less.

Since 1947, when for the first time a governor was elected by general franchise, there have been only four governors. The average postwar tenure has been more than a decade. Only one mayor in early Shōwa served a full four years. Only one governor since the war has not been elected to serve three full terms, or twelve years. The present governor is in his third term. The one exception was the "Olympic governor," who thought it best to leave after the Tokyo Olympics of 1964.

The chief causes of the prewar instability seem to have been the power of the council and the cumbersome system, typical for municipalities before the war, whereby a body of select councilmen presided over by the mayor had perhaps even more power than the council. Prey to factionalism, susceptible to malfeasance, and very intrusive in the matter of appointments, this select body could cause trouble whenever it was in a bad mood. The strong and imaginative Gotō tried to curb it, but his successor, who had been his vice-mayor, did not follow his example. The successor was the mayor who may be counted twice. He presided over the two great events of the decades between the wars, the earthquake and the expansion of the city limits in 1932, which suddenly made Tokyo the second most populous city in the world.

Scandal was endemic in the affairs of the metropolitan government. There were scandals in rich variety during the post-earthquake years: over the purchase of city buses from private hands, over the fish and produce markets, over the election of a council president, over the purchase of land for cemeteries, over gas rates. Two interesting ones may be related, if not very directly, to the earthquake itself and the reconstruction.

The Keisei (Tokyo–Narita, the name means) Railway, a private line serving the eastern wards and suburbs, had long wanted to come across the Sumida River into the main part of the city. It wanted to come into Asakusa, there to join the first subway line, initially from Asakusa to Ueno and presently to Shimbashi and Shibuya. It kept petitioning and getting rejected. In 1928 the mayor recommended rejecting a sixth petition, on the grounds that another private railway, the Tōbu (which from 1929 had the rich tourist business to the ornate Tokugawa tombs at Nikkō, some eighty miles north of Tokyo), had already been given permission to come to the subway terminus, and that the Keisei, entering through Sumida Park, would be an eyesore. The latter seems a peculiar argument, since the elevated Tōbu line, put through in 1931 to a multi-level transportation and shopping complex somewhat resembling that at Shibuya, is very visible from the park. It could not have been made, in any event, if the new park had not been among the results of the earthquake. The council overruled the mayor, and then it became known that the Keisei had spent very large sums of money on the council.

The mayor recommended to the home minister that the council be dissolved. The council got even by passing a vote of no confidence, during a session that ended in fistfights. The minister did not approve the recommendation. The mayor then resigned, taking his three vice mayors with him. Some eminent men were implicated, including Hatoyama Ichirō, who later became prime minister, and the ubiquitous Shōriki Matsutarō of the *Yomiuri Shimbun*.

Thus prevented from entering Asakusa, the Keisei entered Ueno in 1933. In recent years it has finally been allowed into Asakusa, where it joins a subway line (not the one it originally wanted to join) and whence it sends trains through the heart of the city. Asakusa is not the prize now that it was in the days of the scandal. Nor is the station well situated for such Asakusa business as there is. The Keisei is a poor cousin among the commuter lines.

Then there was the fish-market scandal of 1928. From the early days of the Tokugawa shogunate the market had stood beside Nihombashi Bridge, in the mercantile center of Edo. It was not a pretty place and it did not smell good, and from mid-Meiji there had been efforts to move it from what was becoming a center of modern finance and merchandising. The problem of compensation for traditional rights proved intractable. The market stayed where it was until the earthquake destroyed it utterly.

On the evening of September 3, 1923, a sign was already up at the site of the old union headquarters inviting survivors to assemble and deliberate what was now to be done. The chairman of the union had lost his whole family in the earthquake; he himself escaped by boat. The decision was against attempting to rebuild in Nihombashi. Not everyone agreed. A temporary market opened on September 17, in Shibaura, by the bay. Five hundred dealers were back in business by the end of September. The market was already turning a profit. Holdouts attempted to resume business in Nihombashi, but they were turned away, whereupon some of them went to Shibaura and some withdrew to the provinces. More fighting ensued when former naval lands in Tsukiji, east of Ginza at the mouths of the Sumida, were proposed as a permanent site. Tsukiji was approved in mid-November, at a tumultuous meeting of dealers, a type held to be particularly quarrelsome even among sons of Edo. Opening ceremonies took place on December 1, and the new market (properly, the Central Produce Market, because more than fish is sold there) opened for business the following day. The buildings were not finished until 1935.

Wartime controls were invoked to solve the old problem of compensation for lost rights. It was an imposed solution, allowing less than a tenth of what had originally been asked, and it did not come until after Pearl Harbor. So more than a half century elapsed between the first attempts to uproot the market from Nihombashi and the final settlement.

Tsukiji fish market

The market has now been in the new location for more than sixty years and in its present buildings more than fifty, which may be counted, by Tokyo standards, as forever. There is talk of moving it again. The problem this time is not that it is smelly and unsightly, but that the city consumes too much fish. The market is cramped for space and contributes to congestion. It is also somewhat dilapidated.

Compensation for the old rights was at the beginning of the scandal. Upward of a year after the earthquake the mayor recommended a schedule of payments. The council demurred. It was the view of the council that the market had managed to obstruct the proposed move for more than thirty years. What duty had the city, then, to pay the dealers anything at all? After the change of reigns the matter was brought up again. This time, by a narrow margin, the council approved compensation. One of the sponsors of the new measure was also a director of the market. He had bought a council seat solely for purposes of promoting the interests of himself and his fellow dealers. Bribery seems to have been an open secret. Fifteen people, including ten of the forty-two councilmen, were arrested for offering and receiving bribes. The home minister voided the settlement and dissolved the council late in 1928, after several councilmen had been arrested. In 1929 came the resignation of the mayor, a "purification" movement, and new elections. The prefectural government, which was an arm of the Home Ministry, was all the while relatively free of scandals.

The city and the prefecture shared quarters, a red-brick building in Marunouchi, that red-brick quarter built largely by Mitsubishi and known as Londontown. To the left were the municipal offices and the mayor, to the right the prefectural and the governor. In front of the municipal entrance was a statue of Ota Dōkan, and in front of the prefectural entrance a statue of Tokugawa Ieyasu. Dōkan was the man who first made Edo into something more than a remote fishing village. A fifteenth-century warlord, he saw its strategic importance and put up a fastness where the palace now stands. Ieyasu founded the Edo shogunate and made Dōkan's fastness into the political center of the land. A statue of Dōkan, though not the original one, now stands in the courtyard behind the governor's office.

Metropolitan and prefectural offices, Marunouchi

This sharing of quarters was appropriate, for the two governments were close. The Home Ministry controlled the governorship, which it usually filled with one of its own. A majority of the mayors from the change of reigns down to 1943 also came from the Home Ministry. Several had been governors before they became mayors, which suggests that the mayoralty was the more desirable position. It was, so to speak, the more visible. Gotō was not the only mayor of ministerial rank. The seventeenth (or eighteenth) and last mayor was an army general.

In 1878, when the fifteen wards came to be, the population of Tokyo Prefecture was under a million. It reached a million by the mid-1880s, and two million by 1900. A jump in 1893 was due to the cession of the Tama counties by Kanagawa Prefecture. Figures before 1920, when for the first time there was a careful census, are somewhat conjectural in any event. Definitions and methods shift, as to, for instance, whether transient population is to be included, and how much weight is to be given to family registers.

One has a rough notion all the same of what was happening. The rapid growth of the early Tokyo years was in large measure a return to the population of the late Edo years. Thereafter the rate of growth slowed down, and in times of economic depression and disaster the population even fell. Since the rate was measured from an almost consistently expanding base, however, the absolute increase was massive. The census of 1920 showed three and two-thirds million, that of 1925 almost four and a half million, that of 1930 almost five and a half million. In 1932 the population was estimated at not much less than six million. During two-thirds of a century, 1868 to 1932, the city limits changed scarcely at all. They were becoming unrealistic.

The organization of these great masses of people was haphazard. Of all the large cities in the country, Tokyo was the one whose area was most at variance with its actual population. Negligible in 1878, the population of the "county part" accounted for about a third of the total by 1920. It continued to leap forward in the two succeeding censuses while that of the fifteen wards was falling. In 1920 there were about twice as many people in the "ward part" as in the five counties that bordered on it. By 1932 the proportions had been almost reversed. Not quite two-thirds of the people in the wards and the five counties were in the latter.

All along the limits of the city, which in no direction reached as far as the prefectural boundaries, stretched a patchwork of more or less heavily populated districts incorporated as towns and villages. The only incorporated city in the prefecture besides Tokyo itself was a silk-spinning center rather far out in the western counties. Some of the towns and villages had recognizable centers; some did not. Some, like Shinjuku (which straddled the city limits), were already emerging as major satellite cities. Others were arbitrarily defined accumulations of people. Behind the confusion was the assumption that someone would come up with a good idea someday. Someone had to, for it was a necessity.

In the meantime there was reluctance and intransigence on all sides. The entities chiefly concerned—the city, the counties, the prefecture, and the national government—all wished to gain from the new arrangements, whatever they might be, and stood in danger of losing. There were numerous possibilities, from doing nothing at all, on the grounds that the apparent confusion was not discommoding anyone seriously, to the bold step of unifying the mayor's constituency and the governor's and doing away with the office of mayor. The latter would have meant a loss of autonomy for the city and a reversion to a stage even earlier than the "special cities" one that had kept Tokyo, along with Osaka and Kyoto, without a mayor for a decade in mid-Meiji when all other municipalities in the country, however diminutive, had their mayors. In the counties sentiment ran strongly toward this most extreme reorganization. There would have been economic advantages, bringing rich places and poor places together under one budget, and making the mountain people of the far western counties into children of Edo. The final solution, which fell between the two extremes, did not come until 1943. By then the Crisis, the expression that was used to make the populace aware of the sacrifices expected of it, was worse than those who had brought it about had meant it to be.

Opposition within the old city subsided, in the face of an energetic propaganda campaign by the municipal government. The opposition was partly political. The expansion seemed a stage on the way to making Tokyo different from the other two special cities of Meiji, Kyoto and Osaka, and their prefectures. Originally the distinction had been made to keep these biggest and most threatening cities in the land under tighter control. Was Tokyo to be brought back under control, while the other two went on enjoying their autonomy? And then again (the political argument was by no means clear-cut): it might be good to be rid of City Hall, so extremely subject to scandal and malfeasance, and so cumbersome. The city bureaucracy grew more than a hundredfold between 1898, when the first mayor took office, and 1932. After 1932 the expenses of City Hall seemed even less necessary. The expanded city had more than 90 percent of the prefectural population and paid close to 100 percent of the taxes.

The economic argument was clearer, and perhaps stronger. The old city was more advanced than the county part, and was not especially interested in helping the latter catch up. Just upward of half the houses in the newly expanded city, and four-fifths of the houses in the old city, had running water. The poorer eastern wards were in this regard well served, Fukagawa being an exception. A watery place troubled by land subsidence, it worried more about getting rid of water than about bringing it in. The well-to-do western suburbs, after 1932 the western wards, fell much below the average for the old fifteen, and would be an expense. Almost four-fifths of the old city by area had sewers in use or under construction on the eve of the Second World War, and this was the case with less than two-thirds, again by area, of the new wards. Before the expansion of 1932, nine-tenths of the streets in the city, which is to say the old fifteen wards, were paved or surfaced. Less than a third were after 1932.

The solution of 1932 may be thought rather timid. It left the two governments in place, there behind their twin doors and statues, but the five counties bordering on the old fifteen wards themselves became wards. Absorption of the five counties was approved by the city council and the mayor's advisory council in May 1932 and received the approval of the Home Ministry shortly afterward. On October 1, 1932, eighty-two towns and villages were incorporated into the city. The city limits thus coincided with the prefectural boundaries in every direction except the west. The city shared borders with Saitama, Chiba, and Kanagawa prefectures. So it now covered essentially the area of the prefecture of early Meiji, and what remained of the county part was what had been ceded by Kanagawa Prefecture in 1893. Twenty new wards were added, raising the count from fifteen to thirty-five. This is not to say that the twenty were thoroughly urban. Extensive farmlands remained, and limited ones still do.

If timid in its treatment of political arrangements, the settlement of 1932 was startling in its effect on the population and area of the city. The population suddenly doubled, to more than five million, and the area increased sevenfold. It became the fifth-largest city in the world by area (none of the other four was in Japan, though before 1932 Tokyo was not, by area, the largest Japanese city) and the second-largest, following only New York, in population. Many a boy in the American West, no expert in the demography of the Kantō Plain, said that that was exactly the sort of thing the sneaky Japanese would do to catch up with honest, plodding New York. Two villages from North Tama County were annexed into Setagaya, one of the new wards along the western fringes of the city, in 1936.

It was most natural, given the fact that eighty-two towns and villages were reduced to twenty political entities, that there should be disagreement and some bitterness about the naming of the new wards. Those who made the decisions in 1932 did a better job than those who made similar decisions in 1947, when the number of wards was reduced from thirty-five to twenty-two. Some of the twenty-two names have a distinctly artificial ring to them, as if an advertising agency might have made them up. Only one of the thirty-five, Jōtō, has the genuinely fabricated look, and even it is vaguely descriptive. It means something like "the eastern part of the capital." Some names came from prominent geographic features. Four of the five lost counties had their names preserved in ward names, only Toyotama being left out. The commonest device was to give the name of the most prominent town to the whole ward. This caused the most dissatisfaction. In what was to become Shibuya Ward, only the town of Shibuya favored the name. In the other towns sentiment was strong for Jingū Ward, after the Meiji Jingū, the Meiji Shrine, situated in the ward. Of the old Five Mouths, the stations on the main highways out of Edo, Itabashi became the name of the largest ward by area, the one farthest to the north and west, on the old inland road to Kyoto. Shinagawa also named a ward. Shinjuku, the oldest part of which had been within the city limits since 1920, became a ward name in 1947. So only Senjū was left out. Accounting for two of the Five Mouths, it might have received special consideration, but the name of the old county, and no one could object to that, prevailed.

Three of the new wards had populations of more than two hundred thousand, and two of them larger populations than Honjo, most populous among the old fifteen. Two of the three centered upon two of the three rapidly growing western centers, Shibuya and Ikebukuro. Shinjuku, lying on either side of the old city limits, was divided between an old ward and a new. The most heavily populated ward among the thirty-five was Arakawa, a very different case from the other two. It lay just north of Asakusa Ward, and became urbanized as the poorest of the poor were forced into it, many of them refugees from disasters, especially the great earthquake of 1923. The new wards had on the average a lower per capita income than the old ones, but the western ones were extensions of the middle-class High City wards, Arakawa an extension of the poorer Low City. The two wards east of the Sumida, Fukagawa and Honjo, had the lowest average income among the old fifteen, and the two neighboring counties, including the new Arakawa Ward (as well as Jōtō, the one with the fabricated name), were yet lower.

Asakusa Ward had the largest number of pawnshops in the city, and Honjo the largest number of night schools, for very young people who worked in the daytime. Akasaka, on the opposite side of the old city, had only a seventh as many pawnshops as Asakusa, and no night schools at all.

An important novelist (not Tanizaki, who had already fled) said of the proud new city that it got worse every day, and only made him want to flee. Yet it was tidied up, and the new city limits made sense. The crazy pattern of villages along the old limits went away, most of the population was brought within the mayor's jurisdiction, and the new city had integrity. It stood together, a unit. Almost half the people who used public transportation within the prefecture moved between the new wards and the old. The remainder was divided almost exclusively and almost evenly between people being transported within the old wards and the new wards. Movement to and from and within the remaining three counties was negligible.

The time came when the new city limits did no better at containing the population than had the old ones. There are no longer towns and villages, only incorporated cities, along the limits of the ward part. Two of the three Tama counties have quite disappeared. They have been divided into cities. Some mountain towns and a single village yet remain in the remotest of the three. So why not go the whole distance, one might ask, and do away with the county part completely? Why not have a few new wards, and finish the business left unfinished in 1932 and 1943?

It probably will not happen, at least for a long time, because there are not the compelling reasons there were in 1932 for the city to expand. There are no exploding centers along the ward limits like the Shibuya,

Ikebukuro, and Shinjuku of late Taishō and early Shōwa. Books keep getting written which have the commercial and managerial center of the city, and not merely the population center, continuing to move westward, finally engulfing the tomb of that sad, weak man, the Taishō emperor. A bedroom sprawl all the way to the mountains seems more likely. The pattern of cities is not as crazy as the pattern of towns and villages was. And, finally, it would make more sense for the city—the ward part—to expand into neighboring prefectures, already on the borders of the wards, than to expand westward through what remains of Tokyo Prefecture. The reality is one megalopolis from Chiba on the east shore of the bay to Yokosuka near the mouth of the bay on the west shore. The governor of Tokyo is as likely to get jurisdiction over any part of the neighboring prefectures as the mayor of New York is to get jurisdiction over Newark and Jersey City. Meanwhile Saitama Prefecture, which borders Tokyo on the north, can worry about its own crazy pattern.

On October 1, 1932, the city suddenly had seven times the area it had had the day before, but it was not as big as some people seemed to think it was. The *Nichinichi Shimbun,* now the *Mainichi,* set a competition for a city song. The winning lyrics, by a young man in the city government, glorified the expanse of the new city, all 550,000 square kilometers of it. This would be an area somewhat greater than the squaring of seven hundred kilometers. From a spot seven hundred kilometers northwest of, let us say, Tokyo Central Station, the mountains of Siberia might, on a clear day, be in view. Set to music by a music professor, the song was widely sung.

The prime minister, the third to meet that fate during the years between the wars, was assassinated in May 1932, the month in which the great expansion gained approval by everyone whose approval was needed. The Japanese recognized Manchuria as an independent nation in mid-September, a fortnight before the expansion became a reality. Such were the times. Taishō democracy had expired, reaction and aggression were in the air. Tokyo and Japan were, like most places, in economic depression, which is commonly listed among the causes of the hotheaded activism that swept democracy (such as it was), the political parties, and peace away.

The military persons who were the chief agents of the reaction might in the jargon of a later day have been thought "concerned." They saw injustices and contradictions, and thought they saw easy solutions in a return to the virtues, chiefly loyalty and sincerity, of an earlier and purer day. Some people, such as capitalists and party politicians, seemed to thrive on depression, and far larger numbers of people were too obviously in distress. If the earthquake suggested to some that the heavens and their eight million deities were unhappy, the depression made it intolerably clear to others.

The panic of 1927, the remote causes of which might be traced to the earthquake, came under control, and need not have brought a general depression. Dependent on foreign markets and especially the American market, however, Japan could not escape entanglement in the world depression. By 1930, the year the Casino Folies opened, it had come. The late twenties and early thirties were a time of labor strife. Except for a brief time after the Second World War there has been nothing like it since. The early years of Shōwa were the full summer of left-wing activity, polemical and literary. Almost everything could and can be blamed on the depression. Whether or not the reaction of the thirties would have come had the depression not come, we will never know. Perhaps it was merely time for another seizure of puritan righteousness. Perhaps it was another of those mysterious cycles that seem to operate everywhere and in everything.

The critic Oya Sōichi (today he might be called an opinion-maker) remarked that the two Chinese characters with which printers could not keep their fonts adequately supplied were those for "step" or "grade" and for "woman." Left-wing argumentation and evangelism would have been helpless without the former, because without it such expressions as "class struggle" and "class consciousness" cannot be written. The popularity of the latter had to do with *eroguro* nonsense. Kawabata said that two subjects monopolized the media in those days, depression and eroticism.

As early as 1929 firm measures were taken against the radical left. As for eroticism, both prosperity and depression, as suited the moods and conditions of the day, could be blamed for it. The prosperity of the First World War brought laxness, and depression made people turn to *eroguro* nonsense for distraction and comfort. During the years of the Crisis such pleasures disappeared, to emerge in far opener and bolder form after the Second World War, or, as the Japanese call it, the Pacific War. A flood of girls poured in upon the city from the poor northeastern provinces in the mid-thirties. Rural poverty and the depression were the general causes, and crop failures the immediate ones. The fact that crop failures cannot be explained in social and economic terms made no difference. The poor girls added to the indignation, even as they made work easier for the purveyors of *ero* and *guro*. These were darker days than the days of very early Shōwa.

In *Scarlet Gang of Asakusa,* Kawabata reports on the beggars. More of them than usual were living in Asakusa Park in the summer of 1930. Perhaps the number was as high as eight hundred; but Kawabata was reluctant to make an estimate himself, and did not trust the estimate made by the ward office. Someone stole the hilt from the sword on the statue, up behind the temple, of the celebrated Kabuki actor Danjūrō. Asakusa had drinking places that specialized in beggars. Bare-legged waitresses would come and sit upon the tables. Kawabata observed the forbearing code of the beggars. The park benches were full on a warm night, and each of the regulars had his place, which was respected. Asakusa had in those years a beggar chief, or chief beggar, known as Goldtooth, because much of his money was in his mouth. An intelligent man rumored to be a college graduate, he lorded it over the other Asakusa beggars and took a share of their earnings. He was finally incapacitated by stab wounds.

On a level just above beggars and vagrants, ragpickers decreased in numbers in the last years of the Taishō reign, and rapidly increased during the early years of Shōwa. Their number almost quadrupled between 1925 and 1932. About half were in the new ward which many wanted to call Senjū, after the old mouth, but which was called Adachi after the county of which it was a part. Urbanization and disaster forced the very poor outside of the city limits, into what was to become Arakawa Ward, and then beyond the Arakawa, as the Sumida is known in its upper reaches, into the fens of Adachi. In late Meiji truck gardens were islands among fens and lotus ponds.

Drainage brought industrialization, and ragpickers from the old Low City put together a community on lands still too watery for industrial or ordinary residential use. It was rather as Asakusa had been a few centuries earlier, before reclamation of the wetlands along the Sumida: pilgrims made their way to a great temple, in this case the Yakushi temple at Nishiarai, through bogs and queaches among which the few permanent dwellers eked out a subsistence livelihood. The best days for the ragpicking vocation lasted down to about 1960. Thereafter a modest amount of capital was required for what before had required none. Collectors of scrap and wastepaper now make their rounds in small trucks. In the years after the Second World War there was a smaller but more famous community of ragpickers on the right bank of the Sumida just above Asakusa. It seems to have given the language the commonest word for "ragpicker." The last syllable of *bataya* applies to any kind of mercantile enterprise, and the first two seem to be from *kawabata*, "riverbank."

Ragpickers' hovels at Nippori in Arakawa Ward

The Shōwa reign was a decade old on Christmas Day 1936. Had it ended then the reign designation, suggesting peace and accord, would have been somewhat ironic. The decade had moved rapidly in the direction of obfuscation and strife. A time of some pluralism and tolerance gave way to jingoism and repression. Quite aside from the effect on left-wing radicalism, the harmless if by some standards wanton pleasures of the populace were being affected. So was the appearance of the city. The most extreme internal bloodletting of the thirties took place on February 26, 1936, precisely ten months before the end of the first Shōwa decade. The military rising of that day had among its secondary results the chopping down of the palmettos that were among the symbols of Hibiya Park, the central park of the city, immediately south of the palace plaza. The insurgents had their last fortress at the Sanno Hotel, a short distance to the west. The park became artillery emplacements and the palmettos got in the way of the guns.

The Olympic Games were a somewhat later casualty. Soon after the Los Angeles games of 1932, at which the Japanese and especially their swimming team did well, sentiment began to grow for having the 1940 games in Tokyo. By the time purposeful campaigning began Hitler was chancellor of Germany. So, had circumstances not intervened, the world would have had two sets of fervently nationalistic games in a row. The Japanese returned the franchise even before developments in Europe made the games impossible. Developments in Asia had already made them impossible, or so the official view was, for Japan. The war with China, which the Japanese go on calling the China Incident, began the year after the Berlin Olympics.

A delegation set off for Berlin in the summer of 1935. It went by the Trans-Siberian Railway and had trouble with the Russians. Among the lavish presents to Hitler was a gold sword. It was confiscated at the border, but eventually reached Berlin by diplomatic channels. The Tokyo city representative at the Berlin Olympics did not come home. He stayed on in the United States, by way of which he was returning, and took a position at Northwestern University.

Tokyo was awarded the 1940 Olympics on the day before the 1936 (or Nazi) Olympics began. The Japanese did well in them too (for the first time a Japanese woman won a gold medal), but behaved so badly that the Japanese embassy in Berlin got off a special report to the minister of education. Fighting and slashing occurred on the ship back to Yokohama. The samurai spirit was in command.

It was in firmer and firmer control at home too. The turnover of prime ministers was brisk in those days. Three of the six men who held the office during the four years after the Berlin Olympics were from the army or navy. Midway through the four years the Japanese announced that they must give up the Olympics. The reason was that not enough steel for a stadium could be spared from the China Incident. The original plans called for enough steel to build a destroyer. They were cut almost in half, but the government decided that even that quantity would be difficult to come by. The main installations were to be on the Komazawa golf links, far out in Setagaya, farthest to the southwest of the new wards. There was to be a gymnasium in Kanda. The golf links are now Komazawa Park, where a part of the 1964 Olympics took place.

Had the games been held, they would have been doubly nationalistic. The year 1940 was the Zero Year from which the famous fighting plane took its designation. It was the year 2600 by the traditional, mythical reckoning of the age of the Japanese empire—which was, in the patriotic view, now twenty-six centuries old. It was a year to be observed.

Besides the Olympics, there was to be a world's fair, which was also called off. It too would have been markedly nationalistic, and it was changed to something explicitly so, the Zero Year celebrations. The sense in high places was that something was needed to shake the populace out of its gloom and make it buoyant and positive once more. By 1940 it was becoming apparent that the Chinese problem did not admit of a simple solution. Most of the Chinese cities had fallen, and yet resistance went on, pertinaciously. Sacrifice or humiliation, or perhaps both, seemed to lie ahead.

Plans for the fair got as far as Shinto propitiatory rites to the gods whose land, by the bay in Yokohama and at the mouths of the Sumida in Tokyo, was to be disturbed. Tickets went on sale and sold well. Kachi-tokibashi, Bridge of the Triumphant Shout, the farthest downstream of the Sumida bridges and the newest of the prewar ones, was built for the occasion. Missions were sent abroad to stir up interest. And then, also in the summer of 1938, the government announced its opinion that the fair, along with the Olympics, should be postponed. So the city got the less expensive Zero Year observances instead. There was talk of moving City Hall to Tsukishima, the reclaimed island that was to be the fair site. Reports of profiteering caused the idea to be dismissed. The mayor, who had earlier been governor, was among the cleaner ones. It seems a pity now that City Hall did not move then. It might not now be moving out of Edo.

The twenty-six-hundredth birthday of the nation fell, by traditional if unreliable reckoning, on February 11, 1940. There were parades and a river carnival on that day, but, because February is one of the coldest months of the year, the culminating celebrations occurred in clement November. In the summer the city (not the nation) had an eminent guest, Pu-yi, the puppet emperor of Manchuria. The city itself invited him, doing so, said the mayor, in cooperation with the cities of China and Manchuria, the two treated of course as separate political entities. The mayor went on to say that he had no doubt of the resolve of the city to attain to the lofty ideals upon which the nation was founded and climb to the pinnacle of world culture. Such was the rhetoric of the day.

The nation held rallies in the palace plaza on November 10 and 11. Their Majesties attended. The second rally was a big picnic at which everyone, including Their Majesties, ate army field rations. The nation was much moved, newspapers tell us. On November 12 the city had a big banquet in a restaurant across from the plaza, and on November 13 a rally in the Meiji Gardens that was twice as big as the one on the tenth. It wistfully imitated the lost Olympics. A sacred flame was brought by relay from the Kashiwara Shrine, south of Nara. Built in Meiji, the Kashiwara occupies the legendary site of the palace where the first emperor assumed the throne. The flame arrived on November 11 and was kept in the mayor's office until time to run it to the gardens.

Festive observances had been banned because of the Crisis, but the ban was lifted for five days. Floats and portable shrines (*mikoshi,* or "god seats") and lantern processions were so numerous that it was as if local festivals, usually scattered over the landscape and the seasons, were taking place all together. "Flower trolleys," the vehicles decorated for great public occasions, ran all through the city. And then on the fifteenth there were posters: "The fun is over. Let's get back to work."

Secondary observances furthered the cause of bringing the eight directions (as the slogan of the day had it) under one roof, the Japanese one: international conferences for writers, educators, and young people, a conference on "building the new East Asia," a tournament in the martial arts and a more conventional athletic meet.

The closing pages of Tanizaki's *The Makioka Sisters* include scenes set in Tokyo in the autumn of 1940, as the Makioka family makes another attempt, this one successful, to marry off its third daughter. Tanizaki conveys very nicely the fervor which the Japanese are so good at mustering up on such occasions; he manages to suggest as well, from his Kansai vantage point, that it is a peculiarly Tokyo-like kind of silliness. Among the principals in the marriage negotiations is a bustling lady journalist who is busy as can be. She is speaking.

"And the day after that a meeting to organize the Rule Assistance Association. And the festival of the Yasukuni Shrine is

A flower trolley

going on, and on the twenty-first there is a parade. Oh, Tokyo is just full of excitement. All the hotels are overflowing. That reminds me—the Imperial has twice as many people as it can handle. We got you a room, but not much of a room."

The Rule Assistance Association was an invention of Prince Konoe's to advance "spiritual mobilization," which is to say totalitarianism. The Yasukuni, northwest of the palace, was and continues to be the shrine where war dead are venerated. The Imperial is of course the Frank Lloyd Wright building that was completed just before the 1923 earthquake and came safely through it.

Among the proposals by way of getting ready for the Zero Year celebrations was that the palace plaza be made a broader and more continuous expanse by putting the streets that crossed it underground. The proposal was rejected as undignified and risky, with the sacred royal presence so near at hand, though, relying on private contributions and voluntary labor, the city did tidy the plaza up somewhat. Proposals for tunneling under the palace grounds have been dismissed in the years since for similar reasons. Far larger than the grounds of Buckingham

Palace or the White House, they go on inconveniencing rapid public transit. Everything moving between Tokyo Central Station and the busiest station in the city, Shinjuku, must make a detour around them.

The authorities were having their repressive way in matters that may seem trivial and even ludicrous but to them must have seemed important. They could clearly have their way in the naming of cigarettes, tobacco being a public monopoly. So cigarettes formerly known by the English names Golden Bat and Cherry took Japanese names. Yet it is not easy to judge how much was done by force and how much by suggestion. The pressure on popular entertainers to do the popular thing must be very strong, and so it may be that some of them acquiesced in what was expected of them before they were told. A singer who had called himself Dick Mine became Mine Kōichi. Back in freer days a comedian had taken a name, Fujiwara Kamatari, that now was deemed irreverent. There had been a historical Fujiwara Kamatari a dozen centuries before, the founder of the great Fujiwara clan and so a forebear of the royal family. The comedian took a different name.

The pattern was by no means consistent, however. A minister of education sought to extirpate the words "mama" and "papa" from the language, and he was not successful. The pair was so firmly rooted that many a child would not have known what to put in its place. A comic ensemble known as the Akireta Boys, who provided song and patter to the accompaniment of a guitar, became the Milk Brothers. The second word in the earlier designation had been the English one. Now both words were English. *Akireta* means something like "absurd" or "egregious," and was thought not to accord well with the solemnity of the times. Two of the boys called themselves Shiba Rie and Bōya Saburō, which is to say, Maurice Chevalier and Charles Boyer. "Chevalier" died before the change from Akireta Boys to Milk Brothers. "Boyer" did not change his name.

Though more gradually, the war was doing to the reviews what the earthquake had done to the opera. A little Kafū vignette written in 1942 is set in the dressing room of the Opera House in Asakusa, among the places he loved best. A cannon booms onstage and the smell of gunpowder comes drifting up to the dressing room; the actors are in military uniform. Guns and gunpowder had come to the review houses some years earlier, as inspirational pieces came to prevail over eroticism.

Kafū was strongly opposed to the war, and once it had entered its Pacific phase he did almost the only thing a dissident could do: he lapsed into silence. Yet his writings for the Asakusa review houses tell us that he engaged in a kind of self-censorship, and suggest too what was happening to the houses. In 1938 he did the libretto for a two-act operetta called *Katsushika Romance* (*Katsushika Jōwa*). It had a ten-day run at the Opera House. Katsushika is the name of an old county and a new ward, the farthest northeast of the thirty-five wards. After the war he wrote three skits for the Asakusa burlesque houses. One senses in these skits the somewhat lubricious thing he would have liked to write, in the operetta the sort of thing he felt constrained to write if he was to write for his girls at the Opera House at all. It is a very moral piece, preaching the good old virtues of loyalty and sacrifice. It is tearful, thin, abstract, and didactic.

There are three principal characters, each of whom has solos, and a chorus. In the first act the tenor is courting a bus conductor. Almost all bus conductors, from the earliest days of the calling, were young women. She is swept off to the city by a gang of movie people who will make her a star. They have spotted her on her bus and noted a close resemblance to a person who is already a star. This is her solo as she gets swept off:

> Location
> Through the long spring days
> Location
> Such a happy path
> Such an amusing way to live
> Sing, dance
> Dance, sing
> The scarlet lights of the city beckon
> They beckon, those lights
> Hurry home
> Fly away, automobile
> Sing, make haste
> Make haste, sing

The word "location," indicating a movie location, is in English. The syllable count irregularly follows the alternation of sevens and fives that is standard in Japanese balladry.

In the second act the tenor is married to a girl who in the first act kept a little refreshment stall on the far bank of the Arakawa Drainage Channel. The young wife is about to go off and buy medicine for their colicky baby. The tenor goes in her place, for he is a good husband and it is beginning to rain. The erstwhile bus conductor enters, forlorn and bedraggled.

It is all a dream now
The city excitement I yearned for
I cast off love
And soon was cast off by the world
Mired in filth and shame
A scrap of paper blown by the wind
Down among the fallen leaves
Trampled at the wayside
No one to pity me. . . .
Bars, cafés, here, there
And I, homeless
A fallen leaf, soaked by autumn rains
Going where the wind blows
Clutching at my breast

Having allowed just enough time for the solo to finish, the young wife's uncle enters. Her father is in jail. Money is needed for the defense. It saddens him deeply to ask it, but will she not indenture herself to the pleasure quarters? The bus conductor steps forward and offers to make the sacrifice herself. She is in any event "mired in filth and shame." The young husband and wife must live out their lives, long ones, be it hoped, in happiness.

Let it be so
A body sunk in the slough
Does not matter
Filthy

Let it sink
What matters it where
To make up for the betrayal
To help him who was betrayed
I gladly make the sacrifice

It is the world of Meiji Kabuki, whose mission was to praise virtue and chastise vice. Even more, perhaps, it is the world of Shimpa, "the New School," a hybrid melodramatic form, its origins in mid-Meiji, that retained female impersonators but experimented with more realistic styles of acting. The women of Shimpa are always sacrificing themselves to men who are happy to let them do it, and scarcely seem worth the trouble. They tend to be nobler the deeper mired in filth they are. Little of the early eroticism remains in Kafū's operetta save the scantily clad figure of the ruined woman.

After the war, with enfeebled police and an American Occupation indifferent to such matters, Kafū let himself go. The most amusing of his skits for the burlesque or strip theaters is called *What Happened the Night the Lights Went Out (Teiden no Yoru no Dekigoto)*. It is without music, one act and three scenes. The central figure is a woman kept by an elderly man whose business is unclear but conveniently has him out of town for protracted periods. In the first scene she is out of the house and her housemaid is dallying with the laundry boy.

" 'Don't. It tickles.' As she writhes and seems about to fall face up from the window frame, Yamaoka takes her in his arms. Her legs inside, her torso outside, she reveals her thighs as she pulls herself upright. At that moment there is a sound in the hall." It is the woman, who gets measured in delicious detail by her seamstress.

Her patron appears and tells her that he must be in Osaka for some days. She cajoles and caresses, and when he goes out she says, "This isn't the easiest business in the world to be in." The second scene is a dream. A young lieutenant and a baby figure in it. "When," he asks, "will war disappear from human affairs?" Antiwar platitudes were de rigueur in the postwar years. It may be said for Kafū that he had more right to utter them than did most writers and intellectuals.

In the third scene the lights have gone out. It is something they often did in those years. A police admonition is circulated. People must be on guard, this dark night, against robbers. A young robber appears. She invites him to stay the night. He is in the process of stripping her when an elderly robber appears. (There is kissing, taboo before 1945, in the first and third scenes.) She sends an inquisitive policeman on his way, allowing the elderly robber to escape. The lights have meanwhile come on again. "Aiko smiles and turns off the light. Putting tissue in the bosom of her kimono, she kneels on the bedding. The curtain falls. Only a humming of insects breaks the silence."

What Happened the Night the Lights Went Out was presented at an Asakusa theater in March and April 1949. Another skit, called *Love Suicide at Hatonomachi (Shinjū Hatonomachi)*, was presented at the same theater in 1949, and again in 1950, this time at the Rokkuza (House of the Sixth District), most famous of the Asakusa strip places. Kafū himself appeared in both versions. With a different title, which might be rendered *Springtide Passion in Hatonomachi (Shunjō Hatonomachi)*, the piece was made into a movie. Hatonomachi was a "private" or unlicensed pleasure quarter east of the Sumida, successor to the Tamanoi district that had attracted Kafū a decade earlier (see page 53).

All the varieties of girls and their customers pass in review, sincere

In the Tamanoi "den of unlicensed whores," about 1932

ones and frivolous ones, responsible ones and irresponsible ones, girls who rather enjoy their work and girls who are in it because they have no other way to help straitened parents and siblings. A sincere man who has been betrayed by a woman and a sincere woman who has been betrayed by a man go off and commit suicide together. The high moral posture of the Katsushika piece is certainly not wanting in the postwar pieces, and we have a new strain of didacticism, the pacifist sermon. There is, however, a pronounced strain of the *ero* and the *guro,* even though it may seem bland and inoffensive by the standards of our own day. It is missing from the Katsushika piece. Patriotic ideologues made Asakusa do without these little pleasures as its best day was coming to an end.

Like Asakusa itself and its reviews, chronicles of Asakusa come to have a thin, attenuated look. Kawabata wrote little about Asakusa after his interest moved on to the snowy parts of the land (specifically, Niigata Prefecture—the first installment of *Snow Country* appeared in 1935). Kafū's diary is full of interesting bits about Asakusa and the pleasure quarters to the north and east, and he wrote poignantly of the warmth and dirt and uselessness of life in the review halls.

The most famous chronicle of Asakusa on the eve of the "Pacific War" is *Under What Stars (Ikanaru Hoshi no Shita ni)* by Takami Jun. Although almost three decades younger, and although a bar sinister intervenes, Takami seems to have been Kafū's first cousin. His mother was unmarried, and his father, a governor of Fukui Prefecture, was a younger brother of Kafū's father. *Under What Stars* is commonly treated as a "novel of customs and manners," specifically those of Asakusa. It was published in 1939 and 1940, and is set a year or two earlier. Asakusa does not by any means emerge as the sensual, tactile presence that it is in Kawabata's *Scarlet Gang of Asakusa.* The consensus is that Takami's work is the better novel of the two, and so the trouble may be that Asakusa was not, at the end of the thirties, the presence it had been at the beginning.

Much of the reporting does not go beyond what we already know. We hear, for instance, about the unjust and rigid class structure of the review houses, with the dancers forever at the bottom. We learn, as we learned from Kawabata, that they worked hard. "The Asakusa theaters are such hard work that the girls immediately begin to put on weight when they leave. Misako was doing it too, in that particular way, like a sudden bursting when the hoops that have held the staves together are removed."

There is a conspicuous new institution in Asakusa, but it lies outside of the Sixth District. Shōchiku opened its Kokusai Gekijō or International Theater (which has recently been torn down that a hotel might be put up) in 1937. Takami reports that its devotees, mostly women, marched eyes-front from the subway to their theater and back again, and did not set foot in the Sixth District. Devotees of the opera and the reviews had been mostly male. For obscure reasons, all-girl troupes attract overwhelmingly feminine audiences, and the Kokusai had one of these.

Under What Stars is occasionally amusing. It obliquely informs us that the patriots were not wholly successful at stamping out corrupt Western influences. One of the review performers has the most unlikely name Bottlemouth. This is so that his full name can be pronounced Bingu Kurosubei, which is to say, Bing Crosby. What is best about the book, however, is less a matter of character and action and (what *Scarlet Gang* is so good at) reporting than of mood. The good days are over. The action is coming to an end.

"The famous old places of Asakusa had been abandoned. The aquarium, said to be the birthplace of the Asakusa reviews, was in a state of advanced neglect, the subject of weird stories. Late at night, it was said, you could hear the sound of tap dancing on the roof. It has since been torn down, and so those who loved the Casino Folies have lost all trace of their dream." The time is late 1938.

Asakusa owed much of its vitality in the late Edo years and on into the first Tokyo century to the fact that it was on the edge of town. To keep mischievous things from the center, the shogunate moved the Yoshiwara there, and, much later, the Kabuki as well. Still on the edge of all the urban excitement, but now on the wrong edge, Asakusa could not keep them. It had a terminal department store, the Matsuya, where the subway ended and whence a private railway departed for Nikkō and other points in that direction, but for the most part it was a district of small family shops. Old ones held on with admirable tenacity; new ones did not come.

In a 1939 essay called "Nesoberu Asakusa," which might be rendered

The Asakusa subway tower

"Asakusa All Sprawled Out," or "Asakusa Supine," Takami compares Ginza and Asakusa.

Asakusa does not have face and obverse. Ginza has a provocative surface and little of substance, a certain emptiness, behind it. Asakusa sets forth a peculiar kind of warmth right there in front of you, and does not hide an inconsistency, a makeshift quality. It is like a jazz record blaring forth in an alien tongue. When it does not blare it goes to the other extreme and becomes all shyness and awkwardness, as of a girl with an old-fashioned coiffure and an advanced bathing suit. There are none of the voguish places which, in the Ginza fashion, have cover charges.

That is not quite true. We have recently witnessed the opening of "grand tea salons," such as the Purple Gold and the Grand Harbor. They do have minimal cover charges, but, like the places that depend on the subway, they lie outside the Sixth District. In sum: there may be a surface resemblance to Ginza, but it is like a ringworm. It has not penetrated to the heart of Asakusa conservatism. . . .

Here too there is an inconsistency. The young heirs to the Asakusa shops are modern boys, not apparently conservative at all. Their hair is in I forget what advanced style and their trousers are tight. Dance halls no longer interest them. In their spare time they speed about in borrowed Datsuns. And their talk is all of Ginza. . . .

[The girls in Asakusa drinking places] spend their holidays in Ginza. I could give any number of examples. Asakusa yearns for Ginza. . . . And does Ginza do the reverse? Do Ginza people come to Asakusa on their holidays? They do not. They have a low opinion of Asakusa.

At this point Takami refers to Kawabata's view that nothing in Asakusa is of the highest quality. Takami continues:

Asakusa has an unshakable standing as a place of crowds and noise [sakariba], but it is indeed of a lower quality than Ginza. The pull of Ginza for the child of Asakusa may well be the pull of the best for the next best.

Ginza, the best, always seems ready for battle. Asakusa lies supine. Pleasure seekers in Ginza are always on their mettle. Pleasure should mean relaxing, letting things go.

Further evidence that foreign poisons had not been completely expunged, the adjectival element in the name Grand Harbor is in English.

It is an ambiguous passage, and it may seem inconsistent with certain statements in *Under What Stars*, in which we learn, for instance, that girls from Ginza places choose Asakusa for their private conversations because they are not likely to encounter Ginza customers there. It does not much matter which is literally true. Takami is praising the openness and the conservatism of Asakusa, but he is also telling us that there is something a bit less than truly professional about Asakusa. For that, one goes to Ginza. If a Ginza girl does sometimes have a little tête-à-tête in Asakusa, that is because the Ginza clientele is the one that matters, and it is sometimes to be avoided. Takami did not think to make the comparison that would be the most obvious today, between Ginza and the western *sakariba,* Ikebukuro and Shinjuku and Shibuya.

Kafū never seemed to give up on Asakusa. One cold night during the last full year of the war he recorded the closing of the Opera House, his Asakusa favorite. It is a touching entry. "As I passed the lane of shops . . . on my way to the subway, I found myself weeping again. . . . I have been witness to it all, Tokyo going to ruins."

The closing of the theaters brought an end not only to the reviews but to Asakusa as a leader of popular culture. After the war came the burlesque and strip houses, which tended to lack imagination, and in which Asakusa often seemed to be imitating and following Shinjuku. Yet Kafū went on liking Asakusa better than any other part of the city. When, in his last years, he went into the city at all from the suburban dwelling that was his last, it was most commonly to Asakusa.

Nor did Takami immediately give up. Through the war years he went on finding reserves in Asakusa. It goes on drawing factory workers from east of the river, he observes in a 1944 essay called "Enticement and Solace" ("Ian to Miryoku"), as Kinshichō, a *sakariba* built especially for the district, does not. Kinshichō is an entertainment cluster, mostly of movie houses, in Honjo Ward, since 1947 a part of Sumida Ward, near the eastern limits of the city as they were before 1932. It was developed in the thirties by entrepreneurs who thought that what was happening along the western fringes of the city might be made to happen along the eastern fringes as well. Though it was not a complete failure, it fell very far short of becoming a Shinjuku. Not inclined to go as far as Shinjuku, the proletariat of the eastern wards still preferred Asakusa to the more convenient Kinshichō. Takami has an interesting explanation. Kinshichō "has all the facilities, but the attraction of Asakusa is simply not there. Unlike Asakusa, it has no tradition. It has theaters and they have nothing behind them. We may draw a moral from this."

It is an interesting theory, but one which the facts do not support. Shinjuku and Shibuya flourished. Newest and smallest of the Five Mouths of Edo, Shinjuku was a place with a thin tradition, and Shibuya was a place where scarcely the most delicate film of it was to be detected.

The bourgeoisie and the intelligentsia were more important than the proletariat, and they were going west.

Takami did lose interest in Asakusa after the war. So did many others who had been among the celebrities during the good years. In his postscript to a collection of essays he edited about Asakusa, he says that his initial inclination was to decline the task. The Asakusa of recent years has meant so little to him. It is a statement repeated with variations in responses to a questionnaire about Asakusa carried in the same collection. "I never go there," says Enoken. "The Asakusa I knew is thirteen and fourteen years in the past," says Mochizuki Yūko, Japan's mother. Tokugawa Musei, most famous of the *benshi* movie narrators, responds with a poem in seventeen syllables:

> The end of the year.
> The day has come
> When I neglect the place.

When Kawabata said that Asakusa offered nothing of the first quality, he cannot have been thinking of literature. The Asakusa coterie, if we may call it that—Kawabata himself, Kafū, and Takami—was superior to anything Ginza or Shinjuku has succeeded in putting together. Asakusa attracted the attention of gifted writers as no other part of the city has been able to do, and when it went into its final decline the city lost something irreplaceable.

In a coffeehouse near where the Kokusai Gekijō, the International Theater, once stood there is a somewhat naïve mural by the writer Kata Kōji. It is charming and it is sad. All the Asakusa celebrities of the interwar period are there, with Enoken in the middle. Many of them are dead and none hold forth any longer in Asakusa. The girls of the all-girl troupe at the Kokusai once patronized the coffeehouse. The guests at the hotel that has taken its place do not.

The Ginza district, generously defined so that it spills over toward Marunouchi and Hibiya Park on the west and Tsukiji on the east, had almost as many movie theaters on the eve of the war as Asakusa had. Ginza proper, in terms of movies and the performing arts, was a sort of

A memento of Asakusa between the wars—Kata Kōji's mural in the Peter coffeehouse.
Chaplin is seated at right; the rumpled, full-length figure in the foreground is Enoken;
and Nagai Kafū stands at left, holding an umbrella

valley between two ridges, Marunouchi-Hibiya on the west and Tsukiji
on the east. Ginza proper was a place of drinking, eating, and shopping.

A large movie company dominated each of the two ridges, Tōhō the
western one, Shōchiku the eastern. An Osaka firm that moved in on
Tokyo late in the Meiji period, Shōchiku came to dominate Tokyo Kabuki. Its canny impresarios quickly recognized the importance of movies,
and moved into them as well. Tōhō too was from Osaka. Its origins were
in the all-girl Takarazuka review, Takarazuka itself being a suburb of
Osaka. From the mid-thirties Tōhō began making movies. In 1932, as a
company called Tokyo Takarazuka, it launched an assault on Tokyo, as
Shōchiku had done some decades earlier. It was never able to loosen the
Shōchiku grip on Kabuki, though it tried mightily, but it did very well in
the staging and distributing of reviews and movies. By the end of the
decade it controlled most of the movie palaces and review and concert
halls to the west of Ginza, including the Imperial and the grandest of
them all, the Nihon Gekijō, or Japan Theater, on the outer castle moat.
In 1943 Tōhō became the legal name of the company. It condenses Tokyo
Takarazuka, making use of the first and third of the four Chinese characters with which this last is written.

The Nichigeki, as everyone calls it, had big and little movie theaters, a chorus line, and strip shows. It was not quite as big as the Shōchiku property, the Kokusai, or International. They were the two largest in the land, the one seating three thousand people, the other a few hundred more. The Kokusai was in Asakusa, however, and so fell victim to the Asakusa malaise. As has just been noted, a hotel now stands on the site. The old Nichigeki too is gone, but the Tōhō movie complex to the west of Ginza, of which a new Nichigeki is a part, now quite overshadows the Shōchiku equivalent to the east. Ginza has tended in a westerly direction, even as the city has.

Asakusa and Ginza were not in the close competition that a theater count might suggest. Greater Ginza had the Kabukiza, the "cypress stage" (the Big Apple, so to speak), which overshadowed all other Kabuki theaters. It had two other big theaters for live productions of a traditional sort. For concerts and recitals to please cosmopolitan tastes it had the Imperial and Hibiya Hall. It had the Nichigeki and the Takarazuka (known to Americans of the Occupation as the Ernie Pyle). Most important, it was the leader, the center of things, the place where one went in search of Culture. The girls at the Nichigeki could be fairly *ero* and those

Cafés and coffeehouses in Ginza

at the Takarazuka rather *guro,* but quality was there, as it was not at Asakusa, for those who wanted it and could pay for it.

Ginza had almost a monopoly on foreign performers, who began streaming in at about the time of the First World War, and continued to do so until the Crisis began looming too threateningly. The Shimbashi geisha was on the rise and the Yoshiwara geisha on the decline, surviving, indeed, only vestigially. The geisha of the Asakusa district proper, just behind the temple, had never had great prestige. The few children of Edo who were still around to observe Ginza so much at the center of things must have thought it all very odd. The Ginza of late Edo had not amounted to much in the realm of refined pleasure and vulgar entertainment, and Asakusa had been everything.

The Meiji elite had sought to improve Kabuki, by which was meant to remove it from its crass mercantile origins and make it into something elevated and edifying. The West came into Kabuki. The first and second Sadanji, gifted actors, father and son, experimented seriously with Western forms and a new realism, which did not go to the extreme of using actresses. And Western spectators came to Kabuki, and found it good, and so the Meiji effort, based largely on feelings of cultural inferiority, came to seem meaningless. Meiji wanted a theatrical form which it need not be ashamed of before the world, and was surprised to find that it already had one.

Kansai Kabuki was all the while declining. Tanizaki's Makioka sisters, all of them thoroughly and almost aggressively Osakan in their tastes, prefer Tokyo Kabuki. Several of the most famous and gifted actors of our day have Kansai origins, but they have had to make names for themselves in Tokyo.

During the interwar years geisha had their go at improvement. In 1905 the metropolitan police banned public performances by geisha. In their search for a way around the ban, the Shimbashi geisha hit upon the idea of seeking permission to sing and dance in their own theater. Determination prevailed, permission was granted, and the theater was built. Work on the Shimbashi Embujō (the second element in the name means something not far from "dance hall," though the spirit is very different) began in 1923. It ran into the earthquake and was not completed until 1925. The opening program, in April of that year, was a gala recital of classical dances by Shimbashi geisha, the Azuma Odori, Dance of the East, in contradistinction to the Miyako Odori, Dance of the

Capital, or Kyoto. The geisha at first used their theater three months a year and rented it out for the other months. Having made their point, they allowed improvement to withdraw into the background. In 1934 they leased the Embujō to Shōchiku. Thereafter it became a sort of adjunct to the Kabukiza, a few paces up the canal. Dances of the East, and geisha, were less prominent. The grand recital is now an annual affair, a springtide observance.

Whatever Kawabata may have meant by the high-quality thing that was not to be found in Asakusa, the suggestion is very strong from *Scarlet Gang of Asakusa* that the sideshows in the tents and huts scattered around Asakusa Park were near the bottom. From them grew a little genre that had a very brief career and may be considered an original Japanese contribution to the performing arts. It was done in by television, a form, or device, for which Japan can claim no credit. From as early as Meiji, storytellers had used silhouette figures by way of illustration, a little as the shadow performers of southern Asia do. Early in the Shōwa Period they emerged from their shelters and took to the streets, taking with them not cumbersome figures but readily transportable cards. So the *kamishibai,* the "paper show," came to be. *Kamishibai* persons, mostly men, went the rounds of the city with their cards and boxes of sweets on bicycles. In vacant lots and the like they would summon together very young audiences, whom they would hold with illustrated stories and sell the sweets to. Their best days were in the thirties. They fell in nicely with the nationalism of the time, and those who were very young when they were flourishing tell us that their representations of Anglo-American beasts were very vivid indeed. These disappeared after 1945, though the appeal to manly little fellows who went around beating one another with bamboo swords continued. *Kamishibai* seemed an indispensable part of the city and its street life, but it quickly surrendered before television, its career having lasted a generation or so.

Another graphic form, much nearer the bottom, many would say, than *kamishibai,* also had its beginnings in the years between the wars, and continues to flourish. What are called comics are probably today the only presence gigantic enough to rival television. The cartoon, often comic, has a venerable and estimable tradition, centuries old. The panel narrative, the form that so inundates our day, had its beginnings just after the earthquake. The very earliest ones were self-contained episodes in four frames. The *Asahi* and the *Hōchi* both had cartoon strips, tending toward slapstick, from late 1923. The first extended narrative was also something the *Asahi* thought up. It began in 1926, and so "comics" became earnest. Today, in their pursuit of sex and violence, they are more than earnest. They are grim. Whether or not their origins can be blamed on the confusion that followed the earthquake, that is where they are.

Though, as we have seen, there had earlier been faltering essays in the direction of professional baseball, Babe Ruth, Lou Gehrig, and some others came to Japan in 1934, and that same year Shōriki and the *Yomiuri* put together their Giants. So professional baseball began in great earnest. A very young Japanese pitcher became a national hero by holding the Babe to one hit out of three times at bat. He finally lost this now-legendary game, 1−0, but it was a moral victory if ever there could be such a thing. In 1936 a professional league got underway. It had three Tokyo teams and two each from Nagoya and Osaka. One of the Nagoya teams, the Goldfish, beat the Giants in the initial game, but the Nagoya Dragons, successors to the Goldfish, have had nothing like the success and popularity of the Giants. "Goldfish" is not a good translation. They really were the Gold Leviathans of the Castle Donjon, with reference to Nagoya Castle and the maritime monsters that decorate the ridge ends of its donjon. The names in general were more imaginative than they are today, when lions and tigers and giants, all in English, predominate. One Tokyo team was named the Senators, also in English, albeit Japan may have seen some senators but has never had one. Only the Giants (Tokyo and the *Yomiuri* still) and the Tigers (Osaka) survive of the original names.

Baseball was required to pretend, as the Crisis deepened, that it had never been anything but a Japanese game. All the American terms, "strike" and "ball" and "pitcher" and the like, part of every young person's vocabulary, were translated into Japanese. There is a very funny scene in a movie about the war in which a game has trouble proceeding because no one can remember the words with which to make it do so. The Crisis cast its shadow in other ways. A grenade-throwing contest was offered as a special attraction at a Giants game in 1942. This occurred at the Kōrakuen Stadium, which, in 1937, became the premier baseball park of the city. It stands on what had been the main Edo estate of the Mito Tokugawa family. In 1943 baseball players changed to un-numbered khaki uniforms and were required to salute one another. Professional baseball held out longer than many other diversions and in the end disbanded voluntarily. In November 1944, the Patriotic Base-ball Association, as the league had become, announced a recess in its activities.

The Japanese in these years were acquiring a certain amount of international sports fame not for their baseball playing but for their swimming. If the 1940 Olympics had come to be, they might well have been a demonstration of national (not to say racial) superiority such as Hitler hoped to offer at Berlin in 1936. Though a source of great pride, however, swimming produced only intermittent bursts of enthusiasm. It was becoming sadly that way with Sumō as well. The national accom-plishment has not in recent decades held the continuing interest of the nation as baseball has. Here too there were bursts of enthusiasm, a very intense one coming during the years before the Pacific War. It was brought on by the achievements of Futabayama, the most famous modern wrestler, and probably the most famous in the whole long history of the sport. He had the attention of NHK, the national broadcasting system, as no talented wrestler had had it before him.

January 15, 1939 (the year of the nonaggression pact with the Soviet Union), was a day on which the whole nation gasped. Until that evening Futabayama had had a streak of sixty-nine victories, extending over a half dozen tournaments and three years. It was and continues to be the longest in the history of Sumō. January 15 was the fourth day of the Tokyo spring tournament, so called although it takes place in the coldest part of winter. Futabayama failed to win his seventieth victory. He lost to a younger wrestler of lesser rank who some years later reached the top rank but whose place in history was really achieved during those few seconds.

Futabayama retired in 1945. For a time after the war his image suffered because of his adherence to a parvenu religion (there were scores of them in those days) that did not seem very dignified. He returned to head the Sumō Association in 1957 and clear up the confusion that had caused his predecessor to attempt suicide. This unhappy episode is one in the long history of making Sumō, or so it is said, modern and not feudal. Futabayama died, still in his fifties, in 1968. Because of the demands which great corpulence makes on the vital organs, wrestlers tend not to live long lives. Sumō did not, like baseball, declare itself out of business. It persisted through the war. Two tournaments were held in 1945, one before and one after the coming of the Americans.

In these darkling days there were other matters to keep the city interested, incidents sometimes sentimental and sometimes chilling. The city and the nation have never been afraid to risk being sentimental—or perhaps the point is that they define the expression differently, being tolerant as other places might not be of effusive emotional outpourings.

High among the warming items is the story of the faithful dog Hachikō. The name means something like "Number Eight," or possibly, since it has an intimate, affectionate ring and is masculine, "Good Old Octavius." Hachikō was an Akita dog that died on March 8, 1935. For a decade or so before that he had appeared regularly each evening at Shibuya Station, faithful to his practice of seeing his master home from work. Each night he lay waiting as train after train came in. No one could explain that the master was dead. A statue of Hachikō was erected in front of the station about a year before his death. The statue fell victim to the wartime shortage of metals, but a replacement has gone up since the war, and is one of the objects in the city almost everyone knows. Shibuya is now a most bustling *sakariba* (it was not yet within the city limits when Hachikō's master died). When people meet at the station, at Hachikō's feet is the place where they most commonly arrange to do it. There can be no mistakes.

At least one noted European was swept up in the outpourings. Shortly before Hachikō died the German architect Bruno Taut spoke admiringly in his diary of the dog he kept seeing in front of the station. (Because of Taut's writings it was standard for a half century, especially in Japan, to deplore the architectural endeavors of the shoguns and to glorify those of the Kyoto court. A reaction has recently set in, and it is possible once more, without demonstrating one's own bad taste, to aver that that of the Tokugawas and their minions was not uniformly bad.) Hachikō had a very grand funeral, and now, stuffed, is in the collection of the National Science Museum at Ueno.

As with so many warming stories, there is another side to this one,

The statue of faithful Hachikō, as it is today in Shibuya

having to do with Hachikō's motives, of which we will never know the whole truth. Such observers of his behavior as the novelist Ooka Shōhei have held that he did not go to the station in the evening at all, but hung around it the whole day through, waiting to be fed. The station attendants were kinder to him than the people at home—and it may be that they recognized a good story when they saw one. If so, they were very successful. They gave Shibuya its most famous landmark.

Tokyo criminals have always had a certain flair, and sometimes it has seemed that a wish to be apprehended is among their peculiarities. The Tokyo police probably deserve their reputation for effectiveness, and yet one sometimes wonders. How would they perform if they had the unruly, uncooperative citizenry of Chicago or Marseilles to put up with? There was, for instance, the preaching thief who broke into more than a hundred houses from 1927 into 1929. He never harmed anyone, and did not mind being seen. After having chosen what he wanted to take with him, he would stay for a while and talk with his victims, pointing out to them the advantages of watchdogs and well-bolted doors. He left behind fingerprints in the house of a rice merchant in Itabashi, in the northern suburbs, and yet he went on stealing and preaching for some months before he was apprehended, early in 1929. He proved to be a craftsman in the building trades.

The most celebrated criminals of Meiji were murderesses, and the most celebrated criminal of early Shōwa was a murderess. The early decades of the twentieth century did not produce a Tokyo murderess whose accomplishments became legendary, as did those of Takahashi O-den in early Meiji. To say, as is often said, that the newspapers turned with eager delight to the case of O-sada for relief from the gloom of the February 26 Incident, the military rising of that day in 1936, would probably be to exaggerate. They probably would have loved O-sada in any case. The gloom seems to have dispelled itself rather quickly, especially in the poorer parts of the city, in which O-sada did her thing. Retail sales fell off drastically in rich Nihombashi, and especially at its richest store, the Mitsukoshi, but were relatively unaffected at the Matsuya in Asakusa. Expensive seats at the Kabukiza went unsold, but not cheap ones. It is true that there were also empty seats at the Asakusa review houses—but we have seen that they had High City intellectual types among their fanciers.

It was in May 1936, in any event, that Abe Sada, familiarly known as O-sada, did it. For a week she had been staying at a *machiai,* an inn catering to amorous trysters, with her employer, a restaurant owner in the western part of the city. The *machiai* was in Arakawa, that most populous of the new wards, near the northern limits. The man was in his early forties, she in her early thirties. On May 18 he was found strangled. His sexual organs had been cut away and were not on the premises. On May 20 O-sada was apprehended near Shinagawa Station. She had the organs on her person, and his underwear as well.

She was sentenced to a prison term and released from the Tochigi Women's Prison in 1941. For some years she ran a drinking place on the outskirts of Asakusa. Then she disappeared. Recently she has been traced to a Buddhist nunnery in the Kansai. Predictably, she had imitators, none of them remotely as famous as she.

Much black humor was inspired by the O-sada affair. The verb "to cut" also functions as "to punch," as of a bus ticket. Great was the merriment, therefore, when the "red collar" girls on the buses would go about with their standard petition: "Allow me, please, to cut those that have not already been cut." The murder also inspired a superior work of art which demonstrates that the Japanese can still turn out fine pornog-

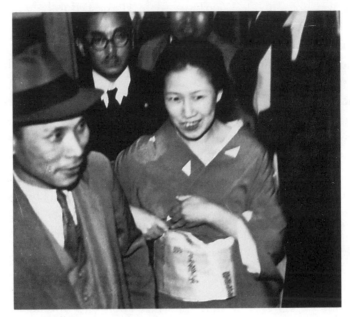

O-sada the murderess under arrest

raphy, as they did under the shoguns. The moving picture *In the Realm of the Senses* contains hard-core scenes, and has great visual beauty and a suffocating intensity; and it is a reasonably authentic retelling of the O-sada story. The actor who played O-sada's friend is still very prominent. The actress who played O-sada has quite disappeared from sight.

Voguish words of the time inform us with concreteness and immediacy of what we would have known anyway, that Taishō democracy was over and more somber times had come. Neologisms stream in and out of Japanese at a rate perhaps unrivaled among major languages, and tell us what is fashionable and socially acceptable. The minister of education did not succeed in evicting "mama" and "papa" from the language, but newspapers and radio and the advertising agencies, overwhelmingly in and controlled from Tokyo, could be brought into line and made to use only worthwhile words, appropriate to the Crisis.

As late as the mid-thirties we still have foreign words and expressions in ample numbers, some of them imported in finished form, some of them fabricated from imported elements. "Air girl," for stewardess, has disappeared from the language. "Yo-yo" might still be recognized by fair numbers of people, but the word itself is no longer to be found in standard dictionaries. "Hiking" is still very much with us.

Sufu was among the last foreign words in vogue before the decade of exclusiveness and xenophobia began, and widely used neologisms came for the most part to have native or Chinese origins. It would be as difficult to eliminate a Chinese influence from Japanese as a Latin one from English. One might as well try to eliminate the language itself. *Sufu* remains in the language, but probably most Japanese would be as slow as most foreigners to recognize its foreignness. It is an acronym from the Japanese pronunciation of "staple fiber," the phonetic patterns of the language requiring a muted "u" after each of the initial consonants. Good cotton and wool almost disappeared during the war. *Sufu* took their place. Some varieties tended to go to pieces in water, and so sea bathing suffered. Being foreign and decadent, it would have suffered anyway.

Many neologisms from the xenophobic decade, such as "spiritual mobilization," are merely cant. They do not say what they mean, in this instance "totalitarianism." Others have sinister, threatening overtones. One hopes that the age which produced them will not come again. They speak of loyalty and patriotism gone mad, and they speak of mindlessness. "The eight directions under one roof" could mean nothing more baneful than that all persons are siblings, but the mood of the times left only one possible interpretation, that it was a kind of manifest destiny for the whole world to become Japanese.

It must be admitted that some of the patriotic coinages of the decade are rather clever. "The ABCD encirclement" is good, and contains delicate irony, perhaps unobserved by the coiners. The encirclers are the Americans, the British, the Chinese, and the Dutch. It may be that the French, down in Indochina, got left out because they did not fit the alphabetic sequence. That and the nonaggression pact may be the explanation in the case of the Russians. Be these omissions as they may, the expression could not have caught on without the aid of the Roman alphabet. So a device from hated Europe was put to the uses of Great Japan and its xenophobia.

Kokutai meichō is the sort of thing that lay in wait for Taishō democracy. It is rendered by the biggest Japanese-English dictionary as "clarification of the fundamental concept of national polity." The expression "national polity" *(kokutai)* may be put in the realm of cant. It sometimes seems that among the claims of the Japanese to superior uniqueness is that they alone have a polity. The longer expression speaks of an anti-intellectual response to a reasoned and intellectual position.

In 1935 the constitutional scholar Minobe Tatsukichi, whose son was governor of Tokyo from 1967 to 1979, following "the Olympic governor," published what has come to be known as the theory of the emperor as an organ of the state. This produced a violent reaction on the part of those who thought that the emperor, if not identical with the state, presided over it as a father presides over a family. The "clarification" movement found its highest expression in *The Essence of National Polity (Kokutai no Hongi)* of 1937. Put together by the Ministry of Education, this treatise condemned individualism, and informed Japanese that they belonged unquestioningly to the emperor as head of the mystical family state; fulfillment lay in service and submission and self-denial. Minobe was prosecuted for lèse-majesté, but no sentence was handed down. He resigned from the House of Peers, to which he had been appointed after his retirement from Tokyo Imperial University. All his works were banned. In 1936 he was attacked by right-wing radicals but escaped with minor wounds. After 1945 he unsuccessfully opposed rewriting the Meiji constitution. He died in 1948, a legend and something of a national hero.

It is but one four-character expression and one series of incidents having to do with one man and his ideas, but in it we have the mood of the times and the travails of the city, intellectual center of the land. Minobe was an independent thinker and a survivor of Taishō democracy. The left wing had already been broken as a concerted movement before his great agony began. *Tenkō* is among the voguish words of the early thirties. It means something like apostasy, recanting, or disavowal, and is applied to persons, and especially writers and intellectuals, who renounced Marxist beliefs and turned to serving the national polity with more or less enthusiasm. There are many ways, chief among them, perhaps, geographic isolation, to account for the fact that Japan had no organized resistance and no selfless underground martyrs. In any event, it had none. *Tenkō* prevailed.

In 1946, after such grim wartime expressions as "Anglo-American beasts" and "a hundred million fighting to the end" (four Chinese characters state this succinctly), we again have bright and often flippant cosmopolitanism, with such expressions as "après-guerre," suggesting sometimes hedonism and sometimes new beginnings, and "hubba-hubba."

As there were voguish, trendy words, so too of course there were vogues and trends. All cities have them, but at least since a cult of rabbit fanciers sprang up in early Meiji, Tokyo has had them more furiously and frequently than most places. In 1932 women suddenly all had permanent waves, Japan having learned to produce the equipment necessary for creating them. The year 1933, as we have seen, was that of the yo-yo. Slightly later there was a craze for stamps, not the postage kind but the rubber kind, provided by famous places to give evidence that the earnest, thorough traveler has been to them. The American writer Helen Mears describes, in *The Year of the Wild Boar,* how the acquiring of stamps seemed to take on its own obsessive importance, greater than the sights behind them. Her boar year, last in the Chinese cycle of twelve, was 1935. As cycles went in the first half of the twentieth century, it was a tranquil one, despite assassinations and the beginnings of the Crisis. The preceding one contained the earthquake, the succeeding one the Pacific War.

Nagai Kafū lamented the loss of harmony when Western techniques and motifs began intruding upon the streets of Edo. Yet it may be said that the Western buildings of Meiji had their own kind of harmony. When, in monumental public building, the wildly fanciful architecture of early Meiji gave way to brick and stone, the major buildings and complexes that resulted, such as Mitsubishi Londontown in Marunouchi and the Bank of Japan in Nihombashi, may not have looked much like Edo, but they did look like one another, and like Western prototypes, a statement that cannot be made about the very earliest excursions into the Western. Now concrete and all its plasticity were coming to the fore, and so, in the years after the earthquake, the eclectic jumble—the miscellany—of today began to emerge. It began to take shape, one might say, but it really has no shape. The twentieth century is the century of fragmentation, and it had come to Tokyo, which was pulled in more directions and ended up with a larger fragment count than most cities.

There were the old and new European styles, modern utilitarian box and Queen Anne side by side in Marunouchi, and there were old Japanese styles done in modern materials. The main building of the National Museum in Ueno and the Kabukiza are probably the chief surviving examples of this last, but there are many others, such as the priestly lodgings behind the Asakusa Kannon. Though gutted in 1945 and renovated with a simpler roofline, the Kabukiza is not much different from the building that went up after the earthquake. The museum is relatively plain and utilitarian, with a roof like that of many a lecture hall in many a temple, though none are so big, and an entrance bay that also looks like a temple. It was finished in 1937, on the site of a Meiji building by the English architect Josiah Conder which was badly damaged in 1923. (The National Museum did not become that until 1947, when jurisdiction passed from the royal household to the Ministry of Education.) An earlier and a later building flank this main one: a Renaissance building in stone put up late in Meiji and a very modern glass-and-concrete structure put up since the war. They are an interesting progression: reading from left to right as one faces the entrance to the main building, a replica of something Western, a somewhat traditional building in Western materials, and a building which eschews Japanese forms but in its basic principles is not far from traditional Japanese architecture. Many will

The Kabukiza, as reconstructed after the earthquake

say that the central building is dishonest, pretending to be something that it is not. None of the three is shockingly unpleasant, but they are diverse. They are what the twentieth century has made the city.

It must be added that many buildings from the interwar period, such as Hibiya Hall and the Daiichi Hotel in Shimbashi, built for the Olympics that never happened, are distinctly unpleasant. They look as if no one, least of all the architects, had expected them to last so long.

Then there are curious exercises in styles neither Western nor Japanese. Chief among them, probably, is the Honganji Temple in Tsukiji, not far from the fish market, the villa where General and Mrs. Grant stayed, and the site of the Meiji foreign settlement. The principal east-country temple of the pietist Shin sect, the Honganji was in Edo from the early seventeenth century and has been in Tsukiji since the great fire of 1657. It was twice burned in Meiji. At the time of the earthquake the complex—much grander than now exists—had a main hall in an imposing courtly style. This too was lost. The rebuilding, in stone, from 1931 to 1935, is a representation of an Indian temple. So it seeks to take us back to the origins of Buddhism, to which the name Honganji also adverts. One of a kind, it looks stranger, there in one of the more

The post-earthquake Honganji Temple, Tsukiji

unchanged parts of the city, than would a glass block from New York. A lady in Tanizaki's *The Makioka Sisters* calls it "that odd building." It is highly unlikely that she would have so characterized a foreign exercise of the Western sort.

The wards of the old Low City, inundated at increasingly brief intervals through Meiji, have been relatively free from flooding since the completion of the Arakawa Drainage Channel shortly before the earthquake. (It was on the banks of this that the young lady in Kafū's *Katsushika Romance* had her refreshment stand. See page 107.) Parts of the city traditionally immune from such troubles, on the other hand, came to be readily and regularly immersed when rain waters were too much for drains. Hibiya, right at the heart of the city and in front of the royal palace, is an example. The explanation is that waters which once went into canals had now, the canals having been filled in, nowhere to go. (Similarly, the disappearance of paddy lands in the suburbs is blamed for the greater frequency of floods in the Meiji Low City. They acted as storage reservoirs during heavy rains.) Land subsidence, chiefly from the consumption of underground water, has been worst in the wards east of the river, parts of which lie below sea level; but such central and technically advanced places as Hibiya have also been affected. Some of the older buildings have their foundations exposed, so that they stand an awkward distance above the ground.

The city limits had been expanded in 1932 to include the five contiguous counties, but the debate over what to do about the duplex government, municipal and prefectural, went on for more than a decade afterward. The interests of the ward part, the county part, and the prefecture did not coincide, especially as regards money. There was increasing agreement, as the Crisis dragged on and deepened, that Tokyo as the capital called for close scrutiny, and perhaps direct control by the national government. In July 1943, by which time it was becoming clear to intelligent and informed people that the Pacific War was not going to end happily, reform of the Tokyo government was put through by proclamation.

The proclamation was issued on the first day of June and went into effect on the first day of July. The discussions that led up to it were kept secret, for it was believed that they might reveal information useful to the British and American beasts. The Doolittle raids of just upward of a year before would seem to have produced the necessary sense of urgency. Reorganization fell short of the more sweeping proposals, which would have made prefecture and city one and done away with the old county part. The latter remained. What the proclamation did chiefly was abolish the city government and the office of mayor. Tokyo-fu, the Tokyo Metropolitan Prefecture, became Tokyo-to, the Tokyo Capital District.

The powers of the wards were a matter of concern, since nothing now stood between them and the prefectural government. Fears that reform would lead to a loss of autonomy proved to be well founded. The wards had fewer powers than cities and towns elsewhere in the country.

In a sense the proclamation and reorganization only made explicit what had already become fact. It brought the city more clearly and openly under the contol of the Home Ministry, which already had control over the police, including the notorious thought police, and over the appointment of prefectural governors. Even before 1943 the Home Ministry had a very large say in the functioning of the city government. Of the nine men who were mayor during the less than seventeen years between the change of reigns and the abolition of the office, five were former officials of the ministry. By way of emphasizing that Tokyo was different from the other prefectures, the governor was called not a *chiji,* like other governors, but a *chōkan,* which means something like "chief executive." The first chief executive had been home minister under Hiranuma Kiichirō, who spent his last years in Sugamo Prison as a first-class war criminal, and mayor and military governor of Singapore, which the occupying Japanese renamed the Shōwa of the South. He had been in charge of preparations for the reorganization of 1943.

The defeat of the Olympics by a metal shortage and the expunging of foreign words from baseball were by no means the only signs of the austere times that lay ahead. The age of the ersatz arrived soon after the beginning of the China Incident. Bamboo and ceramics replaced metals for cooking and tableware. The hegemony of *sufu,* staple fiber, has already been remarked upon. In 1938 appeared the smelly, fuming, sometimes asphyxiating charcoal taxicabs that continued to symbolize deprivation in the years after the war.

The General Mobilization Law and charcoal-burning cabs came into being at about the same time. Essentially the direction of the nation's efforts was turned toward technology and production, toward bringing the Crisis to a happy conclusion. There is a similarity to the tactics used in the great postwar trade campaign. A nation's inclinations and institutions do not change easily. A major difference is that big business objected, late in 1938, to certain provisions having to do with dividends and loans, and forced a compromise. This was the only serious snarl in application of the law. When the great trade campaign was being launched after the war, the army was not strong enough to return the favor. Neither was the other natural enemy, the labor movement.

The economic mobilization of recent years has not taken the joy from life as the military kind did. Two installments of Tanizaki's *The Makioka Sisters* appeared in the magazine *Chūō Kōron* early in 1943. Then it was banned, the contents, about life in a bourgeois suburb of Osaka during the early years of the Crisis, being deemed frivolous. Tanizaki went on writing, but the novel was not published in full until after the war.

The years of the Pacific War and the years immediately preceding were grim, certainly, but the authorities did not go as far as they might have gone. Tanizaki and Kafū were never compelled to break their silence, as they might have been in a thoroughly totalitarian state. Some movie directors managed to pursue their own interests; some almost managed to make fun of censorship. Not all movie houses were required to close, though all of the big ones, and most of the Ginza ones, had closed by the spring of 1944. Some were allowed to reopen again before the end of the war. Late in 1944 the Nichigeki (the Japan Theater), near Ginza, the Imperial Theater in Marunouchi, and the Kokusai (International) in Asakusa were commandeered for the manufacture of the incendiary balloons that were intended to drift across the Pacific on westerly winds and set America afire.

Kabuki did not entirely disappear. In its very worst days there were traveling companies. The largest theaters in Tokyo, Osaka, and Kyoto were all closed in March 1944, but the Shimbashi Embujō was allowed to reopen after a short recess. The great Kikugorō was playing there on the day in 1945 when the Embujō, along with the Kabukiza, was gutted by American firebombs. Performances after the reopening were limited to five hours a day, with the same program twice repeated. This was a sad falling off from the days when the devotee could sit for nine and ten hours in a theater and not have to put up with any repetition at all. The Tokyo Theater (Tōkyō Gekijō), third in the Shōchiku trio east of Ginza, survived the bombings, and Kabuki was playing there down to mid-August 1945. It was soon to find itself belabored by the other side.

Wartime censors disliked the raffish heroes of the early nineteenth century, whom, with the best Kabuki of that day and perhaps of all days, they found decadent. The American Occupation was suspicious of the grand historic tradition, which it thought militaristic.

Already a year and a half before Pearl Harbor, the Crisis was having its effect on the geisha districts. The expensive restaurants at which they entertained (the establishments commonly called "geisha houses" in English) were required to close at eleven, and geisha to cease entertaining at ten. The districts were not required to close down completely until the spring of 1944. People in a position to close them down both needed and enjoyed them. Some geisha belonged particularly to the military police, some to the ordinary police. Then there were army and navy geisha and the geisha who enjoyed the special patronage of the civil bureaucracy. They formed a considerable part of the intelligence network. This was in an old tradition. The Shimbashi and Akasaka districts had become prosperous in large measure because the military and civil services condescended to use them.

New taxes after the beginning of the Pacific War made geisha more expensive. Then finally, on March 5, 1944, all the geisha restaurants closed. They stayed open almost until dawn the night before. Many geisha donned the baggy trousers that were the feminine uniform in the last months of the Crisis and went off to work in munitions and supply factories. The apprentice geisha (*hangyoku*) of Shimbashi formed a brass band which, toward the improvement of morale, had concerts in the palace plaza. In 1942 Kafū had seen the ladies of Tamanoi mustered at a shrine to give thanks for the fall of Singapore.

The all-girl troupe at the Takarazuka Theater, immediately west of Ginza, had its final performance on March 4, 1944. The crowds were so great and dense that the police faced them with swords unsheathed.

Western popular music, so strongly under the influence of the American beasts, virtually disappeared. It did disappear as public performance, and people had to keep their gramophones low if they wanted to listen to records. Classical music was another matter. There was an inherent contradiction in the great campaign to purify Japanese culture: two of the most musical of peoples, the Germans and the Italians, were Japanese allies, and the Japanese went on hoping that the Russians would stay out of the tiff with the A, the B, the C, and the D. Russian and German music were performed almost to the end. Hibiya Hall survived the May 1945 raids that destroyed almost everything in the vicinity, including the prefectural library. The Japan Philharmonic had its last concert there in June. It presented Beethoven's Ninth, a remarkable achievement in a city many of whose musicians had gone to war and whose communications and transportation had broken down. The exhortation in the last movement that the masses hug and kiss may have been taken as another way of inviting the eight directions to assemble under one roof.

The more expensive and elegant restaurants, such as those with geisha, had all closed their doors before the heavy bombings came, but lesser establishments in large numbers—some three thousand of them, the best estimate is—remained in business all through the war. Then there were drinking places known as "people's saloons" (*kokumin no sakaba*), which provided rather chilly comfort. Takami Jun, in his diary, described a visit to one, in Ginza. Each customer was allowed a bottle of beer, a glass of draft beer, or a flagon of sake. Discipline was not good. Customers were divided into parties of ten for admission, but when the time came for Takami's party to be admitted it contained eleven people. Someone had sneaked in. It was possible to get special favors if you knew the manager. This information Takami had from a Yose performer who did know a manager.

The Crisis had some benevolent aspects. It brought, as we have seen, a fall in the suicide rate. Whether or not the closing of gambling establishments is benevolent, it too occurred. Takami reported that until the beginning of the China Incident the regions north of the Asakusa Kannon were dotted with little gambling places, each with a lookout patrolling the street. Their patrons were such people as the wives of the neighborhood greengrocers. Then the Incident began, and they all closed down. The war was a good time for those who wished to get married. If the Japanese were a superior race and if the eight directions were to do the wise thing, why then they must be numerous. They must increase and multiply. So a metropolitan wedding hall was opened, for the inexpensive and efficient production of weddings. During its best times, midway through the Pacific War, it produced some two or three hundred a month.

The Ueno Zoo had its happy events and its great sorrow. A baby giraffe born in May 1942 was named Minami, "South," by way of encouraging the Japanese push into Southeast Asia and the islands. Then the time came, in August and September 1943, to kill dangerous animals. The corpses were dissected at an army veterinary hospital and the notable ones were stuffed. The remains were buried under a memorial stone in the zoo. In a search for funds to maintain what was left, a third as many birds and beasts as in 1940, the zoo took to breeding and selling chicks, ducklings, and piglets. At the end of the war there were vegetable patches on the grounds. The largest animals left were three camels, two giraffes (including Minami), and a water buffalo. A hundred forty fire-bombs, more or less, fell on the zoo on April 13, 1945. The saddest stories one hears are of the elephants. The animals were to be disposed of by poisoning. The elephants refused to eat the poisoned food. The keepers could not bring themselves to shoot their charges, which went on begging until they starved to death. The most vigorous and truculent died first. There was talk of sending the smaller of the remaining two off to Sendai, but this was rejected by the chief keeper as impractical. In their cages, out of sight behind black-and-white drapes, the two struggled to get to their feet as ceremonies for the repose of their spirits proceeded. They seemed to think that if they did tricks they would be fed.

The first American air raid, the raid commanded by Lieutenant Colonel James A. Doolittle, came just after noon on a fine spring day, April 18, 1942. Thirteen carrier-based B-25 bombers flew in low enough for straf-ings, earlier and from a greater distance than had been planned. A Japanese patrol boat spotted the carrier that morning and sent off a wireless message before it was sunk. The message arrived in Tokyo and was treated carelessly. The view was that there might or might not be a raid and in any event it would not come for a while. Ten minutes elapsed after the planes were sighted before an alarm was sounded. A similar insouciance, having to do perhaps with the myth that the Japanese spirit would prevail over all, is to be observed in later and far more serious raids. Three of the thirteen aircraft dropped their bombs on Kanagawa Prefecture to the south of Tokyo, and three of the sixteen that took off from the carrier went to bomb Nagoya, Osaka, and Kobe. Nagoya got more than its intended share, because the Osaka flight bombed it by mistake.

In Tokyo the damage was chiefly along the northern and southern fringes of the city, although there was also damage in Ushigome Ward, just to the west of the palace. The palace itself was not damaged. The casualty total was 364, including thirty-nine dead. About two hundred fifty buildings were damaged.

Two-thirds of the deaths were in the southern part of the city, but the single one in Katsushika Ward, at the far northeast, aroused the greatest indignation. It was the one the newspapers settled upon. A thirteen-year-old schoolboy was killed by strafing. Probably he would not have died had he not lived in a district notorious for its want of medical facilities, but evidence of what the American beasts were capable of was there for everyone to see.

So was evidence of fibbing by Japanese military authorities. The first announcement from the Tokyo army command was that nine planes had been downed. It was, as we have noted, a fine, clear spring day, and no one in the city had observed the downing of a single plane. Perhaps, the joke had it, the defenders of the city meant that they had succeeded in shooting empty air. The Japanese are great punsters, and the words for "nine planes" and "thin air" are homophonous. In fact the Japanese downed none of the planes. All sixteen flew safely across Japan and on to or just short of the Asian mainland. There the crews had varied experiences. Eight men were captured by the Japanese and three among them were put to death. The largest number fell into the hands of Chinese guerrillas and made their way home through India. General Tōjō, the prime minister, chanced to be in the air that afternoon, flying off on a military inspection. He had a close brush with the raiders.

Hibiya Park, which had lost its palmettos and become an artillery emplacement in February 1936, now lost the tops of all its trees in the direction of the palace and became an antiaircraft emplacement. Certain of the Doolittle pilots had been so brazen as to fly over His Majesty, although they had done him no harm. This must not happen again. Things got worse and worse for the park, as for other parks. The lawns and parterres presently became vegetable patches. Iron artifacts were stripped away. Some bronze remained, to meet the hostility of the Americans, who found certain of its applications warlike.

The first serious raids, on the southern island of Kyushu, were mounted from China. The Saipan landings occurred in mid-June 1944. When next, on November 1, American planes were sighted over Tokyo, they came from the Marianas. They were for reconnaissance and dropped no bombs. Bombs came on November 24. The early raids, through February, by both island-based and carrier-based planes, were heavy ones aimed at military targets, mostly in the northern part of the city and in the counties. There were waves of planes all through February 16 and 17. The chief targets were air bases in the suburbs. The Japanese loss of planes was heavy, and the ability to defend the city was grievously reduced.

The Hama Detached Palace, by the bay just south of the Tsukiji fish market, may be called a military target because, like Hibiya Park, it had been devastated to make antiaircraft emplacements. Originally the bay-side villa of the shoguns, it was until 1916 the place for large royal receptions, and until the late nineteenth century it provided lodgings for eminent foreign guests. General and Mrs. U. S. Grant stayed there in 1879, though the building in which they stayed was demolished in 1899. All of the central buildings went in the raids of late November 1944.

The incendiary raids began in March. The most dreadful of them, on the night of March 9–10, did very much what the fires after the earthquake had done: destroyed the Low City. Waves of bombers came in for two and a half hours from just past midnight. The planners of the raids had hit upon what may have been the urban concentration most hospitable to fires in the whole world, and they had hit upon the proper season. As is so often the case in early spring, strong winds were coming down that night from the north and west. The progress of the war had probably made the decision for the planners. The capture of Iwo in February and March and the decimation of the Kantō air defenses in the heavy raids that preceded the incendiary attacks made mass, low-level runs as nearly safe as they could be.

Nagai Kafū's house in Azabu was among the hundreds of thousands burned that night (the damage was not limited to the Low City). Having finally found refuge in the house of a relative, he lay down to sleep, his diary entry concludes, with columns of sparks in his eyes and the shriek of the wind in his ears. No incendiary bombs landed near his house. Sparks were blown in from a considerable distance away. We have vivid descriptions of what it was like to be in a rain of incendiary bombs. It was like "a fox's wedding," a profusion of fox fires or will-o'-the-wisps. Many of the bombs burst in midair and sent out hissing blue tendrils.

Some two-fifths of the city went up in flames. The four wards between the Sumida River and the Arakawa Drainage Channel almost disappeared. Between seventy and eighty thousand people are believed to have died that night. This is some three-quarters of the death count from all raids on the city.

It was a night of horror, and the Americans and their bombers were the agents. Yet a few words may be slipped in by way of mitigation for what they did. The wards east of the river were, along with the wards nearest Yokohama, the most heavily industrialized parts of the city. The pattern of industrialization beyond the Sumida was so fragmented that it would have been impossible to separate implicitly military targets from purely civilian ones. Foresight was, moreover, lamentably bad, and measures to prevent the disaster scarcely existed. Through the first months of 1945 people were actually discouraged from leaving the city. Their patriotic duty was to stay at their posts. The contrast between the March raid and the August one on Hachiōji, out in the county part of the prefecture, is telling. Warned by handbills and quite prepared to believe them, the people of Hachiōji fled. There were only two hundred twenty-five deaths, and the number and weight of the bombs were higher than in the March raid.

Defenses were totally ineffective, even though there had been de-

Looking eastward across the Sumida after the major air raids of 1945

fense drills from as early as 1943 and though the bombers came in low and along predictable courses. The first alarms were not sounded for the March raid until several minutes after the first bombs fell. A false alarm would have had a bad effect on morale—and who would have taken the blame if the emperor and his lady, to no purpose, had been required to dress themselves in the middle of the night and move to a shelter?

Along with most of Asakusa, most of the great Kannon Temple was destroyed that night. It had survived the earthquake. In 1923 the temple precincts had been for Kawabata a field of flowers, bright with refugees from regions to the north. Several bombs fell on the main hall at about one-thirty in the morning. It was consumed in about two hours. The pagoda went too, though some outbuildings and one gate survived. A common view was that it had been a great mistake on the part of the authorities to requisition the statue of the great Meiji actor Danjūrō that stood on the grounds and send it to war. The statue had been given credit for turning back the flames in 1923. The innermost sanctuary, a small, portable shrine or feretory, was removed and brought back to a temporary hall late in 1945, and, a decade later, to a partially rebuilt main hall. Almost no one knows whether or not it contains, as averred by the clergy, a small golden image of almost indescribable antiquity, because almost no one has been allowed to look inside. The lost buildings, from early in the Tokugawa Period, were among the oldest in the city.

Because the corpses had to be disposed of speedily and neither fuel nor manpower was available in large enough measure for cremation, most were given temporary burial. The parks along and east of the river became cemeteries. Of some ninety thousand reburials in the years after the war, eighty-five thousand were in a mass grave at the Earthquake Memorial Hall (see page 12). Identification was next to impossible. Only the remaining five thousand had claimants. Wandering through cemeteries, one is always coming upon tombstones that bear the date March 10, 1945. Few of the graves beneath contain bones.

The next big raids came in April, from the thirteenth to the fifteenth. They did great damage in the northern and western parts of the city and along the industrial belt from Tokyo into Kanagawa Prefecture. Among the casualties were the main buildings of the Meiji Shrine, southwest of the old city limits. Raids in late May took away about half of what remained of the old city, chiefly in and around Ginza and southward and westward into the High City. The main building of the palace was destroyed on May 25, and the royal family moved to a secondary building. There had earlier been talk of moving the royal residence across the Tama River into Kanagawa Prefecture. Now there was talk of moving it to the mountain fastnesses of central Japan. The move would doubtless have taken place if the army had had its way and the nation had fought to the end. It would have meant moving the capital, for the capital is where the head of state resides.

Several newspaper offices were gutted, as were the Kabukiza and the Shimbashi Embujō. Two large universities, Keiō and what was to become the University of Education, suffered heavy damages. The great Zōjōji, the southern of the two Tokugawa mortuary temples, was almost completely destroyed. The May raids also did great damage to the public transportation system. The trolley lines were virtually incapacitated. These were the last important raids on the ward part of the city. The raid on Hachiōji, the main population center of the county part, has already been mentioned.

The total number of American flights over Tokyo in 1944 and 1945 was upward of four thousand. The number of bombers in the March raid was smaller than in the major raids of mid-April and late May. There were about three hundred, as against more than five hundred on May 24 and almost as many on the two following days. If the term "casualties" is taken to include homeless as well as dead and wounded, then the effects of the April and May raids, though far behind those of March, were to some degree comparable. More than half as many people were affected in both cases.

The air raids produced rumors and magic. The rumors tended to be wishful. One of the grander ones held that Japan had developed a fleet of bombers powered by pine resin and capable of flying off to bomb America and flying back again. The Shiseidō, the most prominent maker of cosmetics and the like, active since Meiji in the endeavor (as its advertising said) to give Japanese women pellucid skins like Western women, had a big order in 1944 for expensive perfumes. Everyone learned about the transaction, which produced ominous rumors. The Russians were coming. The perfumes were to please the wives of their elite. Actually they seem to have been traded for Chinese metals.

Just as today there are magic potions, such as bean soup or a brew made from pine cones, for warding off the AIDS virus, so there were charms for keeping bombs at a distance. One was a very simple breakfast of rice and pickles—but it would not work unless others were let in on the secret. Goldfish also did good service in fending off bombs. The owners of houses that survived sometimes had a bad time. People would move in on them uninvited. Since everyone had a share in the disaster, what could be more natural than that housing should be common and undivided as well? Pilferers and looters had the same justification.

A program of offering temporary shelter to victims of the raids was abandoned as hopeless after the March attack. Thereafter the emphasis was on relocation. For the weak and obscure much of it was forced. Fearing that they might never be allowed to return, people were reluctant to leave. Those who wanted to go and were not part of mass relocations could find it difficult. The novelist Satomi Ton, in an autobiographical story called "Putting the Old Woman Out to Die" ("Obasute"), described the undignified process of obtaining tickets. "Bribery at the market rate seemed to him a nearer thing to honesty and a more manly thing than mingily going from acquaintance to acquaintance of acquaintance, finally getting an introduction to a railway functionary, and escaping with only a modest gift."

Between February and August more than four million people left Tokyo, both voluntarily and under various degrees of duress. A great many of the three million or so who stayed were without adequate shelter. The police estimated that on September 1, 1945, one in ten among the Tokyo citizenry was living in an air-raid shelter or some other sort of temporary abode.

The main municipal library had since late Meiji been in Hibiya Park. Plans for relocation in a remoter part of the prefecture took shape after the Doolittle raid. At first it was by truck, then (one is reminded of the Chinese under Japanese attack) by handcart and knapsack. It was not completed in time for the May raids. The library building and some two hundred thousand volumes fell victim to the bombs. The Hibiya library opened temporary offices in the Kyōbashi library, the only one among the branch libraries that escaped damage, and did not return to Hibiya until 1947.

Maps of the areas affected by the fires show much wider destruction than in 1923. The pattern was similar: far worse damage to the east than to the west. One of the fifteen wards of 1923 escaped fire. None of the thirty-five of 1945 did, though the scattering is sparse around the fringes, save to the south, where the northern extension of the Tokyo-Yokohama industrial belt had grown up. If a line is drawn north and south a bit to the east of Ueno and Tokyo stations, then almost everything east of it as far as the Arakawa Drainage Channel—farther east than the eastern limits of the Meiji city, this is to say—is gone. To the west large pockets were spared in the vicinity of Ueno Station. As in 1923, the flat part of Shitaya Ward disappeared and the hilly part remained. This last was suburban when Tokyo was Edo and a part of the Meiji High City distinguished for its intellectual and artistic sorts, and today it is probably the part of the city in which we can best sense what mercantile Edo and Meiji were like. It would not have survived if the wind had been blowing in the opposite direction that night in March.

The High City was, as in 1923, a patchwork of places burned and places spared. Of the twenty new wards, Jōtō, along the lower reaches of the Arakawa Channel, was almost totally destroyed, and all of the other wards along the fringes of the old fifteen, including the one that contained a part of Shinjuku, were badly damaged. An almost solid expanse of burned-over wastes stretched westward from Shinjuku as far as Nakano and the eastern borders of Setagaya Ward, the farthest of the thirty-five to the southwest. A solid and unbroken if somewhat winding band of wastelands stretched all across the city from the westernmost wards to the Arakawa Channel. There was no band by any means that extensive after the earthquake. Starting from the eastern part of Setagaya Ward and Suginami Ward and proceeding past Shinjuku and Kanda, or, alternatively, along the south side of the palace and on through Nihombashi, one could in the summer of 1945 have walked all the way to the Arakawa Channel upon nothing but cinders.

Four of the thirty-five wards suffered more than ten thousand fatalities. All were in the Low City, and among them they accounted for more than 80 percent of the total. It is a situation that once more calls to mind 1923. Punishment was then said to have come down upon decadence, and it might now be said to have come down upon military aggression. It descended most cruelly, however, on people who had little to do with decadence in the first instance and the making of aggressive schemes in the second.

Parts of the Low City were virtually depopulated. If one takes the population of February 1944 as 100, the populations of Honjo and Fukagawa, the two wards east of the river among the old fifteen, were down to 4 and 6, respectively. Fewer than ten thousand people were left in Honjo. Of the fifteen old wards, the southernmost, Shiba, had a higher proportion of bitter-enders than any other. Its population in June 1945 was still more than a third what it had been in February 1944. Of the twenty new wards, Jōtō, immediately east of Fukagawa, was down to 5 from the 1944 base. No other among the twenty suffered a loss of as much as four-fifths of its population. The old city was the worst hit, and, as in 1923, the flat parts of it worst of all. Some districts along the fringes of the city had larger populations in the spring of 1945 than in early 1944.

The war cabinet, that of General Tōjō, resigned in the summer of 1944. In May 1945 the Germans surrendered. Early in August came the atomic bombs. On one of the two days between them the Russians entered the war, invading Manchuria and Korea. On August 15, for the first time in the history of the land, the emperor made a radio broadcast. He announced acceptance of the Potsdam Declaration. Since less than half the Tokyo citizenry is old enough to remember the bombings, less than half is old enough to remember the broadcast. Many who do remember it did not understand it. Reception was generally poor, and the language was stilted. The general import was soon clear enough, however. He was obviously not exhorting them to get out their bamboo spears and await the enemy along the beaches and in the hills. So only one explanation seemed possible for so extraordinary a performance.

Some soldiers gathered on Atago Hill north of Shiba Park, thinking to hold out as supporters of the shogun had held out on that other "mountain," Ueno, three-quarters of a century before. There were suicides. The American occupiers would not have been surprised if they had encountered guerrilla war. The Japanese rather hoped that the Americans would occupy the government buildings at Kasumigaseki, and leave the commercial and financial heart of the city alone. Perhaps they already sensed that the next war would be economic. Advance scouting parties thought that Marunouchi would be easier to defend. General Douglas MacArthur agreed to the choice of the Daiichi Insurance Building for his headquarters. It is a thick-walled citadel with windows recessed behind solid square pillars and the open spaces of the moat and the royal plaza in front of it. The ineffectual defenses of the city had had their command post there.

Takami Jun's wife said that if the emperor had told them to fight to the last man and woman they would probably all of them have done it. Takami was inclined to agree. In the event, there was no resistance. The general would have been as safe if he had gone to Kasumigaseki or pitched a tent in the wastes east of the river.

The "chief executive" of the prefecture, a general, resigned late in August. A very quick succession of executives followed him, six of them between August 1945 and May 1947. The last of them, Yasui Seiichirō, who had had a brief term earlier, resigned to run for election and became the first popularly elected governor of the prefecture.

Americans were in Tokyo from late August. An advance party, heavily armed, set up tents, well surrounded by barbed wire, on the Yoyogi parade grounds, where a few days earlier some boys of the radical right had committed suicide. The purposes of the party were to test the land and to scout out buildings suitable for requisitioning. General MacArthur landed at Atsugi, southwest of the city, on August 30. He spent his first nights in Yokohama, where the guerrillas would be easier to fend off than in the middle of the gigantic capital. The surrender documents having been signed aboard ship in Tokyo Bay on September 2, the occupation of Tokyo began in earnest on September 8. The city could turn its thoughts to another in its venerable series of reconstructions.

4

THE DAY OF THE COD
AND THE SWEET POTATO

In the early years after the war, praise for Nagoya and blame for Tokyo were much in fashion. Nagoya took advantage of the bombings to refashion itself. Tokyo was a growth which, flattened, lay flat for a time and then pulled itself together much as it had been. The redesigning of Nagoya brought wide avenues, sufficient, one might have thought, for all the vehicles likely to pass through the central business district. The corresponding district of Tokyo has a street pattern scarcely different from that of Taishō.

It is more challengeable now than it was forty years ago that Nagoya benefited greatly from the changes. Not many today think that the widening of streets can keep up with the flood of automobiles. Nagoya has its traffic jams too. Nor do wide streets seem to be among the things the Japanese are good at. They range from featureless to ugly. In Nagoya the wide streets took away the past. The bombings, it might be argued, had already taken it away; but one has no sense, along the broad avenues of central Nagoya, of all the people who lived there over the centuries. Not much is old in Tokyo, but the street pattern is, and makes Tokyo seem warmer and cozier than Nagoya, a much smaller city. There can be no final conclusion to arguments over the Tokyo way and the Nagoya way. Yet a person may feel that if there is going to be congestion anyway it is better had on comfortable old streets.

Tokyo might not have been able to do as Nagoya did even if it had had the wish and the will. For one thing, there were all those buildings in the way. A walk east and west through the cinders of 1945 could have taken one close to Tokyo Central Station. The prefectural offices were heavily damaged. Mitsubishi Londontown, however, the heart of financial and managerial Marunouchi, escaped. Only a very iconoclastic prefectural government could have persuaded itself to destroy good, solid buildings in a city that had lost so much.

Then there were the Americans. They left the Japanese the Marunouchi Building, the largest office building in the city and the land, but they took almost everything else in Marunouchi. Unsuccessful at persuading them that the bureaucratic quarter of the city would admirably serve their needs, the Japanese had no way of dislodging them from Marunouchi. Harassment might have worked, but there was none of that. If the Japanese had any policy in those days it was to smile and accommodate and hope that the invaders would soon go away. By 1947, when popular election of the governor brought a measure of stability to the prefectural government, retention of the old street pattern was the established condition all over the city. We cannot know whether the opportunity to do something with Marunouchi would have kindled a zeal to do something all over the city. Nagoya did not do much with its outskirts either.

As after the earthquake, the first thing that had to be done was to clear away the cinders. Again they were dumped in huge volume into the canals. There were not enough vehicles and there was not enough gasoline to take them out and, as was done with garbage in later years, dump them in the bay for landfill. Canals, along with such wide streets as Shōwa Avenue, put through east of Ginza after the earthquake, provided convenient receptacles. The streets, though piled high with rubble for a time, presently became usable again. The filled-in canals did not come back as usable canals; and one wonders where all the cinders will be put when the next disaster comes. Some of the canals were already so silted in that they were little more than broken puddles of stagnant water, and some of the important ones, such as the Kandagawa, the "Kanda River," were in the years of rapid economic growth to become so filthy that, as popular wisdom had it, not even typhoid germs could live in them. They bubbled and seethed with noisome gases. The old canal system thus became a broken ruin. It had been left behind in any event, and when economic growth kills something one is foolish to lament over it. Still the canals were a necessary part of Edo, for which one may pardonably feel nostalgia.

The filling in of canals and the disposition of the land that resulted were among the first stirrings as the city began coming to life again. The conspicuous presence of the Americans in Marunouchi may have been in part responsible for the new prosperity of what had been the back side of Tokyo Central Station. Perhaps more important was the filling in of the portion of the outer palace moat that ran along that east or back side, also known as the Yaesu Mouth. In the early years of the station, railroad yards and the canal cut it off in a most unfriendly way from the old Low City. Now the canal was filled in, and an eating, drinking, shopping, and watering complex arose where it had been. A Yaesu station building went up in 1947, across the tracks to the east of the old station. It burned down a few months after its completion, but it would soon have gone anyway, as the Yaesu Mouth reached up into the sky and down into the earth.

In 1953 a *meitengai*, which might hesitantly be translated "shopping center," began business at the Yaesu Mouth. The reason for the hesitation is that a *meitengai* does not provide accommodation for the automobile. It is more like a bazaar. The city had long had such places, and the one at the Yaesu Mouth led the way to ever vaster ones. It began going underground, and in the next fifteen years or so had become the largest underground complex in the Orient. The first multistorey building after the war started rising, eight floors aboveground and two below, near the north end of the landfill even before the Korean War brought a great building boom. By 1954 the number of persons passing through the Yaesu Mouth exceeded that for the Marunouchi Mouth, the old front entrance, and a dozen years later the Yaesu figure reached a half million a day. So the Low City could have thought, if it wished, that an old wrong had been righted.

A similar instance is Sanjūsangenbori, the "thirty-three-*ken* [two-hundred-foot] dig," which ran north and south just east of Ginza. The back streets to the east of the main Ginza street do not seem to have been very lively before the war. The canal, which cut Ginza off from the Shōchiku entertainment center, farther east, became a cinder dump. When it was completely filled in, by about 1950, the land was divided among people who could be expected to make it a bustling pleasure center. It had pinball parlors, drinking places, cabarets, and a burlesque hall which was in business for less than a year, even though it offered such celebrities as "the queen bee of Anatahan." (The queen bee had spent several postwar years with several men on Anatahan, a small island in the Marianas.) And it had the Tokyo Onsen, the "Tokyo Spa," a pleasure palace not of a completely new kind, perhaps, but of a bold sort that seemed to bring an end to the years of deprivation. It was until 1986, when it was torn down to make way for a much higher building, a four-storey watering place. There are no natural hot springs within a great distance of downtown Tokyo, but since Meiji there had been fabricated ones at, for instance, Shinagawa, at the southern limits of the old city.

The Tokyo Onsen contained big communal baths, said to incorporate the latest techniques from Turkey and Scandinavia, and private rooms as well, and for a tariff of a hundred yen, not much in those days of inflation, one could have a bath attended by a pretty masseuse. It all seemed rather shocking at the time, not because of the sexual abandon, so much a part of the life of the city that only a missionary or a policeman could object, but because of the prodigality. It seemed a luxury which the city and the nation could not afford. The builders of the Onsen were presently vindicated. They led the way into a future in which the pleasures their enterprise offered came to seem modest and even demure, and it may be that their boldness was just what the city needed in those difficult times.

The filling in of the "dig" had one consequence that cannot have been foreseen: it brought the entertainment complex east of Ginza closer to Ginza, by which it was presently absorbed. The old Kobikichō became East Ginza and then plain Ginza. The change of names had no great practical effect. The smaller districts into which the Tokyo wards are divided have no more administrative or political significance than the streets of an American city. Nor has the entertainment complex been in the television age what it was in the movie age. Yet a grand old place name was lost. Elderly people still go to Kobikichō, not Ginza, for their Kabuki. It will take time for the old name to fall completely into oblivion.

Like the cinder-filled canals, the black markets helped to get things started again. Probably they were necessary. Rationing did not provide adequate sustenance. In 1947 the death of a judge in the Tokyo District Court received much attention from the newspapers. He died of mal-

A reconstruction of the Ikebukuro black market

nutrition, because he refused to eat anything purchased on the black market.

Every little station along the commuter lines had its little market for illicitly acquired foreign products. When the need for them passed, with the passing of rations and the presence of adequate supplies, they became the clusters of eating and drinking places where, at the end of their day, office workers fortify themselves against the rigors of home and family. There have been such places ever since there have been office workers and commuting, but the black markets contributed to the huge increase in their numbers, a far more rapid increase during the postwar years than that for enterprises in general.

The Occupation left the Japanese to do what they could by way of controlling the black markets, though they would have been impossible without the generous cooperation of many a commissary sergeant. It did wish them to keep out of its sight, and show reticence in operating where most of its operations were. So in the center of the city black marketing did not contribute to the first stirrings of revival and reconstruction as it did along the big transfer points of the Yamanote loop line.

The most thriving among the black markets was what came to be known, and still is known, though its functions have changed, as Ameya Yokochō, just south of Ueno. The Americans had their own name for it, the Ueno PX. Yokochō is "alley," and Ameya is a pun on "American shops" and "sweets shops." Sugary items, in cruelly short supply in those years, were important to Ameyoko, which offered sweet concoctions from beans and potatoes. There were repeated raids on the district. On a day in May 1946 six hundred armed police staged a very big raid. They could not cope with Ameyoko's resilience, however, and it is doubtful that they really tried very hard. A raid might briefly diminish the flow of American goods, but only briefly. Unless they were suspected of having committed more serious crimes, stallkeepers and shopkeepers were treated leniently, as if by way of recognizing that at least they were doing something, and *someone* had to do something. When Japanese started going abroad again,

The Ameya Yokochō black market as it looks today

they of course had to come home bearing gifts. One would hear that those who were too busy or too timid to do their shopping abroad would go to Ameyoko for it.

During the second postwar decade Ameyoko began to shift from American goods to marine products, which no one would dream of importing from America. The change may be taken as a sign that the worst deprivation and confusion were coming to an end. In 1983 an Ameyoko Center, all shining metal and glass, was finished. The small retailers who moved in dealt mostly in manufactured goods. Purveyors of foodstuffs remained along the street and far outsold the food department of the gigantic Matsuzakaya department store a few steps away. In very recent years Ameyoko has been the center of a new kind of black market. Japanese (or whoever) can buy easily transported goods in, for instance, New York, bring them back to Tokyo without paying duty, and sell them at a lower price than they sell at in Japan through legal channels. All of these changes, and many others, are symbolic of larger change. Step by step, Ameyoko has kept up with a changing city, and, after a fashion, represented it.

If a black-market stallkeeper risked being raided and losing a few commodities and spending a few nights in jail, things could also be risky for a more pitiable kind of black-market person: he, and very often she, who circumvented rationing by buying rice in the country and bringing it to city markets. There were occasional roundups, generally at railway stations in the northern and eastern part of the city where *katsugiya,* "bearers," as they were called, were likely to leave or change trains. (The big Japanese-English dictionary renders *katsugiya* as "runner," with a warning that this is an Americanism.) The policeman on the beat seems to have been reluctant to take action against *katsugiya* when he did not have to. The story was told of a policeman who tapped a woman on the shoulder and said, "Your baby is wetting its pants." In those days when the almost universal way of transporting babies was by strapping them to adult backs, a woman would seek to disguise her black-market rice by strapping it and cosseting and posseting it and making soothing noises to it, quite as if it were a baby. This poor woman's sack had sprung a leak and rice was trickling out.

At the beginning of 1946 Tokyo contained an estimated sixty thousand black-market stalls. Sad reminiscences of those hard days persuade us that most of the stallkeepers were desperate men and women who

Police search a woman smuggling rice into Tokyo

would gladly have done something else if there had been anything else to do. Many, however, were under the control of gangs. Very soon after the surrender, extortion and protection gangs occupied land at each of the main entrances, the "mouths," east, west, and south, to Shinjuku Station. The motto of the gang at the most important of them, Eastmouth, was "Let light spread forth from Shinjuku." Court action was required to return the land, now not far from the most valuable in the world, to the rightful owners, some of them, such as the Takano Fruits Parlor, among the most venerable and esteemed of Shinjuku retailers. Gang warfare was endemic at Southmouth, and we may be grateful to very great complications at Westmouth that we still have the relic of the postwar years known as Piss Alley (see page 213). A farrago of rights and claimed rights made it possible for keepers of little drinking places to buy their own land. It was a decade and a half after the war that the old black market at the Ikebukuro Westmouth was finally leveled, by court order.

There was in those days the problem of the "third nationals." It was conspicuous in the underworld and in gang squabbling. Third nationals were for practical purposes Chinese and Koreans resident in Japan. The expression put them in their place, distinguishing them both from Japanese and from the Occupation, which favored them, treating Chinese as allies and Koreans as quasi allies (enemies of the enemy). It is hard to deny that they took advantage of their position.

If the police could not intercede in behalf of Japanese gangs that thought of themselves (or at any rate advertised themselves) as Robin Hoods and defenders of the Japanese spirit, there is much evidence that they managed to aid them surreptitiously. In the "Shimbashi Incident" of 1946, American military police and Japanese police intervened to prevent an armed battle between Chinese and Japanese gangs for control of the market. The nonbattle was in effect a victory for the Japanese. It showed the Chinese, who were progressively weaker, that they could not have everything their way even in that day of confusion and demoralization. Across the bay in Chiba, later in 1946, the police seem to have actually encouraged a showdown between Japanese and third-national gangs. It would be the occasion, the Chiba police and the American military police agreed, for rounding up gangsters of whatever nationality. The Japanese police told the Japanese gangs what was to happen and invited their cooperation. The Americans do not seem to have accorded the same favor to the third nationals. The encounter took place, a few minutes of gunfire in which several men were wounded but no one was killed, and in the end only third nationals were rounded up.

The problem of relations between the police and the underworld has always been a delicate and elusive one. At the very least the police seem to prefer organized crime to the more scattered and diffuse kind. Some elements in the police force would have to work harder if the gangs were to go, and the gangster for his part prefers police whom he knows and who know him to outsiders who might come meddling if an incident were to be prolonged.

The most powerful force in getting things moving again came fairly late. The Korean War broke out in June 1950, almost exactly at midpoint through what we may call the decade of the rebuilding. For Korea it was a terrible happening, for Japan a momentous one, with little sense of the terrible. The calm with which Tokyo and Japan assumed that someone would do something was rather wonderful. It was perhaps natural in an occupied country that had no foreign policy save to get rid of the Occupation and export things whenever and wherever possible; and an eminent editor once remarked that two subjects certain to send readers away in droves were Korea and education. Still it was rather wonderful. The prospect of losing Korea to the people (in those days the Chinese and the Russians seemed monolithic) from whom it had been won less than a half century before was received with huge indifference.

Momentous the event certainly was for all that. Japanese profits from the Korean War were massive, and they went into rebuilding city and land, and bringing them back somewhat near, in material terms, the position that had been theirs before the folly of the forties. Procurement contracts in the remaining months of 1950 ran to $180 million, and before the Korean War was over they ran to $2.3 billion. Production returned to and passed prewar levels. Direct American aid, which had been necessary in the immediate postwar years, now ceased to be. Brave beginnings had already been made toward putting things together again, but it was in the early fifties that matters went forward with speed and purpose. No one can blame the Japanese for having a delightful fish in troubled waters, and someone else would have done it if they had not. Yet it is ironic that the prosperity of a country which has renounced war (see Article IX of the postwar constitution) is founded on a war.

The days just after the surrender were very hard ones. When a middle-aged or aging Japanese remarks upon the terrible time, one must listen carefully to know which time is meant. One may instinctively suppose it to be the last months of the war, the time of the bombings, but for many the really terrible time was the first winter after the war, a time of cold, disease, and hunger. Typhus was the worst plague. There were almost ten thousand cases of it in Tokyo Prefecture during the winter of 1945 and 1946, and almost a thousand deaths. Smallpox and cholera may not have reached such epidemic proportions, but in a more settled day they would scarcely have been present at all. Typhus bespeaks lice and unclean bodies, very distressful to the well-washed Japanese. In those days not even a good hot bath was easy to come by. The city has always had fleas and chinches in ample numbers, but lice are a different matter.

A tenth of the populace that clung to the city through that winter lived in such emergency places as air-raid shelters and warehouses. The underground passages at Ueno Station, at that time the most considerable in the city, though they do not bear comparison with the honey-

*A postwar census-taker at work among the homeless
in the Ueno subway station*

Dance hall scene, 1946

combs that have been dug since, had the largest and most famous accumulation of beggars and vagrants in the city. From time to time they were rounded up, and ineffective attempts made at dispersal. On a night in mid-December 1945, some twenty-five hundred persons were taken in. There were deaths from exposure. Temperatures in Tokyo do not go much below freezing, but dampness can bring great discomfort even to the well-fed person. Through the last months of 1945 vagrants were dying in Ueno at a rate of two to three every day, and sometimes the number was as high as six. The second postwar winter brought improvement in the sense that exposure was not for the most part the immediate cause of death. Eleven people died in the Ueno Station complex during the first week of 1947, most of them from pneumonia.

Students sat and shivered in their overcoats in unheated classrooms, professors stood and shivered. An office in one of the best buildings left to the Japanese, such as the Marunouchi Building or the Bank of Japan, might be heated only by a charcoal brazier or a scattering of them, to which typists would turn from time to time to thaw their stiffened fingers. The bravery of dancers in unheated theaters, such as the Rokkuza, the Sixth District Theater, in Asakusa, was something to arouse admiration. Everything was rationed. One had to have coupons to eat in a restaurant. The cod and the sweet potato were the staples. Many a Japanese of a certain age cannot look at either without shuddering.

Yet there was a communal spirit over the city and the land which, in the recall, makes the shabby Japanese of the day seem more estimable than the dapper (or chic) Japanese of today. It was beautiful the way in which people shook themselves from daze and shock and looked about them, and, military expansion having proved impractical, set about having a try at another kind.

As after the earthquake, huts began going up almost immediately on the burned-over wastes. Street stalls were back in the bustling places where they had always been—Shinjuku, Ginza, Ueno, and the like. They offered food and drink before less flimsy shops were doing so. The Occupation did not like the stalls. It ordered in 1949 that they be done away with, and on New Year's Eve 1951 the last of them finally went. Efforts at coaxing stallkeepers into other businesses were not entirely successful. Many of the stalls were finally subsumed into covered markets, in such places as the filled-in canal east of Ginza and the revetment beneath the statue of the Meiji rebel Saigō Takamori, the most famous of Ueno landmarks.

The streets of Ginza and Shinjuku thus became more passable for people and automobiles in a hurry, but what they gained in that regard they lost as gathering places. The stalls probably would have gone anyway, as the city and the country became more affluent. Occasionally an aging stallkeeper is interviewed in a newspaper, and almost always he says that he would not for the world go back to the old business, with its prickly heat and chilblains. An unsuccessful experiment with stallkeeping a quarter of a century before had demonstrated that it was not a business for dabblers and dilettantes. In the summer of 1930, as a device for relieving unemployment in those bleak depression years, the prefectural police opened some ten miles of streets in the city and the suburbs to amateur stallkeepers. More than sixteen thousand stalls quickly lined them, but within a year more than fourteen thousand had gone out of business.

Charcoal-burning taxicabs also went away, not to reappear, on that New Year's Eve of 1951. Scarcely any remained—perhaps fewer than ten still puffed about the city, as against three thousand or so during the war. Many liked the street stalls, no one liked the charcoal cabs. They were forever fuming and sputtering to a halt, choking their passengers along with themselves. Like the sweet potato and the cod, they were the embodiment of bad days.

In a sense the black market never really disappeared. We have seen that smuggled goods, often of Japanese make, can be purchased at, for instance, Ameyoko. It stopped dealing in necessities, however, as they became plentiful and were no longer rationed. The process of derationing began early. Retail derationing was slower than wholesale, which ended in 1950. Not many who visited the city for the Olympics in 1964 can have guessed that the system of coupons for meals in restaurants still prevailed. It was not discontinued until 1968, by which time it had long been meaningless. The black-market price of rice fell below the rationed price in 1959. So retail rationing withered away.

There may already have been huts among the cinders when the first Americans arrived, but the city has not done strikingly well in the matter of housing. One person in twenty was still living in a temporary shelter at the end of 1946, as against one in ten the year before, but the population had grown. The first public housing went up, on old army land, in 1948, and had three hundred applicants for every small house available. A survey of housing by the Construction Ministry showed that Tokyo had rebuilt about a third of its housing by early 1949. This was a better performance than that of Osaka, but not as good as those of a number of other cities, including Hiroshima and Nagasaki, the cities of the nuclear bombs. Despite its poor record in new buildings, Osaka had more living space per capita than Tokyo, which had fewer than three *tatami* mats per person. (A *tatami* is about two square yards.) The figure has gone up gradually and continues to go up, but in 1986 Tokyo still had fewer than eight mats per person, the lowest for any prefecture in the country except Okinawa—and Tokyo is the richest of the prefectures, and Okinawa the poorest but one or two. The average citizen of Tokyo thus has a space of about twelve feet square to call his own. Seven people may be expected to share a house or apartment with a thousand square feet of floor space. This is the average, including the affluent wards along with the poor. The eastern and northeastern wards are well below the average. Of land prices and the distance from the center of the city to which an office worker must go to find a bit of land he can afford, more must be said later. They seem to be spinning out of control. All that "planning" can really hope to do is make things more convenient and expeditious for people who must commute long distances.

Nor has the city done very well with parks. Some considerable tracts, notably along the Sumida River, were left open after the earthquake and presently developed into parks. Little of the sort happened in 1945. The problem of what exactly did happen is complicated by the fact that several sets of parks are involved: national parks, royal parks, prefectural parks, and city and ward parks. The area of park lands has increased, but the prefecture was initially slow about adding to them, other than with small playgrounds. More considerable accessions to the system or the several systems resulted from donations. An example is the Hama Detached Palace, where in 1879 General Grant and his lady were accommodated. Once the bayside villa of the shoguns, from whose hands it passed to the royal household, it was donated to the city late in 1945. Somewhat halfheartedly, the Occupation requisitioned it a year and a half later. When it was needed for American training purposes the public was excluded, but it was open during periods when the Occupation had no specific need of it.

So the city itself did not do much when so much could have been done with the charred wastes. Some prewar parks actually disappeared. Conspicuous among them is Asakusa Park, one of the original five established early in Meiji. For this the Occupation may be held in part accountable. It returned the park lands to the Kannon Temple. The temple, hard pressed for reconstruction funds, made them utterly commercial. The famous ponds in Asakusa Park existed for perhaps three generations. Only the tract behind the main hall of the temple remains unbuilt upon. Hard-surfaced, it provides parking space for tourist buses.

Per capita the area of parks is equal to that for Kyoto, larger than that for Yokohama, and smaller than those for Osaka, Nagoya, and Kobe, whose per capita park area increases in that order. It is only one-twentieth that of Washington, D.C. The absolute area is well under that in Philadelphia and only a bit over that in Detroit—both of them much smaller cities. It may be, though much depends on definitions, that Tokyo is worse off in the matter of parks than Edo was. The proportion of parks to the total areas of the city today is smaller than was that of the shrine and temple grounds that functioned as parks in Edo.

To the credit of Tokyo must be admitted the fact that large areas of the center of the city are freely open to the public. Tabulations always give Seoul a much larger per capita park area than Tokyo, but fail to note that one must pay an admission fee to every considerable park in or near the center of the city.

In these regards the city has not done well. In building to make itself more firmly what it already was, the economic center of the land—and to make it a strong challenger as well to the traditional economic centers of the world—it has done far better. The Korean War, crucial to the economic revival of Tokyo and Japan, speeded up the concentration of managers and executives in Tokyo. Gradually, it came to mean as well the waxing of Marunouchi and the waning of Nihombashi as a managerial center. Before the war and in the early years after, new construction of offices was smaller in area than new construction of residences. In the early 1960s the former area passed the latter.

The Crisis of the thirties put a stop to monumental office building, and the Korean War set it going in earnest once more. In 1951 work began on a second Marunouchi Building, across the station plaza from

Tokyo Central and across the street from the first Marunouchi Building, which was finished just before the earthquake and suffered damage in it. The foundations of the second building had already been laid before the war. The prewar excavations filled with water and remained a stagnant pond through the Occupation years, with an occasional corpse floating upon it. There was a great treasure hunt when drainage and filling began, for rumors spread that a trove had been dumped there at the time of the surrender. Nothing was found.

Viewed from the station, the two buildings look like twins, both of them with uninspired tiled fronts. The second one has a somewhat different floor plan, however, with more space for Mitsubishi to rent, and so it now became what the first one had been, the largest building in city and land. It did not long remain so. A third Marunouchi Building, more properly called the Otemachi Building from the district in which it reposes, was finished in 1958. Many a yet larger building has been put up since.

Very little was being done, meanwhile, to accommodate commuters to these new buildings. For the first decade after the war transportation to the center of the city remained as it had been before the war. The third Marunouchi Building held forty thousand workers, and the crush on the National Railways was becoming frightful. The most painful (to some amusing) pictures of station attendants pushing people in tighter so that the train doors will close date from these years. A segment of a second subway line, the first to pass directly under Marunouchi, opened from Ikebukuro to Ochanomizu in 1954. It cannot have done much good for anyone except a scattering of students and scholars on their way to browse in the Kanda bookshops. It opened as far as Tokyo Central in 1956 and Ginza in 1957, but did not go through to Shinjuku, whence and whither the largest floods of commuters came flooding, until 1959, a year after completion of the third Marunouchi (or Otemachi) Building. Free transfer between the two subway lines, that from Asakusa to Shibuya and that from Ikebukuro to Shinjuku, did not come until later yet. It would probably be unfair to say that metropolitan policy consciously favored business over convenience, but that is certainly the ordering that prevailed.

In one respect things became easier for the office worker—or at least the messenger boy who ran from office to office. In the original Mitsubishi Londontown, the complex spread out before the station, the pattern had been vertical, with a company renting several floors of a segment of a building. Now it became horizontal. A company that did not have a building of its own would rent a whole floor or two from Mitsubishi or someone else.

In 1951, the second year of the Korean War and the year in which the boom in office building began, the city received the first considerable increment to its hotel space since the Daiichi of 1938, built for the Olympics that never took place. The Nikkatsu Building, with shops at ground level and below, offices on the next several levels, and hotel rooms at the top, rose at the Hibiya crossing. The hotel space is now gone, and would scarcely be noticed in any event among all the huge hotels the city possesses. The builder was a movie company later done in by television. Great was the wonder in those days at the daring. Would enough foreign tourists and businessmen come to fill the rooms? They never had before. Not many seers guessed that the foreign clientele would be of so relatively little importance in keeping all the hotels filled.

Until the completion of the Daiichi, hotels, in contrast to inns, had catered almost exclusively to alien tourists and businessmen. Despite its Olympian origins, the Daiichi wished to attract Japanese businessmen

The Nikkatsu building

and even an occasional family group, and in a measure succeeded. The tiny rooms and especially the tiny bathtubs seemed meant for them, a way of luring them gradually into something new. This new adventure in lodging lasted but briefly. The war came and hotels were destroyed, and the remaining ones, led by the Imperial and the Daiichi, were taken over by the Occupation, either for its own personnel or for "foreign traders," as they were called. When the Occupation ended, the adventure was resumed with enthusiasm, and by the time of the 1964 Olympics five times more hotel rooms were available. The clientele, especially for lavish receptions, was increasingly Japanese.

The distinction between a hotel and an inn has never been very clear. (It is a little like that between a geisha and a prostitute.) The earliest hotel in the city, the Tsukiji Hoterukan, which was of wood and went up in flames in 1872, seemed to think itself both, since the first three syllables of the generic part of the name are "hotel" and the last is a part of the commonest Japanese word for "inn." There has recently gone up in the Ueno district a place that calls itself the Hoteru Yado, to show that this ecumenical tradition perseveres. *Yado,* another reading of the *juku* of Shinjuku, "New Station," signifies a traveler's lodging.

One cannot say that hotels are in the Western style and inns in the Japanese, since many places that anyone would call an inn have beds and chairs, and numbers of large hotels have rooms in which one sleeps on the floor. Nor can it be said that hotels are expensive and inns are cheap, since either can be both. Perhaps the most definitive statement that can be made is that a hotel tends to be big, high, and fire-resistant, and an inn tends to be small, no more than two or three storeys high, flimsily built, and often rather combustible.

By the end of the first postwar decade there were almost four thousand inns in the city and a dozen or so hotels. There were scores of rooms at an inn for every one at a hotel. Of the inns, more than three-quarters were of the "dubious" *(aimai)* kind, their mark the "upside-down jellyfish." It is the mark of the hot spring, the jets of steam from the water resembling a jellyfish supine, its tentacles in the air. Their business was sex, and ladies of the night were an important part of their clientele.

There is dispute as to when and where a Japanese establishment first took for itself the American designation "motel." Some say that it was in Atami in 1963, others that it was as early as 1957 at a rather remote place on the "back side" of Japan, the coast of the Sea of Japan. In any event it does not seem to have been in Tokyo, and it does seem to have been in the pre-Olympic years. Soon Tokyo had numerous specimens, and soon the secret was out in the open. The expressions "upside-down jellyfish" and "motel" had been suggestive but not explicit; "love hotel," in English, was very explicit.

Yet there remained something furtive about love hotels. A night at the Yoshiwara, in another age, had an open, rather companionable quality about it. A night in a love hotel does not. The Edo wife had no right to complain if her husband went off occasionally to the Yoshiwara. The wife of our day and days recently past thinks herself much put upon if she or a gossipy friend sees her husband emerging from a love hotel. A good part of the furtiveness has to do with arrangements for making as sure as possible that he is not detected. Family life has changed.

Officially, the recovery of Tokyo from the great earthquake was accomplished in less than a decade. There were no observances after the surrender corresponding to those in 1930 that felicitated recovery from the earthquake. In another way the reconstruction was different from that of 1923 and after. It did not stop. Building did not of course come to a complete stop in the Tokyo of the Crisis years, but depression and Crisis kept the city from changing greatly after the 1930 celebrations. It was as if they announced the end of a period of great constructive endeavor and the coming of a less active period in which to await the next storm.

Nothing of the sort has happened since the war. The building has gone on and on. There have been recessions, but there has been no major depression. Japan has been free of international involvements as probably no other major nation in modern times—free to manufacture, to export, and to build. One may expect to see from time to time in the newspapers and magazines the announcement that the postwar period is *finally* over. They are like announcements that Edo has finally died. Even as we may expect them, we may be sure that the most recent one will not be the last. "The postwar period," an expression for practical purposes interchangeable with "the period of reconstruction," will probably go on as a cultural and economic era until the next disaster brings it to a close.

Yet we may say that by the middle or late fifties Tokyo was essentially back where it had been in 1940 or so, and everything that has come since has been new growth. It took about a decade to recover from 1923, and it took about a decade to recover from 1945. In the middle fifties one started hearing Japanese say that their standard of living had returned to the prewar level.

Affluence is never evenly distributed, and the growing affluence of the city was not. Some wards had ampler housing than others. Besides taking over most of the Marunouchi business district, the Occupation requisitioned houses, more than six hundred of them in Tokyo Prefecture. With all the houses in the city and the prefecture to choose from, it naturally chose the most luxurious, and so the pattern of requisitioning follows the pattern of the domicile of wealth. A quarter of the requisitioned houses were in what is now Minato Ward and before 1947 was the three southern wards of the old city, Shiba, Akasaka, and Azabu. The American embassy is at the northern edge of it. The addition of two other wards—Ota, southernmost of the new 1932 wards, and Shibuya, centering on the bustling place of that name in the southwestern part of the city—brings the total to more than half. No houses at all were requisitioned in six wards along the northeastern and eastern fringes of the city. Scarcely any would have been left along the inner fringe even if the Occupation had wanted to have places there, but the three wards along the outer fringe were not badly damaged. Nothing in them caught the Occupation eye.

In 1956 Edogawa, one of the two easternmost wards, had the lowest per capita income. It was in those days still heavily agricultural. Of the thoroughly urbanized wards, the two immediately east of the Sumida River had the lowest income. In 1957 the weight of vegetables brought into the Kanda wholesale produce market was twice that of those brought to the Kōtō market east of the river (the two were among seven wholesale markets in the city), but the sales value was three and a half times as much. Kanda was where the expensive Ginza retailers and restaurants went for their supplies. Kōtō had no such clientele. (In 1956 Kanda sold, by value, 14 percent of the vegetables and 26 percent of the fruits for the whole nation. The value of the fruits was higher than that for any single city other than Tokyo itself, and that of vegetables higher than for any other city except Osaka.)

The population of the prefecture, which had risen above seven million in 1939 and stayed there until 1944, fell to about three and a half million in late 1945. It climbed by about a fifth during each of the following two years. Thereafter the rate of growth fell off sharply. The population once more passed seven million in 1952, and in 1962 it passed ten million. Of the seven and a third million inhabitants of the prefecture in 1940, six and three-quarters million lived in the thirty-five wards. Of about eight million inhabitants in 1955, fewer than seven million lived in the wards. This is to say that the population of the old "county part," beyond the limits of the 1932 city, had doubled, while the population of the wards had risen only by some two hundred thousand people.

The population of the wards rose to almost nine million in the late sixties, and never passed that figure. The ward part of the prefecture was saturated, while the population of the county part continued to grow. Since 1967 the population of the wards has been stable, though in slight decline over the long run. The population of the central wards and some wards in the eastern and northeastern parts of the city has, in the long view, been in decline since before the disaster of 1945. In all the wards there was an increase in population after 1945, but in the wards in question the population has never returned to the highest prewar figure.

Chiyoda Ward and Chūō Ward, the former including the Marunouchi business district and most of the government bureaus, and the latter Ginza and Nihombashi, both declined in population between the census of 1955 and that of 1960. Minato Ward had more people in 1960 than in 1955, but declined thereafter. The same was true of Taitō Ward, including Ueno and Asakusa, and Bunkyō Ward, including the haughtiest of the national universities and the Kōrakuen baseball stadium. (Estimates for noncensus years suggest that the last two wards may have been growing at a very slight rate for a year or two after the 1960 census.) Setagaya Ward, at the southwestern limits of the ward part, lost less than a tenth of its population from 1944 into 1945, and already in 1946 had more people than in 1944. It has not flagged on its way to becoming the most populous ward in the prefecture. If we combine the populations of the thirty-five antebellum wards into the twenty-three of today, then Setagaya was in 1935 fourteenth among the twenty-three, and Taitō and Sumida, which face each other across the Sumida River and neither of which has returned since the war to its highest prewar population, were the most populous.

Eight of the twenty-three wards, among them all the wards that lay entirely within the old city (the city as it was to 1932), lost population between the censuses of 1960 and 1965. Two that straddled the old city limits, one of them Shinjuku, gained slightly, but estimates for noncensus years suggest that they too were already in decline by 1965. All of the new wards outside the 1932 city limits were with a single exception gaining population. The exception was Arakawa Ward, that district to the north of Asakusa where the very poor went when disaster and rising costs drove them out of Asakusa.

So it is that Tokyo moves away from Edo. The new wards grew as the old ones declined, the county part continued to grow as the ward part (seen as a bloc) declined, and when the prefecture in general started to lose population, the neighboring prefectures went on growing enormously. Inevitably there was diffusion, as the tight heart of Edo emptied and the circle around it widened, and the mass of people who might be expected to be paying attention to the same thing at the same time grew enormously. The marvel is that the city has gone on having a center at all. The daytime population of the central wards is several times the nighttime population. That is true, however, of many a large city whose center is incapable of attracting people for any purpose other than making money. People still swarm to the center of Tokyo to dissipate their money and their energies, and to consume.

The average term of governors since, in 1947, the first one was popularly elected has been ten years and a little more. This figure is certain to rise, since the incumbent has most of his third four-year term yet to serve. Such longevity in office, as has been noted (see page 88), is in sharp contrast to the breathless comings and goings of the prewar years.

Japanese local government since the war has followed the American presidential pattern, with popular election both of chief executives and of legislative bodies. The national government has followed the British parliamentary pattern. The Japanese example does not provide strong arguments in favor of either system, since both have produced stability. The mayor before the war had endless trouble with what were in effect two city councils. The prefectural council since the war has been on the whole manageable, though since 1965 no single party has had a majority of the seats. Only one governor has completely lost control. That was the Olympic governor, most of whose attention went into staging a model sporting event. A larger part of his attention should perhaps have been on a scandal that broke shortly after the event was triumphantly staged.

Since the war, scandals have been neither as frequent nor as interesting, for the most part, as before the war.

One powerful force in the workings of the city and the prefecture is not entirely under the control of the prefectural government: the police. The chief of the Tokyo prefectural police is appointed by a national police agency with the approval of the prime minister and upon the advice of a prefectural police commission, which is ineffectual. None of these agencies is under the control of governor and council. Tokyo becomes a police city when it is thought necessary to guard against the embarrassment of having someone shoot at a president or a queen or a pope. It has more than twice as many policemen as Osaka, though it is less than twice as large in population. The problem of police excesses is by no means limited to Tokyo—it was in Kanagawa Prefecture that a case of illegal eavesdropping was uncovered in 1986—but it is most conspicuous in the prefecture in which national embarrassments are most likely to occur. People complain that most of the police budget is provided by the prefecture, which does not control the size of the force. Much of it would come from Tokyo even if it were routed through the national government. The richest prefecture naturally contributes the most to national revenues. In 1946 the Tokyo police, under the influence of the Americans, had policewomen for the first time. It still has them, though many another American idea, such as decentralization, has long since been forgotten.

Even before 1947, when for the first time a governor was popularly elected, the view had come to prevail that the ward boundaries were ill drawn. They had since 1932 varied greatly in size, with the old fifteen wards on the average much smaller than the twenty new ones of that year. Now, with bombings, evacuation, and the return from evacuation, population differences were also extreme. Sources do not agree as to whether the initiative in the matter of reducing the number and the inequalities came from the Americans or from the prefecture. The best evidence is that the prefectural government brought the Americans into a matter of little concern to them as a way of making sure that it would have its way.

In 1946, in any event, the Occupation indicated that some of the wards should be amalgamated. The chief executive set up an advisory commission in the summer of 1946. Having obtained the approval of the prime minister, he submitted a report later in the year that called for reducing the number of wards from thirty-five to twenty-two. Eleven wards would retain their present names and boundaries. They were all among the twenty new wards of 1932. The old fifteen of 1932 would all be amalgamated either with other old wards or with new ones. In a single instance, Shinjuku, two old ones were combined with a new one. All would most probably lose their old names.

The probability brought resistance, for there was great pride in the old names. Only four among the councils of the old fifteen wards indicated immediate approval. Six of the nine new ones facing amalgamation approved, for with these the pride was less considerable. Palaver ensued. It was a foregone conclusion that all thirty-five would, when talked out, agree, and all presently did; and this was despite the fact that popular opinion was in several obvious cases ignored. Thus a small residential ward in the northern part of the city wanted to join the residential ward bordering it on the south, but was joined instead to a very dissimilar industrial ward to the east. The history edited and published by the new ward, Kita, tells us that the decision was carried out quickly and without publicity.

In March 1947, very shortly before the first gubernatorial elections, the chief executive, with the consent of the prefectural council, proclaimed the reduction from thirty-five to twenty-two wards. All of the old wards did in fact lose their names, and here too public opinion was little respected. Early in 1947 the *Tokyo Shimbun* conducted a poll among residents of the twenty-four wards to be amalgamated. They were asked what names they would prefer for their eleven new wards. Only four of the names finally adopted were even mentioned. Some of the new names seem appropriate. The time did seem right for Shinjuku, that principal rival to the old business district, to become the name of a ward. Others seem merely fatuous. The worst is Bunkyō. It means something like "literary capital" or "cultural capital," probably with reference not to the Kōrakuen baseball stadium but to Tokyo University. The name has that bureaucratic ring to it.

There was no attempt to equalize the area of the wards. Even after amalgamation the central wards remained much smaller than most of those remoter from Marunouchi and the palace. The smallest of all, an amalgamation of the old Shitaya and Asakusa, was only an eighth the size of Itabashi, the farthest of the wards to the north and west. Though

Itabashi had had the same boundaries since it became a ward, with the same name, in 1932, it was now thought unwieldy. It was big, certainly, some ten miles across at its widest point, and rapidly growing in population. Later in 1947 it was split in two, and so the count of wards became the twenty-three it has remained.

The new ward lines had more to do with population than with area. Looking to the future, they anticipated a ratio of one to three between the smallest population and the largest. It is not surprising that the eye to the future did not serve well. Few could have foreseen that affluence and prosperity would return and that the outer wards would grow so hugely. If Itabashi had stayed whole it would today have some twenty-two or twenty-three times the population of Chiyoda, where the palace and the Marunouchi business district are. Setagaya, the farthest to the south and west, today has the largest population, upward of eight hundred thousand, seventeen times that of Chiyoda.

In the functions permitted the wards we may see a small instance of a successful popular rising. Outbreaks of resentment at this and that policy of the government have not been unknown, but few have produced even minor change. As a part of the reforms in local government that brought popularly elected governors, "ward heads" (this is the official translation, appearing on alien registration certificates and the like) were also popularly elected. In September 1952 the national government, one of several led by the strong-minded Yoshida Shigeru, replaced this method with something less direct, the announced reason for the change being that the wards were too small to go their own undirected way. Most of the cities in the prefecture, it may be noted, were smaller than most of the wards, but they continued to elect mayors. The ward heads were now elected by the ward councils with the agreement of the governor.

Two decades later the councils of five wards adopted as their policy the designating of ward heads by plebiscite. The candidate with the highest popular vote would be commended to the governor. Three wards actually held plebiscites. This happened, we are told, in response to a popular view that a certain decentralization might be at least a partial solution to the increasingly complicated problems of the city — and indeed it was getting smoggier and more debt-ridden all the time. In 1974 the Local Autonomy Law was amended to return to the earlier system of popular elections. Under the new law the prerogatives of the wards became as they had been under the Occupation, similar to those of incorporated cities.

There have been other little shows of independence at this lowest of administrative levels. Nakano Ward, to the west of Shinjuku, has gone against the wishes of the Ministry of Education and elected its school board by popular vote. Probably not much of significance will emerge from this smaller rising. Tokyo had a radical government, supported by both of the major left-wing parties, from 1967 to 1979. Faced with a choice between ward heads elected by popular vote and ward heads whose appointment required the consent of the governor, the Local Autonomy Agency was of the view that it did not much matter one way or the other, and that elections might actually be an improvement in Tokyo, where all the fuss was. We will never know what would have happened to the popular rising in other circumstances.

It is a bleak city that loses its sense of fun and pleasure. Tokyo did not. Pleasure quickly came back, and humor went the rounds. The jokes about General MacArthur and his Occupation may not seem exactly sidesplitting by American standards, but then Japanese humor is not American humor. The general emerged with more dignity, on the whole, from Japanese jokes than from American ones.

"Why is General MacArthur like a navel?"

"Because he is above the *chin.*"

The italicized word is a first-person pronoun used only by the emperor—he used it in the broadcast of August 15, 1945. Here it signifies His Majesty himself. It is also a ribald though not grossly indecent word for penis. So the general and the navel were above the *chin* in its two senses.

Nationalist sophistry has in recent years maintained that Japan did not surrender unconditionally, since the emperor remained in place. But popular wisdom had no doubt as to where the place was, and the first meeting between general and emperor clearly established it: The emperor called on the general, and not the reverse. The general did not go to the door to receive his guest or to see him off. In the famous photograph of the occasion the general is large and relaxed, the emperor small and tense. The emperor called on the general five times thereafter, and the general never paid a return call. Among the expressions used on every possible occasion during the autumn of the surrender was: "It's Mac-Arthur's order." He was an imperial presence, and probably he saw less of Japan than any other American who came during the Occupation years. He shuttled back and forth between his offices by the moat and his residence in the American embassy, perhaps fifteen or twenty minutes' walk away.

One major Kabuki theater, the Tōkyō Gekijō or Tokyo Theater, a part of the Shōchiku complex to the east of Ginza, came through the bombings and burnings. The Shimbashi Embujō and the Kabukiza, the other two major parts of the complex, were both gutted. Kabuki was playing at the Tokyo through the first half of August 1945 and was still there on August 15. The theater was closed for the rest of the month, but opened again on the first of September, even before it was known how the Americans would behave. They behaved in a way that may, from a certain remove in time, seem peculiar.

Ichikawa Ennosuke, a very popular actor who had led the troupe at the Tōgeki in early August, was back there leading it again in September. In October the Shimpa, a melodramatic form less stylized than Kabuki,

General MacArthur and the emperor, 1946

was at the Tōgeki, and the sixth Onoe Kikugorō, one of the most celebrated actors of the century, was at the Imperial Theater in Marunouchi. Relations with the Americans seemed to be progressing nicely.
Then, in November, there was trouble. It was almost as if the grand
satraps of Kabuki were asking for it, or at any rate probing the limits of
American permissiveness. The first Nakamura Kichiemon, another
highly esteemed actor, chose as his November vehicle at the Tōgeki a
play which, unless one is used to its sort of thing, may seem demented,
pushing the old military virtues, and especially loyalty, to the point of
insanity and still holding them to be virtues. So it seemed to the Occupation censors, who ordered the play closed. There were censors of the
arts and literature in those days, not the most democratic of people, but
people who must be tolerated, perhaps, in a crisis. There was a certain
air of crisis about the Occupation. It had a great deal to get done in a
short time—and a half dozen years is, in the long view, a short time.

Censorship was not new to Kabuki. Wartime censors had been stern
with what they thought to be frivolous and immoral elements, and especially with the idealized rogues of late Edo. There was no attempt to
resist before 1945, and there was none after 1945. The effort in both
cases was to accommodate. Since the show went on in both cases, it may
be deemed successful.

Shōchiku promptly organized a committee to select plays that no one
could object to, and to negotiate with the censors. The latter accepted a
list of 174 plays of a soundly democratic nature, and said that new plays
might be a solution to the problem. Kabuki has never had a fixed repertory, a canon. New plays are always being written. To this Shōchiku
acceded with an appearance of heartiness. Early in 1946 it announced a
sad fact it had come upon. Kabuki was in danger of fossilization. New
plays were the thing.

Had the early views of the censors and the announced ones of Shōchiku prevailed, dance might have become more central to Kabuki than
it had traditionally been. Kabuki has always been a highly ritualized and
choreographed form. The repertory contains pieces that are entirely
dance. These would have come to prevail. The "feudal" old classics
quickly started coming back, however. Plays not on the approved list
were being performed from as early as 1947, and the censors did not
object. The play that was the cause of all the trouble in 1945 was being
performed before the end of the Occupation in 1952.

The Tōgeki, where Kabuki survived the most difficult times, perhaps, in its history, does not itself survive. The building does not, this is
to say, though the institution does, under a dozen or so storeys of offices
and restaurants. As a place for Kabuki it did not last through the postwar
decade. It became a movie house with the reopening of the Shimbashi
Embujō and the Kabukiza. Redone on the inside, looking very much as
they had before the war on the outside, the two reopened respectively in
1948 and 1951. As had been the case on its original opening, the Shimbashi geisha who had built the Embujō had the use of it in March 1948,
the month of the reopening. Once again they gave their recital of Dance
of the East. To save money, Shōchiku did not attempt to rebuild the
ornate prewar roof of the Kabukiza, which had collapsed in 1945. The
building is nevertheless one of the grander relics of the interwar fondness
for old styles in new materials. The facade, still elaborate, is in a Tokugawa style.

The Tōgeki was the only major Kabuki theater to come through the
bombings, but the Mitsukoshi department store in Nihombashi helped
fill the gap until the Embujō and the Kabukiza could be redone. Ever
since the mercantile revolution that produced department stores, around
the turn of the century, they have been cultural and amusement centers.
They became these things to draw people away from the old specialized
stores and make them feel at home in a confusing and threatening emporium. It is to their credit that, having drawn the crowds, they have
gone on being cultural and amusement centers. Ever since its rebuilding
after the 1923 earthquake, Mitsukoshi had had an auditorium which it
rented out for meetings and performances. The name was changed from
Mitsukoshi Hall to Mitsukoshi Theater in 1947, at which time it became
a full-fledged, full-time theater. In addition to providing another place
for Kabuki, a somewhat more sumptuous and elegant one than the Tōgeki, the Mitsukoshi Theater was very important in passing Kabuki on
from an aging generation to an emerging one.

The postwar decade was, like the first decade of the century, a time
when everyone seemed to be dying. People announced the death of Kabuki itself. The great Kikugorō, the leading Kabuki actor of his time,
died in 1949, within two months of two other major actors. His last
performance was at the Mitsukoshi. (In the last year of his life, Kikugorō
became the first actor of any sort to receive the Culture Medal, the
highest honor the nation can bestow on its literary and artistic talents.

Kabuki had climbed a great distance since, a scant century before, it had been beneath the notice of the Tokugawa military aristocracy.) The first Kichiemon, who would have been on most lists as Kikugorō's leading rival, died at the end of the first postwar decade, in 1954. But death announcements for the Kabuki form as a whole were, as they had been in late Meiji, premature. The actors who are the old masters today were establishing themselves, and the Mitsukoshi Theater, more than the Tōgeki, was the place where they were doing it. The Mitsukoshi was last used as a Kabuki theater in 1951, the year the Kabukiza reopened. Since 1953 it has returned to its earlier duties, as a place for recitals and meetings.

The Meijiza in Nihombashi, the oldest Kabuki theater in the city, reopened a few months before the Kabukiza, in November 1950. Before the new decade was over it had been gutted and restored yet another time, the fifth since its original construction early in Meiji. Early on an April morning in 1957 a fire started in the illumination room. There were no casualties.

The Tōgeki narrowly escaped requisitioning by the Occupation. The story of how it escaped is a pleasant one, though there is considerable possibility that it is apocryphal: Early in 1946 Ennosuke, he who was playing at the same theater in August 1945, appeared in a modern sort of play with Mizutani Yaeko, probably the most esteemed actress of the day. They kissed, unabashedly, right there in front of the public. Never had it happened before. The critical reception was mixed, but the public approved. So did the Occupation, which thought this display of independence and emotional honesty promising and did not requisition the theater.

The Takarazuka, that big Tōhō property across Ginza from the Kabukiza and the other big Shōchiku properties, did not escape being taken over. As the Ernie Pyle, known to every American who visited the city during the Occupation years, it was a movie and stage theater in the hands of the Americans for almost a decade. It had a huge staff and served as a sort of public-works project for unemployed Japanese theater people. When Tōhō got it back, in 1955, it launched a brave effort to break the Shōchiku monopoly on Kabuki. Some famous and accomplished actors joined the Tōhō Kabuki, and Shōchiku seems to have been genuinely unsettled. It responded by having popular singers do recitals (or something of the sort) at the Kabukiza, and by finding new Kabuki talent.

The brightest among the new Kabuki actors was Bandō Tamasaburō, a female impersonator who made his debut in 1967 in the play the American censors had taken objection to in 1945, and who today, in his thirties, is the most popular Kabuki actor. In the end the Tōhō undertaking was not a success. Shōchiku still has its monopoly. The Takarazuka has returned to what it was originally meant for, light and popular musicals, prominent among them those of the all-girl Takarazuka troupe. Yet a decade later the troupe was to have its most smashing hit, *Rose of Versailles,* in which, as in *The Marriage of Figaro,* a woman impersonates a man (in attendance upon Marie Antoinette) impersonating a woman.

Not long after its release by the Americans and its return to the Takarazuka troupe and others, the Takarazuka Theater was the scene of another famous fire, one which, unlike that in the Meijiza, resulted in deaths. The first day of February 1958 was opening day for a musical comedy (not all-girl) about the Ainu, the aborigines who survive vestigially on the northern island of Hokkaido. The play was in progress, the house was packed. On a higher floor an audience was having a movie afternoon, and on a level yet higher a program of the Yose variety theater was underway. Along toward the end of the performance in the main theater the Ainu village which was the setting was attacked by the Japanese. The effects were partly achieved by a fire machine, a sort of flame thrower. It seems that not all the sparks and flames it threw were extinguished. Still later in the performance a curtain began to smolder. The fire quickly spread. The audience applauded these yet more dramatic effects, and did not realize that they were unintentional until a barrier was lowered between the stage and the pits. There was panic and there were injuries from trampling, but no fatalities among the spectators. Those in the theaters above, not witness to the excitement, were evacuated quietly by emergency exits. The three deaths occurred backstage—two child actors and a woman dancer.

Yose too had its troubles with censorship. Although certain feudal tendencies, such as an emphasis on loyalty and submission that runs all through Japanese society, are to be detected in Yose, the censors found nothing in the comic Rakugo monologue so undemocratic as to call for action. They did object, however, to the serious, didactic Kōdan, also done by monologuists. They thought, and they were right, that it glorified the military virtues. They were particularly suspicious of revenge and righteous violence. The form accommodated itself by devices similar to those resorted to by Kabuki. As with Kabuki, the attention of the censors presently flagged.

The most popular Yose theater in the city was for a time near the Sumida River in the Ningyōchō district of Nihombashi. It closed, for want of a clientele, in 1970. Ningyōchō, in which something of old Nihombashi yet survives, is not the bustling place it once was. It escaped the bombings, though the Meijiza, to the east, did not. In the years just after the war it seemed to beckon across the wastes to western Nihombashi, where big business and finance resided, as if asking it to come home again.

In late Edo and through much of Meiji, until the movies came along, Yose was the entertainment for the masses who did not have much money. Presently radio and baseball also came along, and then television, and a far bigger city now contains only one percent as many Yose halls as during the best years of Edo. Yet one need not despair for Yose. It has come to terms with the newer media, and they have extended assistance. The Suzumoto in Ueno, the oldest hall in the city, and now the largest, seating upward of two hundred people, was having a very hard time during the depression years, 1930 and thereabouts, and fees from NHK, the public broadcasting system and the only one there was in those days, helped it come through. Radio and television fees still give a comfortable living to the better-known performers. Yose seems moreover to appeal to the young. Scarcely a university is without its Rakugo study society. Most of the active professionals, a scattering of women among them, were born in the last reign. A single one was born in Meiji, and fewer than twenty in Taishō.

So it seems that Rakugo, and, more tenuously, Kōdan, will survive. There is today a single house in the city and indeed in the nation that specializes in Kōdan. Also in Ueno, it opened in 1950, before the censorious Americans had gone away. The name, Hommokutei, is interesting. It once belonged to the Suzumoto, which was founded in the year of Commodore Perry's landing. The Hommoku district of Yokohama was made famous by that event. So we may infer that Edo had a good idea of what was going on and was much interested.

The name Ernie Pyle does not seem to have suited Japanese taste. Takarazuka came back. Piccadilly did better. The British Commonwealth Occupation Force gave the name to a theater west of Ginza, and it was kept. We are not to understand, however, that American movies and the American movie business were held in low esteem. Marilyn Monroe and Joe DiMaggio came visiting in 1954, to huge acclaim, more of it for Marilyn than for Joe. The pack of reporters and photographers at the airport was so huge that she was hustled off the plane through an emergency exit. They had a parade into the city and up Ginza.

It was a most advantageous thing in those days for an actor or actress to have a trip to Los Angeles on his or her record. The expression *ameshon,* a most graphic one, had some currency. It is another acronym, made of "American" and *shomben,* "urination," and it refers to a sojourn in America just long enough for a good trip to a urinal. When the actress Tanaka Kinuyo returned from her *ameshon* in 1949, she too had an open parade up Ginza and on to the *Mainichi Shimbun,* from a balcony of which she blew kisses to the crowds, not at all a common or accepted thing for a Japanese lady to do. Her first word to the reporters upon disembarking from her plane is said to have been *haro* ("hello"). She was for a time an object of ridicule, but her career, a brilliant one, did not suffer. She gradually moved from ingenue to gerontic roles.

The two decades after the war may have been the golden age of Japanese moviemaking. The great directors, Ozu Yasujirō and the rest, were doing their best work. It was not, however, the best for box offices. That came between the wars. There was a boom in the building of movie houses during the first postwar decade, at the end of which there were four times as many such places in Tokyo as at the beginning. And then, with television, came the decline in audiences, and bankruptcies and closings. Ginza has dominated the age of the movie in decline. The big, fashionable "road show" theaters are almost all near Ginza, if not precisely in it. Road shows (the expression is in English), chiefly of foreign movies, are offered in a single theater per city at a high price for an indefinite run. They have held their own as the cheaper domestic film has declined.

As the legitimate theater had its first undisguised kiss in 1946, so did the movies, in an otherwise forgotten film. The very first postwar commercial film has not been forgotten. It was made in what is now termed Greater Tokyo, and its name is Zephyr (*Soyokaze*). From it came the first postwar hit song, a swinging smash of a hit and a charming piece of nonsense after all the fustian and doctrine of the war years. Everyone

was singing "The Apple Song" in that autumn of 1945. The lyrics are by
Satō Hachirō, a well-known humorist and writer of light verse.

> To this red apple
> My lips draw near
> The blue sky watches in silence
> This apple
> Is silent too
> And yet I know how it feels
> How agreeable is this apple
> How agreeable

The utter want of a message, and indeed of meaning, may account for
the huge appeal. The tune is agreeable as well, and, remarkable for a
popular Japanese song, there is not a tear in sight, not a sob to be heard.

The age of television, both public and commercial, began in 1953. Those
of us who thought television a luxury beyond the means of the Japanese
could hardly have been more mistaken. Already in 1958, as rapid economic growth was getting underway, NHK had a million sets from which
to extract fees. Early in 1962, the first full year in which the joys of color
television were to be had, the figure passed ten million. It is hard to
imagine today that commercial television could have gone with other than
complete slickness, but the first commercial, in the sense of advertise-
ment, was run silently backwards.

Such idols of the radio age as Dick Mine may have been required to
change their names as being out of keeping with the contemporary Japanese spirit. He had many a successor in the television age, however, that
spirit once more being receptive to exotic things. Tony Tani, Peggy
Hayama, Frank Nagai—the list is a long one. Tony, on the staff of the
Ernie Pyle for a time, was very popular as a master of ceremonies on
radio and television. He invented new words, or catchy variations on old
ones, such as *o-komban wa,* adding an honorific prefix to the standard
expression for "good evening," so that it becomes something like "estimable good evening." They seemed to have entered the language for
good, but one does not hear them today. The matter of which neologisms

stay and which go, in this language so extremely fond of them, defies explanation.

Puritans disapproved of those first public kisses, on stage and on screen, both for what they were and for what they foreshadowed, and they were right that more was coming, on stage and on screen. Toward the end of the first postwar decade there was a vogue for sex films that professed to be educational. They contained a great deal of suggestive posing but not much that was very revealing. More and more has been revealed in the decades since, but not, on the screen, the ultimate, not even in movies with titles like *Flesh Gate* (see page 188) and *Women of the Night*. The hard-core masterpiece about Abe O-sada has not been shown publicly in Japan except in an expurgated version.

The live stage has been bolder. It is more firmly under the control of the local police than the movies, and, for reasons which are not easy to grasp, they have been spottily permissive, not to say arbitrary, in deciding what may be staged and what may not. The strip show, in any event, was something new in popular entertainment. The shows that titillated and even shocked in the early postwar years would not be worth the trouble of producing today, so mild are they compared to what everyone over eighteen (in theory—practice seems more generous) can see. More and more has been stripped away.

January 15, 1947, is recognized by historians of the subject as the day on which the strip show was born. What was known popularly as "The Picture-Frame Show" and properly as "The Birth of Venus" had its premiere on that day on an upper floor of a Shinjuku theater. In the middle of the stage was a large composition resembling a picture frame. In it a girl posed as Venus being born. She was not completely nude; she wore panties and a brassiere, and the rest of her was enclosed in gossamer. She posed for some thirty seconds. It was all, witnesses say, very artless.

This public display of flesh was far more extensive than anything the Casino Folies had ever dared offer. The house was so silent that one could hear a pin drop. People came time after time for those few seconds, and the lines at the box office were as long as ration lines. The show ran until August 1948.

The performers who had such a quelling effect on the Shinjuku audience were at Asakusa slightly later in the season. In June, Asakusa had a completely nude performance, a young lady modeling a model, so to speak. The scene was a painter's studio. It was very popular. Asakusa now proceeded to go wholeheartedly for the strip show, which expression referred at the outset not to the process of stripping but to the stripped condition. (The English word "strip" has always been used, though there are native expressions that would serve as well.) In the early years, when it was bringing comfort and diversion to large numbers of men, even as radio and television were bringing these things to large numbers of women, Asakusa had wider expanses of naked flesh than Shinjuku. Many were heard to lament the falling off which this represented from the days of the opera and Enoken.

The years immediately after the Shinjuku opening are known to cultural historians as the golden age of the strip show. Despite the strip theaters in Shinjuku and some time later in Ginza, Asakusa was the place for them. With bold competition from places beyond the prefectural boundaries and so beyond the jurisdiction of the prefectural police, Asakusa too became bolder. Posing moved into stripping, onstage and not in undressing rooms. Panties and brassieres went away, and even butterflies. In the early days of stripping (not mere posing), more than half the girls in Asakusa rid themselves of Japanese dress. In Ginza Western dress prevailed. Shinjuku occupied a point in between. Asakusa soon adopted the Ginza way. Western dress comes off more quickly than Japanese.

The strip show had its rivals. Light dramatic skits such as Kafū's were still there and popular enough. For a time, midway through the postwar decade, Onna Kengeki, "women's swordplay," threatened to eclipse even the strip show. The form had its origins in the interwar period (see page 85). For a time a half-dozen troupes were performing simultaneously in as many Asakusa theaters. Somewhat erotic from the start, Onna Kengeki held its own in the competition by taking bold steps in the direction of the strip show. The latter prevailed. The early fifties were the best years for the Asakusa strippers. A "bathtub show," replete with bubbles, made its appearance in 1951, and is credited with the triumph of the strip show. Tightrope strips and acrobatic strips also had their time of popularity.

The rebuilding of the Asakusa entertainment district was swift. One might have thought at the end of the post-surrender decade that it was in a position to hold its own against the upstarts out west. Only a dozen

Oe Michiko, the great star of female swordplay, 1959

Asakusa theaters, a bit more than a third of the prewar number, survived the war intact. Some, including Kafū's Opera House, which was never rebuilt, were torn down during the war to make firebreaks, others closed for other reasons; eight were either partially or completely gutted during the incendiary raids. By the mid-fifties the count of theaters, stage and screen, was almost back to the prewar level, and for a time a few years later it was even higher.

For one not armed with sociological statistics (see page 42), the Asakusa of the postwar years may well have been the part of the city with the strongest, warmest sense of life. Ginza and Shinjuku were already coming to seem impersonal by comparison. All the hum and bustle made the in-between light, coming after great darkness, seem like a dawn and not a dusk.

But the revival was illusory. A 1966 history of Taitō Ward, which includes the old Asakusa Ward, quotes a newspaper article with the headline: "Deserted Place, Thy Name Is Asakusa." This is only a little extreme. The same history refers disparagingly to "Asakusa County, Chiba Prefecture." By this is meant that sophisticated, urbane crowds have gone elsewhere, and such crowds as Asakusa still draws are predominantly rural ones from the prefecture to the east, held in low esteem. Chiba Prefecture lies within Greater Tokyo as legally defined, but that fact has not much helped the prefectural image.

Old Asakusa hands have blamed the filling in of the lakes for bringing on the decline. Kubota Mantarō, a poet, playwright, and novelist who was a native of Asakusa and wrote with great nostalgia about the old Asakusa, vowed that he would never return to see the place without its lakes. He cheated on the vow, for he was seen there by many a person; but the sorrow and anger ring true. Both lakes were filled in, or all three of them, if one thinks of the larger as divided in two by a causeway. When, in the declining months of the Occupation, Asakusa Park was returned to the big temple, the latter promptly started looking for buyers. The southernmost portion of the lakes went to a movie company, which excavated part and filled part, and put a movie theater on the excavated part and an amusement park on the filled. The northern part went to a syndicate which included the ubiquitous Mitsui and which put up a pleasure emporium, practically everything except bawdy houses under one roof. The amusement park and the emporium now are gone. The movie theater remains. The old hands cannot be completely correct, for such changes are never simple. Yet Asakusa was greatly altered by what the temple and its successors to title did with the old park; and it may well be that when even the topography of a place has changed people who knew it before the change will look for other places, where the wrench of memory is less painful.

Other explanations are possible for the fact that so promising a start came to so little. Kata Kōji thinks that Asakusa was doomed because no swarms of students have campuses nearby. Enoken thought that Asakusa made the mistake of trying to be all classy like Ginza. This is interesting, and it does have a certain applicability to Enoken's Asakusa reviews. But if Asakusa imitated any of the other bustling places it was Shinjuku, and Shinjuku has not been much noted for its classiness. As for the Kata view, one may point out that Roppongi is not favored with campuses either. Students come from afar.

The essential facts can be stated simply. The Japanese seem to enjoy moving as if to the sound of a drum, and one of those sixth senses (there are many) of which they are proud seems to tell them in which direction everyone is moving. The great thrust of the city was westward, into the hills and away from the flatlands, and the best advice in the world from all the people who had explanations for the decline of Asakusa could not have done much to stop it.

Such first-run movie houses as the Tokyo Theater and the Japan Theater (the Tōgeki and the Nichigeki), to the east and west of Ginza, also had their strippers, with names like Mary Matsubara, Gypsy Rose, and Frieda Matsumoto. Early performances were elegant by comparison with what was going on in Shinjuku and Asakusa. The first performance at the Nichigeki Music Hall, in March 1952, had a pair of French artistes live from the Folies-Bergère, as well as Koshiji Fubuki, one of the great figures, and not at all a bawdy figure, in recent popular entertainment. The Music Hall loosened up a bit as time went by and it became apparent that much would be permitted which had not earlier been. Yet Ginza maintained a certain tone that the other places did not.

Even as the Meiji government had essayed to provide ladies of pleasure for early foreign visitors and residents, so the Japanese government thought to do it for the Occupation forces. Soon after the surrender there was a poster in Ginza inviting young ladies to join a "recreation and amusement association" for the entertainment of the Americans. It had a few gatherings in the basement of a Ginza department store, but soon became a cabaret for Japanese. The government early indicated a willingness to set aside a generous number of pleasure quarters for the exclusive use of the Occupation. Unfriendly to the idea, the Occupation responded by declaring houses of prostitution off limits. So they remained. Even today the person who knows where to look can find off-limits signs on the crumbling tile and plaster fronts of what once were such houses, in districts left behind by economic growth.

Of the old licensed quarters, the two within the old city, Yoshiwara and Susaki, prospered. The Shinjuku quarter was doing well enough too. The Shinagawa quarter actually received public subsidies, because, pleasantly and conveniently situated beside the bay and the Tokyo–Yokohama highway, it was popular with Americans. Under certain con-

ditions they were permitted the company of geisha, held not to be prostitutes. The haughtier Shimbashi geisha quarter refused a proffered
subvention.

The most famous of the "private" or unlicensed quarters, Tamanoi,
did not come back after the bombings, but another such quarter east of
the Sumida River was probably the most famous one of the immediate
postwar years. Called Hatonomachi, "Pigeon Town," it was the setting
for a minor Kafū work, one of his burlesque skits (see page 110). Without
having known Tamanoi, one may imagine that Hatonomachi was very
much like it, though with the addition of an off-limits sign at every door.

A quite new kind of quarter also sprang up, becoming one of the
things people went to see. Kafū went to see it on February 25, 1947.

> Clear, and warm again. I enjoy cooking beside the well and eating
> under the eaves. In the afternoon I walked through the Koiwa
> district. Some five or six hundred yards to the west on the Chiba
> highway is a den of unlicensed prostitutes. The Kameido quarter
> picked up and moved itself en masse to an imposing complex
> which during the war was a Seikō factory and dormitory. At the
> cement gate is the name of the place, Tokyo Palace, and at the
> entrance is a clinic for diseases of the quarters. To one side is a
> dance hall which opens at five every evening and always has, I am
> told, thirty girls in attendance. There are five two-storey dormi-
> tories, each with fourteen or fifteen rooms, and passageways join-
> ing them, and sellers of vegetables and repairers of footwear. One
> is initially startled at the size of the place. By the gate and all
> through the grounds are signs: "Off Limits," "VD." Until Octo-
> ber of last year American soldiers streamed in and out, but now
> the clientele is entirely Japanese. For a half hour, a hundred yen,
> I was told, and for an hour two hundred; eight hundred to spend
> the night from nine o'clock and six hundred from eleven o'clock.
> I bought an apple apiece for two or three women who were taking
> sweets at the confectioner's and had them show me about. Then
> I walked back to the station by a different route.

The off-limits warning is reproduced in Roman letters. "Palace" is the
Japanese phonetic representation of the English word. Both Kameido and
Koiwa are east of the Sumida, the latter near the boundary with Chiba

Prefecture. Kafū was then living in Ichikawa, on the Chiba side of the boundary. Kameido had a "den" of unlicensed prostitutes before the war, larger than Tamanoi. Bombed out, it seems to have done as Kafū here has it doing. Another such den grew up in the Koiwa district after the war. Seikō is of course the clockmaking enterprise famous the world over. Tokyo Palace, one of the sights along the Chiba highway in those early years, was a temporary expedient. The girls started moving to more central locations as soon as they could, and nothing was left in 1958 to outlaw.

These who had shelter were among the luckier ones. It was the day of the streetwalker. She was among its symbols, and her gradual disappearance, not that she has ever disappeared completely, was among the signs that a better day—not a day of improved morals but a day of material improvement—had come. Streetwalkers were everywhere in the early years, most conspicuous in places where the after-office crowds were densest and soldiers most numerous. Their paths as they plied their trade in Shinjuku were a factor (see page 216) in changing the map of the place. In the golden age, so to speak, there were as many as five hundred girls in the vicinity of Yūrakuchō Station, just south of Tokyo Central, and immediately west of the main Ginza crossing. (Yūrakuchō is often abbreviated Rakuchō, literally "Pleasureville.") On a November evening in 1953 a drunken American soldier threw a pimp over the bridge that still ran across the outer castle moat between Yūrakuchō and Ginza. The fellow drowned, and the incident got much attention from the media. Anti-Americanism was strong in the days after the San Francisco Treaty. ("Yankee go home" was among the expressions that enjoyed great vogue. The English was used.)

Streetwalkers gave the language at least one neologism which has survived. They were and still are known as "*panpan* girls." The origins of the first word are unknown. The second is the English. They had their literary spokesman. The novelist Tamura Taijirō was the leading exponent of the "carnal literature" (*nikutai bungaku*) of the day. His most famous work, a novella published in 1947, has the same title, *Flesh Gate (Nikutai no Mon)*, as the very popular movie made from it. A group of streetwalkers work the district from Yūrakuchō eastward through Ginza to the Sumida River, and live a communal life in the ruined dockyards. They have their code: they do not give themselves to men except for money; business is business, and any suggestion that sex is other than business is a threat to them all. The main action has to do with the punishment meted out to girls who violate the code by indulging gratis and with pleasure. The first stage, exposure, made the work obvious material for the strip theaters, which did not overlook it. The girls have such vivid names as Borneo Maya. Maya has never been to Borneo, but her brother was killed there, and she is always talking about it. Poor Maya is awaiting punishment as the story ends.

It is sometimes the case that a minor work of literature captures the sense of a time and place better than any major one. *Flesh Gate* must be called a minor work, but one would have trouble thinking of a work that better catches the desperation of those grim years, and the determination to survive. The code may not be of a very elevated sort, but the girls are expected to live by it, one for all and all for one.

So much for the flower of the old pair, flower and willow, courtesan and geisha respectively. The sad decline that was to overtake the willow profession of the geisha was not apparent in the immediate postwar years, although there were shifts and changes. Because of a rumor that Americans would be widely requisitioning to the south of Yanagibashi, the Willow Bridge from which the old and elegant geisha quarter derives its name, the houses farthest to the south moved north, and the whole

Poster for the film Flesh Gate

quarter came to lie north of the bridge. The Shimbashi district was meanwhile moving eastward, though there was no similar threat, and leaving the Ginza district entirely to the dancer and the bar girl. In hindsight it is as if they were leaving the future to these latter types. Aficionados talked, as they had for a century or so, of the decline of the geisha. The new geisha had neither the accomplishments nor the brains of the old one. Doubtless the complaints had, for a century or so, been valid. The problem of the decline of the geisha, not numerically apparent until later decades though adumbrated by these complaints, is essentially a moral one. The old sense of pride and responsibility was declining. The flower and the willow were less and less distinguishable.

Already in October 1945 the police permitted the reopening of bars and cafés. The profusion of such places presents taxonomic difficulties. One is hard put to grasp the distinction between a dance hall and a cabaret. They may have been much the same thing, with the former predominant before the war and the latter after. So it is too with the café and the bar. Ginza led the way. It had the only high-rise building, six storeys of it, that was cabaret from top to bottom. The opening in 1947 was segregated. There was a floor for foreigners, by which was meant Occidentals. Soon after the San Francisco Treaty it became exclusively Japanese, not admitting "foreigners" at all. Even today, this sort of racism (so it must be called) is not uncommon. Many a deal that contributed to the economic miracle, we are told, was arranged amid the din. The big Ginza cabaret came upon bad times toward the middle of the fifties, as the Akasaka district, near the bureaucratic center of the city and still the abode of elegant geisha, began to have cabarets that were tonier and more convenient. The building was sold to a large magazine in 1955.

One does not often hear the word "café" anymore. "Bar," on the other hand, is everywhere, and unquestionably English, while "café" could be French. Connoisseurs may draw distinctions between them. To the person who has not known the prewar cafés except from literary sources, they may seem very much the same. Young women of varying degrees of elegance, depending on the price, provide company in bars even as Kafū's café girls did before the war. The most elegant and expensive ones have continued to be in Ginza.

Then there were the coffeehouses, the *kissaten*, literally tea shops, though this is misleading. In them persons of more limited means could take more moderate and innocent pleasures. They proliferated in the years after the war, and the years after the San Francisco Treaty may be seen as their best ones. There were coffeehouses where a person could watch newsreels for the price of a cup of coffee until he had had his fill of them or concluded a deal of some description, and places where one could do the same to the accompaniment of popular or classical music. There were "chanson" coffeehouses, where some very famous performers got started. The coffee was not cheap, but one could stay all afternoon and evening and not feel rushed. Coffeehouses got bigger and bigger until, in the mid-fifties, they perhaps got too big. In 1955 a six-storey coffeehouse opened in a busy part of Ginza, very near the six-storey cabaret. It had life-size animated female dolls to greet customers at the entrance, and several live bands, and the dominant color was purple. It could accommodate six hundred fifty customers. It was not a success. People seem to have gone once and decided that it would not do for every day.

Also toward the middle of the fifties, coffeehouses started becoming less innocent. The matter of the "late-night coffeehouses" attracted the attention of the media, and in 1956 the prefecture handed down regulations for their governance. Licensing of such places had been lax. Some stayed open all night, offered curtained-off and otherwise sequestered nooks, and were much frequented by prostitutes and petty criminals. They provided inexpensive substitutes for inns. The 1956 regulations forbade such places to take customers under eighteen and overnight customers. There were raids. Intermittent fits of police sternness did not succeed in eradicating them. It may be that this was impossible in so energetically sensual a city; and it may be that the police did not try very hard.

Then there was the "*arbeit* salon," abbreviated *arusaro*. The first word is of course German, and it has since the war indicated part-time nonprofessional work, chiefly by students piecing out their income. The *arbeit* salon was a sort of cross between the coffeehouse and the cabaret. Office girls, girl students, and even housewives with spare time would be companionable waitresses during the daylight hours and dancers in the evening. It was less expensive than the cabaret, and for a time customers found the amateurishness of the hostesses pleasing. The vogue for such places had largely passed by the end of the fifties.

In 1947 an imperial edict (for the Meiji constitution was still in force) did away with publicly recognized prostitution. This in theory meant the end of prostitution. What it meant in practice was that the old public quarters, the Yoshiwara and such, turned private, like Kafū's beloved Tamanoi. The operators of the old houses became "special purveyors of beverages," and the women who wished to could work as waitresses. They were free agents, got a share of the earnings, and could depart whenever they wished. The Yoshiwara women formed a union and set up their own clinics, replacing the ones that had sought to control venereal disease among licensed prostitutes. They were supposed to be over eighteen, but many were not.

The evidence is that the change from public to private prostitution made things worse for them. It had been harder to obtain work in the Yoshiwara than elsewhere, because the Yoshiwara required stronger assurance that women would not run off leaving debts behind them. The private operators had pimps and gangsters to assure that this did not happen.

The events of 1947 have a cyclical look. Much the same sort of things had happened in early Meiji when, out of deference to what were thought to be Western notions of propriety, the ladies of the quarters were liberated. It was to happen again in 1958, when, this time by act of the Diet under the new constitution, prostitution was finally outlawed. The new law was opposed by the union, which organized an anti-anti-prostitution movement.

A clerk for the Supreme Court wrote in 1955 of the 1947 edict (Edict 9) outlawing prostitution, and the reasons for its ineffectiveness: "Many Japanese laws fail to work as their drafters intended them to, and this is because of a failure to investigate, thoroughly and in detail, the manner in which society is likely to react. A reaction sets in, and the law becomes incapable of imposing the controls which are its reason for being. It is like an old sword that has no function except as a family heirloom. The assigned function of the law does not accord with reality. So it was with Edict 9."

In a word, society was not ready. Four decades have passed and it is still not ready. Yet the sword that has become the family heirloom does swing occasionally. It is true of many laws in Japan that they are ignored until it suits someone's convenience to enforce them. Heads then may fall.

Baseball may have replaced Sumō as the national accomplishment, but vogues for other diversions have blazed so violently that they have seemed capable of sending even baseball into eclipse. There blazed the yo-yo, and the Hula-Hoop, which even appeared on the Kabuki stage. Shiga Naoya, one of the dignified elders of Japanese letters, aroused some interest when, in Japanese dress, he had a try at it. When it began, a half-dozen years after the surrender, one might have thought that *pachinko* would blaze and fade. It has not faded. Even today, looking for pursuits that keep people mindlessly happy, one might well come up with a trio— baseball, television, and *pachinko*.

The word is an onomatopoeic one that had several uses before it settled upon the pinball machine. It was a slingshot, a catapult, and a pistol. The vogue for *pachinko* as pinball began in Nagoya, not Tokyo, but Tokyo had more than five thousand pinball parlors by 1952, after which the number fell off somewhat, though the number of machines and customers remained constant. Some were and are very grand, veritable casinos of parlors, blazing with lights and sending forth their metallic clangor to be drowned somewhat in amplified music. The balls fall vertically and not, as in Western prototypes, along an incline, and so speed and noise are increased. With premiums offered for skillful play, *pachinko* became a gambling game. Skillful players were willing to sell their premiums at prices that undercut the retail market. The underworld therefore entered the scene. Petty racketeers would loiter about to buy up premiums.

In 1956 the prefecture, along with other local bodies here and there across the country, took action against automatically fed machines, which greatly increased the speed of play, allowing as many as two hundred balls to flow through a machine in a minute. Automatic feeding led to bigger premiums and a bigger role for the underworld. "Third nationals" have always been prominent in the *pachinko* business, as owners and as buyers of premiums. More than a decade later the automatic feeders were back again, though with the proviso that no more than a hundred balls were to be admitted to a machine per minute. In the mid-fifties upward of one divorce in ten was on grounds of prodigality. *Pachinko* often figured in the matter.

Playing pachinko

Why has *pachinko,* among all the fads that have come, most of them to go again, shown this perdurability? That it is a flight from reality, a refuge from nagging worries, seems almost too obvious. But there are many such refuges, and why the Japanese have taken to *pachinko* as no one else has, save imitators elsewhere in East Asia, is mysterious. Probably there is no simple answer, but it does seem to be the case that the Japanese would prefer to be knocked into happy oblivion by sheer noise than by most things. *Pachinko* is in any event an instance of Japanese originality.

Baseball came back quickly after the war, both the professional kind and the semi-amateur kind that draws large crowds. The Patriotic Baseball Association returned to its old name in October, and returned as well to the corrupt old terminology, largely English. The Kōrakuen Stadium once more took the English for the second element in its name, the professional teams went back to their old names, Giants and Tigers and the like, also in English, and the best pitcher by far, a Russian, reverted to his real name from the Japanese name he had been required to take during the Crisis. The first professional games took place in November, in Tokyo and Osaka. They were anticipated slightly by a resumption of the Keiō-Waseda rivalry. A game between "old boys" of the two schools was held at the Meiji Stadium on November 18. The stadium had been requisitioned by the Americans and was lent for the occasion. The Occupation was all in favor of baseball, which was peaceful and democratic and which it thought would cement relations, not that it had done much toward this end during the preceding decade.

The novelist Funabashi Seiichi was at the Keiō-Waseda game and set down what it meant to him.

The gates having been closed off by the Americans, we had to go in over concrete rubble along the passage between infield and outfield. This was unpleasant, but I suppose inevitable. . . .

In the violence of the war, so recently over, we thought that we would never again see a baseball game. And here we were already, under autumn skies, listening to the crack of the baseball bat. It was like a dream. Today, even now, behind the net, I was witness to a squeeze play, a fielder's choice, a pitcher giving an intentional walk, a two-three count with two out and the bases full.

I wanted to feel my eyes and make sure that they were open. But it was no dream. American officers, viewing a serious university baseball game for the first time, seemed to take a different view of us Japanese.

Funabashi uses the old and revived terminology, laced with English.

The Occupation was sensitive to the argument that baseball would be good for the national morale, and Funabashi's remarks suggest that the view was not groundless. The Kōrakuen Stadium, the main grounds for professional baseball in Tokyo, was in a very dreary state at the end of the war. The scoreboard was a twisted ruin from the April bombings, the stands were artillery and machine-gun emplacements, the field was vegetable patches. Unpromising though it was, the stadium had to remain in Japanese hands if professional baseball was to survive. This was the view of the magnates of the sport, who gathered in emergency session early in November. Their resolve was initially frustrated when the Occupation requisitioned the stadium a few days later. They did not give up, however. They argued eloquently that baseball was necessary to restore the shattered morale of the nation. The requisition order was revoked in February 1946. The first postwar season began in April, at the Kōrakuen and at the Nishinomiya Stadium in the suburbs of Osaka. The morale of Tokyo was not helped by the fact that the Giants did not win the championship that year. An Osaka team did.

The Kōrakuen Stadium was surrounded by potholes in the early years after the war. Then in 1955 it came to be surrounded by an amusement park, the brightest and best in the city, quite overwhelming the Hanaya-shiki, the "Flower Garden" in Asakusa. It had roller coasters, of course, and it had skating rinks and gymnasiums too. There it was that Mishima Yukio took up boxing and body-building to reshape the rather fragile endowments with which he had had to be satisfied in his earlier years.

Professional baseball had enough players and sponsors that by the end of 1949 it had enough teams to split into two leagues, the Central and the Pacific. So 1950 was the first two-league season, and in that autumn occurred the first Japan Series, on the American model. Again Tokyo was disappointed. A Tokyo team won the series, but it was not the idolized Giants. Lefty O'Doul, who had given the team its name, came visiting with his San Francisco Seals in 1949. The first night games were held in 1950, and so the language received a new word, "nighter," in modified English.

Shōriki Matsutarō, the father of Japanese professional baseball, became the first chairman of the baseball commission, overseeing both leagues. The circumstances leading up to the split into rival leagues suggest that, besides the national morale, baseball was interested in money. The Giants and the Osaka Tigers had initially been on opposite sides in the matter of admitting new teams to the old league. But then the possibility arose to haunt the Tigers of having to give up games with the Giants, the most lucrative games, if the two remained at odds. So the Tiger organization switched its vote, the teams were admitted, the split occurred, and Giants and Tigers remained lucratively matched.

The promptness with which the Occupation returned the Kōrakuen may have been responsible for the survival of Shinobazu Pond, a part of Ueno Park, and one of the prettiest spots in the city, especially in mid-summer, when the lotuses are in bloom. A very shallow pond, it was drained after the war and put to the growing of cereals. There was a nasty scandal having to do with the disposition of the cereals thus grown. (A large part of the pond disappeared again in 1968, when excavation for a new subway line accidentally punched a hole in the floor.)

Water came back in 1949, but there was talk of putting the site to uses other than pleasure boating and the growing of ornamental water plants. A suggestion which had strong backing was that it be made into a many-level parking garage—for even in those thin days it was apparent that the number of automobiles and the proportions of the traffic problem would not stop growing. Another suggestion, and one that was very popular with businessmen who thought that Ueno, like Asakusa, might be languishing, was to make the site into a baseball stadium. The faction in favor of filling in the pond and making it useful had a majority on the Taitō Ward council, and the death of the pond seemed a matter of time.

Cultivating the drained Shinobazu Pond,
Ueno, 1946

Opponents lobbied here and lobbied there, and sought to stir up public attention and concern through such devices as fireworks displays. Finally they summoned up their last measure of courage and went to see Shōriki. He listened in a friendly manner and made a call to the president of the league. It seemed, he said, that the locals did not want a baseball stadium. He thought it might be well for the league to take action appropriate to this state of affairs. So the petitioners went to the president. He nodded smiling assent to their every word and suggestion, and thus ended a battle that had lasted three years. We often hear the word "consensus" with regard to Japanese decisions. The incident might offer evidence as to its deeper meaning. One of Shōriki's visitors said that for the first time he really understood the expression "a single call from the crane." The principal Japanese-English dictionary renders the proverbial call of the crane as "a word *ex cathedra*." Shōriki might not have been as ready with his cathedral pronouncement if the Giants and those other teams had not already had the Kōrakuen at their disposal.

The Occupation was not as kind to Sumō as to baseball. The Sumō arena east of the Sumida River, the domed Hall of the National Accomplishment, was requisitioned the day after Christmas 1945. Like several big theaters, it had been used during the closing months of the war to make incendiary balloons. Except for a single tournament permitted by the Occupation in 1946 in the old arena, Sumō spent the next forty years west of the river. Its main grounds through the Edo centuries and most of the first Tokyo century had been in the east.

After several temporary sites during the immediate postwar years, including the Kōrakuen, Sumō settled on the west bank of the Sumida, just below Asakusa, and remained there for more than a third of a century. At the entrances to the temporary arenas was the warning: "Off limits to all Occupation and non-Occupation personnel." Those who spoke the Occupation dialect understood the meaning: that no foreigners, whether with the Occupation or not, were permitted within. As a practical matter this meant persons of European or African extraction, who could be apprehended, chided, and evicted. The reasons probably had to do with overcrowding, the Occupation taking the sensible position that Japanese crowds were quite large and dangerous enough already.

When the old arena was finally returned, on April 1, 1952, the Sumō Association found the cost of rehabilitating it, and especially of removing the huge masses of concrete that had been poured into the pit, prohibitive. In 1958 it was sold to a university, which in 1981 sold it to the prefecture, which in 1983 tore it down. The site is now a parking lot. (The Meiji Stadium and the Imperial Hotel were derequisitioned on that same April Fools' Day of 1952. Important things happen on April Fools' Day in Japan because it is the first day of the fiscal year.) In 1985 Sumō returned east of the river, but not to the old grounds, which were never reoccupied. The new arena lies a short distance to the north of the site of the old one, on the other side of the railway line to Chiba.

Probably all authoritarian regimes have their arbitrary side, and the American Occupation, despite its high democratic rhetoric, was authoritarian. It was not evenhanded in its treatment of the two sports. Perhaps the Sumō Association, being somewhat insular, was not as persuasive as the baseball magnates, and of course it did not have the bond of friendship and mutual admiration which each crack of the bat calls up. Because it was very old and very traditional, it may have been, like judo, associated with the martial arts. Certainly judo did help many a soldier, Japanese and American, offensively and defensively. It is hard to believe that Sumō ever did anyone much good in a martial way.

A dozen years after the war Sumō went through another in its series of crises and challenges on the road to what is known as modernization. It has already been mentioned for its place in the career of the great wrestler Futabayama (see page 122). There were hearings in the National Diet on the obstinate refusal of the sport to become modern. Pressures mounted periodically through the first "modern" century of the sport. The president of the Sumō Association was a man who had held the highest rank and taken the professional name of Tsunenohana, which means something like "Everlasting Flower." (Sumō wrestlers often take flowery names.) The pressures became too much for him. One day in May 1957, in what was then the Hall of the National Accomplishment, on the west bank of the Sumida, he attempted a premodern kind of suicide, by disemboweling.

He recovered, but Futabayama replaced him, and in the autumn was able to push reforms through. The problem was the nagging one of how tickets should be sold. The solution was a compromise, as they all have been. Should they be sold directly through a box office managed by the association, or should they go through the traditional teahouses? Well, some would go the one way, some the other. It was a problem that also nagged Kabuki, but Kabuki reformers were more energetic and resolute.

The teahouses have vanished from Kabuki sales arrangements. The formal status of the teahouses was also changed, but the change made little difference in their operations.

There were other gestures toward modernization or (another magical word) internationalization. Chairs were put into some of the stalls in which spectators had hitherto had to hunker down on straw matting. The pillars were removed from the roof over the wrestling ring. Like Nō actors, Sumō wrestlers had long performed under two roofs, that which closed the larger arena or theater off from the heavens and that which gave the stage or ring the aspect of a smaller, more intimate building. In 1952 the pillars disappeared from the smaller, lower roof of the Hall of the National Accomplishment. It has since been suspended from the higher ceiling. Safety and visibility were given as the reasons. Wrestlers were always injuring themselves against the pillars.

Futabayama retired a few months after the end of the war, and everyone said that his like would not come again. It may be true, and it certainly is true that Sumō as popular entertainment has been put in deep shadows by baseball. Yet Sumō more than survived. It returned from the ashes to have one of the most remarkable periods in its modern history. From about the end of the first postwar decade two fine wrestlers, Wakanohana and Tochinishiki, began their rise to the top, which both of them reached toward the end of the fifties. (Wakanohana is another of those floral names. It means something like "Flower of Youth.") They may not have been the very finest of postwar wrestlers, but each was a worthy rival of the other, and it takes two to make a match. There was excitement in the Tochiwaka period, as the Japanese fondness for acronyms has it, as there has not been since.

The two provided moments of great excitement, and Wakanohana won the important matches. They fought to a draw in 1958, at the end of the tournament as a result of which one or the other was certain to be promoted to Yokozuna, the top Sumō rank. Wakanohana won the rematch. In 1960 both went into the fifteenth and last day of the March tournament undefeated. It was the first time in the history of the sport that two Yokozuna had gone into the final day in that condition. Again Wakanohana won. It is true that the rank has been debased in recent years, so that there may be stars to attract crowds and the television audience. Yet it was a fine moment. The pair provided fine moments as we have not had them since.

*The great Sumō wrestler Futabayama being
arrested. The religious group of which he was an
adherent was suspected of black market activities*

We often hear that the invasion of the old national accomplishment
by "foreigners" did not begin until the late sixties, when a Hawaiian
came into prominence. In fact there had earlier been Koreans. One of
them, whose Sumō name was Rikidōzan, started something, the huge
popularity of professional wrestling, that would probably have started one
day even without him. As in all places, professional wrestling in Japan is
less sport than show. Rikidōzan, a moderately successful and popular
Sumō wrestler, though he did not reach the very top, left Sumō in some
pique at the feudal ways of the Sumō world, and in October 1951 was
the big attraction in the first professional wrestling matches. He became
a great hero. He had come upon something the age and the nation
yearned for, doing brutal things to monstrous persons of European stock.
It was the Bruce Lee act. Rikidōzan was proclaimed "world champion"

in 1954. He had close ties with the underworld. Feeling that he needed bodyguards, he used gangsters. In December 1963 he was stabbed during an altercation in an Akasaka cabaret. The assailant was a member of the gang that controlled the place. Rikidōzan died a week later.

Besides the black market mostly provisioned by Americans, there was another market, blackish, at least, that is not often remarked upon. The Japanese armed forces had huge commissary supplies at the end of the war. Indeed they were almost the only organizations that might have been deemed affluent. The more lethal portions were for the most part turned over to the Americans and destroyed, and those that were less so found their way into the civilian market by various routes. They got many a Japanese company started on its way to recovery, and they also got Akihabara started. The Akihabara electronics market is today among the marvels of Tokyo. At Akihabara, it is said, and we who do not know must take the statement on faith, the electronically sophisticated person can find anything that has been invented.

"Akihabara" is literally "the meadow of the Akiba Shrine." Nagai Kafū insisted to the end that anyone who did not pronounce it "Akiba-gahara" was a barbarian. Alas, the barbarians have quite taken over, for everyone today says Akihabara. A freight yard since Meiji, it became an important passenger station when, after the earthquake, the Yamanote loop line was finally completed. In Meiji the district was known for domestic handiwork, combs and split-toed socks and the like. Between the wars it was known for its bicycle wholesalers. Such of these as remained after the bombings withdrew some distance from the station.

The radio was very important during the last months of the war and the hard times after. Often it was the only bit of advanced technology a family took with it to the air-raid shelter. Radios were the way to know when danger was coming and when it seemed to have passed. The nation might not have surrendered so meekly if it had not been told to turn on all its radios at high noon on August 15, 1945. The radio became a kind of status symbol in the months after the war. To say that one had an all-wave radio was to say that one had a particular pipeline.

So everyone wanted radios, not as easy to come by as the television sets everyone was to want in a few years' time. Akihabara was ideally situated to take advantage of the blackish market in military supplies.

The first to come in were from the Chiba Peninsula, to the east of Tokyo Bay. Akihabara stands at the junction of the Yamanote loop and the line that runs eastward to Chiba and westward to Shinjuku and beyond. The last of the electronics stalls still scattered over the Kanda district moved north when, at the end of 1951, street stalls disappeared.

Electronics emerged dominant at Akihabara for another reason. Penniless young men back from the war were trying to get ahead with their schooling, and Akihabara was near the Kanda-Hongō university district. Many stood on the sidewalk and sold peanuts. A much better way to do it, for those who could, was to build radios. So they combed the Akihabara shops for parts the shopkeepers themselves often did not know the functions of, and built.

Thus began the Akihabara market, assuredly a wonder. Many of the makeshift devices and institutions of the postwar confusion have gone away, and some have stayed and prospered. Chiyoda Ward still has the largest volume among the twenty-three of retail sales in electronics equipment. It is peculiar that that place of big-time managers should lead in retail sales of anything at all, but we must remember that Chiyoda is a mating of two very unlike wards, Kōjimachi, where the managers are, and Kanda, a place of students, universities, and small enterprises.

On April 28, 1952, the great actor Kichiemon led the audience at the Kabukiza in three cheers. It was the day on which the Occupation ended and the San Francisco treaties—the peace treaty and the Japanese-American Security Treaty—went into effect. The undoing of the Occupation, the reassembling of the old combines and the like, is a long and complex story, and of course not limited to Tokyo. Neither is the story of what happened to "summertime." This last is an instance, however, of an American miscalculation that could be and was swiftly repaired. The expression is in English, and it signifies daylight-saving time, which was imposed by the Americans in April 1948 and abolished just four years later, in the month in which the treaties went into effect. It was something American that could be readily disavowed, though more rational arguments were offered. Better to have an innocent and healthy extra hour in the morning, went one of them, than an extra hour in the evening to waste on drinking and mah-jongg. Just a year later the American practice of giving women's names to typhoons was discontinued.

Since then they have had only numbers. Kitty, which struck in the autumn of 1947, did more damage to Tokyo than any other typhoon in all the years since the war.

Though he cannot have intended them so, Kichiemon's three cheers might have been taken to announce the beginning of the radical years. Those who read only the newspapers during the Occupation years cannot have been prepared for what happened immediately afterward. The newspapers had suggested little except delight with the Americans and their Occupation and ways, and a resolve to move upward into the light, equal partners (in an expression much favored by a later ambassador) with the United States. Those who went occasionally to the university campuses and saw what was on the student posters may have been vaguely aware that another current was waiting to burst forth.

It did, explosively, on the third day of Japanese independence. May Day had been among the annual festivals of Taishō democracy. Laborers and progressive thinkers got out and marched. With an estimated half-million people in attendance, the observance was resumed in 1946. The seventeenth May Day rally, after the loss of a decade's worth to the Crisis, was held in the palace plaza. In succeeding years that was the place for it. Then, in 1951, the last year in which the Occupation had a say in the matter, the use of the plaza was banned. This happened again in 1952.

Progressives and laborers assembled in the Meiji Gardens. After a big rally there they set forth on marches over five approved routes. The march that was supposed to end at Hibiya Park was seized with an urge to go on to the plaza, just across the street. Erstwhile headquarters of the Occupation lay across another street from the plaza, and a few paces up from the intersection between the two. So General MacArthur, if he had been there, would have had among the best views in town of what happened. The marchers crossed the street and poured into the plaza, and there were met by the police, who used truncheons, tear gas, and even pistols. As they retreated back across the street the demonstrators overturned and set fire to a few American automobiles. A large proportion of the automobiles in the city in those days were American, and they still were allowed to park along main streets.

Initial announcements had one young man killed, by pistol fire. Actually two were killed. More than a hundred, more of them policemen than demonstrators, were seriously injured. More than a hundred dem-

Riots in the palace plaza, May Day 1952

onstrators were arrested on the spot, and eventually more than a thousand. Of the two hundred or so brought to trial, more than half were declared innocent by the Tokyo District Court—in 1970. Not quite eighteen years had passed. Justice grinds more slowly in Japan than in most places that have it. In 1972 the Tokyo Higher Court declared most of the convicted ones innocent. Fewer than twenty sentences were served.

Such clear-eyed witnesses as the novelist Umezaki Haruo, not of strongly radical inclinations, put the blame on the police. The first acts of violence, he said, were on their side. It may be true. The police, not the well-oiled machine they are today for containing such manifestations, may well have been overzealous. Whatever the rights and wrongs, May Day 1952 stands symbolically at the beginning of a remarkable period. Those who controlled the media seemed intent upon making the nation accept a most simpleminded orthodoxy. Every unpleasant question had a simple answer: blame it on capitalism and imperialism, and join the peaceful socialist force. Many an explanation has been given for the phenomenon, but the sudden clap of pacifist, socialist thunder after the quiet of the Occupation was certainly very startling.

The rioters of 1952 still had another dozen years to go with their court travails when it all began to quiet down. In 1960 the attempt to prevent revision of the Security Treaty failed, and showed that the media were not after all omnipotent and that the movement may have been more sound than substance. There followed fragmentation and (as in the thirties) apostasy, and the golden radical years did not return. Today they are (as the saying has it) a dream within a dream. They were remarkable while they lasted, and Tokyo was where the noise was made. Having a demonstration in Osaka or Nagoya would have been like marching on the wrong Washington.

There had been numerous instances under the Occupation of violence with political origins. In 1946 there was an occurrence the likes of which had not often, perhaps never, been heard of in earlier Japanese history, a demonstration not against evil, corrupt ministers surrounding the emperor but against the emperor himself. In the spring of 1946 a "give us rice" rally in the western part of the city was turned into a march upon the palace by the communist firebrand Nosaka Sanzō, recently back from China. Only a direct confrontation with the emperor would serve, he said. The rally marched upon the palace and breached one of the palace gates before it was dispersed. A demand was presented: that the contents of the royal pantry immediately be communized. "I have plenty to eat. You people can starve," said one placard. The first-person pronoun was the sacred *chin* (see the ribaldry on page 172), reserved for the emperor alone. A result was arraignment for lèse-majesté, the last before that crime ceased to exist. The Occupation was less sure thereafter that communist agitation was a welcome part of the new democracy.

A prominent instance of possible political violence remains a mystery. Was the violence wrought by the victim upon himself, or was it at the hands of others? We do not know. In the spring of 1949 the National Railways began a drastic personnel retrenchment. On July 4 the railway offices announced plans to dismiss forty thousand workers. The president, Shimoyama Sadanori, was last definitely seen alive on the morning of July 5, near the main Mitsukoshi department store in Nihombashi. The next morning his dismembered body was found on a track of his own National Railways in the northeastern part of the city. The finding of the official autopsy was that he was dead before being run over, but there was expert opinion to the contrary, holding that he had placed himself upon the tracks and been killed by a train. There were also those who averred that someone very like him had been seen near the fatal spot on the night of July 5. No arrests were made. If Shimoyama was indeed murdered, then his murderers were most likely radical unionists. They were much inflamed in those days, both because of the layoffs and because of a hint from General MacArthur on that same July 4 that the Communist Party might be outlawed.

Through the month of July there were literally thousands of instances of sabotage and obstruction throughout the National Railways system. The most famous incident occurred not in Tokyo but at Matsukawa in Fukushima Prefecture, on the main line of the National Railways to the far north. Three train crewmen died on August 17 in a derailment. The union members taxed with the act were not finally acquitted until 1963. Some weeks earlier there had been a bloodier though less celebrated incident at Mitaka, in the western suburbs of Tokyo. On July 15 seven railway cars ran loose down a sloping track from the Mitaka railway yards. They crashed into a house, killing six people. The suspicion was strong that the runaway was not accidental. Two union men were arrested and one was sentenced to death. The sentence was never carried out. He died in prison.

If the Matsukawa defendants were guilty (they were acquitted for want of evidence) and if Shimoyama was murdered, then the most likely explanation for all three incidents is union unrest. The thought that Japan once had militant unionism is like a faint echo from a legendary past; but indeed there was such a time. A strike against the *Yomiuri Shimbun* in 1945 brought a brief period of democratization, by which is meant control of editorial policy by the labor unions. General MacArthur interdicted plans for a general strike in 1947. Concerning the most celebrated instances of violence, the railway cases, there have been theories that someone else did everything, some strongly anti-union entity wishing to make it *seem* that the unions were responsible. The Occupation is prominent among the suspects. In the Shimoyama instance, it is said that a peculiar grease used by Americans in ministering to their weaponry was found on the dead man's shirt.

The Mitsukoshi department store figured peripherally in the Shimoyama incident, possibly a product of labor strife, and it had some strife of its own which was rather amusing and showed how quickly the militancy was subsiding. This occurred during the year-end rush of 1951. A

The train wreck at Mitaka, 1949

popular saying resulted: "You can find anything at Mitsukoshi, even a strike." Management, with the help of nonunion and part-time clerks, was prepared to open the store on the morning of December 18, but some two thousand pickets from the Mitsukoshi union and others sealed the entrances. They were joined by thirty concerned clergymen from the aggressive Nichiren sect, who marched up and down banging on ritual drums. The police informed the pickets that they would not be allowed to interfere with business, and that was that. By noon customers were pouring in.

A history of labor strife in Tokyo over the past third of a century would surely be among the shortest histories ever written. It has consisted mainly of ceremonial stoppages of which the public is informed in advance. They can be fun. Office workers who know that they cannot get back to the suburbs disport themselves later than usual and sleep in the city.

. . .

The hardships of the first winter after the war caused the death in March 1946 of the eminent Kabuki actor Kataoka Nizaemon. He was the twelfth in a line of actors bearing that name, its origins in Kyoto in the seventeenth century. He was murdered, along with four members of his family. The murderer was a young man who lived with the family. His complaint was that he was cheated on rations, given less to eat than members of the family. Having been scolded by Nizaemon's wife for stealing food, he seized an ax with the intention of punishing only her, and was surprised into attacking the rest of the family.

(In the case of the other postwar Kabuki actor of eminence to die in extraordinary circumstances, the circumstances were much more luxurious. The seventh Bandō Mitsugorō died of *fugu* poisoning in 1975. Certain parts of the *fugu*—blowfish—are poisonous. Much prized by gourmets, it is safe when prepared by professionals. Real gourmets, however, approach close to the poisonous parts and, it is said, experience a delightful tingling of the palate. Mitsugorō seems to have approached too close.)

Some of the crimes and misdemeanors of the postwar years, though they produced pains and losses, seem in retrospect chiefly amusing. On the evening of November 22, 1948, the chief of the prefectural police, off having a look at Ueno Park, a most disorderly place, was beaten up by a male prostitute. The following month the park was declared closed at night to everyone but policemen. In September 1950 a teenage chauffeur for Nihon University made off with a large sum of money, stolen from a university functionary, and also with the daughter of a university professor. The two were apprehended in bed. In the two days between their absconding and their capture they had spent some twenty-five times the beginning monthly salary of an office worker. As the police entered the room they had taken, the boy sat up in bed and said, in English, "Oh, mistake." He never explained himself, and there were several theories as to what he meant. Probably he wanted the officers to think, back in those Occupation days, that he was an American. "Oh, mistake" was among the new expressions that went the rounds that year, along with "nighter" signifying an after-dark baseball game.

Some crimes were dreadful. A man named Kodaira took advantage of the postwar hardships to rape and murder women, ten of them. He would lure them to secluded spots with promises of food and work, and there do it. The body of the last victim was found in Shiba Park on the heights behind the Tokugawa tombs, where Tokyo Tower was later to go up (see page 251). He was apprehended in August 1946. Then there was what is known, with black irony, as the Kotobuki affair. *Kotobuki* means something like "good luck." In this instance it was the name of a lying-in hospital, in what was before 1947 Ushigome Ward, to the west of the palace. In January 1948 the police apprehended an automobile taking a dead infant from the hospital. Investigation revealed that the man and wife who ran the hospital had since 1945 been taking in unwanted infants for money. They had disposed of more than a hundred in several ways. Some had been allowed to die of exposure and pneumonia, some had starved to death. The largest number had been quietly suffocated.

There was a young man named Yamazaki who was eminently representative of nihilistic postwar youth. He was a member of the elite, a student at Tokyo University. He set up a usury business. It failed, and he committed suicide, in November 1949. Life is an empty play, he said, and death is nothing at all. The affair caught the fancy of Mishima Yukio, who a few months later began serialization of the novel *The Green Years (Ao no Jidai)*, based on Yamazaki's brief career.

It may be that the crime most celebrated the nation over during those postwar years was the Matsukawa derailment mentioned above. That is because it aroused intense political passions, and won the services of an eminent writer, Hirotsu Kazuo, who thought of himself as a Japanese Emile Zola and made it his mission to establish the innocence of the defendants. Probably the most celebrated Tokyo crime was the Imperial Bank robbery. (The Imperial, or Teikoku, subsequently reverted to its earlier name, the Mitsui Bank.) On the afternoon of January 26, 1948, just at closing time, a man of perhaps fifty wearing what seemed to be an official armband entered the branch of the bank at Shiinamachi, on the Seibu Ikebukuro line a short distance west of Ikebukuro. He said that he had come to administer a dysentery preventative and that all the employees must drink it. They did, all sixteen of them, and twelve died. What they had drunk was potassium cyanide. He too had a drink of the liquid, by way of demonstration, but seems to have drunk only from the layer of water on top. He made off with a considerable sum of money and a check.

A painter named Hirasawa was sentenced to death for the crime. The sentence was confirmed by the Supreme Court in 1955, and numerous petitions to reopen the case were dismissed. The sentence was never reversed, nor was it carried out. In 1985 Hirasawa was returned to Tokyo from Sendai Prison, where capital punishments are carried out for Tokyo criminals. He died in a prison hospital in 1987, at the age of ninety-five. He had been imprisoned for almost forty years, and had lived with the death sentence for almost a third of a century. All that was required to carry it out was the seal and signature of the minister of justice, and no minister ever signed and sealed. Since 557 executions did occur between 1947 and 1985, believers in his innocence have found support for their position. There had been more than thirty justice ministers during the more than thirty years between Hirasawa's final conviction and his death. Every one of those many ministers—who replaced each other at a dizzying rate so that all manner of politicians might have their time— apparently had doubts about his guilt.

The devices which led to Hirasawa's arrest, on the island of Hokkaido in August 1948, were certainly very ingenious. There had earlier been two similar incidents, one late in 1947 at a bank in the southern part of Tokyo, one a few days before the Imperial affair at a bank very near its Shiinamachi branch. Both of the latter banks were within walking distance of Hirasawa's residence. In both of the earlier cases a man of great assurance had said that, by way of disease prevention, the bank employees must drink of the liquid he offered. He was thwarted in both instances. The similarity among the three led the police to suspect the same culprit, and their attention was drawn to the name cards he (if indeed it was a single person) had left at the two earlier banks. One of them bore a fictitious name, but the other bore the unusual name of a physician living in Sendai.

Certain peculiarities in printing, having to do with the unusual name, established that the card indeed belonged to the physician. So he was set to the task of remembering the people he had exchanged cards with. Among those he remembered was Hirasawa. The two had met and exchanged cards in 1947, on the ferry from Hakodate on Hokkaido to Aomori. Hirasawa was singled out as the most suspicious, and arrested. It was all very ingenious, but it did not, in itself, prove much of anything.

Interrogation was intense. Initially it revealed nothing about the Imperial affair, but it did seem to reveal something else of interest. As the time approached for Hirasawa's mandatory release, evidence emerged that he might be guilty of fraud. At yet another bank he had, or so it was suspected, taken advantage of loose procedures and made off with a sum of money intended for another customer. So he was arraigned for fraud, and the interrogation continued. He signed a confession in the Imperial Bank matter. He later retracted it. Most of it was composed by the detectives, he said, and mental torture caused him to sign. All three of the courts that imposed or upheld the death sentence accepted the validity of the confession.

It was not quite the only evidence, though we are often told it was. A large amount of money that went into Hirasawa's bank account shortly after the crime was never adequately explained. His statement that it was in payment for a work of pornography which someone had commissioned him to do was not a part of the sworn testimony and is not convincing. Several of the experts summoned, though not all of them, said that the endorsement on the check, which was cashed on the day after the murders, was in Hirasawa's hand. Like the handwriting experts, the four Imperial Bank survivors were not in agreement. Neither were the employees of the other two banks. Some were certain that the criminal, or the would-be criminal, was Hirasawa, some were not.

Many a court would in these circumstances have held that there was reasonable doubt as to his guilt; and many a person has held that a third of a century awaiting the seal and signature of one of those justice ministers constitutes unusual and inhuman punishment.

It was a fascinating case, and not the least fascinating element is the

Detectives inside the Imperial Bank after the robbery

air that hangs over it of postwar confusion and deprivation. Even the bank in which the crime occurred has a make-do look about it, not at all a Mitsui look. To judge from photographs, it was a quite ordinary dwelling house made to do until something more banklike could be put up. One cannot imagine the cool clerks and branch managers in the glossy banks of our day accepting an unidentified drink from a stranger; but epidemics raged in those years, and the faculty called common sense had come unmoored.

Another line of investigation proceeded parallel to that of the name card. It is much favored by the radical left because it brings in the possibility of American skulduggery. The police thought it possible that the criminal was skilled in the use of chemical poisons. The biggest pool of expertise was in the Japanese army, and particularly a chemical-warfare unit once active in Manchuria. This second investigation was frustrated by the Americans, its supporters aver, because they took the unit under their protection. The Korean War broke out a few weeks before the first Hirasawa conviction was handed down, and, with a mind to launch chemical warfare against the Koreans, the Americans wished to use Japanese skills to reinforce their own inadequate ones. Rumors of chemical warfare were rife in those days. One can say for the case that it might possibly be true, but that the evidence is flimsier than that which led to Hirasawa's conviction.

The child of Edo, who had nothing to compare his city with except the cities of the Kansai, which were not worth the time of day, may not have noticed something that early foreign visitors were quick to discern. They thought the city a cluster of villages. They were right in the sense that it was a scattered city with more than one center. What they remarked upon has been among the unchanging elements in a city of violent change. The city has gone on having not one "downtown" but several. It did not have to start decentralizing when decentralization came into vogue among planners. The process was already well advanced.

In the fifties we started hearing the word *fukutoshin*. It is literally "secondary heart of the city," and it might also be rendered "subcenter" or "satellite city." In 1960 it entered specifically into the official plans of a city that has never (and it is among the pleasures of the place) really done much effective planning. A commission presented and the prefectural council approved a plan that had specific reference to Shinjuku, Shibuya, and Ikebukuro. They were to be the first *fukutoshin*, dispersing the oppressive strength of the traditional center. The plan and the concept are notable for their westerly inclination, which is realistic, that having been the inclination of the city ever since it became Tokyo.

Shinjuku was well ahead of the other two in those days, and it is well ahead now, the only one among them that can seriously challenge the old Ginza-Nihombashi-Marunouchi center. How successful the challenge has been is a matter that must be treated later. Shinjuku grew up at the point where one of the main highways out of the city, that to the province of Kai, crossed the railroad which in 1885 commenced service from Shinagawa through the western suburbs to a point near the northern prefectural boundary. The inland road to the Kansai had in premodern times departed the city in a northwesterly direction, through Itabashi. The railroad that was to replace it began service as far as Hachiōji in 1904. It headed uncompromisingly westward from Shinjuku. Itabashi languished. Already in the early decades of this century two important private commuter lines, one of them the Odawara Express of lyric fame (see page 70), terminated in Shinjuku. Their commuter clientele fell into the habit of taking a few cups and other pleasures at Shinjuku before resuming the outward passage. Shinjuku was the place in the western suburbs that drew the biggest crowds.

In the years when the word *fukutoshin* was gaining currency, Shinjuku saw the possibility of widening its lead yet further. Indeed the possibility was becoming a certainty that it would in the near future have a big piece of land to develop. The Yodobashi Reservoir (Yodobashi was the name of one of the three wards which in 1947 were amalgamated to form Shinjuku Ward) covered a tract of more than eighty acres just to the west of the Shinjuku Nishiguchi, the "Westmouth" to Shinjuku Station. From the Taishō Period there had been talk of moving the reservoir farther west. The move actually took place in 1965, and so the story of what was done with the land can be left to later.

The Westmouth was in those years the neglected, backward one. It was not without its places for reveling. We have seen that immediately after the war underworld gangs opened markets at all three of the mouths, west, south, and east. Traces of that at Westmouth yet survive, in the cluster of one- and two-storey "barracks" known popularly and affectionately as Piss Alley (Shomben Yokochō). It would much prefer that the public call it Chicken Alley, for skewered chicken is, along with alcohol, the commodity it chiefly purveys, but the public does not oblige. Piss Alley it is and will be so long as it survives. It may not smell very good, but it is an object of great nostalgia for those who wish that the city had not rebuilt itself quite so thoroughly in the four decades since the war.

A more delicate vestige remains at Southmouth. A few paces east of the south entrance to the station, in against the revetment where the broad, constantly jammed successor to the old Kai highway crosses the railroad tracks, is a cluster of "barracks," shabby wooden buildings with that postwar look about them. They were once drinking places. The Construction Ministry has announced its intention to make the tract a decorative public plaza. Something of the sort is probably needed, for the pedestrian crowds at rush hours spill over onto the highway; but the owners of the buildings, or some of them, will have nothing of it. They say that the ministry does not own the land and has no right to expel them, even though it has effectively rendered most of the buildings derelict. They squatted on land that belonged to the National Railways and now belongs, in their view, to the successor company, and they them-

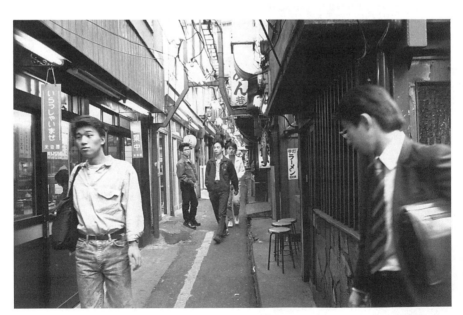

Piss Alley, Shinjuku

selves claim obscure rights. A court battle is in prospect. Rights are clearer in the Westmouth case. If the decorative plaza ever comes to be, it is not likely to be remotely as interesting as the vestige. In a corner of the tract is a public latrine less than ten feet square. The value of the land is estimated at not far from two million dollars at the current exchange rate. Piss Alley has no latrines. That is why it is that.

Westmouth and Southmouth were not without their reveling places, then, but Eastmouth was the really bustling part of Shinjuku. The center of the bustle had shifted in the modern century. Shinjuku, like the others of the "mouths" on the main highways out of the city, had its licensed quarter. It lay just to the north of what is now the Shinjuku Royal Garden. The railway station, somewhat to the west, pulled shopping and other pleasures toward it, and in the interwar years the busiest part of Shinjuku, and the center of its café culture, was a short distance east of the station, where two roads to the west forked. With its big department stores, this is still the part of Shinjuku where women have the most fun shopping. Men came to have places farther north.

There was what was first called the Hanasono Block, from the name of the shrine against which it nestled, and then the Golden Block, the first word in English. It has never been very golden. With the clearing away of black markets from the eastern approaches to the station, a snug little pocket between shrine and trolley line became jammed with tiny drinking places, accommodating no more than a dozen customers and occupying a space no more than perhaps that many feet square. Up a very steep flight of stairs would be space for more private drinking and other activities. The district began calling itself the Golden Block from about the time of the Olympics. Even with the disappearance of the trolley line, it remained a little apart from and a little different from the much brighter and larger district that grew up to the west, and it has shown great powers of survival. The indications are that it will not survive much longer. The Seibu enterprises are buying it up, and a warren of little two-storey wooden buildings is not in the Seibu class.

The story of how that brighter, larger district came to be is a most remarkable one of industry and enterprise, with a strong admixture of luck as well. Kabukichō may today be—the matter is arguable—the liveliest part of the city. It is without doubt the leading center in the city and quite probably the land for what is called "the sex industry." The industry is not quite as open, perhaps, as in Times Square, but it is more varied. There can be few proclivities to which Kabukichō does not minister. And until 1948 the name Kabukichō, much less the fact, did not exist.

Until it was reduced to cinders in 1945, the district was a nondescript one of small shops and dwellings. Noting the regularity and apparent inevitability with which the paths of the ladies of the night, as they plied their trade in the aftermath of the war, led through the district, a man named Suzuki had a dream. He had in his youth been a cook in the British and American embassies, apparently a good one. (His teacher was a man who later became head chef at the Imperial hotel.) At the end of the war he was in the food-processing business and the head of the neighborhood association of a district to the north of Shinjuku Station. His dream was that the district might be made over into a cultural center, with a variety of theaters, including a Kabuki one. It did certainly become a center, and it does have one big theater and numbers of lesser ones, but "cultural" might not be the word that best characterizes it. "Raunchy" might do better.

Suzuki and others busied themselves, and their labors seem to have been enormous, with such matters as providing utilities for and assigning lands to the owners of establishments, mostly eating and drinking ones, that would cater to the theater crowds. A new name was needed, for easy reference, because the district with which the planners were concerned extended over two of the older districts in what from 1947 was Shinjuku Ward. This gave it a divided and scattered look, when identity and integrity were required. In elaborate ceremonies in 1948, attended by such dignitaries as the first elected governor of the prefecture, it became Kabukichō.

The new name does undeniably have style, and it was expected to have a certain talismanic function as well. It was to break a jinx regarding Kabuki, to refute the old notion that Kabuki was an art form particular to and inseparable from the old Low City. Like a wildflower, it could survive only on its native grounds. As a matter of fact Shinjuku Ward had had instances supporting the generalization. A theater in the old Yotsuya Ward had what historians call second-rate Kabuki from 1917. It also had the usual history of burnings and rebuildings, and a brief period of prosperity just after the earthquake, when it was back in business before any of the Low City theaters could be. It declined as they returned and had its last Kabuki in 1937, although it survived in other capacities, to be destroyed just after the war as unsafe. A Shinjuku theater called the Shinkabukiza, the New Kabuki Theater, opened in 1929. The name having changed to Shinjuku Daiichi Gekijō, or First Shinjuku Theater, it gradually became less a place for Kabuki than for concerts, reviews, and theatrical performances of a more modern and exotic sort: For a brief period after the Second World War, when so many of the Low City theaters were gutted shells, it was again among the main places for Kabuki. It does not survive.

Possibly, depending on definitions, the jinx has been broken by the National Theater, which stands on one of the most awesome expanses of land in the High City, just across the moat from the palace. It was not, in any event, broken by Kabukichō, which never got its Kabuki theater. The first movie theater opened in 1948 and closed a decade later. It was popular with the chic left, whose great decade its one decade approximately coincided with. Kabukichō was becoming all the time more strategic, and did not really need Kabuki. The Shinjuku line of the metropolitan trolley system was rerouted in 1949 so that its Shinjuku terminus was at the southern edge of the district. The Seibu railways extended one of their lines to Shinjuku in 1952. The Shinjuku terminus was at the western edge of Kabukichō.

There was an exposition. When in doubt have an exposition: this seems to be a part of Japanese folk wisdom. In the Meiji Period there was a series of national expositions, most of them at Ueno, designed to rally the nation in the endeavor to catch up with the world. They do seem to have had an enlivening effect. Suzuki decided that Kabukichō would have one. It was held at three sites in the spring and early summer of 1950. It was a complete disaster—or would have been if good luck had not come upon the scene at this point. The fact that it was such a fiasco attracted attention, and Kabukichō was, so to speak, on the map. In 1951 Suzuki was able to arrange a land transaction between the largest landowner in the district and a movie company. It included the site of the biggest and most famous of Kabukichō theaters, the Koma Stadium. The Koma opened as a movie house in 1956, and a year later changed over to stage. The most popular entertainers in the land, such as Enoken, performed there.

Kabukichō emerged as the most bustling part of Shinjuku. The district of the interwar café bustle did not languish, but it was rather lost in the glare of Kabukichō. The pleasure quarter that was attached to the old post station did well in the years just after the war. The count of its ladies was in 1951 ten times what it had been at the end of the war. Some of the houses modernized themselves by becoming joint-stock companies and by arranging exchanges with the Yoshiwara, the most venerable of the licensed pleasure quarters. The advantage of this arrangement was that a girl could have more than one debut, and debuts were highly profitable. The two quarters had the most expensive brothels in the city.

With the second postwar outlawing of prostitution in sight, that of 1958, many a little drinking place emerged as a cover for the old business. By the time Shinjuku Ward had been in existence long enough to publish a history of its first thirty years, almost a half million people were partaking of Kabukichō each day. As many as 80 percent of them were under thirty. It is the young crowds that give a bustling place its life and its future, and so Kabukichō was doing well.

But if Kawabata thought that Asakusa had nothing really first-rate to offer, what would he have said of Kabukichō? Being of the crowd which commuted south from Ginza rather than that which commuted west from Shinjuku, he does not seem to have paid much attention. The Koma did offer performances of some quality, but, except for first-run movie houses, it was the only place all up and down Eastmouth that can have been said to do so. Shinjuku has in this respect never been a rival of Ginza. Nor does it offer the variety of stage performances that interwar Asakusa did. Eastmouth is essentially a purveyor of drink and sex. It has been increasingly that ever since it became Kabukichō. One does not wish to sound censorious, for it is all very interesting and amusing; but one would have liked to have, while it was still possible, a comparison of Eastmouth and Asakusa from Kawabata.

If Suzuki and the others who worked so hard to get Kabukichō going had a sense of where it would go, they did not say so. Perhaps those initial observations about the habits of the ladies of the night pointed in an inevitable direction.

Shibuya, a glance at a map may inform one, is so like Shinjuku that its failure to grow as rapidly, though it grew quite rapidly enough, may seem puzzling. Like Shinjuku it grew around a point where a road out of the city crossed the first railway line through the western suburbs. The highway, to a sacred mountain in the Kantō hinterlands, was not, however, as important as the two that forked at Shinjuku. Nor did Shibuya, like Shinjuku, stand at a crossroads of the National Railways. Private railway systems were slower to take shape. Shibuya had its subway line into the heart of the city a quarter of a century before Shinjuku did, but Shinjuku had its railway connection decades before Shibuya had its subway.

Perhaps the most important difference is in the lay of the land. Both Shinjuku and Ikebukuro are on tablelands and look as if they could sprint off in any direction. Shibuya is hemmed in by hills which have had a confining effect.

When, in 1883, the forerunner of Aoyama Gakuin University moved to the campus it still occupies, there was not much below it in the Shibuya valley. In those days the city limits more than encompassed the city, and the new Aoyama Gakuin, founded by missionaries in the Tsukiji foreign settlement, was in open countryside. The first Shibuya Station, a private one later nationalized, opened in 1885. It was with the Sino-Japanese War and the Russo-Japanese War, and especially the latter, that Shibuya began to turn into something more than a sleepy country village. Army training grounds lay in the countryside beyond. The road that crossed the railway tracks at Shibuya was much used by military conveyances. So the army is back at the beginning of all the bustle, today so little martial and spartan. As with Shinjuku, rapid growth came after the earthquake. What in 1932 became Shibuya Ward had a far larger population than that legally required for incorporation as a city.

As the Olympics drew near, it came to seem that Shibuya would have a large, open tract of land with which to do as Shinjuku did with its reservoir. A place called Washington Heights was returned to the Japanese in time for them to make it over into the athletes' village. It lay just north of Shibuya and adjacent to the Meiji Shrine. The American Occupation had used the old Yoyogi parade grounds for family housing and called them Washington Heights. The Olympics past, the land was put to other use, but it never did for Shibuya quite what the Westmouth reservoir did for Shinjuku. The story of what it did do may be left for later.

Shibuya has continued to lag behind Shinjuku. Until the subway went through to Shimbashi in 1939 it had no direct link with the heart of the city, and until 1932 only one private railway ran from Shibuya into the suburbs. That one is today a minor part of the Tōkyū system that dominates the district. Shibuya has until recently had more the look of a one company town, if town it may for convenience be called, than Shinjuku. It had that look even more during and immediately after the war. The two private railway systems were amalgamated in 1942. In 1948 they resumed independent operations.

So Shibuya would *seem* smaller even if it were not. In fact it is. The count of persons passing through the complex of mass-transit stations is much smaller than that for Shinjuku. One crucial indicator, however, suggests that Shinjuku may not always be dominant among the *fukutoshin*. The very young today prefer Shibuya, and vaguely distrust Shinjuku. It is dirty and it has gangsters. Someone might come up and accost a young gentleman, or sell a young lady into prostitution.

Of the thriving centers along the western arc of the Yamanote loop, Ikebukuro seems the accidental one. Highways from Edo passed through Shinjuku and Shibuya, and any speculator would have seen them as promising places when railway stations went up beside the roads. It was not so with Ikebukuro, which was boggy, as the name, Lake Hollow, suggests. No significant road led through it, though a very important one, the inland road to Kyoto, along which many a noble procession made its way during the Tokugawa years, passed through Sugamo, just to the east, and the Itabashi way station, where travelers could rest and indulge themselves.

If the development of the railway system had been different, our speculator might have looked to Sugamo or Itabashi as the place to plunge. The first railway station in the district was put at Mejiro, to the south of Ikebukuro, on the line that passed through Shibuya and Shinjuku and continued northward past Ikebukuro. Had the loop line gone through before the north-south one, Sugamo would have been the obvious place for the germination of a *fukutoshin*, but it was not until 1903 that the loop began its turn to the east. The original plan was for the two lines to fork at Mejiro. Not as alert as it might have been to the speculative possibilities which this proposal opened, the local populace opposed it vehemently. So the forking was placed at Ikebukuro, too insignificant for a local clamor to be heard, and a station was built there, and so began the third of the *fukutoshin*.

It was slower to develop than the other two. Until a subway line went through to Tokyo Central Station in 1956, there was no direct and rapid transportation to the center of the city, and Ikebukuro had no surface link until a freeway went through in 1969. One had to wander back and forth on this and that street or take the roundabout sweep of the Yamanote if one wished to get to Ikebukuro from Ginza or Marunouchi.

Ikebukuro, like Shibuya, acquired a missionary school, but much later, when rapid urban growth was beginning. St. Paul's or Rikkyō, another product of Tsukiji, moved there at about the time of the earthquake. Also like Shibuya, it has been dominated by a single railway company. In 1915 what is now the Seibu Railway opened a line from Ikebukuro to a town in Saitama Prefecture. It has greatly expanded, and now goes into Shinjuku as well as Ikebukuro.

Inevitably, the Seibu went into the department-store business, though it was late in doing so. Ikebukuro was the natural place (not that there was anything very natural about the growth of Ikebukuro) for it to choose. A Musashino Food Company began business just before the outbreak of the Pacific War. It became the Musashino department store, and in 1949 the Seibu. Musashino was the original name of the Seibu. It means Musashi Plain, Musashi being the province in which Edo was situated. Seibu, more modestly, is Western Musashi.

The Seibu enterprises, one of which is headed by the man named by *Forbes* magazine in 1987 as the richest nonroyal person in the world, are very big all over the city, and they loom over Ikebukuro. One may complain in both Shinjuku and Ikebukuro about the impediment which the railroads and their stations present, requiring a detour for anyone who wishes to go from Westmouth to Eastmouth or the reverse; but in the case of Ikebukuro one's complaints might better be directed at the Seibu department store, which blocks off the eastern approaches to the district like the Kremlin or the Berlin Wall.

The stroller through the Ikebukuro Eastmouth has the Seibu department store to the west of him, and until 1971 there was an even more darkly glowering fortress to the east. Had Sugamo Prison been built in later years it might better have been called Ikebukuro Prison, for it was much nearer Ikebukuro Station than Sugamo Station. The reason for the name is that the institution dates back to a time when Ikebukuro was but an inconspicuous part of the rural expanse called Sugamo. Several prisons occupied the site from 1895. The last of them, the Tokyo Deten-tion Center (Tokyo Kōchijō), was put up in 1937. It replaced the Ichigaya Prison, where such celebrated Meiji criminals as the murderess Taka-hashi O-den were beheaded. The last persons to be executed at Sugamo were seven Class A war criminals, including the wartime prime minister, Tōjō Hideki, who were hanged two days before Christmas in 1948.

The prison was returned to the Japanese in 1958, and seemed pre-pared to go about its old business. Opposition was intense, and powerful, having commerce behind it. Ikebukuro was by then emerging as one of the great shopping and entertainment centers along the Yamanote. A person could look right down on the prison grounds from the Seibu or the Mitsukoshi, which has a branch at the Ikebukuro Eastmouth. This was altogether too grim a prospect, and the prison was torn down in 1971. The site resembling all that newly opened space which Shinjuku had at its Westmouth, the debate was intense as to what should be done with it. Some favored recreation, some favored commerce, and the latter won. The highest building in the city, if Tokyo Tower (see page 251) be excluded as not quite a building, now occupies the site.

Sugamo Prison

. . .

All three of the *fukutoshin* grew up as strategic points in the mass-transit system. These they have remained in the automobile age. Despite the Olympics and the building of freeways, the inadequacies of the street system have been an automatic limitation on the automobile. In 1947 forty thousand automobiles were registered in the city. By the end of the first postwar decade the number had reached a quarter of a million, and in the next two decades it was to increase another tenfold. Already by the mid-fifties the busiest intersection in the city was accommodating three times the number of vehicles considered the maximum for free and easy movement. This was Iwaitabashi, at the south end of the palace plaza and the north end of the Kasumigaseki bureaucratic complex. Thirteen other intersections at the heart of the city were accommodating traffic above the ideal maximum. Subsequently the "doughnut phenomenon" saw the worst congestion moving out to places like Shinjuku. Subsequently too there were freeways; but the problem is insoluble, and there are alternatives to the automobile, as there are not in most American cities. Trains on various levels go almost everywhere. The sensible person takes them.

The number of trolley passengers rose rapidly in the years after the war. It reached a peak of more than six hundred thousand per day in 1955—and even this was a mere trickle compared with the clientele of the suburban railway lines, public and private. There was modest expansion in total trackage as well, and from 1960 it too began to decline. With the approach of the Olympics, as Tokyo was getting itself ready to appear before the world, there were rumblings about doing away with the trolley system; it was almost completely accomplished during the post-Olympic years.

Meanwhile there had been an experiment with the trolleybus, making use of trolley wires but doing away with rails. Its career lasted from 1952 to 1968. The routes were predominantly in the northern and eastern parts of the city (the non-Olympic parts). The arc of its waxing and waning lagged somewhat behind that of the postwar trolley. The total mileage of the routes began to fall off from 1961, and the last route was discontinued in 1968. The trolleybus was the product of a gasoline shortage, and occupied an uncomfortable middle position, less of a drag upon the freedom of the automobile than the trolley, but more than the unattached bus.

Public transportation on the streets was thus left to the bus and the taxicab. The fifties were a time when cabdrivers were uncommonly lawless even for a lawless breed. The refusal by cruising cabs to take passengers, quite without explanation and quite without legal sanction, became so common that the police staged roundups. One series of them, toward the end of the decade, netted two dozen miscreants, surely a tiny fraction of the total. All manner of contradictory explanations were given for the phenomenon, but it was chiefly a matter of too few cabs and inadequate incentives. At one time it was so bad that Ginza bars were hiring buses to take their employees home after work.

The fifties were the time of the Kamikaze cabdriver, who acquired the designation from the suicide pilots in the last stages of the Second World War. The phenomenon had to do with fare and meters. When the meters were changed so that the fare mounted even during motionless intervals, drivers became more tolerant of them, and calmer. Until 1959 all drivers worked for companies. In that year for the first time owner-drivers were permitted, specifically for purposes of alleviating the abuses; and indeed it was from about then that things started getting better. Owner-drivers were older men with good records, and of course it was their own property they sent hurtling through the streets and their business that would suffer if they happened to be in the tiny minority caught in a roundup.

Among the voguish words of 1955 was *noiroze,* from the German word for neurosis. Affluence was returning, and indispositions of affluence. The Japanese may have disliked giving names to typhoons, but each of the periods of especial prosperity that have come along has had its name. The earliest was Procurement Prosperity, following upon the outbreak of the Korean War. At the time of the first postwar decade there was the Jimmu Prosperity. Jimmu was the legendary first emperor of Japan, and the name implies that nothing like it had been seen in all the days since his reign.

Then there were the *zoku,* the "tribes" or "breeds" that were in the news. The progression of *zoku* also tells of increasing affluence. Shortly after the war there was the Shayō Zoku, the Setting Sun Tribe, the name deriving from a novel about a ruined aristocratic family. The novelist, Dazai Osamu, was himself a ruinous type, but his malaise went back to his youth, long before the disaster that ruined so many once-eminent families. A couple of years later we have Shayō Zoku again, but written differently, to tell us that business is getting back on its feet. The tribe in question is the expense-account one. At the end of the decade, along with Jimmu and neurosis, we have the Taiyō Zoku, the Sun Tribe, whose designation is from the title of a short story about pampered and rebellious youth. The author, Ishihara Shintarō, may once himself have been a member of the tribe, but he is no more. He is a conservative member of the National Diet.

The dispelling of darkness, from the busy entertainment districts at least, was becoming as nearly complete as human hands can make it. Tanizaki Junichirō may have deplored it in his famous eulogy to shadows, but only limitations on fuel cut down the voltage. In 1953 Ginza acquired the largest neon light in the world, a globe eleven meters in diameter which, set atop a building near the main Ginza crossing, advertised Morinaga sweets. Though it was turned off immediately after the "oil shock" of 1973, it came back again, and was for three decades among the marvels and symbols of Ginza. Finally in 1983 it was judged obsolescent and torn down.

Toward the end of the first postwar decade the drug problem emerged. It was and continues to be mild compared to the American one, but transgressions were frequent, and profits huge. There were fourteen thousand arrests in Tokyo in 1954 for selling illegal pep pills, and profits were fifty and a hundred times costs.

In 1951 tuberculosis slipped into second place as a cause of death. By the end of the first postwar decade it had fallen to tenth, and the fatality rate was only a quarter of the highest prewar rate. Midway through the fifties we started hearing complaints about how difficult it was to find domestic help, and how expensive, incompetent, and intransigent such help was when found. Tokyo had its first supermarket, not at all inexpensive, in 1953. We started hearing too of luxurious physical examinations known as *ningen dokku,* which might be rendered as "human dry dock," and luxurious surgery. Young ladies would go to plastic surgeons with photographs of those they wished to be made over into. Wide, round eyes were especially popular.

The day of the cod and the sweet potato was rapidly withdrawing into the past.

5

OLYMPIAN
DAYS

Baseball may have helped to restore the shattered national morale, and the Korean War did much toward restoring the national economy. Yet strong feelings of inferiority persisted, and a sense of isolation. Japan continued to be something of an international pariah. Any sign of recognition was eagerly received. In 1957 an international literary gathering in Tokyo was front-page news. It would probably have taken a terrorist bomb to put such a gathering on the front pages of European and American newspapers.

The Japanese seemed to take the view that any international notice is good notice. Arthur Koestler came to Tokyo in 1958 and denounced the literary organization (it was the Japanese branch of the International PEN) that had arranged the gathering of 1957. He thought, and he was right, that its attitude toward freedom of letters was tepid, not to say contradictory. This was the great day of easy left-wing solutions, when apology was made for most actions of the Soviet Union, including the obstacles interposed to Boris Pasternak's receiving the Nobel Prize that same year. Koestler's views were also front-page news.

The first postwar Olympic games came and went, and Occupied Japan had no part in them. That Japan would have had a superb swimmer to show off if only it had been there was a matter of great chagrin. He was a genius (and he had only nine fingers), the best swimmer Japan has produced since the thirties. He had blossomed and, as swimmers will, rapidly faded by the time the next Olympics came. He had to make do with a few international victories in America. No one but the Japanese paid much heed to them, but he probably did as much for the national morale as baseball.

In 1951, the last full year of the Occupation and the first of the Korean War, and the year General MacArthur went home, Japan was readmitted to the Olympics. A Japanese team went in 1952, and did less than brilliantly. But the important thing was being there—as the Olympic charter suggests. The next task was to repair the loss incurred when the games of 1940 failed to take place. London, the other city that lost Olympics because of the war, got the first postwar games.

Already in 1952 the governor announced that Tokyo would bid for the 1960 Olympics. The bid was duly made, and was unsuccessful. There were seven candidates. Tokyo placed last in the vote. When the 1956 Olympics were over the prefecture set up a special office to entice the 1964 games. In January 1958 a commission went to work on particular and specific preparations. In May the bid for the Olympics was formally entered. The persuaders sent off to Munich, where the International Olympic Committee met in 1959, included the governor, his predecessor, and a prince of the blood who (unlike most of the imperial family) was a man of great personal charm. This time there were four candidates: Tokyo, Detroit, Vienna, and Brussels. They placed in that order on the first ballot. Tokyo had a solid majority. Literary gatherings could not again expect to make the front pages.

The city and the prefecture took the games very seriously. A new governor, Azuma Ryūtarō, was elected in the spring of 1959 as if for the specific purpose of presiding over them. He was also chairman of the Japanese Olympic Committee. The only one not to run for a third term and the only one who utterly lost control of the prefectural council, he was perhaps (though some would give the nod to his successor) the least successful of the four governors the prefecture has had. His was the administration that had the best scandal of the postwar years, one which turned into a political fiasco. Yet the whole world seems to agree that the city, the prefecture, and the nation did a superb job of staging the Olympics. They were an opportunity to show the world what Japan had been up to since 1945. The opportunity was made good use of, and Japan regained much of its self-esteem and international standing.

"Direct expenses" for the Olympics were a small fraction of those generally listed as indirect, perhaps as small a fraction, depending on definitions and categories, as a thirtieth. Direct expenses and indirect provided a good way to get money from outside the prefecture for solving a few prefectural problems. The national government took care of more of the direct expenses than the prefecture. There are no surprises on the list of these. The money went for athletic installations and accommodations for athletes and the like.

As for indirect expenses, funds came overwhelmingly from borrowing. The "bullet express" to Osaka made up about a third of the total. Its relation to the Olympics was certainly very tenuous, although the showing of Japanese organizational and technical skills was among the main reasons for having the games in the first place. Another third, almost equally divided between the two, went into streets and subways. Had the games come at a later day the division might have been different. The traffic problem was at crisis proportions, and freeways and wide nonexpress avenues were seen as a solution. The system of freeways went on growing after the Olympics, but the time passed when it was seen as a solution to much of anything. The athletic installations, and especially the main stadium and the gymnasium, are some of them very imposing, but the "Olympic thoroughfares," as they were and sometimes still are called, the freeways and the widened streets, were the most prominent change which the Olympics brought to the contours (as the regent's post-earthquake proclamation had it) of the city. It would have been remarkable if the effects had been distributed evenly over the city. The concern was to get people from the airport, then in the farthest south of the wards and near the bay, to the downtown hotels and then to the Olympic installations. These were concentrated, though not exclusively, in the southwest, the athletes' village and the gymnasium in Shibuya Ward, the main stadium in Shinjuku Ward, and a considerable complex in Setagaya Ward, out beyond Shibuya. Had someone been away for a couple of years before the Olympics and (sensibly) come back when the excitement had died down, and been asked, as the returning person always is, whether he did not find the changes in the city perfectly astonishing, he might with reason have replied, "In Shibuya, yes, perfectly."

In the old center of the city the freeway system was relatively inconspicuous because it used old public rights-of-way. Only a tenth of the land used for the whole system had to be wrested from private hands. The rest was in the public domain, as streets and canals. The original system passed discreetly by the bustling center of Shinjuku. Shibuya was the *sakariba,* the bustling place, which it cut uncompromisingly through, opening a way into and out of the very heart of the place which had not been there before. Dropped down at Shibuya Station and suddenly surrounded by the concrete and the roar, the returning person (and we are to assume that he knew the place well) might have wondered where he was.

Minato and Shibuya wards, to the south and southwest of the palace and the old downtown district, were the wards in which the Olympic freeways were the most conspicuous. Among the most affluent of the wards, they were the ones upon which Olympic blessings, perhaps mixed, poured in the greatest profusion.

A very small beginning toward a system of elevated and subterranean freeways had been made before it was even known that Tokyo would have the Olympics. After all the cinders had been dumped and such pleasure and consumer centers as Tokyo Spa and the Yaesu Mouth complex at Tokyo Central Station had been built, the filling in of canals went on. In Kawabata's *Scarlet Gang of Asakusa* there is a boy who is the son of a boatman and whose home is the boat. His father drops him at Asakusa in the morning so that he may attend school on the temple grounds. He must wait until night and sometimes all through the night for the boat to come again, and so he becomes a child of the park and its gangs. It is a way of life that has quite disappeared. The filling in of canals brought a loss of channels and moorings, and a new law that had to do with longshoring brought complete extinction to life upon the waterways, so important in Edo and Meiji.

The canal that had been the outer moat of Edo Castle was in the late fifties filled in along the border of Chiyoda Ward (which lay within the moats and the old castle revetments) and Chūō Ward (which lay without). This was the canal between Yūrakuchō and Ginza into which the American soldier threw the pimp (see page 187). The bridge from which the unfortunate man was thrown was Sukiyabashi, where all the modern boys and girls wanted to be photographed. It was especially famous in these years because it figured in a tear-provoking, Evangelinesque, and very popular radio serial called *What Is Your Name? (Kimi no na wa),* about love frustrated by the bombings and their aftermath. (Frank Nagai's biggest hit was based on the serial.) The bridge was demolished in 1957, and at the site a wistful plaque now says, in the hand of the *What Is Your Name?* playwright, "Sukiyabashi was here."

The freeway, extending less than a mile from a point just north of Shimbashi Station along the filled-in canal, did not amount to much, and did scarcely anything toward relieving congestion on the main north-south Ginza streets. Today it is joined at either end to the larger system of freeways and is used mostly for parking. In another respect it was put to better use than most of the newer freeways have been. Two shopping arcades went into business in 1957 and two more in 1958, making use of the space beneath. In two of them the shops occupy sequestered space, cut off by walls from neighboring spaces. The other two are more like the "blocks of famous shops" (*meitengai*) or "shopping centers" in the basements of the big department stores. Stalls share a common space.

The city financed the filling and the building and sold some of the space and rented out some at less than it was worth. The leases will soon expire. The site of the old bridge is at about midpoint through the complex, which is the boundary between the two wards. Except for a rare happening such as the pimp incident, which the police to the east of the canal initially took charge of, the canal area did not much matter while it was an expanse of mud and stagnant water. Now, with money coming in, the two wards started fighting for jurisdiction. A boundary line was presently drawn that runs now down one side of the old canal and now down the other, and sometimes down the middle.

The system of Olympic freeways, which is to say, the freeways that were ready in time to serve the Olympics, extended for some twenty miles, and affected only the central district (Ginza, Marunouchi, and Nihombashi) and the wards to the immediate south and west. Freeways ran northward from the airport to the center of the city, and westward along two routes, to the heart of Shibuya and to the vicinity of the main Olympic stadium. The gymnasium and the athletes' village lay between the two.

It was not for some time that the northern and eastern parts of the city were favored with freeways. Early post-Olympic accretions were also in the central and southwestern wards. The first considerable extension to the north came only in 1969, when a freeway joined Ueno with Nihombashi. The northern and eastern parts of the city are in general the more slowly changing parts. Though slow to come, such improvements as freeways have had a more pronounced effect in uglifying the backward parts of the city than the advanced and affluent. It might almost be argued that freeways, clearing away some postwar shabbiness, have been an improvement for parts of the south and west. The argument would be quite impossible in the case of the freeway that runs along the east bank of the Sumida and onward to the north. It sits like a lid on the famous line of cherry trees. This is not to say that the freeways have not had unhappy effects elsewhere in the city. Nihombashi Bridge, the most celebrated in the land, is still there, and it still crosses a canal, but it has been sadly diminished by the freeway that passes overhead. Even the sacred view from the palace has been blemished by freeways. The mileage has grown to upward of four times what it was in 1964.

The widening of nonexpress streets was also most evident in the southwestern wards. Aoyama Avenue, as it is called from a district through which it runs, is much the most conspicuous instance. A street was widened to twice its earlier width all the way from the outer castle moat to Shibuya. The expense was huge. On charts of indirect Olympic expenditures the cost of nonexpress streets runs to some five times that for freeways. Low buildings had to be bought up one by one and moved back into the somewhat higher buildings that line the widened street. So we came to have "pencil buildings," several storeys high, thin as pencils. They are said to be earthquake-proof, but they do not look it.

Less than a month before the Olympics began, a monorail was opened from the airport to Hamamatsuchō, some distance south of Ginza and Shimbashi. Neither the worst nor the best location that could have been chosen, Hamamatsuchō is not within easy walking distance of anything except the park on the site of the old Hama Palace. Not many people can get there without changing a time or two from some other mode of transportation. Despite this disadvantage and despite initial unpopularity —people may have been frightened at the Olympic crowds—it has been a commercial success. It is the best way to get to the old airport, whence domestic flights still depart, and it is fun. In 1980 it was carrying more than two million passengers a month. It was not the city's first monorail; several years earlier one had been put through joining two sections of the Ueno Zoo. But it was the most ambitious in Japan and, indeed, the whole world.

Diggings for new subway lines began at about the time the Korean War began, and much digging had been accomplished in time for the

Olympics. It has gone on since and is still going on. Besides its freeway Shinjuku now had a subway line to the center of the city. The same line, the first postwar one, sweeps southeastward through the center of the city and then westward, and had earlier joined Ikebukuro with Ginza. By 1962 it had pushed on past Shinjuku to Ogikubo, near the western limits of the ward part of the prefecture.

It encountered an interesting difficulty as it made its way past Ginza. Near Hibiya Park the diggers came upon great boulders, which had to be demolished, at a great cost of time and money. It was established that they were underground foundations for the outer revetments of Edo Castle, most probably abutments for the Sukiya Gate from which Suki-yabashi took its name. They were probably put there in the seventeenth century by Date Masamune, most famous of the lords of Sendai. Not many old things remain above the Tokyo ground, but under it many an archaeological specimen is yet to be discovered.

A new and most imposing Ginza subway station was ready just in time for the Olympics. It joined the new line with the prewar Ginza line. Probably more than the underground complex at the Yaesu Mouth of Tokyo Central Station, to which few visitors from distant lands were likely to go, it showed the world what marvelous diggers the Japanese are.

It cannot be charged that the northern wards were left out in the building of subways as they were in the building of freeways. They were present at the creation of the subway system, and the earliest trackage of the second line (the first postwar one) ran to the north and northwest of the palace. The farthest northern wards were linked to the center of the city by Olympic time, and work had begun on yet another line, its eastern stretches aboveground, which would in the post-Olympic years cross the city east and west from beyond Shinjuku to well beyond the border with Chiba Prefecture. It too passes north of the palace. The increment to the system between 1954 and October 1964, the Olympic month, was almost a hundred kilometers, or upward of sixty miles.

As if by way of confusing Olympic visitors, the subways were complicated in those years by the founding of a new system. The prefecture had long wanted to take over the old system, which, though a public corporation, was not under prefectural control, and among the most striking attributes of which was that it was very profitable. Failing in this endeavor, the prefecture started its own system. Digging began in

1958, and when the first stretch of tracks was opened, in 1960, it offered service to the wards east of the Sumida River, untouched by earlier diggings. The first city-owned line was in operation through the center of the city and on to the vicinity of Shiba Park in time for the Olympics. Transfer between the two systems is possible but not easy, and it is expensive. The city-owned system has higher fares and does not show a profit. It got started too late, and for that reason might better not have started at all, though it did serve the neglected eastern wards. The old system had already dug its way through the best routes on several levels in the Ginza-Marunouchi district.

The expansion of the trolleybus system in the years before the Olympics looked ahead to dispensing with the clumsy old trolley cars. The latter were among the things Tokyo would as soon not have shown the world, but it could not do everything. The Olympics had trolleys as well as the proud new freeways and subways. The almost complete demolition of the system was left to the Olympic governor's successor, who set aggressively to work on it in 1967. Trolleybuses had their largest passenger load in 1965, and, as the trolleys went, they went too.

After streets and transportation, the largest items on compilations of indirect Olympic expenditures are for water and sewers, the latter slightly larger than the former. The Tokyo region had a severe drought in the summer of 1964, and a water shortage. For a time in August, seventeen of the twenty-three wards had water only nine hours a day. Parts of the High City were completely dependent on water trucks. The national government, prudently, had a special minister of state in charge of Olympic affairs. He turned so energetically to the drought problem that he became known as the minister of the waterworks. The present governor of Tokyo, Suzuki Shunichi, had made a career in the national bureaucracy before the Olympic governor appointed him vice-governor and assigned him particularly to Olympic preparations. He too was much concerned with the waterworks.

Tokyo did not at the time have access to the Tone River, the largest in eastern Japan, but water was coming across Saitama Prefecture from the Tone to the Higashimurayama Reservoir, in the county part of Tokyo Prefecture, in time for the Olympics. Water continues to be a problem which the prefecture has not really solved. Farming has prior rights to a considerable portion of the water that flows into the city supply when farmers do not need it. When they do they get it and the city does not.

There was a serious water shortage in 1987. The governor would like to dam the Shinano River, which flows into the Sea of Japan, and bring water across the mountains to the Tone, whence it would flow into the Tokyo system. The governor of Niigata Prefecture is understandably in the opposition, for the main mouth of the Shinano is right there in the main city of his constituency. The project is not one which the governor and the government of Tokyo can see to by themselves.

The major part of the sewage effort was directed at hiding the most obvious manifestations of what was still a very inadequate system. In 1964 only about a third of the population of the wards had the use of sewers. Obviously not much could be done to put a bright modern face on the matter, and Olympic visitors would probably not have the inclination or the means to inquire deeply. Something could be done, however, to render the *kumitoriya,* the carters of night soil, less of an assault upon the senses. Vacuum trucks replaced the old cart-and-dipper arrangements in most parts of the city likely to be on display. Statistics released by the city, however, showed that two decades after the Olympics *kumitoriya* had not disappeared from the eastern wards, where fewer than a quarter of the population had the benefit of sewers.

The year of the Olympics brought the opening of the last bridge across the Sumida, from east of Ginza to the oldest bit of filled land at the river mouth. This occurred six weeks before the games began. So the last ferry across the river was discontinued, and Tokyo became a bit more what it seemed to wish to be, no different from other cities. The ferry had been in service for three hundred years. Meiji Village near Nagoya wanted the last boat, but an elderly boatman who had worked the ferry for forty years was successful in his insistence that it remain in Tokyo. This was a most striking success in a day when no one seemed to care much whether anything of historic interest remained in Tokyo.

Also by way of preparation for the Olympics, the Construction Ministry and a public corporation charged with the nurturing and development of water resources undertook to flush out the Sumida River, which was in such a state that the expensive restaurants along its west bank smelled like sewers (and indeed it was a sewer) when the wind was right. In August a channel was completed, expressly for flushing purposes, from the new Higashimurayama Reservoir to the upper reaches of the river. Fresh reservoir water poured through for about a month just preceding the games. An announcement came toward the end of October that the results had not been disappointing. The algae content at Ryō-goku Bridge, just below the Yanagibashi geisha quarter, was down by half, and farther upstream it was down by as much as three-quarters. Oxygen had scarcely existed before, and now was up to a half gram per ton at Ryōgoku, as much as two grams upstream. This was still far from enough to keep fish alive, but it was better than nothing. The smell of the river was much improved. Delicate incenses in the restaurants could overcome it.

During the Olympic years the city began to do something for itself in the matter of parks. In earlier postwar years it had waited for windfalls such as the Hama Palace. In 1958 it bought a famous iris garden at Horikiri, some distance east of the Sumida, a relic of the nurseries that once fringed Edo. The site has changed radically over the centuries, but there it still is, never built upon except for small pleasure pavilions through the three centuries of its history.

The clearing away of beggars and vagrants from the parts of the city the world was likely to notice has a little of the scent of authoritarianism about it. Many went into institutions; harassment caused many to pick up and move to places held by their intelligence network to be more friendly. Such harassment would not have been possible in a litigious city like New York. A few years later, after the "oil shock" of 1973, they all came back (or perhaps they were different ones), and life was some-what easier for them, with so many more diggings to sleep in and so many vending machines to obviate unpleasant encounters with shopkeepers and waitresses.

Preparation for the Olympics was a big effort, national and local, and the Japanese did most of it by themselves. Such was the distance they had come. To point out that they asked for just a little help is not to belittle the effort and the success. Since there were contingency plans for an athletes' village, something would doubtless have been put up somewhere in the couple of years at Japan's disposal even if the decision had been against letting them have the American military housing com-plex called Washington Heights. The complex, in Shibuya Ward, just beside the Meiji Shrine, close to the freeways, and offering space for installations besides the village, was certainly the best of possible sites. It was returned less than a year before the Olympics, with the proviso that the Japanese provide substitute housing for Americans. There is an item on the list of indirect expenses, a small item, less than 1 percent of expenditures on most lists, that is designated "construction of American military housing in the Chōfu paddies." Chōfu is a city out beyond Setagaya Ward in the county part of the prefecture.

So, the degree of readiness very high, the Olympics began, on the Double Ten, October 10, 1964. Rain threatened on the day of the opening ceremonies, but forbore. The general view is that the games were a huge success and marked a great step forward in the emergence of Tokyo as one of the grander cities of the world. Japan won sixteen gold medals, the third-largest number, after the United States and the Soviet Union. A certain amount of arranging was required to achieve this result. Japan had a remarkable women's volleyball team thanks chiefly to the efforts of a relentless coach known as "the demon," and of course it enjoyed a certain advantage in judo. Both of these sports became Olympic events for the first time.

The gold medal won by the volleyball team was only the second to be won by Japanese women, the first having been won at Berlin in 1936. There were sad happenings afterward, signifying that such events can be taken too seriously. A Japanese marathon runner who had been thought a possible winner was in second place, well behind the great Ethiopian Abebe (who this time ran with shoes on), as he came into the stadium. He was overtaken in the last two hundred yards by an Englishman—and right there before the stadium multitudes. A woman hurdler who had been expected at the very worst to win a bronze medal came in fifth. Both later killed themselves.

Perhaps when everything was over some Japanese wished that the arranging had never taken place, for it brought a great national embarrassment. The volleyball team duly won its gold medal on the last day of competition. On each of the three preceding days Japanese won gold medals in the three weight divisions of judo, but on this day, in the contest that really mattered, the open-weight division, a Dutchman, Anton Geesink, took the medal. There was weeping in the streets. He said afterward that the struggle against the hostile crowd was worse than that against his Japanese opponent. That there should be weight divisions in the first place rather damaged the mystique of judo, which held that the little fellow, the Bruce Lee, uses the big fellow's weight to defeat him.

*Aerial smoke rings mark the opening
of the 1964 Tokyo Olympics*

The famous director Ichikawa Kon was commissioned to do the official film document. The minister of the waterworks did not like it. He
said it may have been art but it was no document.

The 1956 games were the first ones held in Oceania, one of the five
Olympic circles. They had not yet been held in Asia, another of the five.
That the prostrate country of 1945 should have held them made it feel
that it had, perhaps, something which the rest of the circle did not have.
National feelings of inferiority did not disappear in 1964, but the emergence of confidence was striking. That year is sometimes put beside
1867, 1923, and 1945 as the momentous ones in the history of the city.

This is surely an exaggeration. Yet the Olympics were an event of great moment in the life of the city, spiritual and material.

"The Tokyo Olympics were not merely a sports festival. They were a ritual marking the fact that for the first time since the defeat Japan had formally been accepted by the world. For a time on opening day, traffic in the city came to a stop. A happy excitement welled up that the nations of the world were extending their hands in congratulation. And then, after a time, all the noise and confusion of people and vehicles came back again." So wrote one observer of the scene.

The nation gave voice to its happiness in what might be called poetry, but would more safely be called verse. It has been much given to expressing itself thus, in joy and in sorrow.

> Seventy thousand see Abebe into the stadium,
> No change upon his face or in his pace.

And again:

> One and then another, ninety-four flags.
> Some, perhaps, have met on battlefields.

The "perhaps" may be taken as a mark of the Japanese tendency to soften things a bit.

On December 8, in Japan the twenty-third anniversary of the attack on Pearl Harbor, though the choice of date can hardly have been intentional, the Seibu department store in Ikebukuro had a big sale of furniture and utensils from the athletes' village. It sold out in an hour.

Tokyo acquired its first important hotel since the thirties in 1951, and then there was a pause, and then a great rush in preparation for the Olympics. A half dozen big new hotels went up near the palace and along or near the avenue that had replaced the outer castle moat. One of them, with seventeen floors, was for a time the highest building in the city. Another, the new Imperial, went up on a part of the land occupied by the old, or second, Imperial. The management did not get around to destroying this second building, designed by Frank Lloyd Wright, until several years after the Olympics. Wright's niece, the actress Anne Baxter, stayed in the then newest Imperial, which has since been replaced by a glossy tower, and delighted in it. She said that it made her uncle's work look better than ever.

A new pattern was emerging, in which the Japanese home market, reserved almost exclusively for Japanese, made foreign businessmen bilious with envy. It quickly became apparent that all these new hotels would rely very heavily on the home clientele to keep themselves profitable. The building of hotels did not stop when the Olympics were over. In 1986 there were well over twice as many hotel rooms in the city as in the Olympic year.

There was another indicator, initially somewhat disheartening. Retail business actually suffered from the Olympics. In Ginza and Shinjuku sales during October 1964 were well below the average for the run of Octobers preceding it. Japanese customers stayed away, even as they at first stayed away from the monorail. They did not want to get caught in the press of foreigners. Cameras were almost the only items that sold well, but not the more expensive ones. Shopkeepers found the tendency of customers to haggle over prices not to their taste. The important matter, the drop in sales, had its sunny side. It showed that the Japanese custom, which would come back when all those foreigners had gone away, was the one that mattered. Japanese retailing has not suffered perceptibly from foreign competition. The growth of a huge Japanese domestic market skillfully shielded from foreign incursions is among the important developments of our time.

Among the *sakariba,* the bustling places of the city, Shibuya was the one that was most visibly affected by preparations for the Olympics, and it was the one most directly caught up in the aftermath. The Shibuya district proper, the vicinity of the mass-transit complex, did not change at an especially dizzying rate compared with the other bustling places even after the freeway went through. It became part of a larger complex, however: a triangle northward from Shibuya to the Meiji Shrine and, beside it, the site of Washington Heights and the Olympic village, eastward to Aoyama Avenue, the street widened in preparation for the games, and back to Shibuya along this last. The northeast corner of the triangle came close to the outskirts of Roppongi, another rampant pleasure district, and on to the north Roppongi merged with Akasaka of the cabarets (such as the one in which Rikidōzan was stabbed) and the geisha. So one vast entertainment, shopping, and to a degree managerial district was growing up all the way from the outer castle moat to Shibuya. For convenience, though the expression has no currency in Japan, we may call it the Southwest.

With the Olympic village at one end of the main street leading through the Harajuku district, and Aoyama Avenue, the main access by rapid transit to Ginza and the old center of the city, at the other, the Olympics brought a great increase in the number of late-night purveyors of pleasure. In the beginning it was a matter between athletes and purveyors, but the female adolescent crowd loved all the exoticism and lingered on. A decade earlier the idle young tended not to have money to spend. Now they did. The fame of Harajuku spread, and it became a place with a powerful attraction for curious and mildly rebellious youth the whole land over. Great swarms of schoolboys and schoolgirls have always converged upon the city, especially during the clement seasons, to improve themselves. In days of old they came in tightly mustered groups and looked reverently at the royal residence and the Diet building. Now they preferred to look at Harajuku, and the teachers who were their wardens were powerless to stop them.

There, in the post-Olympic years, one seemed to see the future most clearly. In those years we first started hearing of the Harajuku addition to the *zoku*, the "tribes" which followed one another through the postwar decades. Harajuku has disappeared as the official name of a district, but it survives as the name of the Yamanote station next north from Shibuya, that nearest the Olympic village (and that whence the bodies of emperors depart for their final repose). In popular usage it signifies the regions eastward from the Meiji Shrine and the Olympic village to Aoyama Avenue—the northern side of the triangle. The expression "Harajuku Zoku" might be freely rendered "flaming youth." They have been perhaps the most perdurable of all the tribes, for, changing as fads and rages change, they are with us yet. They have their sports cars and their hot rods and motorcycles, and the police have seemed unwilling or unable to stop them as they race back and forth along that northern side of the triangle, Yoyogi Park, where the Olympic village was, to Aoyama Avenue.

They also have flamboyant styles of dress and lawless ways, among them the taking over of any bit of unguarded and unoccupied property. It was in the post-Olympic years that the English words "event" and "happening" entered the language, to designate the exhibitionist behavior of the young, especially in Harajuku and Yoyogi. The Sunday afternoons

Street performers on a Sunday in Harajuku

of a quarter of a century have been rendered deafening by the noises from their amplifying devices and riotous by their dress and dancing. Happenings and events are concentrated in front of the staid Meiji Shrine, at the northwest corner of the Shibuya triangle.

Many have been distressed by them, some have thought them a hopeful sign—for a small measure of pluralism in Japan, most conformist and undifferentiated of nations, might be good for all of us. Thorstein Veblen thought the Japanese opportunity would pass when, as must inevitably happen, premodern ways of behavior no longer prevailed. It might finally be happening. Yet in some ways the Harajuku tribe does not seem so very rebellious and decadent after all. Detailed maps of Harajuku are striking for the lack of the sort of places so numerous in Shinjuku, the sex places. The events and happenings are alfresco.

The Harajuku-Aoyama district was becoming the center of high fashion in an ever more highly fashioned city. Such expressions usually have reference to feminine elegance, and this one does here. The center of masculine elegance has stayed in Ginza.

Men were wearing Western dress with reasonable competence during the interwar decades. The emperor may look a bit overdressed in the famous pictures of that first interview with the general, but he does not look badly dressed. Since emperors of Japan never wear Japanese dress on public occasions save the most elaborately ritual ones, such as coronations, it was during the interwar years that he got his practice.

And when did it happen for women? The disasters of 1923 and 1945 both brought sudden increases in the frequency of Western dress for women—although the victims of the 1932 Shirokiya fire, as we have seen (page 34), were still in Japanese dress. In the postwar years Japanese dress became so uncommon that it also became uneconomical. Low demand brought high prices. Old weavers died, old techniques fell into disuse, and those who had to have Japanese dress, such as geisha, had to pay high and ever higher prices for superior pieces.

There came a time, along toward the end of the first quarter or third of a century after the surrender, when women at length began to look as if Western dress were meant for them—not women of the diplomatic and banking sets, who came to grips with the problem much earlier, but housewives and students and office girls. With women's dress as our indicator, we may say that it took almost a century from the Meiji Restoration for Western appurtenances to rest other than awkwardly. Today Japanese ones are coming to seem that way, as when young ladies kick at the skirts of the kimonos they put on for graduation day or a wedding. Their stride goes better with Western dress.

Yet another part of Washington Heights, parts of which became Yoyogi Park and the Olympic gymnasium, became a new center for NHK, the public broadcasting corporation. The old building, near Hibiya Park, had been "Radio Japan," whence the Tokyo Rose broadcasts went forth to gladden young American hearts all over the Pacific. In 1972 NHK sold the old building to Mitsubishi. The price was over thirty-four billion and a few-odd million yen. Even in those days of a strong dollar this figure converted to almost a hundred million dollars. The new complex, very glassy, was completed with the opening of NHK Hall, for concerts and the like, in 1973.

Roppongi was the earliest of the brassy, amplified entertainment districts. It had its tribe, its *zoku,* years in advance of the Harajuku one. The origins of Roppongi are similar to those of Shibuya: military. There were training grounds beyond Shibuya, and there were barracks near the main Roppongi crossing. So Roppongi developed in response to the military demand. This occurred during the two big wars of Meiji. The barracks were taken over by the Americans, and Roppongi went on responding. During the American years it was not an especially lively place, though it contained many a little bar that stayed open late at night to please the soldiers. When Tokyo Tower went up in 1958 (see page 251), Roppongi was like the darkness at the foot of the lighthouse. The tower blazed, and Roppongi did not. The place on the edge of Roppongi where the tower went up was a dark, lonely one, well suited for murder (see pages 208–9).

In the early sixties, the pre-Olympic years, Roppongi started to become the sort of place people knew about. The Americans moved out of the barracks in 1959. Providentially, a very big television studio opened there the same year. In those early years of its fame, Roppongi was new among the pleasure centers of the city in more than one sense. It was of course the newest in point of time, and it was the only one among them that took a little trouble to get to. Asakusa languished because it was not an important transfer point and was not served by the National Railways. Roppongi was not served by any kind of rapid transit. It did not have a subway line until 1964, the Olympic year, and it has never had an elevated line, private or public. Young people came in droves all the same. Unlike the hot-rodders and motorcycle gangs that were later to converge on Harajuku, not many of them had their own transportation. And what was it that lured them, despite the inconvenience?

What if not television? When the American clientele departed Roppongi, the television one took its place, and young people went to ogle, and to imitate, and to dance and eat pizza. The mass media were talking about a Roppongi Zoku from about 1960. It did the things just enumerated. The pizza and dancing were exotic, and the people of television were at the bright cutting edge of progress. The exotic and the advanced were what the Roppongi Zoku were after, and what they signified.

The Yoshiwara, when it flourished, was known as "the nightless city," but it was less nightless by far than places like Roppongi have become in the years since the Olympics. Though the Yoshiwara may have been in business all through the night, there were no crowds in the streets during the early-morning hours, and the biggest noise was that of the wooden clappers exhorting caution against fires. It is not so with Roppongi and other parts of the Southwest. Especially before a holiday, they are lighted, crowded, brassy, and amplified all through the night, nightless as no Japanese place had been before. They are like Times Square on New Year's Eve or Greenwich Village on Halloween.

Television has also figured in the prosperity of Akasaka, just to the north. Once dominated by the geisha, it is an older and was a more elegant pleasure center than Roppongi or Shibuya. The geisha dominates no more. Her decline of recent years has been precipitous. Akasaka was one of the great geisha quarters of Meiji, very much of Meiji in the sense that it had been a dark, silent place of noble estates under the shoguns and began to bustle only in Meiji. It lay on one of the guard points along the outer moat and near the southwestern limits of the Meiji city. During the interwar years it was favored with a station on the earliest subway line, and after the war it became one of two points at which transfer between the first and second subway lines was possible (Ginza was the other).

The Akasaka geisha prospered because of her proximity to the bureaucratic center of the city. After the war Akasaka was the most conspicuous place for *machiai* politics, thought infamous by the newspapers, which invented the term. The word *machiai* is rendered by the big Japanese-English dictionary as "an assignation house." It is the institution more popularly rendered as "geisha house." *Machiai* politics had to do with the big deals in which businessmen and politicians worked hand in glove and with the arrangements whereby rival political factions formed their shifting coalitions.

Akasaka supplanted Ginza as a cabaret center. It had the gaudiest ones in the city, both because of *machiai* politics and because of all the big hotels that came with the Olympics. It too had its big television studios, and so, like Roppongi, it was a place to go for a look at the people who were making the future. There was no Akasaka Zoku, however. Only one *zoku*, the expense-account one, seemed made for Akasaka, but it was scattered everywhere.

The Shibuya-Aoyama-Harajuku triangle lies almost completely beyond the limits of the old city; Akasaka and Roppongi lie within. The separate parts have their several histories, some reasonably old and some very new, but none of them amounted to much of anything before Meiji. They are still somewhat separate, though the cordons of quiet between them are not wide.

One would be hard put to say whether the Olympics or television was more important in the rise of the Southwest. Roppongi had taken off well before the Olympics came, and so it may be that the young would have gone to that part of town in search of the future even if the Olympics had not worked their change on the Shibuya triangle. The Olympics did come, however, and they brought other ingredients of the future—freeways and boutiques and high fashion and exoticism. It has long been the case, though the Japanese remain astonishingly faithful to old modes of behavior (whether Veblen was right or not is still in doubt), that they look abroad to see what the material future will be.

While the Southwest was thus leaping forward, Shinjuku and Ikebukuro were in the Olympic years making more modest progress, and plans. The first postwar subway line joined the two, and took a circumspect route that joined both of them to the old center of the city. The old Eastmouth at Ikebukuro became a plaza for automobiles, that at Shinjuku returned to places for eating, drinking, and shopping. Ikebukuro may thus have erred. It has less chance of one day catching up with the old center of the city than has Shinjuku or Shibuya. Its Westmouth is not in serious competition, as a provisioner of drink and sex, with Kabukichō in Shinjuku.

Shinjuku started burrowing as the Yaesu Mouth of Tokyo Central Station had done, and by the Olympics had a grand subterranean promenade leading under the railroad tracks and joining Eastmouth and Westmouth. Grander plans were still largely plans. They had to do with the reservoir, and included everything a planner needed to keep himself happy—streets, plazas, parks, parking, big buildings. Two years before the Olympics water started flowing into the new Higashimurayama Reservoir, out in the county part of the prefecture. The year after the Olympics the old reservoir ceased to function. So the post-Olympic years were the time for making plans come true.

Though Shinjuku went on having a larger count of bodies in transit than Shibuya, it might have fallen behind the Southwest if it had not had the reservoir. Barring the rise of bustling centers out in the county part of the prefecture, however, its decline could only be relative. It has gone on being a gigantic blaze and din, and in one respect it remained well in the lead of the Southwest even before the Westmouth started reaching upward into the light: the sex business. For all the grotesqueries of Harajuku and Yoyogi Park and the kinky clubs of Roppongi, they were places where a boy could go walking with his high school sweetheart, in from the country, with no fear of embarrassing her or giving her the wrong idea about him. The difference is rather like that between Times

Square and Greenwich Village. The Village may offer all manner of perverse pleasures, but it keeps them out of sight. For the open thing, one goes to the Square.

Certain farsighted companies, knowing what was to come, started putting up big buildings at Westmouth even during the Olympic years. An insurance building was finished in 1961; another, about twice the size, in 1964. Neither outdid buildings in the center of the city in size or height, but they looked very big and rather lonely there at Westmouth, the undeveloped side of Shinjuku. Today, viewed from the east, they are like foothills against the range that was thrust up later.

Just after the Olympics, Shinjuku had a *zoku*, a tribe. The Fūten Zoku were more aggressive dropouts from society than the Harajuku Zoku. *Fūten* is the first adjective in the title of the famous Tanizaki novel *Diary of a Mad Old Man*. In this case it means something more like "delinquent" (and indeed the Tanizaki title could have been rendered *Diary of a Senile Delinquent*). The Fūten Zoku had as their habitat the plaza in front of the newly rebuilt Shinjuku Eastmouth, what was then the main entrance to the station complex. They were the equivalent of

The Bankers' Club, a Taishō building surviving in Marunouchi

the flower children of San Francisco, and they could have chosen almost any place in which to loiter had they not craved attention. That they did want it, and so clearly, gave their doings an air of the theatrical. They got their attention as they lolled about, quaffing and sniffing mysterious things. Then they started having a social conscience, and it was the beginning of the end. Japan may be a little discommoded by dropouts, but it knows how to deal with political and ideological dissent. In 1967 the Fūten Zoku joined certain anti-communist (which is to say, more radical than the communists) student factions in a famous attack on the Eastmouth police box. It was the first of several such attacks in those years when the left-wing establishment was falling apart and the student left was growing ever more violent. When the violence died down the Fūten Zoku was no more.

Marunouchi was in these Olympic years tearing down its London-town, those blocks of red-brick buildings left from Meiji. The process was not completed until the post-Olympic years, when the first to go up was the last to come down. There was no murmur of protest when it did come down, but there has since been a vigorous movement to protect from demolition two brick buildings yet remaining in the Marunouchi district, the Bankers' Club and Tokyo Central Station. Both date from Taishō. Only in the past two decades has Tokyo come to have some sense that there might be objects worth preserving in its material heritage. Not quite everything of Meiji has disappeared from Marunouchi. Each of the Londontown buildings contained, high up in its attic, a Buddhist image. The images and the lightning rods are preserved in the basement of the Marunouchi Building, saved by the Mitsubishi executive who oversaw the destruction.

Despite the beginnings at the Shinjuku Westmouth, there was no indication that the business center of the city had any intention of jumping westward across the palace grounds. Except for the two Shinjuku insurance buildings just mentioned, all the major office buildings put up in the early sixties were in the three central wards, Chiyoda, Chūō, and Minato, the largest number in Chiyoda, which is to say, greater Maru-nouchi, the Marunouchi district proper and the districts immediately to the north and south. It is hard to know why insurance companies should have been the boldest in moving out beyond the central fastnesses. Per-haps, feeling less vulnerable to foreign incursions, they have felt less need to be near the bureaucracy. Two years after the Olympics another big insurance company moved its headquarters to the old site of the American school, in Meguro Ward, south of Shibuya.

There continued to be, however, significant movement within the central wards, consistently away from Nihombashi, which in Edo and Meiji had been the unchallenged financial and retailing center of the city, and toward Marunouchi and Ginza. For retailing the new center was Ginza. In financial matters the transfer to Marunouchi was accomplished with finality during the Olympic years. The Bank of Japan and the stock exchange remained in Nihombashi, but twelve of the thirteen metropolitan banks moved across what had been the outer castle revetments to greater Marunouchi.

Only the Bank of Tokyo, postwar successor to the Yokohama Specie Bank, which had been such a help in financing Japanese expansionist policies, remained in Nihombashi. The metropolitan banks are the ones which, though privately owned, are deemed to be national banks, as distinguished from myriads of local banks. The departure in 1960 of the Mitsui Bank was symbolic. It had stood on its Nihombashi site, across the street from where the Bank of Japan had been since late Meiji, for more than eighty years. Its first building on the site, gloriously prominent among early Meiji exercises in "Western" architecture, was the subject of numberless Ukiyoe woodcuts. Now its main office moved to Yūraku-chō, just south of Marunouchi. (As the Imperial Bank, its name from 1945 to 1954, it provided the setting for the most interesting postwar mass murders; see page 209.)

Retailing has not since the earthquake been as centralized as finance and management. Three very big department stores remain at Nihombashi. Two of them were the great competitors in the mercantile revolution of Meiji which produced department stores in the first place. Mitsukoshi still has its old name. Shirokiya now bears the name Tōkyū, from its new owner, the railway company that owns so much of Shibuya. (The Honolulu branch is still called Shirokiya. Perhaps Americans are thought to have stronger sentimental attachments to old names than Japanese.) Then there has been the great surge forward to the *fukutoshin*, the satellite cities along the Yamanote, as retail centers.

It may have been in the Olympic years that Ginza could for the last time confidently claim the fealty of that very important crowd: adolescents and those slightly older. Two other tribes came and went during

Members of the Miyuki Zoku, 1964

the Olympic years, and Ginza was their base. The Miyuki Zoku took its name from the Miyukidōri, Street of the Royal Progress, in Ginza, along which the Meiji emperor passed on his way to the Hama Palace. It was also known as the Oyafukōdōri, Street of the Unfilial, or possibly Street of the Prodigal Son. The first element in Ivy Zoku is borrowed from English, indicating a presumed resemblance to the Ivy League style of the United States. The two came in such quick succession and were so similar that it is not easy to distinguish between them. Perhaps it is useless to try, since both designations were invented by the mass media. Both favored casual dress, plaids and stripes and tight high-water trousers for the boys, long skirts, sweaters, and blouses for the girls, big shopping bags without distinction as to gender. The dress could be rumpled and ill-shaped, but, frequently imported, it tended not to be inexpensive—hence the element of prodigality. Ginza has not had *zoku* since.

The very young crowds have tended to favor the Southwest, though in recent years there have been signs that they may be coming back to Ginza.

The building that seems most representative of the Olympic years, the gymnasium at Yoyogi, is by Tange Kenzō. So is the main prefectural building, the one in which the governor now has his office. So is the building under construction in Shinjuku, where he will presently have his offices. The one in use today was begun in 1953 and finished in 1957. It is not the largest building in the prefectural sprawl occupying an expanse just south of Tokyo Central Station and on both sides of the railway tracks, where there would have been room for rebuilding, had there been a will. It is true that the governor and his people might have been inconvenienced during the rebuilding. A statue of Ota Dōkan, who built the first Edo Castle, had stood in front of the old city hall. A new statue was unveiled a year and two days after completion of the new city hall. At first it stood on the north or front side of the main building, as the old one had stood at the door of the old city hall. Now, because of diggings in the vicinity of the station, it is out in back. No place is set aside for Dōkan in Shinjuku.

The Olympic Stadium, designed by Tange Kenzō

The highest structure of the second postwar decade, and still the highest in the land, is Tokyo Tower, not really a building at all in the sense of an enclosed and roofed space that keeps off the elements. It is a big framework, a third of a thousand meters high, with observation towers at the hundred-twenty-five-meter and two-hundred-fifty-meter levels, and containing four thousand tons of steel. Finished in 1958, it so resembles the Eiffel Tower, though it is a bit higher, that the historian Umesao Tadao called it a monument to the Japanese lack of originality. One might indeed have wished that advances in the almost eight decades since the Eiffel Tower went up might have been put to more novel use; but perhaps it was good for the Japanese spirit, in those days when economic growth was barely getting underway and the spirit craved sustenance of any kind. The chief purpose of the tower, which serves

The Tokyo Tower

few other purposes than sightseeing, may well have been to rise higher than the Eiffel. Hopes that it might be put to use in the electronics age came to little, but as a sight for seeing it was a success from the start. People waited in line two and three hours to take the elevators. If there was symbolism in the date chosen for the opening, it has not been remarked upon. General Tōjō and his fellows were hanged in Sugamo Prison a decade, to the day, before.

The site, on the hilly side of Shiba Park, is a storied one. There it was that the elite of Meiji had their Kōyōkan, House of the Autumn Colors, where they could invite foreign gentlemen to elegant dinners without having to patronize the quarters of the flower and the willow. There too it was that the last of the Kodaira murders occurred (see page 208).

Ota Dōkan is thought to have finished his castle in 1457. Although there had earlier been a fishing and farming village on the site, 1957 could therefore be taken as the quincentenary of the founding of the city. Among the undertakings to mark the event was the erection of a big concert hall in Ueno Park. Mostly for Western music, it was finished in 1961, of proportions not much inferior to the insurance building going up at about the same time at the Shinjuku Westmouth, and was widely regarded as a great step forward on the way of the city and the nation back into the esteem of the world. Certainly it was a great improvement on Hibiya Hall, until then the main concert hall in the city. The exterior of the Ueno Park hall may not be to everyone's taste. Modern architecture has not yet come to grips with the fact that unfinished concrete soon begins to look nasty in a damp climate. The interior and the acoustics are good, however. So even before the Olympics the Japanese had technical accomplishments to show off to the world.

In another part of Ueno Park the National Museum resumed construction after a lapse of a quarter of a century. In 1962 a hall went up to house treasures from the Hōryūji near Nara, the greatest reliquary of early art in the land. It is similar in conception to the main hall, finished in 1937: traditional forms are added to modern materials. For its next and most recent building, finished in 1968, the museum discarded old forms. It is a glassy, flat-roofed building which incorporates old Japanese concepts, such as openness and an absence of supporting walls, even as it discards traditional forms.

So the National Museum is a sort of sampler for modern Japanese architecture, a record of the struggle to come to terms with the West.

All that is missing is the "Western" architecture of early Meiji, the reverse of the main hall and the Hōryūji hall. In the beginning superficial Western details were added to traditional methods and materials. The oldest surviving building, from 1908, is of the day when reproduction of Western prototypes from start to finish was the thing. It is a handsome enough Renaissance building with a central dome and lesser domes at either end—in concept a little like Tokyo Central Station, though it is in stone and not brick. Then come the buildings of 1937 and 1962, in a hybrid style. Then comes the most recent building, the hall of Oriental (as distinguished from Japanese) art. It was beginning to dawn on Japanese architects that modern architecture had come to them and they did not have to go to it. Modern architects, or some of them, were doing something not dissimilar to what the Japanese had been doing from time immemorial.

The Olympic decade was in some respects incoherent. Toward the end of it came the games themselves and the warm glow of cosmopolitanism. Midway through it came a great xenophobic rising, the protest demonstrations against revision of the Japanese-American Security Treaty.

They had the city paralyzed for several weeks during the summer of 1960, and produced one fatality—or two, if the principal assassination of the postwar period, that of the chairman of the Socialist Party, is attributed to anti-treaty unrest. It occurred at a public meeting in Hibiya Hall, but after the summer of discontent had passed and the city was back to something like normal once more. The assassin was a teenage boy of the radical right (he later killed himself in prison).

It was a most xenophobic time, and particularly an anti-American time. "Yankee go home" was among the things people were saying (in English). Even unintellectual, down-to-earth Asakusa was caught up in the mood. In April 1960 the Rokkuza (Sixth District Theater), where one of Nagai Kafū's postwar skits was performed (see page 110), offered a play called *The Tachikawa Base: Ten Solid Years of Rape*. The Tachikawa base was American, a big air base out in the county part of the prefecture.

The play is largely flashback. At the outset a young man is being arrested for murder. The police accede to his request that he be allowed to explain his reasons for killing the young lady he loved. So the flashback begins. The young lady was doing welfare work among ladies who were doing the only thing a lady could do, aside from welfare work, in Tachikawa: selling themselves to American soldiers. The girlfriend was raped by an American and acquired a loathsome disease. That is why he had to kill her.

Such was the mood of the city in those days. The play was erotic entertainment, of course, but it had its message, not too remote from the "one of us will get one of them" principle on which the extremists of the interwar years acted. Japan being a peaceful country, the ladies of Tachikawa, in one of the little sermons with which the piece is studded, are exhorted to get one of them by nonviolent means, such as infecting them with loathsome diseases. It was rather marvelous, the way the people of Tokyo had of assuring one that nothing personal was intended. The dislike for smutchy outsiders seemed very genuine. They threatened the purity of the island nation, left to itself until they came along.

The cabinet fell, but not before the treaty revisions went through; and the left never again rose to such heights of militancy. Indeed it started going to pieces. Violence continued, but it was fragmented and largely internecine. The Communist Party came to seem mild and restrained compared with the factions that broke away from it and went about flailing at one another with pipes and staves and hijacking airplanes. They did great harm to the universities in the post-Olympic years, but this does not mean that they continued to be a significant political force. Universities are defenseless against bands of fanatics unless they call the police. When they refuse to do so and the police refuse to come unless called, they are in serious trouble. The next great rising should have come in 1970, and it did not. In that year either party to the treaty could legally renounce it.

Another sort of political or social violence, if these kinds may be distinguished from ordinary criminal violence, might have developed into something serious in another country. The fact that it failed to satisfy expectations may have to do with the imprecise language that raised the expectations. Loan words, most commonly from English, can be most misleading. News that there is unrest in the Detroit slums is cause for alarm. News that the big police box in the Sanya *suramu,* north of Asakusa and the Yoshiwara, is being stoned again is routine. Such things happen and no one need feel threatened. People go off to watch, as they would go off to a display of fireworks. The stoners may be genuinely indignant at the police, but the Sanya *suramu* is not genuinely a slum.

Sanya is, along with the Kamagasaki district of Osaka, the most famous of the "slums." Purists draw a distinction betwen the Meiji slums, preeminent among them the Samegahashi or Sharkbridge one in Yotsuya, west of the palace, and Sanya. They assign the latter the designation *doyagai*, though "slum" is certainly much commoner. *Doyagai* is from the underworld argot that reverses the two syllables of a bisyllabic word. *Kai* or *gai* is "district" or "street," and *doya* reverses *yado*, which is "inn" or other temporary lodging. "Flophouse" might be the best rendition. Thus a slum is, to purists, a place where poor families dwell as families. Sharkbridge was for the least fortunate of provincial families who came flooding in upon the great city. A *doyagai*, on the other hand, is a place of cheap lodgings for single and transient lodgers. In the popular mind, Sanya is a slum for all that, and a stoning of the police box no different linguistically from a rising in Detroit.

In Edo and on into Meiji, Sanya accommodated people away from home. They were mostly of two sorts: travelers to and from the northern

Sleeping rough in the Sanya "slum"

255

provinces, for Sanya lay where the main northern highway entered and left the city; and the staff and clientele of the Yoshiwara, for it lay on the canal that offered water access to the quarter from the Sumida. In 1976 the canal was filled in except for a hundred yards or so at the mouth. A Meiji edict regarding the operation of lodging places put Sanya in the lowest class. The opening in 1897 of what is still officially called the Sumida freight yards, though more popularly it is Shioiri, Tidewater, gave Sanya the particular character it has had ever since. It is just south of the freight yards, and it provided the most convenient lodgings for workers there.

Sanya has had a public employment agency since late Meiji, but access to work, in recent years mostly in what the Japanese call dirt-wood business, which is to say roads and construction, has been over-whelmingly through less formal channels, brokers often under the control of underworld gangs. The system provides no security and no insurance, but it does provide freedom from embarrassing questions.

The *doya* of Sanya have improved. In the first years after the war they were tents, then there were large common rooms. These have mostly disappeared, though bunking arrangements with eight men in a room some twelve feet square are not unusual. Prices have risen, though not at rates greater than general inflation. Space in a shared room can still be had for under a thousand yen a night, and a man can have a tiny room with television for two thousand. Life in Sanya is not intolerable when there is work. It allows drinking, gambling, and inexpensive sex. Long rainy periods are the bad times.

A 1970 survey revealed that not many very young men lived in Sanya. Sixty percent of those polled were in their thirties and forties. More than half had been in Sanya for five years or more. So, although still a place of cheap, pay-by-the-night *doya,* Sanya was not exactly a temporary abode. The age of the residents has observably risen in the years since. The day may come when the *doya* business will disappear and Sanya will be little different from other residential districts in the northern and eastern parts of the city. The laboring population is well down from a peak of some fifteen thousand during the Olympic years. Even now, during most hours of the day, it looks little different from many another shabby neighborhood. The best hours for observing that it is in fact somewhat different are in the early morning, when crowds of men await transportation by bus and truck to the day's working place, and others lie sleeping in the gutters. In the early-evening hours it can be rather jolly, somewhat like Piss Alley at the Shinjuku Westmouth.

Sanya may not be as grim as parts of Detroit, but it has reason for discontent. The nation started moving ahead in the fifties, and Sanya did not move with it; and there was a common feeling that the police with their mammoth box, which went up in the summer of 1960, were arrogant and threatening. Indeed they are not the most friendly and helpful of police. The first big riot came that same summer, which was the summer of the treaty disturbances. There may have been a spillover. Three thousand men gathered at the mammoth box, and stoned it, and tried to set fire to it. A policeman was injured.

There have been frequent Sanya incidents since, the same police box being the main target. Perhaps because the early ones received much attention from the media, later ones came to seem random and ritualistic.

Ordinary criminal violence was not as big or as horrid as in the early postwar years. There was nothing to compare with the Imperial Bank case or the Kotobuki and Kodaira cases. Perhaps the most widely publicized Tokyo incident was one involving a television "idol," as victim and not as culprit. On January 13, 1957, in the Kokusai (International) Theater in Asakusa, a nineteen-year-old girl flung hydrochloric acid in the face of Misora Hibari, among the most popular and perdurable of postwar entertainers. She appeared as a child at the Ernie Pyle. During her most vigorous period, the Olympic years, she was able to fill all three thousand seats at the Shinjuku Koma twice a day for a run of two months. (A month at the Koma is the cachet, the sign that a popular singer has reached the top.) Her popularity is unabated even now, though her vigor has been diminished by poor health. The girl said that she did it out of an affection so overwhelming that she wished it to be attached to a cicatrized visage. Miss Misora was laid up for three weeks and came back uncicatrized. Numbers of similar incidents have occurred in the years since.

There went on being curious little incidents to suggest that Japanese criminals rather enjoy getting caught and so render the role of the police less difficult than in most places. In September 1961 a man came into the detective offices at the Ueno police station. He wished to say hello to the detective who had sent him up for extortion two years before and to report how well he had been behaving himself since his release from prison. An old man came in to report that someone had taken his watch over by the railway station. He recognized the earlier caller as the thief.

In 1965 a man in Meguro, in the southwestern part of the city, killed his common-law wife and entombed her in cement. Several months later —he had been living with the cement block all the while—he was arrested trying to peddle his interesting story to a weekly magazine.

Crime was becoming more white-collar and intellectual. It was in the sixties that the *sōkaiya* came into prominence. Though their business is rarely thuggish enough to attract the intervention of the police and the public procurators, at its heart are extortion and intimidation. The expression shows how concise the Japanese language can be when it wishes to. The literal meaning is "general-meeting business," but the big Japanese-English dictionary must go to these lengths to make the real meaning quite clear (and thus tells us implicitly that the European languages have no need for such a word): "a person who holds a small number of shares in a number of companies and attempts to extort money from them by threatening to cause trouble at the general meeting of the stockholders."

It is a somewhat longer definition than necessary. The words "attempts to" are superfluous, for the *sōkaiya* have been very successful at getting hush and protection money from the biggest and most highly esteemed companies in the land.

In part the companies have themselves to blame. The underworld and people who occupy the twilight zone between the underworld and the great radiant world of finance and industry might not have noticed how profitable a thing it could be to own a few shares if they had not been called in for union busting and the stilling of protests against pollution and such things. The general willingness to buy off *sōkaiya* must inevitably suggest to the outsider that the great ones of finance and industry have things which they would prefer to keep out of sight. The general-meeting business, in any event, is more subtle than even a subtle bank robbery, such as the robbery of the Imperial Bank, and tells of a day when a certain margin to think things over and make a few calculations had returned.

In the post-Olympic years English-speaking *sōkaiya* began making their appearance at meetings of foreign companies. The most capable among them was a former intelligence interpreter for the American army who had studied in the United States. The labors of the *sōkaiya* have not been limited to Tokyo, but Tokyo, where most of the big companies have their headquarters, offers far the best opportunities. Like all Japanese, the *sōkaiya* are very industrious, to remind us of an important and neglected truth, that industriousness is not in itself necessarily a virtue.

In the summer of 1965 the Olympic governor, Azuma Ryūtarō, announced that he would not run for reelectior He was then midway through his second term. He had ample reason, 'ide from the fact that the Olympics, the occasion for his seeking office in the first place, had been accomplished. Both his predecessor, the first elected governor, and his successor, the radical governor, served three terms, or twelve years. The present governor, another conservative, is effective and popular, and, now in his third term, may well seek an unprecedented fourth one (unprecedented in Tokyo, though by no means unheard of in the provinces). The main reason for the decision not to run was a scandal and its effect upon the conservative base. They might have prevented reelection in any event.

The metropolitan government had an aura of scandal hanging over it most of the time. The prefectural government of the postwar years has not been without scandals, though they have for the most part not been as big or as interesting as the prewar ones. A scandal surrounded the election of Azuma to his second term. Then came the biggest one of the postwar years.

The prefectural council elected a president in March 1965. It was a very dirty election, involving bribery and intimidation. The president himself was arrested, as were almost a score of others. Dissolution of the council was obviously called for, but it had to await amendments to the Local Autonomy Law. In June, pursuant to provisions of the new law, the council unanimously voted its own dissolution. New elections were called.

While the campaign was in progress, from late June into July, a huge plague of flies descended on the wards east of the Sumida River. The skies and the earth were black with them. They came from a spot of land out in the bay called Yume no Shima, "Dream Island." Dream Island is a garbage fill. Initial efforts of the Self-Defense Force (the Japanese army by another name) to exterminate the flies seem initially to have had only the effect of spreading them. Finally a scorched-earth policy worked. Dream Island was for a time a cinder on which not even flies could live. It is doubtful that the governor could have done much to foresee or forestall the scandal, though he might possibly have guessed what garbage fills are capable of. The timing, in any event, was unfortunate.

The election, which occurred late in July, was a free-for-all, great fun to watch, however one may have felt about the results. Councilmen awaiting trial ran for reelection. Several known gangsters were among the candidates. The results were a thorough renunciation of the Olympic governor and his administration—less than a year after they had acquitted themselves so nobly of their main task. The conservatives, who had a majority of the council after the 1963 elections, lost almost half their seats and were left with a third of the total. No single party has since had a majority. Coalitions have been the rule. All of the other parties gained, and the socialists became the first party, with seven more seats than the conservatives.

This fiasco for the conservatives looked ahead to the next gubernatorial elections, when the socialists and communists offered a persuasive candidate, Minobe Ryōkichi, son of the professor whose ideas found so little favor with the radical right of the interwar years (see page 128). Minobe was a television personality with a large following, particularly among women. The problem of garbage disposal, which had such an unfortunate effect on the Azuma administration, was among the consuming interests of the Minobe administration.

The matter of addresses and place names in Edo and Tokyo has always been such a complicated one that efforts to improve it often bring new complications. The theory of the address is two-dimensional rather than, as in the West, unidimensional. A huge effort would be required to change from the former system to the latter, and one of the complexities would only become more complex, the fact that place names are always changing. In possession of a slightly outdated map and an up-to-date place name, a person can find the effort to reconcile the two utterly bewildering. So it can be too with tracing a place name from a century or so ago. Several changes have probably occurred before it at length arrived at the designation which it has today (but may not have tomorrow).

By a two-dimensional system is meant one in which addresses are scattered over a tract of land. In a unidimensional system they are dots along a line. Complications become formidable when there is no perceptible ordering to the numbers here and there over the tract.

Attempts at simplification and rationalization have taken dual form, reducing the number of separately named tracts (which means of course that many houses acquire new tract designations) and bringing some order to the arrangement of numbers within each tract, so that there is at least a reasonable chance that adjacent spots will have consecutive numbers. The amalgamation of tracts to reduce the number has gone on sporadically through the century and more since Tokyo became Tokyo. It became systematic during the Olympic years, and it cannot yet be thought finished. There is still a welter of small tracts in what before 1947 was Kanda Ward, and there is one in the old Ushigome Ward, to the west of the palace. Yet, though the problem of how to match an address with an outdated map has if anything become worse, the endeavor accomplished something. One can often find a new address without the help of the police. It is often true that numbers move back and forth along traverse lines, rather as if the lines of a book were to read alternately left to right and right to left, but one does get the hang of the system, and at least it is a system. The old one was that only in a very primitive way, having to do with the order in which buildings went up, and the outsider could scarcely be expected to know that.

One may carp at the ordering of numbers, and find ways in which it can be improved; but that it is an improvement seems hard to deny. The other half of the endeavor, the amalgamation of tracts (the old *machi* or *chō*), is more controversial. It is here as it was with the 1947 reduction in the number of wards. Old names go, and a coating of history goes with them.

"Reminded that the district around the Shirahige Shrine was known in the old days as Terajima Village, I might once have thought first of the country villa of Kikugorō."

So writes Nagai Kafū at the beginning of A *Strange Tale from East of the River*. On his first visit to the Tamanoi quarter that is the site of the principal action, he passes a secluded villa, and has this thought. It is a little disingenuous, because the region surrounding Tamanoi was still known as Terajima. It would be more to the point today. Terajima is among the place names that have disappeared. It was an old and famous one, giving a family name to a celebrated line of Kabuki actors, the Kikugorō. Today Kafu would not have to pretend that he is remind ed of a name now gone. Its going makes the history of the place seem remoter.

Not all places were unhappy about the change of names. The Yoshiwara and Sanya thought that new names might improve their images, and got them. In neither case has the new name been accompanied by great social improvement, but that is another matter. Suzugamori, at the far south of the Meiji city even as the Yoshiwara and Sanya were at the far north, was similarly pleased. It was known chiefly as one of the places where the Tokugawa magistrates had people's heads lopped off.

One place felt so strongly about its name that its citizenry brought an administrative action suit, in 1965, to keep it. The action was successful. A part of Bunkyō Ward continues to be called Yayoichō. Why the authorities should even have thought of tampering with so great a name is difficult to understand. It was in Yayoichō, in mid-Meiji, that artifacts were found which gave the name Yayoi to a great cultural epoch, some five centuries straddling the beginning of the Christian era.

Most attempts at resistance were unsuccessful. Sometimes the citizenry was divided. Kobikichō, east of Ginza, where the Kabukiza stands, was as important as any part of the city in the history of the Edo theater. Romantics and antiquarians wanted to keep the name. Businessmen thought that having the element "Ginza" in the name would be better for business. So it became East Ginza. (Actually this happened before the systematic rationalization of addresses. In the course of this last, the "East" was dropped, and the district became simply Ginza.)

Sometimes an old name was assigned to a larger district, so that if an old name disappeared at least it was subsumed under another old name. Often the new name was merely arid and bureaucratic. The city is dotted with Easts and Wests and Outers and Middles and Inners. Devotees of the Yose variety theaters used to greet favored performers not with their names but (so much better a way of showing that one was a real connoisseur) with the names of the districts in which they resided. It sounds nothing like as good, one of them pointed out recently, when the names must be Outer A and Middle B.

Simplification produced complication both because many old addresses had to be changed and because sometimes the old names remained in certain capacities. The subways and railways have declined to change the names of their stations merely because at street level the old name has been canceled. The two subway stations between Ueno and Asakusa bear names no longer to be found in the regions above. Shiina-machi, where the Imperial Bank murders took place, no longer exists, but it is the name of a station on the Seibu Ikebukuro line. This can be puzzling. Simplification itself becomes a complication.

August 1, 1965, was a sad day for Asakusa. The name Rokku, Sixth District, signifying the section of the old park where show business flourished, ceased to exist. On the same day the Tokiwaza closed its doors for stage performances and became a movie place. Most of the big Asakusa names from Taishō and early Shōwa had appeared upon its banners.

What was surely among the big events of the second postwar, or Olympic, decade was one in which city and prefecture played no part. Prostitution was again outlawed, this time by the National Diet. Four years after the end of the Occupation, in May 1956, an anti-prostitution law was enacted. It took effect on April 1, 1958. The previous outlawing was at the instance of the Occupation. This time the feminine electorate and women Diet members, both of them postwar institutions, were instrumental. It might never have happened without woman suffrage, and it certainly would not have happened so soon, a mere decade after the much-ignored Edict 9 (see page 191). Men, such as brothel keepers, were certainly behind the opposition to the new law (the anti-anti-prostitution movement), but the openest and most outspoken opposition was feminine. It was an amazonian battle—not that the conclusion was other than foregone. More than one opposition movement took shape early in 1956 as passage of the law, which had languished in the Diet for several years, seemed imminent. Two socialist members of the Diet were expelled from the party for being active in organizing a movement, in Asakusa. The Socialist Party may have wobbled and tergiversated on some issues, such as the need for revolution, but it was firm about prostitution.

There was even a grand coalition against anti-prostitution. It was called the Tokyo Federation of Unions of Women Workers. But the law was passed, of course. In the interim before its tentative application, still clinging to a hope, brothel keepers organized a National Autonomous

Association for the Prevention of Venereal Disease. A Diet member was arrested for taking bribes from it. The 1958 date is the one generally accepted for the disappearance once again of prostitution, but the law theoretically went into effect a year earlier, on April 1, 1957. The following Aprils Fools' Day was the one on which the meting out of punishments was to begin.

Even as it was a foregone conclusion that the law would pass, it was a foregone conclusion that prostitution would not disappear. More than a hundred thousand women the country over were affected by the new law, and they and their associates would find ways. Yet to say that the new law made no difference would most certainly be in error. The great and venerable world of the flower and the willow, so central to the arts of Edo and early Tokyo, had over the years fallen into a malaise, and the new law made it even sicker. Of the two licensed quarters within the old city limits, the newer one, Susaki, went out of business. The Yoshiwara shifted over to a closely related business.

The Yoshiwara and Susaki had both been destroyed in 1945. Susaki rebuilt in a quiet, conservative, and, given the materials at hand, not at all tasteless fashion. The Yoshiwara began its convalescence with the shacks called "barracks," but within a half-dozen years after the war was its gaudy old self again. It had some of the most expensive pleasure palaces in the city, charging the equivalent of thirty dollars a night, a very large sum of money in those days. The architecture of the brothels was as eclectic and uninhibited as it had been before the war. The lavish courtesan processions of an earlier day were resumed, by way of advertising.

Which would have prevailed, the Yoshiwara way or the Susaki way, if the first Tokyo century had not been so rich in disasters? These are usually blamed when someone from outside remarks upon the hodge-podge which the city for the most part is—an eminent European intellectual referred to it as "this tortured use of space." What else can a place be, retorts the son of Tokyo, when it is twice wiped out, and subjected to many a lesser disaster between the two major ones? It is true that such a place has to work hard even to survive. Yet, though we can only speculate, the eclectic and uninhibited Yoshiwara way seems the genuine Tokyo way.

Wandering through Susaki today, one still comes upon a scattering of house and shop fronts that announce what the places once were.

Blocks and blocks of nondescript landfills had in any event removed Susaki from the bay shore that had been among its principal charms. It may have been the newcomer among the licensed quarters in and on the edges of the city (it opened only in Meiji), but the Fukagawa district in which it is situated was prominent among the "hilly places," the unlicensed flower-and-willow districts of Edo. (There is disagreement as to why they were called hilly places, though the word "hill," *oka,* is an element in a number of expressions indicating remoteness from the place where the action is, in this case the Yoshiwara.) People like Nagai Kafū could go there and linger with melancholy pleasure over vestiges of Edo. The going of Susaki brought a sense of loss.

Some of Kafū's "dens of unlicensed whores" went too, including what was probably, along with the Tokyo Palace, the most famous postwar one, Hatonomachi, Pigeon Town (see page 186), east of the Sumida River. The houses of Pigeon Town all closed their doors late in January 1958, some two months before the date from which they could all in theory be fined. Stenciled "Off Limits" warnings to the men of the Occupation grow fainter and fainter as the years go by, but even today

Hatonomachi as it appears today. The small mosaic tiles are among the identifying signs of a bawdy house

they are to be found in the district that still calls itself Pigeon Town, if one knows where to look for them.

The Yoshiwara was not so docile about leaving the old business behind. A few of the more distinguished houses, proud of themselves and their past, quietly closed their doors and sold their land. A great many others became what were called Turkish baths until recently. A Turk objected. Now the standard though not universal designation is "soapland." The Toruko (the Japanese metamorphosis of "Turk") was, and the soapland is, a place, often expensive, where a man can go and have a ritual bath and massage and the undivided attention of a young lady. It is a brothel by another name. The count of soaplands in the Yoshiwara is now almost two hundred, and that of soapland ladies some twenty-five hundred.

The Yoshiwara had since Meiji been noted for its architectural extravagances, often of a fancifully cosmopolitan kind. One may not come upon much that looks Turkish beside a Yoshiwara street, but the more ornate styles of Europe and the ancient Orient are most of them there, with an occasional touch of Egypt among them. It is all very interesting and amusing, but a result of anti-prostitution has been to make the

Exuberant architecture in the Yoshiwara. Once known as Turkish baths, the brothels are now called "soaplands"

Yoshiwara slip yet a bit further from the heights of other ages. The more dignified houses went away, and the less dignified ones stayed and became less dignified all the time.

Many a den of unlicensed prostitutes followed the way of the Yoshiwara rather than that of Susaki and Pigeon Town. The view of the police seems to have been that the law was unenforceable from the outset. It is a view in keeping with that of the Supreme Court expert (see page 191) who commented on the preceding disappearance of prostitution. Those who formed the association for the prevention of venereal disease may have felt themselves vindicated. Police detected a sharp rise among prostitutes during the post-anti-prostitution years.

The years between the next-to-last and the last outlawing of prostitution were those of the *akasen,* the red line. The expression seems to have originated as police jargon, the prefectural police thus designating the districts to which the edict applied. The old distinction between licensed and unlicensed prostitution thus disappeared. The Yoshiwara and Pigeon Town were alike red-line districts. Another distinction now grew up to replace the old one, as if there were a reluctance to let anything go. Places such as the Golden Block of Shinjuku, in which prostitution was covert and somewhat secondary, came to be known as *aosen* or blue-line districts.

In 1963 there came tacit recognition from reliable quarters that prostitution yet survived, and could be a problem. The style manual of NHK, the public broadcasting corporation, decreed that those who had hitherto been called BG would henceforth be OL. Both are acronyms from English expressions, "business girl" and "office lady." Both signify working women, but NHK feared that the former might be taken to signify "prostitute."

The Yoshiwara has had no great fires on its own, none that it did not share with the rest of the city, in more than three-quarters of a century. The fire of 1910 was among the last great conflagrations of which the city has been a victim, save for the disasters of 1923 and 1945. Among postwar fires, one which occurred in the northern part of the city in April 1963 and destroyed thirty-six buildings is the most extensive given notice in the centennial history of the Tokyo Fire Department. The chronology appended to the centennial history of city and prefecture notes a fire that destroyed fifty-eight buildings east of the Sumida in 1957. It does not matter which was the larger. They were of generally the same proportions, and neither would have been much noticed during the full summer of the Flowers of Edo.

The most sensational of postwar fires included one in a department store and one in a hotel. The former, which killed seven people, occurred on August 22, 1963, in the Ikebukuro Seibu. The day was a holiday for the store, but several hundred maintenance men, decorators, and the like were on the premises. Among them, in the seventh-floor dining room, was an anti-cockroach squad. One of its members, about to have a post-luncheon smoke, threw his match into a heap of paper impregnated with insecticide. In the scramble to extinguish the flames, a can of insecticide was knocked over. Though the store really had no one to apologize to, it took the occasion for an act of contrition, a big sale, which almost turned into another disaster. The crowds at opening time were so gigantic and threatening that the store closed its doors in less than an hour. It was not wholly cleared of crowds until noon. Many a housewife demanded repayment of her train fare, and was obliged.

The toll was smaller than that of the Shirokiya fire, but still the third largest from any postwar fire in Tokyo. The hotel fire, in 1982, took thirty-three lives. In 1963 nineteen firemen died in a warehouse fire in the southern part of the city.

The most lamentable fire of the postwar years was a case of arson. It wrought great damage upon the material heritage of a city that has never been very strong in that regard. One of three surviving wooden pagodas in the city stood in the Yanaka cemetery near Ueno. On July 6, 1957, it was damaged beyond repair by fire. A campaign to rebuild it is only now getting underway. The foundation stones remain, a few steps from the graves of the famous murderess Takahashi O-den and Nagai Kafū's grandfather. Two bodies were found among the cinders. The proprietor of a tailoring establishment in the neighborhood and a woman employee less than half his age had chosen the pagoda as the place in which to carry out their suicide pact. The pagoda had been built late in the eighteenth century and is the subject of a famous and once widely read piece of Meiji fiction, Kōda Rohan's "The Five-Storey Pagoda" ("Gojūnotō"). Rohan made his hero, the master carpenter who built the pagoda, the embodiment of all the old virtues.

Yanaka Pagoda, as it was before being
burned in a love suicide in 1957

In 1957 there occurred a double suicide that seemed to have as much potential for setting off a vogue as the Oiso suicides of the interwar years (see page 35). It did not, but, for reasons that quite defy explanation, a suicide in 1972 did. About a hundred fifty people have jumped from the roofs of the Takashimadaira apartment complex in the northwestern part of the city since, in that year, a woman first did so. The setting and circumstances of the 1957 suicides were far more romantic, and set off no vogue at all.

On an early-winter day the bodies of a young boy and girl, dead of gunshot wounds, were found on Mount Amagi, on the Izu Peninsula in Shizuoka Prefecture. It was established that the boy, in accepted fashion, had killed the girl and then himself. They proved to be schoolmates from Tokyo. The girl's name was Aishinkakura Eisei, a most unusual one for a Japanese. The family name is the Japanization of Aishingyoro, the family name of the Manchu emperors of China. (Like Kim, the commonest of Korean names, it means "gold" or "money.") She was the niece of Pu-yi, the last emperor of China and the only head of the Japanese puppet state in Manchuria. The Japanese wife of the emperor's brother appears briefly in the movie *The Last Emperor*. She is conspicuously pregnant, and it is probably with this girl, who was very pretty and not, by all accounts, especially unhappy. The act was probably one of romantic abandon more in keeping with the Japanese half of her nature than the continental. The mystery remains that there were no imitators, while the altogether more pedestrian suicide at Takashimadaira had scores and scores.

The burning of the Yanaka pagoda was the greatest loss by fire which the city has suffered since the war. And what was the greatest loss by death? Perhaps that of Nagai Kafū, late in April 1959. He was the writer among all modern Japanese writers who most particularly made Tokyo his subject, and he was the most industrious and among the best at evoking its moods and describing its places. Toward the end of his life he expressed a wish to be buried among the courtesans in a little temple north of the Yoshiwara. Had he known that the Sunshine Building, highest in the city and the land, would come to loom gigantically over the Zoshigaya cemetery, where he is buried, he might have insisted more strongly on the temple. He did not like such places as the Sunshine, or what it stands for.

Takami Jun and Kawabata Yasunari, who wrote so well about Asakusa, died a few years after Kafū, the former in 1965, the latter, probably a suicide, in 1972. Neither was as faithful as Kafū in his attentions to Tokyo. Takeda Rintarō, who wrote so well about Ginza, died in the spring of 1946, a victim of the postwar confusion. Most biographical dictionaries say evasively that he died of a sudden liver attack. One or two hint at something nearer the truth. His death was indeed sudden, and it was from drinking methyl alcohol in a little place in Shibuya. Inexpensive beverages were not safe in those days.

Tokyo has had no one like any of them since, no writer to express its individuality as his own. The trouble may be that, vast and inchoate, it no longer has much individuality.

Along with its peculiar crimes and its voguish suicides, Tokyo has quirky deaths. On November 10, 1964, exactly a month after the opening of the Olympics, the paid announcement that the Rakugo monologuist Sanyūtei Kimba had died came out in the first person. "I am safely dead. You may put your minds at rest in that regard. It has been my wish all along that I receive no floral offerings, natural or artificial. Asking you to forgive my petulance, I mean to stand by it. We will meet again, perhaps, centuries hence, in the heavenly pavilion, or among the dew-drenched leaves on the banks of the stony river. In the meantime, have long lives, all of you. I thank you for your many kindnesses during my own lifetime. November 8. Sanyūtei Kimba."

The Buddhist writ contains many hells. In the one referred to here, children pile stones in heaps only to have the heaps knocked down by demons. The general sense is that we will meet again one century, in heaven or in hell.

The dozen years between the cooling off from the white heat of 1960 and the "oil shock" of 1973 were years of rapid economic growth. It almost seemed during those summer months of 1960, so completely was the city under the control of the anti-treaty demonstrators, that all they had to do to consummate their revolution was march upon the television stations, the Tokyo equivalent of the Winter Palace. The cooling was rapid. Youthful factions went on fighting, but it was mostly with one another and with the universities. In a land where business has never been below second on the list of important things, it was first again.

Among the loan words in vogue from the late fifties into the sixties were "glamour," "vacance," "leisure," "topless show," "*otomee fujin*," and "instant." Most of them tell of new and affluent ways, one or two ask for explanation. The next to the last is a hybrid, the first element being an abbreviation of "automated" or "automation," the second a Japanese word for housewife. The last refers to instant food, making things easier for the automated wife.

Among the tribes or *zoku* not already mentioned were the *yoromeki*, the *kaminari*, and the *eieki*. The first took its name from a very popular novel by Mishima Yukio called *The Faltering of the Virtues* (*Bitoku no Yoromeki*) and suggests wantonness and infidelity. The second is literally "the Thunder Tribe." Its members raced about on motorcycles. They outraced the police, who were left to pretend that they were not there and to hope that they would go away. The last is another abbreviation, of "electric." It signifies amplified music, and especially the electric guitar.

In these tribes and their names is the spirit of the day. There were also an Anchūha and an Angoha. The first syllable in both cases signifies the Japanese-American Security Treaty, and the second is respectively "during" and "after." The third is "faction." So, in contrast to the faction that was all caught up in the disturbances, there was already by the early sixties a faction that had come to the fore after they subsided. For them 1960 was already ancient history.

Pearl Harbor was prehistory. In 1959 a group of forty-five students at a Tokyo middle (or junior high) school was set without warning to the task of composing an essay about the significance of December 8, the anniversary of the attack, corresponding to December 7 in the United States, that day once expected to live in infamy. Only two knew the principal significance, and many another significance was attached: the day Christmas sales begin, the day on which a famous Sumō wrestler got married, the day Grandfather died. Probably a similar group of American students would not have done much better with Pearl Harbor, but it would most likely have spread its ignorance more impartially, offering little help as to the significance of August 6 (Hiroshima Day) either. This last day, when Japan could claim to be the injured party, is remembered.

There were also the years of (in English) "my car." The word *doraibu* was already in vogue by the beginning of the Olympic decade. It signifies a new pursuit, pleasure driving, and it is the Japanization of the English "drive," used as a noun. At first most of the drivers out on the road for the fun of it were businessmen with expense accounts, and civil servants, but within a few years driving clubs with cars for rent made half their money from students.

In the next decade private automobiles became so numerous that the parking-lot business began, the first Tokyo specimen opening in 1959. In 1963 it was made illegal to keep the family automobile in the street space in front of the family house. Little garden plots all over the city fell victim to the higher demands of the automobile. In general driving conditions were much improved from the days early in the century when Tanizaki was getting his nose bloodied against the roof of a taxicab. By the early eighties virtually all the streets in the wards had hard surfaces.

Conditions were not quite so good in the county part of the prefecture, but the surfaced mileage passed 90 percent for the prefecture as a whole. Three decades before, it had been well under half.

The so-called Jimmu prosperity of the mid-fifties recalled the semi-legendary founding of the Japanese nation, Jimmu being the legendary first emperor and the expression signifying that there had been no such prosperity in all the centuries since his reign. The sixties and seventies were not without their little setbacks, such as the one occasioned by oil shock, but the dominant note was of growth, prosperity, and increasing national confidence. The names given to periods of prosperity suggested that they were getting better all the time. There was the *iwato* or "cave" prosperity, and later, in the years after the Olympics, there was the Izanagi prosperity. Each took us further beyond Jimmu and back into the legendary origins of the nation. The "cave" referred to the one into which the Sun Goddess withdrew after a quarrel with her fractious brother, causing darkness to fall upon the land. Izanagi was an ancestor of the Sun Goddess a few generations earlier. Each of these periods of prosperity outdid the others in department-store sales. If there had been anything like them in the days of the Sun Goddess and Izanagi, there had not been since.

The supermarket, almost everyone agrees, is an American invention. It is among the American ideas that have proved more exportable than American products. It has not developed in quite the same way in all the places to which it has been exported. In America supermarkets began during the depression, to provide food at low prices to the jobless and otherwise straitened. They appeared in Tokyo during the first postwar decade. One might have expected, in those years of the cod and the sweet potato, that supermarkets would have some relation to straitened circumstances; they did not. The first self-service food emporiums that could call themselves supermarkets opened in the southwestern wards where rich foreigners and rich Japanese alike were concentrated. They were expensive.

The food departments of the big department stores had been similarly all-purpose, but they had not been arranged so that the customer could serve himself. As is in the nature of department stores, comestible items had been segregated, kept separate from noncomestible. The supermarket somewhat nearer the original American kind, purveying to the less than wealthy, did not make its appearance until the Olympic years, when almost everyone was wealthier. It put both kinds of commodities, comestible and noncomestible, in the same space, and caught on because of this not very startling innovation.

In 1964 two supermarket chains, one native to the city and the other from Osaka, got started in Tokyo. Their competition, which was intense, took place at first in the western suburbs, where neither commuting husband nor automated wife wished to spend much time shopping. Sociologists associate the emergence of the supermarket with the emergence in those same western suburbs of the two-generation "kernel" family.

The time came in the pre-Olympic years when the Japanese could no longer say with much conviction that they were poor. Consumption was becoming conspicuous. In 1962, to much publicity, an Asakusa clothing wholesaler offered a necktie for fifty thousand yen. It was snapped up. Every thread of the weft was different from every other, and an expert weaver spent three days weaving it. A reasonably expensive tie of the more ordinary sort would have cost no more than a thousand yen.

A government survey in 1964 showed that 50 percent of Japanese thought themselves middle-class. The number was probably higher in Tokyo. Three years later a survey showed that 90 percent of Tokyo women thought themselves middle-class.

Among the new words of 1964, the Olympic year, was *kagikko,* "key child." It gives concise statement to the new realities of life in the High City (the Low City, as in most things, lagged behind): the nuclear family, the apartment, and, her numbers increasing, the automated wife. A key child is one who, the expectation being that no one will be at home when he or she returns, carries a key. The following year a newspaper remarked upon the growing number of fat children. Though the report was highly impressionistic and offered no statistical criteria for its findings, it confirms one's own impressions. Eating habits were changing, in the direction of fatty foods. The key child, since he usually had money and no one to tell him he ought to stop eating and get some exercise, could spend all his time with the vending machines. The number of these the nation over increased a hundredfold during the decade of the seventies. In addition to junk food the key child could, if he wished, put money in the vending machines for whiskey, condoms, and pornography.

The year 1964 may also be counted as the Year 3 of the Mansion Age. "Mansion" is an example of a foreign word put to new use upon arriving in Japanese. "Barrack," another instance, had already been a familiar word in Japanese for almost a half century when "mansion" came in. Given the principal significance which the former word had taken, one might have expected the latter to mean something very like the opposite, the one a flimsy and temporary hut, the latter a grand dwelling. The meaning of *barakku* does bear some resemblance to one of the two principal meanings of "barrack," a large building in which large numbers of people live uncomfortable lives. It has no military significance. Other words fill that gap. The want of comfort is present in a *barakku*, even though the largeness may not be.

"Mansion," in English, is different. In 1962 a developer first used the word to designate his developments, which were condominiums. A mansion became any condominium, large or small, plain or extravagant. (The word is still occasionally applied to apartments for rent.)

There were apartments for rent in Tokyo before the war. A public corporation put up apartment clusters, at least three of which survive, here and there over the city. The individual buildings were small and low. As early as 1910 there was near Ueno Station a wooden building, five storeys high, with more than sixty units, that called itself an apartment house (an *apaato*). The first building said to be in the American style, a four-storey one in fireproof materials, went up near Tokyo University in 1925. It survived as a sort of youth hostel until 1986. One might have guessed from its name, Culture Apartments, that it was from the interwar period.

Mostly such places were for unmarried persons. It was only in the postwar years that very large apartment houses started going up and people started flooding into them. The expression *danchi*, which scarcely a Japanese above infancy can be unfamiliar with, is postwar. It is an abbreviation of "public corporation housing," or public housing in big apartment complexes. Tokyo contains some huge ones. They tend to be not very cheerful places, badly painted and maintained. (That famous suicide place, Takashimadaira, in the northwestern part of the city, is a *danchi*. See page 269.) Surveys have shown that there is even less intercourse among the tenants than in similar American suburban developments. The Japanese run to extremes when a notion such as privacy grips them. The first *danchi* went up about a decade after the war. So there are second-generation *danchi* people who are now adults, have known no other residence, and think of the *danchi* as their hometowns, their "native places." The advent of the mansion and other multi-unit dwellings with common entrances is something new to the Tokyo and indeed the Japanese experience. The "long house" or row house, in which the several dwellers under a common roof have their own individual entrances, is very old. Scarcely anyone wanted to move into the new Ginza brick buildings in early Meiji, and here everyone was moving into buildings little different from them in principle.

Mansions and *danchi* tend to combine American want of community with Japanese flimsiness. The traditional view of a building—that it will not last long in any event and so durability need not be a consideration —has persisted in the construction of multi-storey buildings. There are exceptions, especially in such places as Shinjuku and Marunouchi, but the life expectancy is far lower than for similar American or European buildings. The surviving apartment complexes from the post-earthquake period are historical curiosities. New York is full of apartment houses that are decades older. The problem of rebuilding has not been faced and is bound to be painful. If the owners do not have the means and the will to rebuild, Tokyo may for the first time have slums that bear comparison with Europe and America. It may have slums and not *suramu*.

The expression Capital District has had more than one meaning since, in 1956, it achieved legal status. A Law for the Ordering of the Capital District (Shutoen Seibihō) passed the National Diet in that year. It was modeled on the English plan for Greater London. A more specific plan drawn up two years later defined the expression to signify an area within a radius of a hundred kilometers from Tokyo Station. This includes the whole of Saitama, Chiba, and Kanagawa prefectures, bordering Tokyo on the north, east, and south; a part of the fourth prefecture with which Tokyo shares a boundary, Yamanashi, the old province of Kai, off beyond the mountains to the west; and parts of the three northern Kantō prefectures. In 1966 the district was redefined to include all of the seven Kantō prefectures and Yamanashi.

Faced with opposition from local agencies and developers, the system of green belts that is so important to the London plan may be deemed a complete failure. A pair of bedroom towns out in the county part of the prefecture and some bypass and loop highways are the chief tangible results to be detected from the big plans. Yet the concept is significant, for it tells us what Tokyo has become. So is another expression, Greater Tokyo, variously used. Most commonly it includes all of Tokyo, Chiba, Saitama, and Kanagawa prefectures and part of Ibaragi Prefecture, most importantly the new academic and research complex at Tsukuba. Greater Tokyo has thus grown to well over thirty million people, and the Capital District to not far from forty million. A third or more of the population of the land resides in a space which, were it not for all the motor vehicles, a vigorous marcher could march across in a long weekend. There are still farmlands between Tokyo and the population centers of the northern Kantō, and indeed there are farmlands within the Tokyo wards; but the area of unbroken urbanization includes the bay littoral from Yokosuka on the west shore to beyond Chiba on the east shore. The dwindling of farms means that if the day of the sweet potato comes again it will be worse than last time.

The Sumida was flushed for the Olympics, and has gradually accumulated oxygen and little fishes. In other respects it has not been treated well. The stroller along the banks cannot even see the river for considerable stretches because of high concrete retaining walls, and the boater upon the river can see little except the walls. The ultimate reason for these was a big storm a hundred fifty miles away. In September 1959 a storm called the Ise typhoon—since the center passed over Ise Bay, at the head of which Nagoya stands—left upward of five thousand dead. It was the worst storm to hit in either the Shōwa reign or the one preceding it. Ise Bay, unhappily at flood tide when the typhoon struck, rose by some five meters. The highest point in Chūō Ward (Ginza and Nihombashi) is not that high. The Sumida was already being walled in. Now the walls were made higher, against the possibility that a similar disaster might hit Tokyo. So by the end of the sixties concrete walls six to eight meters above water level stretched for some fifteen or sixteen miles along the two banks of the Sumida. During the following decade the two principal canals draining into the Sumida, the Nihombashi and the Kanda, were also walled in.

Doubtless the sort of vision that protects the lowlands of the city against a disaster which might come one of these centuries is laudable. It has not come yet, and meanwhile we may lament that the walls are so ugly.

The Sumida has been mistreated in other ways. An expressway, put through in the post-Olympic years, crosses it from Nihombashi and proceeds upstream along the left bank to well past Asakusa. Like the walls, it is not beautiful. The Sumida once flowed home to the sea past strands where the gathering of shellfish was among the popular diversions. Now it must pass bleak landfills extending as much as two miles beyond the old coastline. One of them is Dream Island, of the pestilence of flies (see page 259). Again the concept is laudable. The city must expand, it seems, and if it can do so over garbage dumps and not paddy fields, something is saved and nothing is lost.

It should not be impossible to convert reclaimed land into something pleasing. The old Low City demonstrates as much. Yet in recent years it has seemed impossible. The tract called a park on Dream Island is probably the best thing the prefecture has done over the whole reclaimed expanse. It is occupied almost entirely by athletic facilities, freight yards, and apartment complexes. The inability to make a garbage dump look like anything but a dusted-over garbage dump is among the reasons for misgivings about plans for a "city of the future" to occupy yet more of the bay.

All in all, the Sumida is an ill-used little stream. Probably the fact that it is little is the reason. The distance from wall to wall is no more than a couple of hundred yards. The Arakawa Drainage Channel, the artificial stream farther east, is more imposing. A little stream running through a great city is bound to get dirty. When it has the obstreperous ways of the Sumida it may expect to find itself walled in as well. Yet the lady who said "It ain't the Grand Canal" had a point. The Grand Canal too is a narrow little strip of water, and it remains beautiful.

One of the great observances of Edo, the opening of the Sumida, was discontinued for a decade, beginning in 1937, because of the Crisis. It was resumed in 1948 and discontinued again in 1961, because it was thought to be a fire hazard and because the odor of the Sumida had so taken away from the pleasure. The opening came late in July and signified the advent of hot weather, when the river, before it got so dirty, added much to the beauty and pleasure of the city. It was the occasion for a huge display of fireworks, and that these could be dangerous was demonstrated in Kyoto when a display set fire to one of the buildings in the old palace compound. The cessation was presumed to be permanent, but in 1978 the fireworks were resumed, farther up the river, near

One of the few remaining geisha restaurants along the Sumida, squeezed between modern buildings

Asakusa. They attract a million or so people each year, and are among the events most disliked by the police.

The million gather along the two banks near Asakusa, and not, as they once did, near Ryōgoku Bridge downstream. So the Yanagibashi geisha district lost a valuable drawing card. Its restaurants ("geisha houses") had been much the best places for viewing the fireworks, and had commanded huge prices. Reservations had to be made literally years in advance. A place in a Yanagibashi restaurant on the night of the opening was the badge of membership in the Establishment.

Yanagibashi was far more grievously wounded by the walling in of the Sumida. All the indications are, indeed, that the wound is fatal. The river remains visible above the walls from upstairs windows, but mendicant musicians no longer come rowing up to Yanagibashi gardens. The gardens were extensions of the river bottom, and they are no more. Yanagibashi may have been doomed in any event. The geisha business has done badly in recent decades, and Yanagibashi, in the old Low City, is a part of town to which captains of government and industry do not go in the ordinary course of things. Among the once-great geisha districts Yanagibashi is the one that seems nearest to expiring. Aficionados hold that in its good years it was the most Edo-like of the districts, the worthiest successor to the Fukagawa district, which flourished across the river in late Edo.

There was no attempt to make Sumō, like judo, the other traditional sport with a mass following, into an Olympic event. It may have been too utterly Japanese. In most lands and sports, obesity and athletic prowess do not go together. Sumō was not having a bad time. The postwar "golden age," opened by Wakanohana and Tochinishiki, went on. Taihō, the most accomplished wrestler since the departure of the above two, was arguably the most popular champion the sport has ever had. He had the television audience, not comparable to that of baseball and especially the Giants, but no small thing all the same. Although it did not make the Olympics, Sumō was becoming a little more cosmopolitan. The first non-Oriental to reach the top ranks, a Hawaiian, did so in 1967. It was also advancing technologically. In 1969 videotapes were used for the first time in settling challenged decisions. (Any one of several judges may challenge the decision by the referee.) There were technological failures. On September 20, 1960, a light exploded in the Hall of the National Accomplishment while a match was in progress. The two wrestlers, who had been locked in combat, fled. They returned and started wrestling again twenty minutes later, the damage having been repaired. One of them had been treated for burns, from fragments that lodged inside his loincloth.

In 1963 the famous writer Ishihara Shintarō, he whose second published story gave the Sun Tribe its name (see page 225), complained publicly that a Sumō match had been fixed. The match took place in Fukuoka, but Tokyo, where all the wrestlers live, can be held responsible. The Sumō Association said that such things did not happen, and that was that. The common wisdom is that such things do indeed happen. Not exactly the fix, perhaps, but the friendly, warmhearted understanding between wrestlers has long been a part of the sport. A wrestler badly needs a win, or perhaps the association needs one to keep people interested, and the wrestler who is asked to lose would be unfeeling and disloyal, among the worst things a Japanese can be, if he did not oblige.

Somewhat later an accomplished wrestler made an uncommonly frank statement. "Wrestlers going into the last day of a tournament with seven wins and seven losses always win. Even when the matches are big ones you know who is going to win."

A division remains between the northern and eastern parts of the city, not rich and not quick to change, and the southern and western parts, quite the opposite. It is a rough and generalized division, but not invalid for that fact. Those who are looking for old Japan, or unchanged Japan, or something of the sort, would be well advised to do their looking amid dirt and poverty, in Sanya rather than Shibuya. Shabbiness does not change, while the world of the rich and powerful seems to change by the minute.

The idea of having a baseball stadium that the Low City, the eastern flatlands, could call its very own was a delightful one. Geologically the Kōrakuen, home grounds for the Giants, is of the Low City, for it lies in a Koshikawa valley only a few feet above sea level. Historically it is very much a part of the High City, for it stands on land which was the main estate of the Mito Tokugawa family; and in recent decades, because of the Giants, it has been chief among the jewels of commercial television and of advertising.

When plans were announced for a new stadium, to be home grounds for a less popular professional team, within an easy walk of Sanya, the possibility that the Low City baseball crowds might stay home and keep a little life there was buoying. Tokyo Stadium, as it was called, opened its gates in Arakawa Ward, just across the boundary from the old Asakusa Ward, in 1962, and waited for the crowds to come. It waited for some years, and was sold to the prefecture in 1977. Now it is used for sandlot baseball. The stands are gone. The crowds continued to go to the Kōrakuen.

For a time early in the Olympic decade a saying about television seemed almost as popular as television, and it was not a friendly one. It did nothing to diminish the power of television, which has grown and grown. Even the haranguers on the campuses, whose style was once stiff and jerky, have taken on the glibness of television newscasters and masters of ceremonies. The saying was the creation of the critic Oya Sōichi, and it had to do with the Japanese television audience: "A hundred million reduced to idiocy." A neat half-dozen Chinese characters, it had its time of popularity in 1956.

6

BALMY DAYS
OF LATE SHŌWA

On a day in the spring of 1965, the portion of the Shōwa reign to occur after the surrender of 1945 became longer than that which had gone before. On a day early in the summer of 1970 the Shōwa emperor had been on the throne longer than his grandfather, the Meiji emperor, who had reigned longer than any of his predecessors whose reigns can be dated with any certainty. On Christmas Day 1976 the emperor became the first in Japanese history to greet a golden jubilee. On Christmas Day 1986 came his diamond jubilee.

The first of these four dates no one seems to have noticed at all— though it would have been a good day on which to declare that elusive entity, the postwar period, finally over. The second received brief notice in the newspapers. The other two were occasions for formal observances, though in neither case did the observances occur on the precise Christmas anniversary. On November 11, 1976, to celebrate the golden jubilee, there was a gathering in the Hall of the Military Way, the Olympic building north of the palace in which the Japanese had won and lost those judo medals just over twelve years before. On April 29, 1986, the emperor's eighty-fifth birthday, there was a gathering to celebrate the diamond jubilee, in the new Hall of the National Accomplishment east of the Sumida River. Both occasions were formal to the point of stiffness, as if those in charge felt that they must be held, but with limited fanfare.

There is a strong and growing tendency to pretend that the first two decades of the reign never happened. Children learned astonishingly little about them in school. (For evidence of their nescience, see page 272.)

There had been a great deal of peace, and, though the war was still remembered on August 6, Hiroshima Day, and though the nation often found it convenient to go on being postwar, which is to say deprived, the bad days were beyond the memory of most Japanese, and further away each day. In the year of the golden jubilee the number of Japanese born after August 15, 1945, passed the number born before—and of course only those born no later than 1940 or so can have clear recollections of that day and its remarkable broadcast.

As the golden jubilee approached, several events took place that may be held to mark the end of one stage and the beginning of another. In 1968 the dollar started slipping. The exchange rate of three hundred sixty yen to the dollar had been set by the Occupation in 1949 and had come to seem almost sacred. Now it was a failing god. In 1973 came the "oil shock." The international consortium of oil producers had made it certain that the price of imported oil, and Japan had scarcely any domestic oil, would rise.

So the age of rapid economic growth, which had lasted from the years when the Korean War was being put to such good use, was at an end. The years immediately following were ones of hesitation and uncertainty. Bankruptcies occurred with greater frequency than at any other time since the war. It came to seem possible that rapid growth would be replaced by no growth at all, or even a diminution. The effect on the life of Tokyo was immediately noticeable. Most prominent among the lights to go out was the Morinaga globe in Ginza. Elevators were put on furlough, lights in hallways were dimmed. Broadcasting hours and movie hours were shortened. Filling stations took holidays. Another sacred institution, the expense account, seemed threatened.

The city and the nation emerged from it all with greater confidence than ever. It was in those years that one began to hear that Japan, after a century and more, had nothing to learn from the world, and the world, if it had any sense, should start learning from Japan. Though slow economic growth would be the thing, the continuing slide of the dollar was the best indication that the national foreign policy, export and export and export some more, had been a success. The lights started going on again.

By the end of the decade the city gave little indication, in its surface aspects at least, that the shock had occurred.

Inflation proceeded apace. In 1975 prices in the ward part of Tokyo were four times what they had been a quarter of a century before, when the wild inflation of the immediate postwar years had been brought under control. The higher price of energy of course made domestic manufactures more expensive. The lower price of the dollar might have been expected to make foreign products, and especially American products, cheaper. Deflation in this regard was scarcely to be detected. It certainly did not occur at the rate at which the dollar declined. Economic growth would continue, at a reduced pace, and the country had proved itself capable of handling both expensive imports of raw materials and cheap imports of manufactured goods. The new confidence seemed quite justified. Opinion will differ as to whether or not it made Tokyo a pleasanter and more livable city.

Quiet was returning to the campuses by the early seventies. The violence and the apparent ability of students to do as they wished with their universities began to subside with the fall of what the media called Yasuda Castle. Yasuda Hall is the main administration building at Tokyo University. Radical students who had made it their "castle," expelling the president and all the other administrators, were themselves expelled in the summer of 1968. They occupied it again, and were again expelled, in January 1969, after a fierce battle with close to ten thousand policemen, watched by the whole nation on television. Among the popular words of those years were *gebaruto* and *gebabō*. The former is the German *Gewalt* ("force, power"), and the latter combines its first two syllables with a Japanese word for "stick" or "stave." It refers to the staves with which radical students flailed at the police and rival student factions.

Mishima Yukio died on November 25, 1970. It was too complex an incident, and he was too complex and intelligent a person, for us to see it as merely an instance of misguided nationalism. He knew the youth of the land too well, and the changes that were coming over it, now that the turbulent sixties were out of the way, to expect that the army (more properly, the Ground Self-Defense Force) would rise up and follow him in bringing about a Shōwa Restoration. A repetition of the 1960 demonstrations against the Security Treaty was expected in 1970. It did not come off, and 1970 may be seen as the year in which the Socialist Party

*Fire hoses drench students holding out at Tokyo
University during the battle of
"Yasuda Castle," 1969*

lost all credibility as a possible alternative to the conservatives who
had been in charge of the country since 1948. Those who wanted
change became splinter groups. Conformity came to prevail, and an
appearance of democracy in which it would not be possible to turn the
rascals out.

After standing on a balcony for a few minutes and urging the assembled soldiers at the Ichigaya barracks to rise and follow him, Mishima
withdrew into the office of the commanding general, and there, with
help, met his end (it was technically murder and not suicide). The
recorded shouts of the soldiers are more suggestive of amusement and
derision than sympathy—and it is hard to believe that Mishima expected
them to be otherwise.

His death speaks of the times, in a very negative fashion. He did not
like the emerging consensus and conformity. In all manner of ways, from
dress to sexual behavior, he was a nonconformist. He did not have much

Mishima Yukio's last oration, Ichigaya, 1970

to say about democracy in the lands of its origin, but he thought that in Japan it was a sham and a pretense. He had hoped that the anticipated anti-treaty demonstrations of 1970 would bring a genuine confrontation and the emergence of something more honest, even if the honesty might be revealed in ungentle ways. It is clear that he started making preparations for his death during the summer, when the confrontation seemed possible. Motives other than disappointment must have been present in his last, drastic deeds. We may reasonably think that it was among the motives, however. The city was entering a time of ever bigger and brighter material objects and ever greater conformity, and no one turned up to protest, on the last occasion when genuine protest might have been possible.

In the spring of 1977 four young men who had been members of Mishima's private army attacked the headquarters of the Federation of Economic Organizations, just north of Marunouchi. Even as there are splinter groups on the radical left, there are such groups on the right;

and Mishima and his death are among the inspirational sources of the latter. The day when such happenings will be of importance is a great if not infinite distance away, but they serve to remind us that the city and the nation chose to take one course and some by no means stupid people wished them to take another.

For bright young people who conformed there might be a room at the top of one of the high new buildings. These were very new, something the city had not seen before, the first buildings worthy of the name sky-scraper. The city started reaching upward as New York had done a half century before. In this way too the years just before the golden jubilee and after the Olympics seem to mark the beginning of a stage.

The relatively permanent, fireproof, and advanced parts of the city had low, fairly even lines in the interwar period and the years just after the war. On one of her visits from suburban Osaka to Tokyo, Sachiko, the heroine of Tanizaki's *The Makioka Sisters*, finds the avenue with the palace moat and plaza on one side and the office buildings of Marunouchi on the other—it is the avenue on which General MacArthur had his headquarters—almost the only thing in Tokyo, aside from the Kabuki, worth looking at.

It was, by comparison with its condition today, a modest, quiet sort of avenue. The big Marunouchi office buildings, including the Marunou-chi Building, the biggest of them all, did not exceed seven and eight storeys, in a day when New York was flinging the Empire State Building into the heavens. Reasons of dignity and reasons of prudence were argued for this state of affairs. The royal residence must not be dwarfed by huge towers (for the same reason headquarters of the prefectural police, at Cherry Orchard Gate, were kept to a modest level); and skyscrapers would not do in a city of earthquakes.

Somewhat higher buildings began to rise in the years after the Korean War. The biggest and highest of the Olympic hotels was seventeen sto-reys high. The reasons of dignity just mentioned are closely related to aesthetic reasons, and these last seemed to be forgotten. The hotel, the New Otani in Akasaka, looms over a surviving segment of the old outer moat, until the Olympics (when it also got freeways) one of the prettiest places left from the old city. When the time came for *real* skyscrapers, however, aesthetic considerations asserted themselves once more. A race seemed in prospect to see who would have the first such building. The competition was between the Marine Insurance Building in Marunou-chi, on Sachiko's avenue and General MacArthur's, and a building which Mitsui proposed to erect just south of the Kasumigaseki government complex. The former got embroiled in a controversy over the integrity of the avenue. Time passed before an accommodation was reached which cut several storeys from it. The new Mitsui building meanwhile went up, to be the first of the "super high-rises," as the Japanese expression for the genre may be translated.

The Kasumigaseki Building was finished in 1968, and it is thirty-five storeys high. We are told that prudence was kept in mind. The building, along with other supers, we are assured, is perfectly earthquake-resistant. It is in any event a nauseating experience, like seasickness, to be high in one of them when even a mild earthquake strikes. When the building was new the largest annex to the American embassy stood right across the street from it. People would rush to their windows and watch it rock. Looking up at the supers, one may wonder less whether they will stand through a big earthquake than whether all that glass will come showering down into the street. The Kasumigaseki Building was a new adventure for Japanese builders, but it does not look very daring, save for its height. It is a large block.

It did not long remain the highest building in the city. In the years since it was finished it has slipped to tenth place or so. In 1970 a World Trade Center (Sekai Bōeki Sentaa) was put up at Hamamatsuchō, a short distance south of Ginza and Shimbashi. It is forty storeys and a hundred fifty meters high. Though it was not yet built when the Olympic mono-rail was put through to the airport, it now functions as the northern terminus.

The highest structure in the city continues to be Tokyo Tower, and the highest building in the narrower sense of the term—a structure of walls and rooms—is the Sunshine, finished in 1978 on the site of Su-gamo Prison in Ikebukuro. It is sixty storeys and a bit more than two hundred forty meters high, plus three underground levels.

The Shinjuku Westmouth, however, is the true place for supers. It has a cluster of them, while those mentioned above stand in isolation. The cluster too wears an air of isolation when viewed from anywhere except the middle of the cluster itself. From a distance it goes on looking as if the city had not made adequate preparations for it and did not quite know what to do with it.

The prefecture kept a part of the old reservoir site for its own use, and it is there, toward the western end, beside Shinjuku Central Park, that the new prefectural offices are under construction. The rest of the tract was turned over to private developers. The park is made over from the well-wooded grounds of an old shrine that still occupies a corner of it.

A new station building rose at Eastmouth in the year of the Olympics. Besides being the main Shinjuku station for what were then the National Railways, it is an elaborate shopping and feasting complex with an English name, My City. Traffic and crowds were put into a kind of order at Westmouth before the high buildings started going up. The Westmouth plaza was finished in 1966. The pleasant station plaza that had stood near Piss Alley at the undeveloped Westmouth quite disappeared. A complex on several levels took its place, accommodating many, many vehicles, public and private, and people and shops. It became possible to have a covered, rain-free walk eastward from the old reservoir site past

The old Yodobashi reservoir, later site of the Shinjuku Westmouth skyscrapers

one subway station and on to another, a distance of a kilometer or so, with subterranean entrances to shops and department stores and rapid transit all along the way. Not many cities can have the digs that Tokyo has. It is like a coal mine.

No one seems to have foreseen that the Westmouth plaza could easily be clogged by people who chose to clog it. On a day early in October 1968 students for whom the Communist Party was too conservative started hurling chunks of pavement, mostly at the police but somewhat randomly, and occupied a police box. Then, by way of preparation for an "antiwar day" later in the month, all the paving blocks were taken up in the course of a single night and replaced by asphalt. Windows were boarded over. My City closed early in the evening. Some twelve thousand policemen were massed in readiness. The station was occupied by student factions all the same, and in chaos. Fires were set, stones were hurled, tear gas was used.

Thereafter for a time skirmishes were almost nightly affairs, and fun to watch. Folksinging and dancing of a militantly nonmilitant sort succeeded the violence. They too led to clogging and police action. The police eventually succeeded in putting a stop to the singing and dancing, but it was a great bother to them. The Shinjuku Incident of October 1968 and the fall of Yasuda Castle early the following year were probably the most conspicuous events in the great show of youthful spirits. We have seen that the Delinquent Tribe of the Eastmouth was a part of the action, and got dispersed as a result of it. What with mouths and plazas and tribes and factions, Shinjuku was in those days a very lively place.

The first super high-rise on the old reservoir site was the Keiō Plaza Hotel, finished in 1971, forty-seven storeys, but still under two hundred meters. Also in Shinjuku, another Mitsui building, finished in 1974, went up fifty-five storeys and some twenty meters over the two hundred mark. Critics of architecture do not find much to praise in these supers. The new prefectural offices will, however, be something to look at. If they look like big pieces of latter-day Gothic, they will do so with some honesty. Notre Dame of Paris is the admitted inspiration. The offices will be, we are told, a monumental specimen of "postmodern" architecture. This very fashionable expression is elusive, but one of the things it seems to mean is that architectural forms will once more hark back to periods remoter than the present century.

While all this was going on at Westmouth, Eastmouth did not cease to bustle. The immediate Eastmouth remained one of the best places for shopping, and crowds of ladies with money poured in upon it every afternoon from every direction. The district farther east, where the old post station had been, became somewhat specialized. It evolved into the homosexual capital of the nation, and surely it is well in the running for the designation homosexual capital of the world. The homosexuality is not exclusively male, but that predominates.

As a place for masculine bustle of the commoner type, Kabukichō, with its neighbor the Golden Block, was leaving the competition behind in Shinjuku, certainly, and arguably in the land as well (though the Kansai cities were often pioneers in the kinkier things). In 1984 and 1985 the police had another fit of puritanism, and it was generally agreed that Kabukichō provided the occasion. It was becoming altogether too open and brazen with one of its two staples, sex. The other staple, alcohol, was not a problem unless it led to drunken driving, and this was dealt with sternly. Nor has noise, a by-product, been thought a problem. Tokyo and its police have in this regard always had a high threshold.

The puritanical fit removed from the streets the most obvious signs of what was going on. Touts became more reticent about laying hands

Kabukichō at night

upon passersby who seemed in a mood for something; the latter had to look a little harder to find it. Gaudy billboards and lights were no longer there to direct them. Yet it had taken a quarter of a century to create Kabukichō in its present image, and it was not prepared to revert to an earlier existence, or convert to something else. Detailed maps of the place go on showing something of a titillating nature at almost every Kabukichō number.

A recent one is packed full of mysterious runes and codes, and the key to them may be translated thus: "peep show; crystal; health girl; massage in private rooms; telephone club; love room; television games; video; girl companions; private sauna; pantyless tearooms; special baths; adult toys." About half the key is in what seems to be English. It would take a genuine expert to say exactly what all the terms mean, and whether they are carefully defined and mutually exclusive categories. That the sex business is large and subtle, however, must be apparent to anyone.

The most mysterious item is the second, "crystal." It is in the Japanese phonetic syllabary, and seems to be from English. The English word was already present in the Japanese language in such expressions as "crystal glass," "crystal diode," and "crystal microphone." In this case it seems to derive from the title of a popular novel, *Somehow Crystal* (*Nan to naku Kurisutaru*), written in 1980 by a student named Tanaka Yasuo. It is an almost plotless piece, really a novella, which would run to no more than thirty thousand words in English translation; and it contains 442 footnotes identifying details, predominantly exotic, that might otherwise puzzle the reader. We may presume that the use of the word here also signifies something exotic, though a recent inspection of Kabukichō turned up no very convincing answer to the question. The "crystal" places seemed no different from the run-of-the-mill purveyors of "adult" gadgetry.

Another recent tabulation, compiled at about the time the police were beginning to have their puritanical seizure, covered only the southern half of Kabukichō, the half in front of the Seibu station and nearest to Eastmouth proper. It contains twenty "consolidated pornography houses" (pornography emporiums, so to speak), twenty-one places offering massages in private rooms, two strip theaters, twenty-one "nude shows in private rooms," four pornographic movie theaters, seventeen "soaplands" (which would earlier have been called Turkish baths), four houses offer-

RIGHT: *Love hotel in Kabukichō*
BELOW: *A Kabukichō eating and
drinking establishment,
unfortunately named*

ing video in private rooms, thirteen peep shows (including places that offer these in private rooms), two pantyless tearooms, seventeen pornography shops, and eleven enterprises which (most ingeniously) fell into none of the above categories—a total of a hundred thirty-two. There were also fifteen love hotels, and some two hundred touts swarmed the area, no more than five hundred yards across east to west and two hundred north to south.

The strip shows deserve a special word. Always rather demure from the outside, with perhaps no more than a sign saying "New Art Theater" surrounded by a stream of white lights, they were little affected by the police crackdown. They were and are uninhibited. The girl who stood in the picture frame as Venus can scarcely have dreamed what ways she stood there at the head of. Complete nudity and the most wanton of dances prevail. They are under the control of the gangs, some thirty of which, large and small, independent and cartelized, are said to operate in Kabukichō. What the arrangements are between them and the police only the one or the other can tell us.

Many a thing goes on in Kabukichō that the laws of the land and the regulations of the prefecture do not permit. An obvious solution would be to bring the laws and regulations into better accord with what actually prevails; but righteous forces would rise up against that. Probably the police could not stop all these things if they had the will to. Their solution seems a sensible one: keep them out of sight as much as possible.

The events of 1985 were known to American devotees of Kabukichō as the Valentine's Day Massacre. It was on and near that day that the disappearance of the strip girls of Kabukichō seemed imminent—or at any rate their return to the frills and furbelows of an earlier era. Indeed, a certain hush and sense of caution did come over the scene for a while. The hush remained upon the streets, but behind doors things were soon as noisy and abandoned as ever.

The political center of city and prefecture will soon shift to Shinjuku. Does this mean that a great reversal has taken place, comparable to the great shift through the first half of the Tokyo century from the Low City, the cultural center of Edo, to the High City, where almost everything of an original and "creative" nature is today? Has there been a great reversal, with Shinjuku—the leading one among the *fukutoshin,* or satellite cities—now the main center, and the old center—Marunouchi, Ginza, Nihombashi, and southward and westward into Minato Ward—now the satellite? It is a view that has been commonly argued since Kabukichō became so big and sinful and the cluster of supers went up at Westmouth.

There is little evidence to support it. In only one field, or set of fields, related to sinning and toping, might it be asserted with some force that Shinjuku is ahead of the old center. It has most definitely not become the managerial and entrepreneurial center. That is still Marunouchi, somewhat broadly defined. Big insurance companies do have their headquarters at the Shinjuku Westmouth. The first considerable building to go up there, aside from the terminal department stores, was an insurance building. For the rest, headquarters have stayed mostly in the old center. The huge real-estate companies, Mitsui and Mitsubishi and Sumitomo, have stayed there, and rented out space in their Shinjuku supers to lesser companies, cultural institutions, and the like.

In 1982 almost three-quarters of companies with capitalization of a billion yen and more had their headquarters in the three central wards, and the figure was 80 percent for those with capitalization of ten billion and more. Close relations between business and government make Tokyo offices essential even for companies (such as Toyoda) whose head offices are elsewhere. The Tokyo offices of the biggest among these are also in the central wards. All of the "metropolitan" banks, the ones held to be national in their operations, have their head offices in the central wards, most of them in Chiyoda (Marunouchi).

Shinjuku is not a very cultural sort of place, unless "cultural" is defined as signifying all the things that make a culture what it is, which is to say, all the things that people do. Though people do many things in Shinjuku, it does not excel in high culture. Recently there have been reports of schools in Kabukichō to teach Japanese to foreign persons. These might in another place suggest culture and that yet higher cultural entity, international cultural exchange. Kabukichō is a curious place for them. They seem in fact to be arrangements to get easy visas for pretty Southeast Asian girls, especially Filipinos, and put them to work in the bars and cabarets and strip halls of the district.

Kabukichō set out to become a dramatic center, and it did not. It does have its Koma Stadium and the largest cluster of movie theaters in the city. The Koma is the largest theater in the district for concerts, recitals, and stage performances. Popular entertainers are dominant. The "road show" movie houses are mostly in the Ginza district. The inner wards, with Ueno, a bit to the north, are where a symphony concert or an opera is most likely to occur, or a foreign performer to hold forth (sometimes commanding ticket prices that run to four hundred and more dollars at current exchange rates).

None of the big newspapers—the national ones, to correspond to the metropolitan banks—has moved its offices to Shinjuku. They are no longer in the Ginza district proper, but they remain in the three central wards. There has been no tendency on the part of publishing houses to move to Shinjuku. Some big ones have their offices in Shinjuku Ward, but in places where they have been for many years, along the eastern or inner fringe of the ward. (The station and its Westmouth and Eastmouth are at the southwest corner, a couple of miles away.) One big television company has its studios in Shinjuku Ward, but they are in the center of the ward, at a considerable distance from the station. The others are all in the inner wards save NHK, the public broadcasting corporation, which is in Shibuya Ward. A great deal of printing occurs in Shinjuku Ward. That too is most of the way across the ward from the station and its mouths. The heart of the advertising business—the Madison Avenue of Japan—continues to be in the central wards. So it cannot be said that in this day of information the huge and growing information industry has done much to make Shinjuku the new center of the city.

There is very little chance that Shinjuku or any of the other *fukutoshin* will ever replace Ginza in popular lore. According to a history of Chūō Ward published in 1980, there are almost five hundred Ginzas the country over—places of a more or less bustling nature that have taken the name This Ginza and That Ginza. There can be no doubt about the eponym. The history counted the name Ginza in the titles of fifty-one popular songs. Kyoto figures in thirty-two and Mount Fuji in thirteen. Shibuya and Shinjuku were not even in the running, as place names or as song titles. Where the characters for "new station," which is to say Shinjuku, appear in a place name, the pronunciation is often different from that of *the* Shinjuku, and the origins are almost always independent. Ginza is a part of Chūō Ward and so the historians had an interest in establishing its preeminence. Yet allowance for exaggeration still leaves Ginza unique in the popular esteem. If no other part of Tokyo rivals it, neither does any part of any other Japanese city.

The department stores of the private commuter lines that have their terminals at the Shinjuku Westmouth were renovated and expanded in preparation for the crowds to descend upon them from the super buildings, and the buildings themselves and the underground passages leading off toward them are full of expensive boutiques. At Eastmouth there has been no great change in the merchandising business since the years of recovery from 1945. The inner wards, meanwhile, have been adding much to the supply of slickness and opulence. The most conspicuous addition is a big merchandising and entertainment complex where the Nichigeki (Japan Theater) and the *Asahi Shimbun* used to be. Popularly called, in English, the Yūrakuchō Mullion, though it has a more formal name, Yūrakuchō Center, it does have a great many mullions. Indeed it is all vertical lines, metallic mullions and glass up and down the whole twelve storeys of it. Theaters, one of them bearing the old name Nichigeki, and an assembly hall open from a central well with glistening escalators and hanging illumination. It is dizzying in its shininess and cold whiteness. On either side are two huge department stores, both belonging to private railway lines, the Hankyū of Osaka and the Seibu, which, having consolidated its initial hold on Ikebukuro, has moved on to acquire many other bases.

If shadows and easeful ligneous surfaces were essential to the old Japanese notion of an interior, then it must be said the Mullion is about as un-Japanese as a place can be (except perhaps for a few other places in Tokyo, and the Trump Tower). Doubtless it is also among the places that lead the way into the future. In this regard one can only conclude that Ginza is marching more boldly ahead than Shinjuku. The complex opened for business in 1984. In 1986 some two hundred thousand shoppers and viewers were said to enter it every day. Long before it accommodated the Nichigeki and the *Asahi* the site was that of one of the two Edo magistracies, the southern one. A history of it might without great exaggeration be taken for a history of the city this century and more.

The two Mullion stores were not the only big ones that opened in the Ginza district in 1984. It was the year of what was called the Ginza-Yūrakuchō War. Earlier that year a big supermarket chain opened a most swanky and expensive department store and gave it a swanky French name, Ginza Printemps. It is only a few steps from the Mullion, although it is in Ginza proper and the Mullion is in Yūrakuchō. There were already a half dozen other big department stores in Ginza, three of them prewar, three of them (invasions by Kansai and Nagoya capital) postwar. So Ginza, with Yūrakuchō, has more than Shinjuku to draw the daytime, feminine shopping crowds.

The Mullion must be given its due. It, more than any other force, has brought a rejuvenation of Ginza, which in the post-Olympic years had begun taking on a middle-aged look. (Middle age may be held to begin in Japan with the throwing off of blue jeans and with conversion to the religion that is the corporation.) The Ivy and Miyuki tribes were the last ones to have their main base in Ginza. The glitter of the Mullion had the effect of bringing young people back in the daytime, and there has been a rash of new beer halls, open later hours, to keep them from wandering off to Roppongi and beyond when the big Mullion stores and movie houses close.

The Mullion complex and related complexes nearby have put Ginza more firmly in control of the first-run road-show business, which it has dominated since the war. The Mullion contained five theaters, including the old Nichigeki, when it opened in 1984. Two more have since been added. Tōhō has remade the block across the street from its Takarazuka (later the Ernie Pyle) into one of the slickest things in town. Along with the vast department stores, these vast spaces for sitting and watching things have brought youth back to Ginza.

But in sex and drinking Shinjuku, especially Kabukichō, leads. A count in 1987 established that in Kabukichō alone there were not far from three thousand bars, clubs, cabarets, and other eating and drinking establishments. This is about equal to the count of permanent Kabukichō residents and larger than a similar count for the whole of Ginza, which has hovered at about two thousand. A count for the three central wards combined would outdo that for Shinjuku, but would be a misrepresentation, since it would be scattered over a much larger area. Roppongi and Akasaka in Minato Ward are a considerable distance from Ginza, and there is not much revelry in Shinjuku Ward that is not an easy walk from the station. So the preeminence of Shinjuku and especially its Eastmouth demands recognition. It may be added that Ginza continues to be the more elegant place in ample measure. Perhaps Shinjuku is the genuine successor in our day to Asakusa, a place of crowds in search of diversions varied but not of the most ethereal sort.

The conclusion must be that the center holds. When the prefectural offices move to Shinjuku they will not be moving to a new center. They will be leaving a remarkably strong and durable old center behind. A city that has always been more decentralized than the American cities of the railway age has avoided becoming the doughnut that so many American cities of the automobile age are. It may be that in already decentralized cities the centrifugal pull of the lesser centers is weaker than in a centralized city such as Los Angeles once was. The center remains stronger in almost every regard than any of the bustling places along the outer circle. It is of course possible to view this state of affairs in more than one way. Those who first gave currency to the expression *fukutoshin*, "secondary center" or "satellite city," thought that the center had accumulated too much and a distribution of its assets would be good. Charles Beard—it is true that he was not looking at the same city but at that of a half century before—thought that the outward-moving forces were too strong.

Though concentration of any kind can be excessive, it does seem to be the case that vitality at the center of a city has a vitalizing effect on the whole city. The Ginza crowds, human and vehicular, can be maddening when one is in a hurry; but to have them all abandon the area in favor of the county part of the prefecture would be far worse.

It may be, though precise measuring devices are not to be had, that Shibuya, with the adjoining Aoyama and Harajuku, outdoes Ginza in one respect, the chic and the ultra-European.

Since the Olympics two things that Shibuya has done and had done to it are of importance. It has pushed out of its tight, constrictive valley, and it has come to seem less of a one-company town. It has acquired a Park Avenue (Kōendōri). Few Tokyo streets have official names; some have popular names. Insofar as it had any name at all, the street leading up the hill northward from Shibuya Station to the Meiji Shrine and what was Washington Heights and the Olympic Village used to be called the ward-office street. Now, because it leads up the hill to Yoyogi Park, the old Washington Heights, it is Park Avenue. The name is entirely popular and unofficial. It was part of a forceful advertising campaign, for a department store, and then several of them, called Parco. The English word "park" has established its place in the Japanese language, in both the Central Park and the parking-lot sense. Something with more tone was asked for, and so the Italian word was chosen. (Probably the French one was rejected because it would have been indistinguishable from the English.)

The advertising campaign brought the two important new Shibuya developments together, for it was at the hands of the company that became genuine competition with the Tōkyū railways for hegemony over Shibuya. The Seibu enterprises, their groundings in another private railway system and in real estate, moved aggressively into Shibuya in the post-Olympic years. Both Seibu and Tōkyū opened stores in the direction of the park and at a remove from the main station complex, where Tōkyū had been supreme. It was the beginning of the climb out of the valley.

Soon after the Seibu opened its Shibuya store it opened the first of its

"Park Avenue" in Shibuya

Parco places, also in Shibuya. The Parco slogan was: "Park Avenue in Shibuya, where the person you pass is beautiful." The Parco places are not so much department stores as elegant and expensive bazaars. They have as concessionaires the elite in fashion and food. Affluent Tokyo was by these post-Olympic years becoming one of the ultra-chic places of the world, and Shibuya was becoming what Ginza long had been (and neither Asakusa nor Shinjuku ever was, really), the highest of the highly fashionable. "Shibuya" may here be understood to include the rest of the southwestern triangle, Harajuku and Aoyama. So few years had passed since women left behind the shapeless bags of the years of war and defeat.

The Tōkyū enterprises were not slow or timid in fighting back. They opened elegant and ingenious bazaars of their own on the slope leading up the park, and gave them such names as Hands and 109. The good, solid English of the former suggests everything the amateur builder and engineer can possibly want, and that is what the stores by that name offer. The latter is a pun. Advertising renders it in Roman letters, One-Oh-Nine. It is then divided in two, One-Oh or Ten, and Nine, and the Sino-Japanese readings for these figures are *tō* and *kyū;* and it becomes Tōkyū, the abbreviated name of the railway system.

The Southwest, in the broad sense in which the expression was used in the previous chapter, designating the great shopping and entertainment complex from the outer moat to Shibuya, contains most of the places that are even slicker than the Yūrakuchō Mullion. Most striking among them, it may be, is the complex called Ark Hills, finished in 1986. The second word is English; the first might seem to be as well, but in fact is an acronym from Akasaka Roppongi Kaihatsu, "Akasaka Roppongi Development." A few steps from the American embassy, astride the boundary between Akasaka and Roppongi, or the old Akasaka and Azabu wards, it contains a concert hall, luxury apartments, office space, and a very shiny hotel. It seems to have succeeded in doing what it set out to do in one regard, attracting international finance. Highly advanced communications devices are available around the clock. The hotel is a marvel of shiny surfaces and bright lights. Like many shiny surfaces, it seems impenetrable. It seems to turn away all attempts at getting close to it.

Ark Hills has not succeeded, apparently, in becoming one of the new sights of the city, a place to which all the bunches and buses must go, a magnet like the Yūrakuchō Mullion, drawing hundreds of thousands of people every day. Experts find the reasons for this failure in a certain want of integrity. It is concrete and pretends to be something else. This may possibly be true, though one doubts that the multitudes who have failed to show up are aware of such niceties.

Whether or not it is popular today, Ark Hills has the look of what tomorrow is likely to be. Shinjuku is probably ahead of Ginza in sin and roistering, and Shibuya and the Southwest may be ahead in the shiny things of the future. They are most definitely in advance of Ginza and the land in offering advanced things for women to buy and put on. They also have a stronger hold on the adolescent crowds, despite the return of youth to Ginza and the Mullion.

The Sunshine Building, sixty floors and two hundred forty meters, was finished in 1978 on the site of Sugamo Prison, near Ikebukuro Station. It is the highest building in Japan, though not as high as Tokyo Tower, and it requires getting used to. It may not be as forbidding as the prison was, but it does have a remote look about it. The routes of access from the station, which is a fifteen-minute walk away, are obscure; and, at the northwest side of the city, the direction whence cold winter winds blow in from Siberia, the building has, even more than the cluster of supers at the Shinjuku Westmouth, a lonely, unaccepted look about it, quite the opposite of the sunniness which the name seeks to call up.

When one has overcome obstacles physical and mental and set foot inside the doors, it proves, with subordinate buildings, to be a city in itself. Sunshine City is the name of the whole complex, even as Sunshine Sixty, from the number of storeys, is the full name of the biggest building. The complex contains galleries, a planetarium, an aquarium, all manner of shops, a hotel, a theater, a concert hall, a trade-promotion center (as if that sort of thing were really needed these days), government offices, a branch of the Mitsukoshi department store, which has another branch nearer the station, and many another facility. In a corner of the grounds is a melancholy piece of stone, a memorial to the "war criminals" who were hanged there late in 1948.

Open space yet remains at the Ikebukuro Westmouth. It belongs to the prefecture. This is in itself no obstacle to development, since the prefecture owned the lands at the bottom of the Shinjuku reservoir as well, and allowed a perfect frenzy of development to occur there. It has thoughts of something more cultural for the Ikebukuro Westmouth.

The Sunshine Building, Toyko's tallest, seen from the freeway

The Seibu Parco in Ikebukuro

Despite the presence of Seibu, one of its Parcos, one of Tōkyū's Hands, and Sunshine City, Ikebukuro goes on looking a little insubstantial. The bustle has subsided and the district seems to have exhausted its resources some time before one reaches Sunshine on the walk from the station. It asks for comparison not with Shibuya and Ginza but with Shinjuku. Like Shinjuku, it is somewhat wanting in class, and it is this with nothing comparable to the Shinjuku intensity, magnitude, and variety. The comparison is not to be understood as saying that Ikebukuro is dull and dreary. A want of finish brings a particular kind of vigor, not innocent, perhaps, but eager. A century or so ago Ikebukuro offered little promise indeed, and so it may be called the miracle among the bustling places. It is the boom town way out on the wild prairies.

Greater Tokyo contains half the university students in the land, and there is only one four-year university, the Merchant Marine Academy, anywhere in the Low City. It has been said, probably truly, that many a provincial student goes through his four years of higher education in Tokyo without ever seeing the Sumida.

Some of the Low City wards have done brave and imaginative things of a cultural nature. One of the wards east of the river has established an ethnological museum devoted to the customs and physical aspects of the Edo Low City. It does its work well. Earlier there was a smaller museum, devoted to the same subject, beside Shinobazu Pond in Taitō Ward. This last ward, which has been energetic in preservation and restoration as few Japanese agencies are, has moved and restored a Meiji concert hall which was in danger of being torn down. It sends forth Occidental sounds once more in the setting in which Japanese first heard them. The ward has done the same for an apparently doomed sake shop, also of Meiji, in the Yanaka heights behind Ueno Park.

It has sought to bring drama back to its old center, Asakusa. Kabuki, on which Asakusa had almost a monopoly in late Tokugawa and early Meiji, has returned. So have more "modern" and realistic forms that got their start in Asakusa. They have only short runs, however.

Such accomplishments emphasize the hopelessness of the task. A decade and a half after the surrender, before television had really started having its tyrannical way over other dramatic forms, there were three dozen theaters in Asakusa. They were not very innovative, to be sure, but still there they were, in numbers worthy of the old Asakusa. By 1987 the number was down to sixteen, including two strip theaters and three movie theaters specializing in soft-core pornography (the hard-core thing is not yet to be had in any Japanese movie theaters, though it is present in the strip shows). For mildly serious theater there yet remained a pair of variety halls, one specializing in Yose and the other in concerts and light reviews. Of the eight nonpornographic movie theaters only one showed foreign films, and they were second-run. The point is worth remarking upon, not because foreign films are necessarily better than Japanese, but because new films that have attracted favorable notice abroad are the ones still capable of fetching good crowds and admission fees in greater Ginza. In 1976 the Denkikan, "Electricity Hall," the oldest movie theater in the land, was torn down. In 1985 a hotel went up on the site of the International Theater (Kokusai Gekijō), once the largest in the Orient, and the home theater for the Shōchiku all-girl troupe, now disbanded. This had sought to compete with the Takarazuka company of the other big theater owner, Tōhō. The Takarazuka, its popularity undiminished (and its audience overwhelmingly feminine),

The most extensive remains of prewar Asakusa—the three linked theaters between which one could move for the price of a single ticket

still holds forth at its main theater in greater Ginza and at its original establishment in the Osaka suburbs as well.

Ueno and Kinshichō, the other two somewhat prominent entertainment and shopping districts in the Low City, remain much as they were. This is to say that they have declined relatively. Kinshichō, the only *sakariba* or bustling place east of the river worthy of the name, is still a cluster of theaters with a thin coating of bars and restaurants. Ueno is bigger, but falling behind Shinjuku and the others all the same. It draws the biggest crowds in the city for the few springtime days when the cherries in the park are in bloom. In those days the Sumida embankment also draws crowds, but its famous cherries are sadly squeezed in between the concrete of the freeway above and the concrete of the river wall below.

Of bars and cabarets Ueno has many, but by no means as many as Shinjuku. In 1978 the count for Taitō Ward was only a third that for Shinjuku Ward. Since Taitō Ward also includes Asakusa and the Yoshiwara, the Ueno count was perhaps a quarter that for the Shinjuku Eastmouth. The Shinjuku number has grown more rapidly in the years since. And so, despite its pleasant and interesting ethnological museums, we may say that a blight has settled upon the Low City and will not leave.

There is a tendency to blame those third nationals, the Koreans, for the failure of Ueno to bustle as Shinjuku does. It is true that Koreans own many of the taller buildings in Ueno, but whether, like oak trees, they establish openings around themselves that discourage other life is doubtful. The largest concentrations of Koreans are not in places like Ueno but on the outskirts of the city, in the northeastern wards and the industrial south. They are spread fairly evenly over the city. In only four of the twenty-three wards are they other than the most numerous of alien residents. In these four they are second by only a short distance. There are a few more Americans in Chiyoda Ward (Marunouchi and the palace) and Minato Ward (Roppongi and Akasaka), and a few more Chinese in Chūō Ward (Ginza and Nihombashi) and Toshima Ward (Ikebukuro); and not many people of any description have permanent residences in Chiyoda Ward or Chūō Ward. The largest number of Chinese is not in Toshima Ward, where they slightly outnumber Koreans, but in Shinjuku Ward, where they are slightly outnumbered. The

Chinese and American concentrations are certainly better placed, to harm or to benefit, than the Korean.

The street leading south from Ueno Park past the big department store was one of the *hirokōji* of Edo, the "broad alleys" widened as firebreaks, three of which became lively shopping and entertainment districts. The Asakusa district stagnates, and the Ryōgoku district has been quite left behind by the shifting currents of fashion. One of the great bustling places of Edo, even less apologetic for its vulgarity than Asakusa, it lies at the east flank of the earliest bridge across the Sumida. It now has again, as it had down to 1945, the Sumō arena, the Hall of the National Accomplishment. It was once a gateway to the provinces, minor compared to Ueno, for it served only the suburban regions east of the bay. The station is now almost deserted, because it has been bypassed. Trains go directly from the suburbs to Tokyo Central. A yet bigger ethnological museum having to do with the city and its past will go up on the expanse of concrete and weeds behind the new Hall of the National Accomplishment. That may help a little, but the prospect remains bleak. There has been talk of a fashion center east of the river, from Ryōgoku to the Kinshichō amusement district, to rival Shibuya. It is a brave idea and one wishes it well but cannot be optimistic. Affluent maidens and matrons do not live in that part of the city, nor are many of them likely to think that they can find something better at Ryōgoku than at Shibuya.

The literature of Edo was very much of Edo. In the last century or so of the shogunate it was so self-contained as to approach the autistic, and so happy with its own little part of the world as to approach the arrogant. Yet the best of Edo writing did have the power to make Edo a sensual presence. Something of the sort prevailed for parts of the city, Asakusa and to a lesser extent Ginza, down to the war. One feels Asakusa in the Asakusa writings of Kawabata, and a wider expanse of the Low City in the writings of Nagai Kafū. The intensity is much diminished in the Asakusa writings of Takami Jun, only a very few years later than Kafū's curious tale of that bawdy house east of the river. In stories in which Ginza figures—by Kafū once more, and by Takeda Rintarō—one may get a glimpse of this and that place in Ginza, a bar, a café, a street corner, but one has little sense of what Ginza was and why people went there. Asakusa is dense and palpable, Ginza is diffuse and evasive. Asakusa is an individual presence, Ginza an abstraction.

Many a novel has been set in postwar Tokyo. One has no trouble finding descriptions of the black markets and the burnt-over wastes, or the sun and moon coming through the collapsed roof of Tokyo Central Station. The black market at Ikebukuro figures prominently in one of the best novels of the immediate postwar years, *Drifting Clouds* (*Ukigumo*), by Hayashi Fumiko. In others Tokyo Tower looms over things, to take on what one vaguely assumes to be symbolic functions, though what they are symbolic of may be in some doubt. Niwa Fumio's *Love Letter* (*Koibumi*) gave its name to an alley near Shibuya Station. Tamura Taijirō and his streetwalkers have already been remarked upon. The part of the city in which they have their lynchings is a wasteland, as if to emphasize that they are primordial creatures, not part of any civic body. In a very popular novel called *Free School* (*Jiyū Gakkō*), by Shishi Bunroku, a husband and wife separate that they may have their freedom, and come back together again, having concluded that they can have it only with each other. The husband's ambages take him to such places as the ragpicking village on the embankment above Ochanomizu Station and the company of such persons as a band of smugglers.

Many other examples could be cited. Sketches of this and that place in the city are often skillfully done. If Asakusa and Shinjuku stand in contrast to each other in terms of bustle and prosperity, however, Asakusa consistently getting the worse of it, so also, their positions reversed, they stand in literary contrast. Unless some fine author and his works wait to be discovered, we may say that no novel addresses the subject of Shinjuku as *Scarlet Gang* addresses Asakusa. No novel conveys a sense of Shinjuku as a place, no novel is suffused with affection for it. Shinjuku has no regional literature. It may be said indeed that Tokyo has had none since the war.

Not even prewar writings about Asakusa convey a sense of Tokyo as writings from the closing years of the shogunate convey a sense of Edo. In 1933 the critic Kobayashi Hideo wrote an essay called "Literature That Has Lost Its Home" ("Kokyō wo Ushinatta Bungaku"—the first word is more like "hometown" or, as the Japanese say, "native place").

> Looking back over my life and how I have lived it, I see that it
> is very much wanting in the concrete. I do not see there someone

firmly emplanted, a member of a social entity. I do not see a native of Tokyo but an abstraction, someone who was not really born anywhere. Meditations upon this abstraction can doubtless be made into a kind of literature, but it wants a substantial, tangible backing. From it is likely to arise the peculiarly abstract wish of the weary heart to be free of society and back with nature. Nature set off from society is certainly a world of substance, but literature tends not to come out of it.

Mr. Tanizaki has spoken of "literature in which one finds a home [*kokyō*] for the spirit." My own problem is not literary. It is far from clear that I really have a home.

Kobayashi was born in the far south of the Meiji High City to a family long in Tokyo. He did not, to be sure, have a very long life to look back over. He was but a little past thirty when he wrote the essay. He was always old for his years, however, and we need not make too much of the point. The essay contains an element of the prophetic. Already in 1933, when people like Kafū and Kawabata were finding in the Low City not home, perhaps, for neither of them lived or grew up there, but still a mooring place—even then Kobayashi felt that he had no home.

Almost all Japanese writers live in Tokyo today, and none of them write of it as if it were home; and so the problem has become general. Kobayashi was very much a part of the High City, while Kawabata and Kafū distributed themselves more widely, taking in the smells of the Low City along with the odorless rarefaction of the High City intellectual world. Perhaps what has happened to the High City, now so close to being the whole city, is among the things encompassed by that voguish expression "postmodern." A city that is urban in the abstract may be what the future holds.

An element of the television and baseball age, probably a necessary and inexorable one, has been a diminution of street life. By this expression is here not meant the life, mostly very young, that floods the streets of Shibuya, but rather that which once flooded the streets of any ordinary neighborhood. People may fly up from Osaka to participate in a Sunday afternoon in Harajuku and Yoyogi. They do not pour out upon the streets of their neighborhoods as they once did on fine, warm summer evenings. This sort of street life was more important in the Low City than in the High. The salarymen and professors of the High City have always kept to themselves as the shopkeepers and craftsmen of the Low City have not. Then too there are class differences in the High City, with the fishmonger and the magnate living in close juxtaposition. Despite claims, perhaps in some respects justified, about the communal, consensual nature of Japanese working practices, classes do not mix any better in Japan than they do in most places.

In Edo and Meiji Tokyo, the Low City amused itself in the places that lay readiest, its streets. Especially on summer evenings, they became as much assembly places as corridors for passage. The poorer classes of the city did not have much money to spend and seldom went far from home, and the street in front of home was more interesting than home itself. So the streets of the city teemed far more evenly than they do now.

These tendencies still remained strong in the years just after the war, especially on clement evenings when there was a street fair, perhaps a garden fair or a shrine fair. With television and its nightly baseball game all through the summer, home (or, for the privileged myriads, the baseball stadium) became more interesting than the street, and the street began to lose its life. Now the ordinary and undistinguished street tends to be hushed in the evening and on Sunday, which has become an almost universal holiday. The big summer garden fairs by Shinobazu Pond in Ueno and behind the Kannon Temple in Asakusa attract fewer stalls and strollers each year. They may never quite dwindle to nothing, but they are ever more attenuated.

It may be argued that the people of Meiji and earlier poured forth into the streets because their lives contained so little by way of diversion. For most of them there were only the Yose house and the bathhouse in the cold months, and the street was an addition beyond pricing in the warm months. These things have been crowded out by more interesting things. A life that offered so little was a deprived one, and now life is richer. So it may be argued. Yet variety is lost, uniformity prevails, and for some this is a development to be lamented. Certainly a stroll through the Low City of a summer evening is not the fun it once was.

The Olympic governor still had more than half of his second term to serve when he got the Olympics out of the way. No governor of Tokyo has died in office or resigned since popular elections began in 1947. Governor Azuma decided, as none of the others have, not to stand for a third term. Because of the scandals already remarked upon, he had lost control of the prefectural council.

Conservatives do not get voted out of the prime ministership of the land, but they do get voted out of important regional offices. The shock of the post-Olympic scandals was strong and lasting enough to lose them the governorship, which they had held for twenty years. Two university professors ran against each other in 1967. Minobe Ryōkichi, candidate of the socialists and communists, was the winner. It was not by a landslide. With four and a quarter million votes cast for the two main candidates, radical and conservative, Minobe led the other professor by about a hundred thirty thousand votes, and votes for lesser candidates were enough to keep him from a majority. There were no elections for the prefectural council that year, and so the situation after the 1965 elections prevailed. The socialists and communists did not have a majority. Minobe was able to arrange a working coalition, however, as his discredited predecessor had not been. In succeeding council elections during the Minobe years, the communists did better than the socialists, until, in 1977, both slipped badly, suggesting that the prefecture was ready for a change, which it had in 1979.

Despite the closeness of his initial victory, Minobe was a popular governor. He had no trouble being reelected twice. His popularity was in large measure due to his television personality, of which his famous smile was a crucial part. This is always referred to as the Minobe *sumairu*, and why a Japanese word would not have done as well as the English is mysterious. It would seem that the language requires a constant supply of loan words in order to maintain its vigor. "Talent" candidates (again the English word is used)—television personalities who use their exposure for getting elected to public office—are not in good repute with the media. The media blame them on the conservative rascals who cannot be voted out of power, and forget that Minobe was among the earliest.

He was a successful politician. Whether or not he was a successful governor is open to argument. The city budget was in the red all through the Minobe years, and at the end of them the proportion of prefectural expenditures for debt management was twice the average for other prefectures. Many elaborate explanations are given for this state of affairs, and many external causes cited, such as the oil shock of 1973, which threw everyone's plans out of joint. It is true that Minobe and his administration are not wholly to blame. The budget had already slipped into the red during the first term of Governor Azuma. Yet Minobe made things worse all through his tenure, and it is hard not to believe that prodigality and loose administration were chiefly responsible.

Asked what was so wrong with Minobe, an eminent newspaperman replied: "Almost everything, I think, that he could have brought this rich city to the edge of bankruptcy."

Suzuki Shunichi, who had earlier been important in the national and prefectural bureaucracy, was elected governor in 1979, and continues to serve. The conservatives recovered well from 1965, their worst year. From 1969 they were only a dozen or so seats short of a council majority, and had more seats than the socialists and communists combined. Governor Suzuki immediately began a program of personnel retrenchment. During his first term, after two decades, the prefectural budget returned to the black once more. The matter of the black and the red is a technical one. Since the prefecture goes on issuing bonds, it cannot be said to be paying its way in full. Yet the current account is in balance.

One expects mayors—and Minobe may be considered a mayor, though he was technically a governor—to face such problems as crime and drugs. But, though pep pills have been a nuisance and the occasion for numerous arrests, drugs have not been the problem in Japanese cities that they have been in American. The low incidence of random street crime, however matters may be with organized crime, is something in which Tokyo takes boundless pride. These in any event are police problems, and the prefectural police are not under the control of the governor. It may be that the most considerable problem Minobe faced was garbage. Certainly the "great garbage war" got much attention in the media. For a time it was as famous as the Minobe smile.

It had been smoldering for some time. In 1971 it broke out angrily when the council of Kōtō Ward, east of the river, passed a resolution opposing the passage of garbage trucks through the ward on their way to the fills, such as Dream Island, off its bay shore. It was Dream Island whence all the flies came in 1965 (see page 259). Every ward, the council said, should take care of its own garbage, and Kōtō had no duty to be the dumping grounds for the wealthy and, it thought, irresponsible western wards.

Some two-thirds of metropolitan garbage was then being disposed of along the garbage fills of Kōtō Ward. Nine of the twenty-three wards had no garbage-disposal facilities whatsoever. The governor agreed that this was an inequity, and that disposal plants should be built elsewhere. The indignation of Kōtō Ward was aroused chiefly by Suginami Ward, one of the westernmost and wealthiest of the twenty-three. The announcement in 1967 that a garbage-disposal plant of an advanced technological kind would be built in Suginami brought violent opposition from residents. There was similar opposition in Meguro, a rich southwestern ward that shared with Suginami the distinction of being chosen for the first new plants. Five thousand garbage trucks a day continued to pass through Kōtō Ward, trailing filth and bad smells behind them, and creating traffic jams. In 1973 the Kōtō council voted to use force to turn back trucks from Suginami.

An agreement was finally reached in 1974 that in principle every ward would contain facilities sufficient unto its own garbage. The controversial Suginami plant was built, the feelings of the eastern wards were mollified, and the war was over. Dream Island became the park and athletic field, more the latter than the former, that it is today. In 1971 the twenty-three wards produced more than twelve thousand tons of garbage every day, and three wards in the High City accounted for a third of it. The total was three times what it had been a decade before. The population of the wards had in that decade risen by less than a twentieth. Among the things that the economic miracle produced was garbage. By 1977 the percentage of burned garbage had risen to almost 90 percent. So it may be said for the Minobe government that it did well by garbage.

As for sewage, the whole population of only seven of the twenty-three wards had the use of sewers in 1986. The figure for all the wards was 83 percent, for the county part of the prefecture 64 percent. The easternmost wards were the poorest served. One of them, Adachi, had sewers for only 46 percent of its population, and for the other two the figure was under 60 percent. Kōtō Ward and Suginami Ward, the chief combatants in the garbage war, had sewers for more than 90 percent of their population. The goal of the prefecture is to have sewers for everyone in the wards by the turn of the century. There is still a city out in the county part of the prefecture that has no sewers at all.

There are now ten sewage-disposal plants taking care of the wards.

During the last years of the Olympic governor industrial wastes that had poured into the Sumida began going into one of the plants. The river has much improved in smell, color, and general livability.

Tokyo and New York have been sister cities since before the Olympics, and Governor Minobe, despite his unfriendliness toward American systems and institutions, did nothing to change the relationship. It has for the most part seemed that Tokyo is the younger sister, since it has done New York the honor little sister accords big sister, imitating it in numerous superficial ways. Whether, with its new eminence, it will relax a bit and sit back and wait for others (who knows, even possibly New York) to imitate it remains to be seen.

Certainly in the early sororal years imitation was quite open. Articles of clothing bearing the legend "I" and a heart and "New York" had counterparts in Tokyo with only the proper name changed. It almost seemed that "I-heart-Tokyo" might become the motto of the city. But then during his first election campaign, in 1979, Governor Suzuki came up with a new motto, if not for the city and prefecture, certainly for his administration. "My Town Tokyo" it is, and, as with the other, two of the three elements are borrowed from English. He promised a city free from fires, earthquake damage, and pollution. Much progress had already been made on the first and third freedoms before the governor took office, though perfection is unattainable. As for the second, a great earthquake will one day come to tell us how substantial the progress has been. Governor Suzuki also promised generous welfare programs for the aged, who are an increasingly serious problem in a land without adequate pension programs. By the mid-eighties a million residents of the city were sixty-five and more years of age.

Tokyo is less heavily burdened in this regard, however, than the nation as a whole. Charts which divide the population by age show that it has a higher proportion than the nation at large for all ages between fifteen and fifty-five; for ages above and below the proportion is higher for the nation. For the early twenties, Tokyo has proportionately half again as many people as the nation. After twenty-five the figure drops, though not with complete regularity. So it goes on being, by national standards, a youthful city. People tend to return to the provinces when the time comes to face the end. Many youngish men leave their wives and children in the provinces.

Whether or not the governor's goals, as enumerated thus far, are capable of full realization, at least they are capable of definition. An altogether more enigmatic and elusive part of My Town has to do with its functions as a gathering place for and leader of the world. "Internationalization" has been one of the voguish words of recent years. If it means establishing the city as a financial center to rival London and New York, a place where a person can know instantly and always all that there is to know about the markets of the world, a twenty-four-hour place, then that too is capable of definition, and realization is certainly not beyond the capabilities of the ingenious Japanese. If, on the other hand, it means a magnanimous acceptance of people and their ways from all over, such as characterizes New York, then the matter is more doubtful.

For all the huge physical changes that have come over it and all the talk of the "new people" of Harajuku and such places, Tokyo remains a very insular city. Its inhabitants are far from ready to accept the pluralism of a New York. It has not changed so very much since the centuries when the shoguns kept almost all foreigners out. No one would dream of excluding them today; yet in many ways they are effectively excluded. They are in no significant way a part of its life, and it sometimes seems that the workings of the international economy, making it possible for the Japanese to buy the world and next to impossible for the world to buy the tiniest part of Japan, may work toward seclusion every bit as successfully as the policies of the shoguns did. The permission of the Bank of Japan is required for any purchase of real estate by a nonresident foreigner. It is automatic when the purchase is small and there are no special considerations, such as the possibility of criminal activities; but the unrealistically high value of the yen on the foreign-exchange market discourages if it does not prohibit even small purchases.

Its sufficiency unto itself, precluding the "Americanization" of which it has always been accused, has given the city the individuality that has made it interesting, and a refusal to abandon old values has been the chief strength of the land. It is the Japanese who say that they wish to internationalize, however, and the prefecture that puts internationalization among its goals, and so one is permitted to remark upon the unlikelihood that genuine internationalization will ever occur, to make Tokyo as calmly accepting of variety and eccentricity as New York is.

• • •

The population of the wards, which had been falling slightly since about the time Governor Minobe took office, began to rise in the early eighties.

Then in 1987 it fell again. The fall, only a little more than one person in three hundred, hardly suggests a stampede to get out of the city, whose population may be termed stable. The population of the Tokyo region has continued to grow at a much more rapid rate than that of the nation. United Nations statistics now put Tokyo-Yokohama behind Greater Mexico City in population, but well ahead of Greater New York.

Tokyo has most things thought useful and appropriate to the advanced society. The supply of old things diminishes all the while.

The closing months of 1967 and the early ones of 1968 were a bad time for those who believe that old things should be saved even when they are not making money. Destruction of the "old" Imperial Hotel began in December 1967. The following month screens and scaffolds started going up preparatory to the destruction of the Mitsubishi Number One Building in Marunouchi.

What was then called the old Imperial was not the oldest but the Frank Lloyd Wright building put up just before the great earthquake. A Society to Protect the Imperial Hotel was organized in the summer of 1967. It was not successful in its main endeavor, to keep hands off the Imperial, but that there was a movement at all is significant. Until then the populace of the city had accepted the destruction of old buildings in favor of more profitable ones as among the facts of life. Henceforth the profit-seekers must think of possible resistance if their destructive ways threaten something that may be called "cultural property." The conservation movement continues to be erratic and uncertainly organized, however. Tokyo Central Station and the Bankers' Club, both in Marunouchi and both Taishō buildings, are the objects of well-publicized preservation campaigns; and the last Queen Anne building of Meiji left in the center of the city was recently torn down. Originally the Imperial Hemp Building, it stood at the north flank of Nihombashi Bridge. A glassy thing will go up in its place. Nor were voices raised to save Mitsubishi Number One. It quite went away. Designed by the British architect Josiah Conder and finished in 1894, it too was Queen Anne, and a good if somewhat tattered example of the style. The rooms were dark and moldy and the three storeys were unworthy of Mitsubishi's next-to-priceless land. Yet one misses it.

Fragments of the old Imperial survive, the largest in Meiji Village,

The façade of Frank Lloyd Wright's Imperial Hotel, now standing in nonfunctional splendor in a theme park near Nagoya

near Nagoya. One need not go all the way to Nagoya to see lesser fragments, which are to be found in such Tokyo places as the new Imperial and the Foreign Correspondents' Club. The old Imperial closed its doors on November 15, 1967. Demolition began a little more than a week before the last trolley passed through Ginza. Things moved fast in the early Minobe years. In addition to fragments, reflections of the old Imperial survive here and there over the city. The tufaceous stone to which Wright took a fancy when he found it in garden walls and which gave his Imperial its pleasant brownish tinge had not before been used in buildings. It came much into vogue. The most conspicuous surviving example is the prime minister's residence, done by a Wright disciple. A most marvelous Ginza beer hall, the Lion, erected in 1933, shows the Wright influence clearly.

The city virtually did away with its trolley system during the years after the Olympics. Among the prides of Meiji, it had at its most extensive some two hundred twenty miles of trackage. There were minor additions until 1958, and stretches of track were from time to time put out of service through the postwar years down to the eve of the Olympics. In 1963 and 1966 two long stretches of about five miles each went out of service westward from Shinjuku and northward from Sugamo—outward, this is to say, from the Yamanote line.

The Shinjuku one was troublesome, and in any event had not long been a part of the metropolitan system. A single-track line running west as far as Ogikubo, marketing center for an affluent residential district, it was bought from the Seibu system in 1951. Moving trolleys were a great annoyance for the automobile, and stationary ones were far worse. There were always stationary ones up and down the track, because they had to wait at sidings for moving ones to pass.

Resolute abandonment of the system began in 1967 and was completed by 1971, with a single line remaining. Even before 1966 the prefecture had begun disposing of trolley cars. It might be thought that scrap would be the only fate for a trolley car without tracks, but numbers went to parks and playgrounds, where the nostalgic may still observe them and perhaps clamber aboard. The earliest trolley line in the city was among the first to go. Service was discontinued along twenty miles of track on December 9, 1967, and on that night the last trolleys ran along Ginza, the Number One route. There were outpourings of regret and affection. Thousands gathered to say goodbye to the very last Ginza trolley. Governor Minobe, in his first year of office, made some remarks. Much behind schedule, it passed southward through Ginza late in the evening. All-night operations began immediately to remove the tracks.

By 1972 most of the trackage all through the system had been removed. A single route survived both because there was strong popular sentiment for keeping something, and the Minobe government was not cold and remote in this regard, and because it was a peculiar sort of line, planned and executed in such a way that it inconvenienced the automobile less than the others did. For much of its length it runs on its own right-of-way, and where it shares the way with the automobile there are relatively few of the latter. It runs in an arc through the northern part of the city, from just below Waseda University in Shinjuku Ward to Minowa in Arakawa Ward, not far from Sanya, the most successful of the "slums" in getting its name in the headlines and on the screens, and the unsuccessful Tokyo Stadium.

Like the Seibu line west from Shinjuku, the surviving trolley was built as a private railway, to take fanciers of cherry blossoms and maple leaves to Asukayama, Asuka Hill, a famous place for those things. Now in Kita Ward but in the northern suburbs when the line was built, it

The last remaining Tokyo trolley line

was the only one of the original Meiji parks that lay beyond the city limits. The Oji line, as it was called (it is now called the Arakawa line), was put through westward most of the way to Waseda in 1911 and eastward to Minowa in 1913. It is very popular, and for some reason less expensive than the buses. On a fine Sunday afternoon one must be prepared to wait in line for several cars to depart if one wishes a seat.

The trolleybus, that generally unsatisfactory compromise between the tracked vehicle and the freewheeling one, had a much shorter career, only sixteen years. The last trolleybus disappeared before the last-but-one of the trolley lines. The first line, from Ueno to Imai east of the river, was also the last. At 9:45 on a September evening in 1968 the last trolleybus left Imai for Ueno. It was crowded, though the event did not get the attention which had gone to the last Ginza trolley a few months before. Things of Meiji had been around long enough to be a part of everyone's memory and a part of the city scarcely anyone had known it to be without.

The subway system was all the while growing, and it continues to grow. Besides expansion of subway trackage proper, there has been huge expansion because of linkage between subway lines and suburban commuter lines. Though all four terminal stations for the earliest two lines, the only prewar one and the first postwar one, are at points whence lines depart for the suburbs, no effort was made, and indeed it would have been impossible because of incompatible gauges, to run trains through from the inner-city system to one or more of the suburban systems. The concept was slow to die that the inner system should be sealed off from the other and in the public domain.

The breakthrough came in 1962. Two suburban lines began running trains directly from their own tracks via subway tracks into the central wards. Today every one of the suburban systems has connections with the inner system. The commuter seldom has to exert himself further than a stroll across a platform between trains. It is a splendid system, some will say the best in the world. If land prices prevent the average salaryman from living near his place of work, commuting over considerable distances has been made as easy as one can conceive of it being.

It might seem that the old transfer points, Shinjuku and the rest, had lost their reason for being. The commuter need not pause in them. Old habits do not die easily, however. The old *sakariba* continue to bustle furiously during the after-work hours. Many a salaryman, we may infer, prefers to spend in Shinjuku time that might otherwise go into discussing the household budget and disciplining the children.

The subway system (more properly the two subway systems) carries huge numbers of passengers. The public corporation carries far more than the prefecturally owned system, both in absolute numbers and relative to trackage. The former has some eighty-two miles and so outdoes the latter by only about two and a half to one, and carries more than four times as many passengers. It would be easy to blame public administration for this state of affairs, but the essential fact is that the corporation was in business earlier and got the best routes. The two oldest lines, neither of which is connected to suburban commuter lines, carry the largest number of passengers, the one about nine hundred thousand and the other about seven hundred thousand per day.

The number of automobiles grows, but there are incentives, such as are lacking in American cities, not to drive. Frequent trains, underground and otherwise kept beyond reach of automobiles, departing at predictable intervals, see a person to or through the heart of the city in less time than automotive transportation, even by freeway, can be counted upon to do. The freeways choke up frequently, and so have

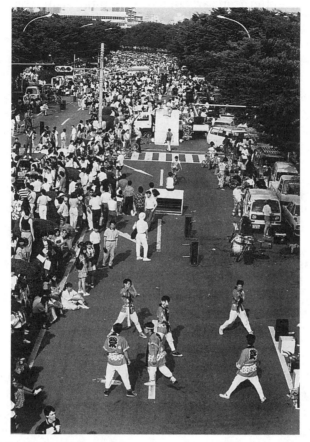

The "pedestrian paradise" in Harajuku on a Sunday afternoon

proven to be what at the outset they might have been expected to be, no solution at all to the congestion problem.

The Minobe administration found a new use for a few of the streets that seems completely laudable. It established the institution of the *hokōsha tengoku*, the "pedestrian paradise." There had been experiments in the United States with closing streets to automobiles and giving pedestrians free use of them, and there had been a brief experiment in Yokohama as early as 1960. The first regular and systematic program of pedestrian paradises began in Tokyo and several lesser cities, the largest of them Kobe, in the summer of 1970—toward the end of the first Minobe term.

On a Sunday afternoon early in that season the main streets of Ginza, Shinjuku, Ikebukuro, Asakusa, and, out in the county part of the prefecture, Hachiōji were closed to automobile traffic. Pedestrians poured forth in huge numbers to enjoy their new hegemony. This was good, for if they had not the experiment would probably have been deemed a failure. In the event the pedestrian paradise became for Tokyo an apparently permanent institution, and it has spread all over the country. Retail sales actually rose on paradise days along the streets affected. There are now paradises in Tokyo places other than the earliest ones, such as Ueno and Harajuku.

Bus and taxi drivers may complain about the pedestrian paradises, which are an inconvenience to them. There are not many success stories that do not inconvenience someone, and the pedestrian paradises are a success story. They have brought new street life to the city, which means a new accession to its supply of life in general. For several hours each week some of the busiest streets turn into parks.

The Minobe administration need not be blamed, at least not in full, for another pedestrian innovation, the overhead crosswalk. This is in theory an increment to the convenience and security of the pedestrian, for it gets him or her across busy intersections without having to wait for traffic lights and without the risk of being run down. Many a pedestrian thinks it a scarcely tolerable nuisance.

The first one went up in the southern part of the city in 1962. By the beginning of the Minobe administration there were more than thirty, and by the end of it they were everywhere. A welcome sign of the Japanese capacity, minute, perhaps, but not completely absent, for civil disobedience was the marked rise in jaywalking. People would march across a forbidden intersection (crossing at street level is generally forbidden when there is an overhead crosswalk) rather than climb all those stairs. If the walks fall in considerable numbers when the next big earthquake comes, fire trucks will be unable to get through, and the fires after an earthquake have a way of being worse than the earthquake itself. We are assured that they are quake-proof. Of that we cannot yet be sure.

Another sort of pedestrian crosswalk, to the theory of which scarcely anyone could object, is the pedestrian bridge across a watery place. The most considerable one is Sakurabashi, Cherry Bridge, across the Sumida north of Asakusa, opened in 1987. It is a pretty bridge, pleasant to stroll across, and it was meant to bring a bit of life back to the Low City. For this it is unfortunately placed. Off to the right as one crosses from the Asakusa side is the famous sweep of cherry trees, one of the most famous since the centuries of the shoguns. Though the trees are confined by the freeway above and the Sumida wall below, they are certainly very handsome when in bloom. The trouble is that they are all of them on the right or downstream side. Cherry Bridge is out of things. Not many people are likely to go out of their way to cross a bridge. It must be at a point where they wish to cross anyway. Not even the soaplands of the Yoshiwara draw people north of Asakusa in great numbers these days, and the flank at the left or east bank is even more remote. Yet Cherry Bridge is pleasant, and the fact that it is there makes the district a little more conspicuous.

It may be that there has been some abatement in the parade of *zoku,* "tribes," in recent decades. One has not heard so much of them. In the post-Olympic years the parade, mostly in Shinjuku and the Southwest, was bewildering. Among those not yet mentioned was the Angura Tribe, which had its main though not exclusive base in Shinjuku. *Angura* is an abbreviation of the Japanese pronunciation of "underground," and it signifies the flamboyantly unconventional young people who frequented the little underground or avant-garde theaters, the most famous of which held forth in a bright red tent on the grounds of the Hanasono Shrine in Shinjuku. The Shinjuku Golden Block (see page 215) nestles in against the walls of the shrine. Performances in the Hanasono tent were most conspicuous for their lurid colors. Another "tribe" that went in for lurid colors was the Saike. *Saike* is from the first two syllables of "psychedelic." They dabbed psychedelic paints over their clothes and the exposed parts of themselves. In 1969 there was a conflict with the law when the shrine closed its grounds to the red tent. Without permission, the troupe moved to the new Central Park at the Shinjuku Westmouth. The riot police took speedy care of the infraction and arrested several people, including the manager, who, however, has continued to prosper. In 1982 he won the most coveted prize for new writers with a story based upon an actual incident, the murder and cannibalization of a Dutch girl by a Japanese boy in Paris.

The Harajuku pedestrian paradise, the closing of the main Harajuku street to vehicular traffic (except stunting motorcycles), has brought a very special kind of street life, associated with one of the more recent tribes to come into prominence, the Takenoko or Bamboo Shoot Tribe.

Takenoko had an unpleasant connotation during the years of the cod and the sweet potato. It signified shedding one's belongings layer after layer in order to buy the necessities. Beginning about 1980 or a little before, it acquired a more cheerful connotation, even though it was not necessarily pleasing to everyone. The name came from the Harajuku boutique which provided the baggy, haremlike dress that was the mark of the tribe. It already had Yoyogi Park in which to do its things, but the Harajuku pedestrian paradise provided more exposure and presumably more exhilaration, a street being a somewhat unconventional place for performances.

The Bamboo Shoot Tribe is still there, but the larger and later Harajuku Tribe dominates things. The Harajuku phenomenon has been likened to the spasms of dancing that have swept the country in times of crisis (see page 36). Since there has been no discernible crisis in recent years, it is more likely rebellion against the boredom of peace, prosperity, and the life of the office worker and spouse. One senses something like a longing for insecurity. The mass media, active in such things as never before, have also played a big part in keeping Harajuku noisy.

The expression "tribe" has become so broad and imprecise in recent years that its meaning is in danger of dissolving. There is the Silver Tribe, which some Americans might call "senior citizens." The appellation derives not, as one might expect, from the color of elderly hair or from silver anniversaries, but from the silver-colored seats set aside on public vehicles for the elderly and disabled. There is the High Yen Tribe, people who take advantage of the high price of the yen as against the dollar, etc., to do things which they would not have dreamed of doing in other years, such as buying Parisian frocks and paintings and weekending in Honolulu.

Tokyo holds itself, and is commonly held by others, to be a model among the cities of the industrialized noncommunist world for its freedom from street crime. The claim is a valid one; but there are other kinds of crime. The elusive nature of organized crime and the police attitude toward it have already been adverted to. Another kind of crime has many apologists and yet remains crime: politically and ideologically motivated violence. The apologists assign sincere motives, and these are not to be gainsaid in Japan.

After the treaty disturbances of 1960 factions of young people first broke with the Communist Party, then started fighting with one another. At first *uchigeba* referred to fights between the Communist Party and the noncommunist (often called Trotskyite) left. Then, the party image having become a peaceful, cuddly one, it became chiefly fighting among nonparty factions, and sometimes fighting for control of a faction. It grew more murderous. The goal was to wound and maim, and eventually to kill. The staves and pipes and even axes of the attackers were aimed directly at the heads of the attacked. There have been scores of fatalities, and the count continues to rise. Extremists in Europe may have been more successful at killing politicians and bankers, but none have been more successful than the Japanese at killing one another. The most murderous incident took fourteen young lives. It was a factional purge which occurred in 1972 at a mountain lodge to the northwest of the Kantō Plain, in a faction whose headquarters (like those of most of them that have not gone overseas) were in Tokyo.

By no means may all violent incidents in public places be blamed on *uchigeba*. There was always the fight against authority and the state of the world. The demonstrations of 1960 were unlawful but nonviolent, except for the occasional use of bare fists against the police. From the late sixties staves and rocks started being used, and then homemade bombs and Molotov cocktails. The argument from sincerity went on being invoked. The first bombing occurred in the Meiji Gardens in 1969. Thirty-seven people were injured. The Molotov cocktail had become a weapon in the anti-Establishment struggle as early as 1952, the year the Occupation ended. The first really damaging one was flung in Ginza in 1968. Sixteen people were injured. This was also the time when assaults upon universities were reaching their high point.

The announcement in 1966 that a new Tokyo International Airport would be built at Narita, in Chiba Prefecture, offered a new outlet for the sincerity of the young. After the fall of Yasuda Castle in 1969 academic turmoil subsided, and so, in Tokyo, did large-scale violence in general. Much of it was exported to Chiba. The airport was not finally opened until a dozen years later. Numbers of violent incidents occurred in the interval, and the airport must still be among the most closely guarded (and inconvenient) in the world. The fact that some of the farmers on the site did not want to give up their land provided a cause.

So did rumors, which may one day prove true, that the airport was really a military base in disguise.

The planting and throwing of small bombs reached a climax in about 1971, when several factions used them against police boxes and the riot police. On Christmas Eve of that year a Christmas tree exploded behind a Shinjuku police box, injuring eleven people. Also in 1971, the wife of an important police official was killed by a bomb that came in the mail.

In 1974 there was a much bigger bombing, the first of a series. In August a bomb exploded in the Marunouchi offices of Mitsubishi Heavy Industries. Eight people were killed. The eight people convicted of the bombings belonged to a faction which called itself the Anti-Japanese Armed East Asian Front (Higashi Ajia Hannichi Busō Sensen). Divided into working parties with far more vivid names—Wolf, Scorpion, Fang of the Continent—it proved to have had its origins among a group of classmates at a private university in Tokyo and was dedicated to rectifying the baneful effects of Japanese imperialism. The faction had no relations with other factions, which is to say that it was not a product of the fragmentation that followed upon the disturbances of 1960. The members passed as quite ordinary office workers and housewives. So

The bombing of Mitsubishi Heavy Industries headquarters, Marunouchi, 1974

discontent may be deeper than one fancies it to be in the conformist middle class.

Public and political crime has overshadowed private, personal crime in recent years. It may be a mark of maturity, of having caught up with the world and shed feudal vestiges. There was much public crime in early Meiji, but there were also picturesque and popular murderesses. The interwar years had assassinations, including those of three prime ministers, but they also had O-sada. Perhaps the absence of women from recent annals of crime has made the annals less interesting.

The most talked-of kidnapping was political, and international as well. On the afternoon of August 8, 1973, Kim Dae-jung, the most prominent leader of the South Korean opposition, was abducted from his hotel room just below the Yasukuni Shrine. Spirited off to Osaka by automobile, he was put aboard a ship and released at his home in Seoul five days later. He seems to have come very close to being murdered at sea. The culprits were Korean intelligence agents. The evidence is that they were not acting on orders from the top levels of the Korean government. The prime minister of Japan, Tanaka Kakuei, who would later be convicted of bribery, told reporters that the incident struck him as *kiki kaikai,* which might be rendered "weirdo." Though the media expressed great indignation, the two governments reached a "political settlement," which meant that the not very adequate explanations by the Korean government were accepted by the Japanese. The Japanese government has never been very skillful in its dealings with truculent Korea. (It does better with fatherly America.) Later, during his American exile, Kim said that he considered the incident still unresolved. He put much of the blame for this fact on the Japanese.

On a less political and more private level, white-collar crime has continued to flourish. The *sōkaiya,* those who specialize in disrupting general meetings (see page 258), are most if not all of them high-class extortionists. Laws have been passed to thwart them, and occasionally a hapless businessman receives unwelcome publicity and a dressing down for having had dealings with them, but they are a resourceful lot and have found ways to persevere. They become publishers of periodicals, for instance, and solicit "advertisements" from the companies that are their targets. They have also made use of a device of which politicians are fond, the coerced sale of very expensive tickets to "parties." Just as American insurance companies find it easier to raise their rates than to fight mischief suits, Japanese companies find it easier to pay off than to face a showdown in the stockholders' meeting. Of some thirteen hundred *sōkaiya* thought to be in business the country over, more than nine hundred do their work in Tokyo.

In 1968 there was a robbery of unprecedented magnitude. It is interesting in itself, and just as interesting for the failure of the police to solve it. The choice of a site suggests that the robbers had a sense of humor. It occurred right beside Fuchū Prison, in the western suburbs of Tokyo. On the morning of December 10, a man on a motorcycle who looked for all the world like a policeman stopped a bank truck and said that explosives were alleged to be planted aboard. The truck contained the year-end bonuses for a Tōshiba plant in Fuchū. Four other men got out of an automobile, and, using the automobile, the party made off with not quite three hundred million yen, which at the exchange rates of today would convert to not far from two and a half million dollars. The automobile and the locker which had contained the money were found in another suburb the following spring, but the robbers were never apprehended. No suspects were announced and no arrests were made, even though the robbers must have been insiders of some description, and the mystery should have lent itself to relatively easy solution. Under the statute of criminal limitations, prosecution became impossible in December 1975. Civil redress ceased to be possible on December 9, 1988.

There was one of those heartwarming incidents, though one over which a suspicion of misdoing hangs heavily. A poor man struck it rich, and, as the newspapers put it, he did so in a fashion so improbable that it was the stuff from which *meruhen* (which word, from the German *Märchen,* "fairy tales," is preferred to anything English has to offer) come. On a drizzly spring evening in 1980 a truck driver noticed a parcel wrapped in a kerchief on a guardrail just east of Ginza. He stopped, picked it up, took it to his residence in one of the poor wards east of the river, and found that it contained a hundred million yen. The money became his when no claimants turned up during the next half-year. The most likely explanation for the absence of claimants is that there was something wrong with the money. It was not counterfeit, but its sources must have been such that it was worth a hundred million yen to someone not to have them revealed. The truck driver sensed something amiss about his trove. He quit his job, resorted to disguises, brushed up on his martial arts, took to wearing a bulletproof vest, and hired himself three bodyguards for twenty-four-hour duty.

It was in the late seventies that we started hearing the expression *yukaihan*, which might be rendered "fun crime." The police seem to have been the inventors of the term. It refers to crimes that create a great stir and the pleasure which the stir gives to the agent of the crime. The most obvious such crime is arson. In 1977 it passed smoking as the chief cause of fire in the city.

The days when General and Mrs. Grant held the city in thrall are more than a century in the past, and they seem every bit that far away. Tokyo is no longer easily stirred. Among foreign dignitaries only the queen of England and the Pope have caught the public imagination with anything like the force of the Grants; and they are unique specimens, the only pope and the only monarch who still moves about with something like monarchical grandeur. Lesser royal personages come and go and few people notice. So it is too with former American presidents—which is what General Grant was in 1879. Incumbent American presidents would probably not much interest the Tokyo citizenry were it not for security measures thought by many to be at best exaggerated and at worst illegal. It would have been a great thing indeed if President Eisenhower had come in 1960. He did not, because of the anti-treaty disturbances. Today presidential visits are next to routine. These evidences of maturity and self-possession are doubtless good, but the eagerness of 1879 must have been good too.

Famous entertainers are another matter. They capture the city with no trouble at all. No one did for a dozen years after Marilyn Monroe, but that was because no one of adequate celebrity made the effort. Then in 1966 came the Beatles. Delayed by a typhoon, their airplane arrived in the dead hours of early morning. This was as well. The elaborate preparations made by the police proved unnecessary. A helicopter was to take the guests to the Ichigaya army (or self-defense) base if the crowds proved unmanageable, and from there to the Hilton Hotel in Akasaka patrol cars would serve. If it seemed clear in advance that the crowds would be unmanageable, the plane was to divert the Beatles to an American air base in the suburbs.

They gave five short concerts in the Hall of the Martial Arts, the Olympic structure north of the palace and near the Yasukuni Shrine. Two thousand policemen were on hand for the opening concert, and more than eight thousand policemen saw action during the five days of the visit. Thousands of overzealous young persons, mostly female, were taken into custody, but no further punishments were meted out. Ringo Starr said that he felt like a bug in a cage. (Prince Philip, also with reference to the elaborate security measures, asked the pearl divers at Toba, beyond Nagoya, whether they had been boiled.)

The Beatles made sixty million yen. Gross proceeds were a hundred million yen, and the impresarios made nothing at all. The security measures cost the prefecture ninety million yen. The sound trucks of the fundamentalist right were on the streets denouncing the event as a national disgrace. They seem to be among the institutions (motorcycle gangs are another) which the police are unwilling or unable to restrain. They make of the regions around the Soviet embassy a constant bedlam.

The city has been repeatedly captured in the years since, by such personages as Michael Jackson and Madonna. Whether the personage be male or female, the crowds are predominantly the latter.

In the realm of high culture and the intellect the French have prevailed. Sartre and De Beauvoir came in 1966, the Venus de Milo in 1964, a few months before the Olympics, and the Mona Lisa in 1974. France got credit for all four even though the last two are not exactly French products. The Mona Lisa was the biggest popular success. A million and a half people, or some two hundred thousand for each of the six-day weeks that she was on display, poured into the National Museum at Ueno and jostled and elbowed each other to have a glimpse of her. It was not much of a glimpse. Railings kept the crowds at a distance. Amplified voices told them in ceremonious but commanding terms that they must not dally.

Among the popular diversions, baseball has pursued its steady way. This is to say that for the Giants the ups have prevailed over the downs. They have gone on being far the most popular team in Tokyo and in most parts of the country (almost everywhere except Nagoya, Osaka, and Hiroshima) that do not have local teams to worship. They are the mainstay of the whole system. It would collapse if they were to.

The Kōrakuen in Tokyo is the baseball capital of the land. It has kept up with the times. We have seen that in 1950 it had the first night games ("nighters"). In 1959 it acquired a baseball museum and hall of fame like those in Cooperstown. In 1976 it had the first artificial turf, a peculiar thing to have, one might think, in a city so rainy that the problem is not to grow natural turf but to keep it under control. Now it has the first covered stadium. This is Tokyo Dome, the second word in English. It is the air-supported kind. Giants fans are advised to come with mufflers and throat sprays. Not even the Seibu enterprises, so capable in most things, have prevailed in baseball. They have their team, heavily promoted, but it has nothing like the popular following of the Giants.

Sumō, the national accomplishment, goes on being at best second to baseball in the national regard. Efforts have been made to liven it up a bit. The ring has been widened so that matches have a chance of being over in less of a hurry, and preliminary rituals have been shortened so that they can get started in more of a hurry. The rituals were traditionally allowed to go on indefinitely, until some sixth sense told the wrestlers that they had gone on long enough. Radio broadcasting brought time limits, varying with the rank of the wrestlers, and television brought further reductions. Now the top wrestlers posture and glare for no more than four minutes. This still is not fast enough for the television audience, which is drifting away from Sumō. Baseball is also thought by many to be a slow sport, but not even a faltering pitcher takes four minutes for his windup. A gigantic Samoan-American has ascended to a higher rank than any non-Oriental had in the past. He weighs more than five hundred pounds.

Publicists and historians of Sumō tell us that it is having yet another golden age. Though there have been two or three very good wrestlers in recent decades, we may be suspicious of the fact that this golden age followed so close upon the last, and of the rate at which Yokozuna, wrestlers of the top rank, have come and gone. Of the sixty wrestlers who have held the Yokozuna rank in the not quite two and a half centuries since chronicles of the sport became reasonably precise, twenty-two have been promoted to it in the last four decades and a bit more. There must be Yokozuna and golden ages if the television audience is to be held. Some Yokozuna have been good neither at wrestling nor at holding the audience. Some have been downright unpopular. In 1987 the Sumō Association took the unprecedented step of stripping a Yokozuna of his rank and his right to compete. He had been behaving in a boorish, overbearing, and indeed violent manner. He had been much touted by the media and the agencies as a "new man." This carries connotations of the liberated and the cosmopolitan. So it may be that the new has gone about as far as it can go if the old is not to disappear completely.

The chronicles of Sumō over the years have resembled those of phoenixes; but if each golden age is going to look more thinly plated than the preceding one, and if the advent of a new one is to be announced every decade or so, the prospects are not bright. At the very worst Sumō will survive vestigially, as do so many "cultural properties"; but that will be a sad survival for those who have known a genuine golden age or two.

A third sport, golf, may have overtaken Sumō as a national accomplishment, or at any rate as a popular diversion. It is participatory. Tournaments get their time on television and crowds follow popular heroes, even as at Pebble Beach and Augusta; but essentially it is the businessman's sport, and that of the politician and the bureaucrat. It has not thrown off the moneyed origins which, as a Japanese sport, it shares with baseball. The first Tokyo golf club, founded in 1914, had among its members some of the most eminent businessmen and politicians of the time. One of them became finance minister and was assassinated. He had tried to teach the Japanese the lesson they have learned so well since the war, that economic penetration is far more tenacious and durable than military. The links, at Komazawa in Setagaya Ward, later provided one of the Olympic sites. There had earlier been golf courses in Kobe and Yokohama. Early amateur tournaments were won by foreigners, but the Japanese came into their own in 1918, at the first one held in Tokyo. They posted the best five scores.

The popularity of golf among politicians, bureaucrats, and businessmen may have something to do with the decline of yet another national accomplishment, that of the geisha, the "accomplished person." That there has been a very sad decline is undeniable. Tastes and ways of life are changing. The traditional music and dance which were the geisha's accomplishments do not interest the ruling classes as they once did, or provide the incentives they once did for a young girl to endure the severities of geisha training.

The "geisha house," which is to say the expensive restaurant where the geisha holds forth, was once the place for concluding big deals, political and entrepreneurial. Increasingly, the golf course is. It has the advantage that electronic snooping is less of a problem. When a business-man or politician is playing golf, he is probably doing more than playing golf. He is making awesome arrangements which he might have made in a restaurant in another day.

The decline of the geisha may be dated from the second postwar decade, when rapid economic growth was beginning. So it would not seem to be true, as is often averred, that the geisha was simply too expensive. It takes dozens of evenings at an expensive geisha restaurant to dissipate a sum equal to the membership fee in one of the golf clubs important people belong to; and the expense-account crowd started turn-ing away from the geisha just at the time when it was beginning to have more than ample money.

Local histories and official publications have become rather demure and coy in recent years. They do not pay the attention they once did to geisha. A Meiji guide to Tokyo published by the city in 1907 obligingly guides its readers to the pleasure quarters and tells them how many geisha they can choose from. It is a rare ward history in recent years that has anything at all to say on the subject. The talk is rather of schools and welfare and day care and the like. It may be that the bureaus and the historians responsible for all these documents are only a little in advance of the times when they treat the geisha as if she did not exist. Such bits of information as one comes upon suggest that it will not be long.

The history of Chūō Ward (Ginza and Nihombashi) published in 1980 is one of the exceptions, rare and refreshing. It tells us that "in the recent past" there came to be fewer than half as many Shimbashi geisha as in the fifties, fewer than two hundred as against more than four hundred. (It will be remembered that "Shimbashi" here really means Tsukiji, east of Ginza.) Matters were even worse with other districts in the ward. The Yoshichō district in Nihombashi and the Shintomichō district near Ginza had almost ceased to exist. In Shimbashi, the district clinging most pertinaciously to life, almost half the *okiya* consisted of an owner-geisha and no one else. An *okiya* is the residence of a geisha, typically, in better days, several of them. *Okiya* were becoming condo-minium apartments, and geisha restaurants were moving into high-rise buildings. Getting into an elevator to go to a "geisha party" represents a change indeed. Before the river wall went up one could enter a Yanagi-bashi restaurant by boat. A sense of the seasons and the elements has always been an important part of the geisha ambience.

All over the city, geisha quarters are disappearing. Shimbashi had been one of the three great quarters of modern Tokyo. Yanagibashi was another. Elegant restaurants once lined the right bank of the Sumida River north of the Kanda. Now only two are to be detected. Akasaka is probably the strongest of the three, because it is so convenient for politicians and bureaucrats, not in a part of town that takes them out of their way; but even there the decline has been marked. Akasaka had only a third as many geisha restaurants in 1984 as it had had a dozen years before. The Maruyama district on a hill above Shibuya had three hundred geisha at its postwar peak, during the years of the Korean War. In 1984 there were only seventy, and most of them were over fifty years of age. They still played the samisen, but few essayed to dance. Presumably the quarter will be extinct when the seventy die or retire. The fall in the count of geisha restaurants was even more striking than the fall in the count of geisha: down to eleven from a hundred forty. So not even the geisha who persisted in the business could expect many engagements.

The same history of Chūō Ward remarks upon the fact that even as the tides of popularity and prosperity withdraw from one part of the ward they flood in upon another. The bars of central Ginza flourished even as the geisha places to the east languished. The theaters and the pleasures of drink and sex always having been in a most intimate relationship, it also remarks upon changing tastes in the latter, corresponding to those in the former: from the stylized traditional forms to more realistic Westernized ones. It might have commented upon a yet deeper change, the decline of the popular theater as it was in the Asakusa of the interwar years.

This is not to be understood as saying that there is no theater. All the varieties, conservative and advanced, that are to be found in the West are in Tokyo, and some traditional, homegrown ones besides. There are more theaters than in New York. When, not long ago, a magazine carried photographs of what it thought to be the twenty most interesting theaters in the city, its trouble was not in finding interesting ones but in choosing among the large number of them. It came upon some that few people can have known of, in such unlikely parts of the city as Fukagawa, east of the Sumida River.

But fragmentation prevails, and in lamentable measure snobbishness. If any theater with its own troupe is as popular as the Asakusa reviews

334

were during the interwar years, it is the Takarazuka of the all-girl troupe. The Koma Stadium in Shinjuku is the Big Apple of popular entertainment, but it does not produce its own performers as the Asakusa theaters did. They are big-time before they get there, and television makes them that.

There certainly are vulgar forms, in the several senses of the adjective. The more advanced and bold of the strip shows, however, are expensive and draw tiny audiences. Yose is not expensive, but it too draws small audiences, and, as we have seen, there are not many theaters left. The largest among them seats only two hundred and a score or two of viewers, and is seldom full save on Sundays and when several tourist buses happen to show up at once. There were until recently tiny theaters —"huts," as the jargon has them—where strolling players held forth with a hybrid of the traditional and the modern. They have gone, though they are still to be found in the provinces. All of these lesser forms combined have less than the drawing power of a single Asakusa theater back when Enoken was playing there.

Television has replaced them all, and a good many other things besides. In place of the devoted local constituency that Asakusa had, there is a single national constituency—or there are as many constituencies as there are channels. Remote local audiences that before had scarcely anything now have something, which is probably good; and the big city has lost something.

Television has combined with another hugely popular form to be a threat not only to traditional forms but to the printed word. Television scenes speed by at such a great rate that no one has time to say much of anything, and there is very little room indeed for what may be called distinguished language. *Manga* dispense with words almost entirely. They are frighteningly popular. In 1987 one and two-thirds billion copies of *manga* magazines were sold. The word *manga* is generally rendered "comics," but it is not a good rendition. The big Japanese-English dictionary has among its definitions "cartoon," which is better. There is little humor in these magazines. The cartoon, humorous and bloodcurdling, has a venerable history in Japan. Of recent years the latter has come to prevail, along with the erotic. Such words as there are to slow the devotee down on his gallop through a *manga* magazine tend strongly toward the imitative or onomatopoetic. They do not convey a meaning so much as an immediate physical experience. They cut through the descriptive functions of language, and splash and splatter and otherwise seek, like Aldous Huxley's feelies, to strike immediately at the senses.

The Japanese language has always been rich in such words. The argument has been made that because of them it is uniquely suited to such anti-rational modes of belief and conduct as Zen. They bear a much larger share of the burden in *manga* than in ordinary language. Some of them are rather amusing. A newspaper article in 1970 listed these: *za-she*, for cutting someone's face open; *zuzu-u-u zuzu-u-u*, for slurping noodles; *chu chuba*, for a kiss; *pattaan*, for a punch in the jaw; *murereri murumuru*, for the impatience of a young lady awaiting her young gentleman. They are many of them sounds that would convey nothing at all independently of their *manga*, which is to say that they are outside of and beyond language.

These developments are of course not unique to Tokyo, and it cannot be said that Tokyo has always led the way. It certainly leads the way in television and advertising, but in sex and violence Osaka is often the pioneer. Many a subtle new direction in the cutting edge of *manga* can be traced to Osaka. Yet it is difficult to describe the city as it is and as it is coming to be without describing such spiritual changes as this, along with all the physical changes.

Even as the Low City and its culture were melted down by the great media waves emanating from the High, so the city itself and the provinces are being fused into one great mass. The mayor of Honolulu has observed that his city is by way of becoming a suburb of Tokyo. Even Osaka, for all its originality in the realm of the sensually explicit, might make the same observation; and the son of Tokyo might complain, as Tanizaki did not cease to complain, that his city too is losing something in the process. Its chief claim today might be that it is more Japanese than Japan, in the sense of having far the greatest concentrations of glass, steel, and computerized information. A loss of individuality has occurred even as the concentration of money and power in Tokyo has approached totality.

It may be almost impossible for foreigners to buy a bit of Japan unless it be in the remote provinces, and it is becoming impossible for most Japanese to buy a bit of Tokyo.

One of the most popular little stunts at drinking places has to do with the ten-thousand-yen bank note and the price of land. The note, the largest printed by the Japanese government, is worth about eighty dollars, though the value shifts somewhat from day to day. A person is told to fold one of the notes as tightly as possible. Take it down to Ginza and drop it, the instructions continue; it will not buy the bit of land upon which it falls.

There are pieces of information that go the rounds, such as that if the lands on which the palace stands were to be sold and converted at going exchange rates, the dollars that resulted could buy the whole state of California. The exchange rate, a product of trade balances, here has its magical effect, because dollars buy far more than yen do in relation to their values on the exchange. So the piece of information has as much to do with exchange rates as with real values. The stunt too is a little exaggerated. Experiment determines that a ten-thousand-yen note can be folded into an area of about two square centimeters. So it would take five thousand of the notes, or fifty million yen, or some four hundred thousand dollars (in which once more the magic of the exchange rate has its effect), to cover a patch a meter square. The annual survey of land prices by the National Land Agency determined that at the end of 1987 the highest price for land sampled in Ginza, near the main Ginza crossing, was thirty-four million yen. So it is an exaggeration, though it is within the bounds of the pardonable, and, as with the matter of the palace and California, emphasizes the fact that land in Tokyo is insanely valuable.

Seven of the ten most valuable pieces of commercial property are in the three central wards, Chiyoda, Chūō, and Minato. As for residential property, the first nine are in the three wards, the tenth is in Shibuya. The most valuable piece of residential property, in Chiyoda Ward just to the northwest of the palace, commanded a price of a little more than twelve million yen, or not far from a hundred thousand dollars, per square meter.

On the assumption that the salaryman cannot risk more than five times his annual pay on a bit of land and a house, the price of the land must be kept within a hundred fifty thousand yen per square meter. Only on the northern and eastern fringes of the old city—the northern part of Asakusa, the wards east of the Sumida—do land prices fall below a million yen per square meter. Nowhere to the west or south do they do so. A square meter may be had for less than a half million along the other fringes of the ward part of the prefecture, and nowhere within the wards does the price fall below a hundred thousand. For this one must go out west where the mountains begin, a distance of some fifty kilometers, or more than thirty miles, from the center of the city.

The situation is little better in the neighboring prefectures, though prices do not rise to such heights. The most expensive land in central Yokohama is worth under ten million yen per square meter. Yet one must go as far as Narita Airport and a kilometer or two onward from the station by other means to find land in Chiba Prefecture for under a hundred thousand yen. One must go to the farther reaches of Saitama Prefecture for such land, and the makers of the survey found none at all in Kanagawa Prefecture (Yokohama).

Narita is about sixty kilometers from the center of the city. This is now considered reasonable commuting distance. One can get to the airport by the fastest express trains in an hour if one happens to be at Ueno Station, but of course commuters tend not to live either in the station or in the airport, nor are express trains always at hand. The commuting life has produced a subculture. The proliferation of sensational photograph and cartoon magazines answers to the needs of people who do not sleep very well on trains and do not want to think. Then there has been the rise of the *chikan,* rendered by the big Japanese-English dictionary as "a molester of women" and "American slang: a masher." No pretty girl who rides crowded trains is free from his attentions, though they are seldom more serious than pawing and pinching.

So the middle class is giving up hope of owning houses in the Tokyo wards. Even the tiny condominium apartment is slipping beyond its dreams. In recent years we started hearing the word *okushon.* This sounds very much like the Japanization of "auction," and was probably in part suggested by it, but more than that it is a variant and pun upon *manshon* or "mansion," which for practical purposes means a multi-storeyed condominium building. The first syllable of "mansion," homophonous with the word for "ten thousand," is converted to *oku,* "a hundred million." So an *okushon* is a condominium apartment that sells for a hundred million yen, not far from a million dollars at present exchange rates. A recent survey by an association of builders and real-estate dealers concluded that the average price for a new condominium of twenty and more square meters within Tokyo Prefecture has now passed a hundred million yen.

There remains a small glimmer of hope, the public-housing condominium. It is very small. Four of the five complexes that drew the largest number of applicants were in neighboring prefectures, and only one, third in popularity among the five, was in Tokyo, in the ward farthest to the north and west of the twenty-three. The most popular complex was on filled land near the western edge of Chiba Prefecture, in the town of Urayasu, which also contains Tokyo Disneyland. There were more than three hundred fifty applications for each available apartment.

The problem is very much one of land speculation, and very much a Tokyo problem. Until recently land prices were rising in the Tokyo region at about three times the national rate, more than three times the rate for the Osaka region, and almost eight times that for the Nagoya region. Very recent surveys suggest that prices may be leveling off and even falling slightly. Real-estate companies are going bankrupt at a rate that cannot be explained by the general state of the economy, and if bankruptcies are ever welcome they are in these circumstances. Government measures, such as tax penalties, restrictions on credit, and licensing in the case of large transactions, may be having an effect. It may be too that a ceiling must inevitably be reached. Speculation works only as long as there is a purchaser who will pay more than the seller did.

The decline, if there is one, is far from enough to make the city once again accessible to the middle class, and a sharp decline is highly unlikely. Bank assets are very intimately associated with land prices. The banks are at the center of the Establishment, which cannot be expected to inconvenience itself unless a massive popular rising forces it to. In some countries we might expect exactly this to happen. In Japan the commuter sighs and goes on commuting. So the "my" in the governor's My Town seems by way of referring to billionaires and ragpickers and scarcely anyone between.

If there is a threat to the position of Ginza as the mercantile heart of the city, it is probably land prices. Perhaps Ginza is being strangled by its own desirability. Transactions in Ginza land are rare, but such recent ones as have occurred suggest that it is even more valuable than the 1987 survey has it, approaching forty million yen per square meter. There are spots in Shimbashi and Shinjuku where land prices approach the Ginza

The huge Westmouth buildings rise beyond the trees of Shinjuku Royal Gardens.

level. Marunouchi, which is managerial and not mercantile, rises to Ginza levels. Yet Ginza is the place that has most clearly the look of being choked by land prices. Ginza shops that have expanded into chains make their money from branches elsewhere and keep their main Ginza stores for advertising. The assets of the ones that have not expanded are mostly in real estate. So it has been aptly observed that Ginza has become a place of advertising and real-estate enterprises. This is worrisome for those who hope that the Ginza center holds, though it does not take into account enterprises, such as the department stores, big enough to make money even on Ginza land.

For about a quarter of a century there has been talk, the first serious talk since 1923, of moving the capital from Tokyo. In 1963 the construction minister, he who was known during the Olympic years as the minister of the waterworks, proposed building a new capital in the hills above Hamamatsu, which is at about the halfway point between Tokyo and Osaka. The National Land Agency has undertaken studies of the matter. The prime minister has directed the removal of minor parts of the bureaucracy from Tokyo. Among other places suggested for a new capital have been Sendai, to the north of Tokyo, and Osaka. The president of the Suntory whiskey company remarked of Sendai in 1988 that it is in the land of the Kumaso. By this he meant "barbarians," but he got his tribe wrong: the Kumaso, mentioned in the earliest chronicles, dwelt at the other end of the realm, in southern Kyushu. He made a political and tactical error as well. The Tōhoku district, of which Sendai is the largest city, organized a boycott which had a pronounced effect on Suntory sales. A politician—not, of course, from Osaka, and therefore immune to reprisals—called Osaka a spittoon. So talk of moving the capital has had its diverting moments.

It is very unlikely to occur, barring another disaster. The interests of too large a part of the Establishment are too much a part of Tokyo. Even effective and outspoken critics of Tokyo as the overwhelming center of everything worth being a center of are doubtful that it will occur. Among the most effective of them has been Hosokawa Morihiro, governor of the land of the Kumaso, Kumamoto Prefecture in Kyushu. He does not look forward to anything very drastic.

"There is talk of several capitals and of moving the capital. The proposal to move the functions now concentrated in the capital to the slopes of Mount Fuji or Sendai or some such place does not seem to me realistic. It will not be practical for the crucial agencies charged with finances, foreign policy, and defense. Yet I do think that when no great weakening of government functions is likely to occur plans should be made for moving to the provinces. I think of the Hokkaido Development Board and the Okinawa Development Board. . . . For the Japanese islands to be a balanced organism and not just an oversized head, greater vitality must be looked for in the provinces, even as Tokyo goes on developing."

Of course the big managers will stay where the "crucial agencies" are. Nearness to the center is very important to them, even though some of them too may feel the Tokyo pinch. Shinnittetsu, the biggest Japanese steel company, owned a Marunouchi building (actually in Otemachi, just to the north) jointly with Mitsui until 1967. Now it rents from Mitsubishi at four billion yen a year, or well over thirty million dollars. Without land in the center of Tokyo, and it has none, not even Shinnittetsu could construct a Tokyo building of its own if it wanted to.

No Marunouchi land has changed hands in the past ten years. If a bit were to come on the market and a potential buyer asked to make an offer, it would probably be: "Whatever you want." Mitsubishi says that some three hundred fifty companies are waiting for Marunouchi space, and that to accommodate them all some fifty acres of new space would be required.

Governor Suzuki agrees with Governor Hosokawa. "The other forty-six prefectures, even Saitama, all have offices in Tokyo. . . . It will not be practical in undisturbed times to move the capital from Tokyo. In the absence of natural disasters and bombings and revolutions such as the Meiji Restoration, it will not be easy."

The three stops in Urawa, prefectural seat of Saitama Prefecture, are the third, fourth, and fifth beyond the Tokyo limits on the main commuter line to the north. Even this proximity, the governor is saying, is not enough. The pull of Tokyo is so strong that even Saitama must have offices there.

The concentration of money and power in Tokyo is to a degree unthinkable in the United States. A reasonable estimate might be that a third of large American companies have their head offices in or near New York. Many of them are trying to get away, and succeeding. There is little indication, despite costs that would seem prohibitive in most places, of a similar efflux from Tokyo and the Kantō region. It has been influx the whole time. Until the Second World War the Kansai might salve its wounded pride at having ceased to be the political center of the land by saying, and not without grounds, that it continued to be the commercial center. While it is true that the Kansai is more wholeheartedly commercial than the Kantō, and may thus make the ancient argument of sincerity and dedication, the argument no longer has much force.

When a big company (examples are Matsushita and the big automobile companies) does not have its head office in Tokyo, it has a branch office so large that the distinction between the two, main office and branch, seems to come down to long-term finance and management on the one hand and day-to-day operations on the other. Some companies make this fact more obvious by having head offices both in Tokyo and in Osaka.

Nor is the concentration only economic and bureaucratic. A "literary" memorandum book which happens to be at hand lists the addresses and telephone numbers of some four hundred institutions and organizations likely to answer to the needs of literary and artistic persons. Only seven of them have the high postal numbers that reveal them to be situated at a distance from the center: an association of photographers in Osaka, a publishing house apiece in Osaka and Kyoto, a paper manufacturer in Shizuoka, and three advertising agencies, in Nagoya, Osaka, and Kobe.

Of the nine hundred or so artistic and intellectual types listed in the same memorandum book, only about a tenth reside beyond commuting distance of Tokyo. Of these a considerable number are university professors residing in Kyoto, to remind us of a rare element in Japanese cultural life in which a modicum of decentralization remains. Kyoto University continues to be the other university, the only one with something like the prestige of Tokyo University, and offering its graduates something like the same ticket of entry to the realm of the elite.

In one field it offers the better ticket. Kyoto University produces winners of Nobel Prizes in the sciences, and so that is where the brightest would-be scientists go. Governor Suzuki recently called our attention, with wry humor, to the fact that his grandson had just entered the college of physics at Tokyo University, and that it was the only college in the university short of new students. Those who passed both in Tokyo and in Kyoto chose to go to the latter. In the realm of power—law, politics, economics—it is the opposite. Most of the very bright boys and girls of the land, when they have passed the entrance examinations of both universities, choose Tokyo. Its ticket is much the more reliable. This fact is behind moves on the part of Kyoto University to have its entrance examinations held on the same day as Tokyo University, and so make it impossible for even the brightest to pass both. They must choose in advance, and spare Kyoto University humiliation.

The concentration of students and universities in Tokyo is impressive, if not quite so impressive as the concentration of big companies, publishing houses, and artistic types. A third of the colleges and universities in the country are in Tokyo, and half the students. There has been some dispersal of universities from the ward part of Tokyo, but the concentration in Greater Tokyo remains. The new Tsukuba university and research complex in southern Ibaragi Prefecture more than makes up for the old University of Education, its core, once situated in the same ward as Tokyo University. (Among the principal attributes of Tsukuba is its dullness. One might have expected an explosion, with tens of thousands of hot-blooded young people suddenly put down in the middle

of nowhere, and Narita Airport and all its controversy so near at hand,
It has not happened. The day of pulverizing universities mysteriously
passed—though the explosion may be hanging fire.)

Such general statistics fade into insignificance beside the fact that
graduates of Tokyo University, and to a lesser extent Kyoto University,
will one day rule the land. The graduate of a provincial university is
lucky if he gets a position with City Hall or the local police force.

Osaka has now been subjected to the indignity of becoming the third-
largest city in the land. It has been passed in population by a Tokyo
bedroom city, Yokohama. Though it is a considerable center in its own
right, the fact that Yokohama is a bedroom city is clear. The proportion
of its daytime to its nighttime population is the lowest for any of the ten
largest Japanese cities.

So Tokyo is and has almost everything, and many a son of the city
might say that it has lost the most important thing, its identity. Americanization, though often blamed, is not responsible. Not much of Tokyo
looks like an American city, and very little of it feels like one. The loss
of identity is the result of the very Japanese process of homogenization.
Everything is subsumed unto Tokyo and Tokyo is subsumed unto everything; and the nation marches victoriously on, untroubled by the insistence on separateness and difference that troubles so many nations.

Plans and dreams for the future of the city do not have to do exclusively
with high technology and company offices, but they tend strongly in those
directions. Nor, though again the tendency is strong, do they have to do
entirely with the central wards. High-rise blocks, many of them under
the auspices of the various wards, will be scattered over the city if the
plans come to fruition. There will be new "new towns" out in the county
part of the prefecture, and better facilities, such as transportation, for
the ones already there.

Though the madness of land prices suggests the saturation of the
central wards, expansion yet seems possible. Open spaces are still to be
found, and landowners see the possibility of more intensive land use than
is presently the case. Mitsubishi says that if Marunouchi can be made to
go the super way, like the Shinjuku Westmouth, it can have ten to
twenty times the office space it now has. The Shiodome freight yards,
just east of Shimbashi and south of Ginza, where stood the first railway

terminus in central Tokyo, will be sold and developed, so that the successor company to the National Railways may ease itself of a bit of its gigantic debt. Something highly advanced, including, like the Ark Hills complex in Minato Ward, residential units, will probably rise. The housing is certain to be for the wealthy. Then there is the expanse of land just south of Tokyo Central Station where the prefectural offices now stand. The prefecture does not, apparently, mean to let commercial developers have it. The thought is rather that it will become a grand convention and "cultural" center.

What is called, usually in English, the "new frontier" remains. It is the waterfront, river and bay, more grandiosely the latter. Claude Lévi-Strauss recently said that he saw the future of Tokyo along the Sumida. When such a person sees something, others start seeing it too. So there are projects for high-rise blocks up and down the river. One is already under construction, on the left bank of the Sumida just opposite the busiest part of Asakusa. It is on land formerly occupied by an Asahi brewery, which Nagai Kafū hated because of its part in making the river unlovely. He would not have liked the replacement either. It is more conspicuous, and not distinguished architecturally. There will be three high buildings and some low ones. The Asahi breweries will have a big beer hall, the most attractive detail of the plans, in one corner.

Arakawa Ward, one of the poorer wards, north of Asakusa and the Sanya "slum," envisions what it calls a *kawanote* complex. The expression derives from *yamanote*. The latter might be rendered "the hilly region," and "the river region" might do for the former. The projected site for the *kawanote* is on the inner side of the bend where the Sumida turns south to flow into the bay. About half of it is the Shioiri or Tidewater freight yards, which played such a part (see page 256) in turning Sanya into a "slum." The rest is athletic fields and a small residential district. The tract is almost four times as large as the reservoir bed on which the Shinjuku Westmouth went up. Plans for the new development are by the internationally famous Tange Kenzō, the man who designed both the old and the new prefectural offices. They are uninteresting, a collection of tubular and cuboid objects. One does not want to think that Tange is losing his touch, but the evidence grows that he might be. His name is omnipresent in plans for the future of the city.

The bay front is the more tempting frontier. Nothing remains in Tokyo of the bay shore of Edo. The woodcut artists of Meiji loved to show steam trains running along the shore en route to Yokohama. Now the east side of the tracks is filled land all the way to Yokohama, where the bay once more comes in sight. Nearly four thousand hectares have been reclaimed from the bay within the bounds of Tokyo. (A hectare is a hundred meters squared, or just under two and a half acres.) There are also ample filled lands in the other two bay-shore prefectures, Chiba and Kanagawa. Yokohama has big plans for putting its filled land to use. They include what will for a while be the highest building in Japan, higher than the Sunshine in Ikebukuro. On the Chiba lands just to the east of the border with Tokyo, in Urayasu, the town in which Tokyo Disneyland is situated, four big hotels have been built and a fifth will follow soon. For advertising purposes the district is called Maihama-Tokyo Bay Resort City. The last three words are in English, and the very last one is commonly written in Roman letters. Maihama is a part of Urayasu.

Of Tokyo filled lands, almost half have been put to use, for factories and docks and athletic grounds and the like. Of the remaining two thousand or so hectares, the prefecture has a scheme for 440, of which it owns 320. On not quite a quarter of it a "teleport," it is said, will be built. By this is meant the ultimate in a communications center, with satellites, etc., at its disposal. There are also to be two dozen high office buildings, condominiums (to accommodate perhaps fifty or sixty thousand people, a very small drop in the Tokyo bucket), and sports and cultural facilities. The land stretches southward from east of Shimbashi to the Shinagawa offing.

Such is the picture of the future that emerges from the drawing boards, and the future that is to an extent already with us. It is a spotty picture, a bit here and a bit there, and a conjectural one. Not all the big projects for doing away with the last frontier will ever be realized. There would be too many of them even if they were not hugely expensive. The teleport has a better chance than most, even though it is estimated to cost more than thirty billion dollars. The prefecture, unless it changes its mind about the whole thing, will need the help of the big companies, which they will be happy to provide.

The picture contains little if anything that offers hope to the middle class, now being driven to the far suburbs and the neighboring prefectures. Nor is it an aesthetically pleasing picture. Such of the filled lands in the bay as have already been built upon can only be described as bleak.

346

Center of the new Tokyo—here, at the Shinjuku Westmouth, the new prefectural government buildings are under construction.

One mile of dust and concrete leads to another. An old district of shops and family houses in, say, the wards just north of the palace may have a somewhat random and discursive look to it, the owner of each building having a slightly different notion from all his neighbors as to what a building should be, but at least it has the feel of having grown from something. The newly filled tracts have none.

It is understandable that the most moneyed city of our day should wish to go on being that, and make its plans for the things that money desires, communications and information and the like. To do much of significance about the greatest problem the city faces, its inaccessibility to the less than heavily moneyed, may well be impossible. With regard to the aesthetic problem, questions may at least be asked. Must what results from doing away with the last frontier, the newly reclaimed lands, have the dreariness of its predecessor, the reclaimed lands already built upon? Must the cuboids to be scattered over the city have the cold glossiness of Ark Hills and the dinginess of the *danchi*, the public-housing complexes? One cannot be optimistic. These are fields in which the Japanese have not shown flair. The jargon that goes with the plans is

347

uninventive and derivative in the extreme. "Postmodern," already remarked upon, is everywhere. So is "space," which almost seems to proscribe aesthetic judgments. So often, hearing an object described as an interesting space, one has wished to stand up in the middle of a lecture and say, "Well, yes, I suppose it is an ingenious sort of air container, what with all those pits and bulges; but isn't it the *ugliest* thing!"

When the United States was the moneyed country of the world, it created the grandeur of New York. When the maritime countries of western Europe had the money, they put together the low, subdued harmonies of Amsterdam, Paris, and London. Tokyo will have unprecedented concentrations of communication and information, but these do not immediately meet the eye. What will is unlikely to have either grandeur or harmony.

NOTES

p.   8 *"avenues and streets."* The Reconstruction of Tokyo, Tokyo, Tokyo Municipal Office, 1933, iv.

     8 *"from our beds."* Quoted in *Tōkyō Hyakunenshi (Tokyo Centennial History)*, Tokyo, Tokyo Prefectural Office, in six volumes, IV, 1972, 1241.

     9 *"field of flowers."* Collected Works, Tokyo, Shinchōsha, II, 1970, 54.

  10 *"mountain of rubble."* Ibid., 55.

  12 *"prayed in silence."* Collected Short Stories, Tokyo, Kōdansha, 1964, 338.

  13 *"fresh autumn wind."* Collected Works, Tokyo, Iwanami Shoten, XIX, 1964, 332.

  13 *"seemed very near."* Collected Works, VIII, 1963, 94.

  15 *"woman out dancing."* Collected Works, XIX, 334.

  18 *"royal death approaches?"* Collected Works, XX, 1964, 86.

  26 *"a generous estimate."* Collected Works, Tokyo, Chūō Kōron Sha, XXII, 1959, 157–59.

  27 *"appearance of health."* Collected Works, XII, 1970, 39.

  28 *"to be beautiful."* Ibid., 33.

  35 *"be your bride."* Shōwa Ryūkōkashi (A History of Shōwa Popular Music), Tokyo, Mainichi Shimbun, 1977, 59.

  39 *"the repellent kind."* Collected Works, XXIX, 1982, 232–34. A more recent version of the collected works than that cited elsewhere.

  57 *"after a rain."* Op. cit., 197.

58 *"into the mirrors."* Collected Works, VIII, 236.

59 *"on their way."* Collected Works, Tokyo, Shinchōsha, III, 1977, 14.

60 *"medical science marvelous?"* Collected Works, II, 28–29.

60 *"just like Osaka."* Collected Works, III, 28.

61 *"not with dew."* Shōwa Ryūkōkashi, 51–52.

62 *"a chain store."* Op. cit., 14.

66 *"spring and autumn."* p. cxc.

70 *"for the dancer."* Shōwa Ryūkōkashi, 48–49.

72 *"into new ones."* Collected Works, II, 30–31.

73 *"song and legs."* Ibid., 31.

74 *"the Fourth District."* Ibid.

78 *"was really listening."* Collected Works, III, 356. The passage is a single sentence in the original.

79 *"stroll down Ginza."* Collected Works, II, 33.

81 *"bags of sweets."* Ibid., 128–29.

82 *"quite radiates eroticism."* Ibid., 109.

83 *"world doesn't have."* Ibid., 86.

85 *"only in Asakusa."* Collected Works, III, 75.

97 *"want to flee."* Chikamatsu Shūkō, quoted in *Tōkyō Hyakunenshi*, V, 1972, 900.

105 *"of a room."* New York, Alfred A. Knopf, 1957, 483.

107 *"make haste, sing."* Collected Works, XII, 1963, 402–3.

108 *"at my breast."* Ibid., 408.

109 *"make the sacrifice."* Ibid., 413.

109 *"in the hall."* Ibid., 422.

109 *"to be in."* Ibid., 430.

109 *"from human affairs?"* Ibid., 432.

110 *"breaks the silence."* Ibid., 437.

112 *"together are removed."* Collected Works, Tokyo, Keisō Shobō, I, 1970, 153.

112 *"of their dream."* Ibid., 241.

114 *"letting things go."* Collected Works, XIX, 1974, 551–52.

115 *"going to ruins."* Collected Works, XXIII, 1964, 439.

115 *"moral from this."* Collected Works, XIX, 570.

Notes

116 *"neglect the place."* Asakusa, edited by Takami Jun, Tokyo, Eihōsha, 1955, 272.

132 *"that odd building."* p. 96.

143 *"a modest gift."* Collected Works, Tokyo, Chikuma Shobō, IX, 1978, 17.

180 *"how agreeable."* Shōwa Ryūkōkashi, 141.

186 *"a different route."* Collected Works, XXIV, 1964, 180.

191 *"with Edict 9."* Murata Hiroo, in Takami, Asakusa, 240.

194 *"of us Japanese."* Quoted in Shōwa no Sesō (Aspects of Shōwa), edited by Harada Katsumasa, Tokyo, Shōgakkan, 1983, 140. The Harada volume is an appendix to the Shōgakkan history of the Shōwa Period.

238 *"came back again."* Akatsuka Yukio, quoted in Edo Tōkyō Gaku Jiten (The Edo-Tokyo Encyclopedia), edited by Ogi Shinzō et al., Tokyo, Sanseidō, 1987, 239.

238 *"things a bit."* Quoted in Harada, op. cit., 254.

247 *"oversaw the destruction."* It may be a mistake to say that nothing else survives of Mitsubishi Londontown. Fragments of the Ginza Bricktown of early Meiji, thought to have been utterly lost, have turned up in the course of demolitions, excavations, and rebuildings.

257 *"helpful of police."* When a friend and I tried to photograph the mammoth police box we were told that regulations forbade it. Inquiry with police headquarters revealed that there are no such regulations.

261 *"villa of Kikugorō."* Collected Works, IX, 1964, 111–12.

264 *"use of space."* Arthur Koestler, as we were having a stroll.

271 *"Sanyūtei Kimba."* Quoted in Shōwa no Sesō (Aspects of Shōwa), edited by Iwasaki Jirō and Katō Hidetoshi, Tokyo, Shakai Shisōsha, 1971, 269.

278 *"had a point."* The lady, obviously American, winked and smiled and made the remark as she got off the riverboat from Asakusa. I was waiting at Shibaura to board the same boat in the opposite direction.

281 *"going to win."* Tamanoumi, in Bungei Shunjū ni Miru Shōwa Supōtsu shi (A History of Shōwa as seen in Bungei Shunjū), II, 1988, 526. The article is reprinted from the magazine Bungei Shunjū for April 1970. Tamanoumi became a Yokozuna in 1970 and died while still an active wrestler.

309 *"have a home."* Shōwa Bungaku Zenshū (a uniform edition of Shōwa writing), Tokyo, Shōgakkan, IX, 1987, 44.

312 *"edge of bankruptcy."* Fukuda Shintarō, president of the Jiji News Service, in conversation.

341 *"goes on developing."* Tōkyōjin (The Tokyoite), March–April 1988, 134–35.

342 *"not be easy,"* Tōkyōjin, special issue, July 1988, 22–23.

INDEX

Index